International Copyright Law and Access to Education in Developing Countries

Graduate Institute of International and Development Studies

VOLUME 10

The titles published in this series are listed at brill.nl/giis

International Copyright Law and Access to Education in Developing Countries

Exploring Multilateral Legal and Quasi-Legal Solutions

By

Susan Isiko Štrba

MARTINUS
NIJHOFF
PUBLISHERS

LEIDEN • BOSTON
2012

Library of Congress Cataloging-in-Publication Data

Isiko Štrba, Susan.
International copyright law and access to education in developing countries : exploring multilateral legal and quasi-legal solutions / Susan Isiko Štrba.
p. cm.
Includes bibliographical references and index.
ISBN 978-90-04-22899-3 (hardback : alk. paper) -- ISBN 978-90-04-23540-3 (e-book)
1. Copyright--Developing countries. 2. Copyright, International. 3. Educational law and legislation--Developing countries 4. Educational assistance--Developing countries I. Title.
K1420.5.S77 2012
346.12404'82--dc23

2012023826

This publication has been typeset in the multilingual "Brill" typeface. With over 5,100 characters covering Latin, IPA, Greek, and Cyrillic, this typeface is especially suitable for use in the humanities. For more information, please see www.brill.nl/brill-typeface.

ISSN 1572-5618
ISBN 978 90 04 22899 3 (hardback)
ISBN 978 90 04 23540 3 (e-book)

This book is printed on acid-free paper.

FSC www.fsc.org MIX Paper from responsible sources FSC® C109576

Printed by Printforce, the Netherlands

My husband, advisor and best friend, Eng. Fridrich Štrba.
Thank you for patiently and lovingly paying the price for this work.

To our children, Patrick, Miriam and Nathanael.

CONTENTS

ACKNOWLEDGMENTS

Several years ago, I got excited when Professors Thomas Cottier and Ernst-Ulrich Petersmann, in separate settings, advised me to write something on intellectual property and developing countries. But it was only after Professor Andrew Clapham, who directed my Masters Dissertation on *Dispute Settlement Under the TRIPS Agreement in Relation to Human Rights* and embraced the idea of me writing a Ph.D thesis on intellectual property and development, that I launched into research on this issue. This book is an improved version of my Ph.D thesis at the Graduate Institute of International and Development Studies. I would like to thank Professor Andrew Clapham for Directing the Ph.D thesis. Professor Joost Pauwelyn was not only a second reader but enriched the research with his insights in WTO law. Professor Ruth Okediji's expertise in international copyright law gave a completely different face to the final outcome of the Ph.D thesis. I sincerely thank them both. A one year scholarship from The Graduate Institute allowed me to take time off work and concentrate on research.

I have been lucky to count on the support of several friends and colleagues, whom I unfortunately cannot list here. Danielle Avanthay of the Ph.D Secretariat at the Graduate Institute provided all the support needed to take care of my children and complete the Ph.D. Sisule Musungu of IQsensato enabled me to test some of the ideas in this book by asking me to speak as a panellist at some of his intellectual property and development seminars. I especially benefitted from the seminar on Copyright and Access to Educational and Learning Materials. Andrew Prosser and Rosalind Wood kindly proof read the manuscript. I especially thank Wend Wendland of the World Intellectual Organization for being available whenever needed.

Lastly, special thanks to my husband Fridrich Štrba, whose unfailing love and support ensured that the book was written, and whose insights in general public international law improved the final product.

ABBREVIATIONS USED

3ST	Three-step Test
ACP	Africa, Caribbean and Pacific
ALAI	Association Littéraire et Artistique Internationale
ARIPO	African Regional Industrial Property Organization
ARV(s)	Antiretroviral(s)
BC	Berne Convention
BIRPI	Bureaux Internationaux Réunis pour la Protection de la Propriété Intellectuelle/United International Bureau for the Protection of Intellectual Property
BLMI	UNESCO Basic Learning Materials Initiative
CAL	Copyright Agency Limited
CDIP	Committee on Development and Intellectual Property
CESCR	Committee on Economic, Social and Cultural Rights
CIPIH	Commission on Intellectual Property Rights, Innovation and Public Health (WHO)
CL	Compulsory Licence(sing)
CODESRIA	Council for the Development of Social Science Research in Africa
COL	Commonwealth of Learning
COMESA	Common Market for Eastern and Southern Africa
Cri	Computer Law Review International
DA	Development Agenda
DCM	Digital Course Material
DFID	Department for International Development (UK)
DOI	Digital Object Identifier
EC (EU)	European Community (European Union)
EFF	Electronic Frontier Foundation
EIPR	European Intellectual Property Review
EJIL	European Journal of International Law
EMRs	Exclusive Marketing Rights
EPIL	Encyclopaedia of Public International Law
FDA	Food and Drug Administration of the US
FDCs	Fixed Dose Combinations
FTA(s)	Free Trade Agreement(s)
FTAA	Free Trade Area of the Americas

GII	Global Information Infrastructure
HAART	Highly-active anti-retroviral treatment
ICESCR	International Covenant on Economic, Social and Cultural Rights
ICJ	International Court of Justice
ICTSD	International Centre for Trade and Sustainable Development
ICT	Information Communication Technology
IDRC	International Development Research Centre
IFFRO	International Federation for Reproduction Rights Organizations
IIC	International Review of Intellectual Property and Competition Law
IIPA	International Intellectual Property Alliance
ILC	International Law Commission
IP	Intellectual Property
IPR Commission	Commission on Intellectual Property Rights (UK)
IPRs	Intellectual Property Rights
JIEL	Journal of International Economic Law
KCAEM	Kenya Coalition for Access to Essential Medicines
KEI	Knowledge Ecology International
LDC	Least Developed Country
LDCs	Least Developed Countries
MCAZ	Medicines Control Authority of Zimbabwe
MFN	Most Favoured Nation
MMV	Medicines for Malaria Venture (WHO)
NAFTA	North American Free Trade Agreement
NCE	New Chemical Entity
OAPI	Organisation Africaine de la Propriété Intellectuelle
OLI	Open Learning Institute
OSI	Open Society Institute
QUNO	Quaker United Nations Office
QIAP	Quaker International Affairs Programme
PCDA	Provisional Committee on Proposals related to the WIPO Development Agenda
R&D	Research and Development
RCADI	Recueil des cours de l'Académie de droit international/Collected courses of the Hague Academy of International law
RMI	Rights Management Information
SCP	Standing Committee on the Law of Patents
S.D.N.Y	Southern District of New York
SPLT	Substantive Patent Law Treaty
TAC	Treatment Action Campaign (South Africa)
TRALAC	Trade Law Centre for Southern Africa
TEACH Act	Technology, Education and Copyright Harmonization Act
TRIPS	Agreement on Trade Related Aspects of Intellectual Property Rights
UCC	Universal Copyright Convention
UDHR	Universal Declaration of Human Rights
UN	United Nations

UNCTAD	United Nations Conference on Trade and Development
UNDP	United Nations Development Program
UNESCO	United Nations Educational, Scientific and Cultural Organization
UNICEF	United Nations Children's Fund
UOLTJ	University of Ottawa Law & Technology Journal
UPOV	Union Internationale pour la Protection des Obtentions Végétales (International Union for the Protection of New Varieties of Plants)
US	United States of America
USA	United States of America
USC	United States Code
USTR	United States Trade Representative
VCLT	Vienna Convention on the Law of Treaties
WBU	World Blind Union
WCT	WIPO Copyright Treaty
WDEFA	World Declaration on Education for All
WHA	World Health Assembly
WHO	World Health Organization
WIPO	World Intellectual Property Organization
WPPT	WIPO Performances and Phonogram Treaty
WTO	World Trade Organization

GENERAL INTRODUCTION

Definition of the Problem and Objectives

The monograph addresses legal issues relating to copyright and access to education in developing countries.[1] The primary objectives are to contribute to the understanding of the legal relationship between copyright regulation and access to education in developing countries and to explore possible ways to facilitate access within the international copyright system. We seek to answer the question whether limitations or exceptions (flexibilities) in international intellectual property law can be utilised to balance the private interest of intellectual property (IP) right holders and the public interest of IP users. In particular, can flexibilities in international copyright law serve to enable access to copyrighted material in the analogue form for educational uses by developing countries? In addition, we explore possible solutions found in the international copyright system, for access to education in developing countries.

Half of the world's population still lives in poverty, having to shoulder a significant share of the disease burden and contend with the challenge of inadequate access to basic human necessities such as food, medicine, education and knowledge. Significantly, education is an indispensable tool in the development of a human being, and it can play a critical role in the attainment of other human necessities such as food.[2] Yet, according to the 2006 United Nations (UN) statistical profiles for Least Developed Countries (LDCs), the Gross National Income per capita of the 48 LDCs (as decided by the UN), 33 of which are found in Africa,[3] range from US $90 to US $2,500.[4] The adult literacy rate for LDCs is only 49.8% for Africa, 53.8% for Asia and Middle East, and 55.5% for other LDCs. Meanwhile, the adult literacy rate in developing countries, not being LDCs, in general is 83.1%.[5]

---

1 'Developing countries' as used in this research refers to countries designated by the United Nations (UN) as least developed countries, developing countries and countries with economies in transition.

2 See section 2.2 on the pertinent elements of education.

3 Office of the High Representative for the Least Developed Countries, Landlocked Developing Countries and Small Island Developing Countries, available at www.unohrlls.org

4 United Nations Conference on Trade and Development, Statistical Profiles of Least Developed Countries, 2006, United Nations, New York and Geneva, 2006, p.10 (hereinafter referred to as UNCTAD Statistical Profiles of LDCs, 2006).

5 UNCTAD Statistical Profiles of LDCs, 2006, *ibid,* p.8.

Of the 48 LDCs, 32 are Members of the World Trade Organization (WTO), which means they are party to the Agreement on Trade Related Aspects of Intellectual Property Rights (TRIPS).[6] Ten more LDC countries are in the process of negotiating to join the WTO.[7] All developing countries are party to at least one international treaty regulating intellectual property in general or copyrights in particular. Consequently, they are obligated to enact national laws protecting intellectual property, and thus cannot freely allow access to protected material.[8]

The last decades of copyright development, at least among industrialized countries, have been marked by a tendency toward the strengthening of the copyright monopoly without commensurate attention being paid to the public's interest in access to copyrighted works.[9] In reality, there exist a number of competing and significant public interest considerations in relation to copyright, such as access to education.[10] The more intellectual property has been at the centre of economic activity, the more its legitimacy has been contested by the public at large and in many other circles. For example, consumers are claiming, their "right" to private copying,[11] and researchers and librarians claim the freedom to access research results.[12] In addition, the visually impaired, librarians and archivists as well as educational material providers are demanding international instruments on access to copyrighted works at the World Intellectual Property Organization.[13]

The conflict between copyright and the realization of public interest goals is not limited to developing countries. Developed countries and particularly many consumer

---

6 Agreement on Trade-Related Aspects of Intellectual Property Rights, Annex 1C to the Marrakesh Agreement Establishing the World Trade Organization, 15 April 1994, in World Trade Organization *The Results of the Uruguay Round of Multilateral Negotiations, The Legal Texts.* Geneva: WTO, 1995, (hereinafter referred to as TRIPS Agreement).

7 These are Afghanistan, Bhutan, Equatorial Guinea, Ethiopia, Laos, Sao Tome & Principe, Samoa, Sudan, Vanuatu and Yemen. Information available on www.wto.org

8 Granting sufficient protection to intellectual property means limitations on its access.

9 See generally, Commission on Intellectual Property Rights, Integrating Intellectual Property Rights and Development Policy, Report of the Commission on intellectual Property Rights, London, September 2002, available at http://www.iprcommission.org (hereafter Commission on Intellectual Property Rights).

10 On Copyright and freedom of expression, the right to culture and access to information and knowledge, see Myra J. Tawfik. "International Copyright law and 'fair dealing' as a 'user right.' UNESCO, e-Copyright Bulletin, April – June 2005.

11 For example, in *Studio Canal et al v. S. Parquin and Union fédérale des consommateurs (UFC) Que choisir*, Paris Court of Appeal, 4 April 2007, Gaz. Pal. 18 July 2007, no. 199, (*Mulholland Drive*), Mr Parquin, supported by the UFC claimed that the anti-circumvention measures prevent him from copying the protected material, thus violating his "right" to private copy. For a commentary on this case, see Christophe Geiger. "Right to copy v. Three-step Test: the future of the private copy exception in the Digital environment." *Computer Law Review International* (*CRi*), vol. 1 no.7 (2005): 1–13 (hereinafter referred to as Geiger, Right to Copy v. Three-step test); also by the same author, "The private copy exception, an area of freedom (Temporarily) preserved in the digital environment." *International Review of Intellectual Property and Competition Law* (*IIC*), vol. 37, no.4 (2006): 371–406 (hereinafter referred to as Geiger, The private copy exception).

12 Intellectual Property Watch, "Panellists outline strategies on limitations and exceptions to copyright," 20 March 2008, p.1 (available at www.ip-watch.org).

13 See generally, current discussions on limitations and exceptions in the WIPO Standing Committee on Copyright and Related Rights.

organizations and other non-governmental organizations as well as academics share concerns about the implications of copyright for access to knowledge, particularly in a digital environment. For example, Benjamin White of the British Library, the United Kingdom's national library, highlighted at a panel on limitations and exceptions to copyright how vital access to library-based information is for education, creativity, culture and industry. A quantitative evaluation conducted by the Library indicated that it returned 4.4 times the monetary value to society as was originally invested.[14] At the regional level, the most recent example of tension between copyright and access to education is the European Communities' Green Paper on Copyright in the Knowledge Economy.[15] The purpose of the Green Paper was to foster a debate on how knowledge for research, science and education can best be disseminated in the online environment. It aimed to set out a number of issues connected with the role of copyright in the "knowledge economy". Such issues include exceptions for libraries and archives, digitisation of works for preservation, making digitized works available, exceptions for the benefit of persons with disabilities and dissemination of works for teaching and research purposes.[16] Civil society organizations such as the World Blind Union are demanding a better international mechanism for access to copyrighted works by the blind and the visually impaired.

While issues of access to information on the Internet or in the digital environment are important to developing countries, it is not as pressing as access to copyrighted material in the analogue form. The present study is confined to issues of access to material in the analogue form because of their salience for developing countries. We exclude issues related to the visually impaired (persons with visual or print disability), not because they are unimportant but due to their not being confined to developing countries. This, however, does not preclude our referring to them when necessary.

As early as 1967, the challenge of access to printed material was emphasized. For example, at the Stockholm Conference[17] for the revision of the Berne Convention,[18] Mr Adiseshiah of the United Nations Education, Scientific and Cultural Organization (UNESCO) drew attention to the fact that, whereas in some countries of Europe and North America the book supply amounted to approximately 2,000 pages per person per year, in India the average was 32 pages per person per year. He further cautioned that India as a

---

14 See for example, Intellectual Property Watch, *supra*, p.1.

15 Commission of the European Communities. Green Paper on Copyright in the Knowledge Economy, Brussels, COM(2008) 466/3, (hereinafter referred to as Green Paper on Copyright in the Knowledge Economy).

16 Green Paper on Copyright in the Knowledge Economy, *ibid.*. The Green Paper comes seven years after the Directive on harmonization of certain aspects of copyright. See Directive 2001/29/EC of the European Parliament and of the Council of 22 May 2001 on the harmonisation of certain aspects of copyright and related rights in the information society, Official Journal L 167, 22/06/2001 P. 0010–0019, (hereinafter referred to as Information Society Directive). The Directive contains a detailed list of limitations and exceptions to copyright in the digital environment, yet it still leaves many questions unresolved.

17 Intellectual Property Conference of Stockholm, June 11 to July 14, 1967.

18 Berne Convention for the Protection of Literary and Artistic Works (9 September 1886), as revised by the Act of Stockholm (1967), and by the Paris Act (1971) and amended in 1979, Publication of the World Intellectual Property Organization no. 287(E) (hereafter referred to as the Berne Convention).

nation ran the risk of dying intellectually and spiritually if the [then] prevailing book famine was not checked.[19] Indeed many developing countries are threatened with the troubling prospect of intellectual "death" should the current "famine" of educational material fail to be addressed.

Why is a study on copyright and access to educational materials in developing countries needed? What is its relevance for international law and the international community? There exists a substantial amount of literature on the relationship between trade and social issues like health, food and culture. A number of studies have examined the relationship between international trade and human rights in general,[20] intellectual property and human rights,[21] patents and health from the perspective of human rights,[22] or patents and access to food.[23] A specific focus has been noticeable with regards to the interplay between WTO law and human rights,[24] although quite often with the emphasis

19 Records of the Intellectual Property Conference of Stockholm, June 11 to July 14, 1967, (vol. II), Summary Minutes, Main Committee II, World Intellectual Property Organizations, Geneva, 1971, p.948.

20 Joost Pauwelyn. *Conflict of Norms in Public International Law: How WTO Law Relates to other Rules of International Law*. (Cambridge: Cambridge University Press, 2003). (hereinafter referred to as Pauewelyn, Conflict of norms); Thomas, Cottier, Joost, Pauwelyn, and Elizabeth, Bürgi Bonanomi, eds. *Human Rights and International Trade*. Oxford, Oxford University Press, 2005. (hereinafter referred to as Cottier *et al*, Human rights and international trade); Petersmann, Ernst-Ulrich, "Human rights and international trade: defining and connecting the two fields." in Cottier, Thomas *et al, ibid*, pp. 29–94; Carlos Justino, Lopez Hurtado. *The WTO Legal System and International Human Rights*, (PhD Thesis, Graduate Institute of International Studies, Geneva. 2006); Thomas Cottier. "Trade and human rights: a relationship to discover." in Thomas Cottier ed. *The Challenge of WTO Law: Collected Essays*. London, Cameron May: 2007, 527–550, (hereinafter referred to as Cottier, Trade and human rights).

21 For example, in Resolution E/CN:/SUB.2/RES/2001/21, of 16 August 2001, the Sub-commission on the promotion and protection of Human Rights, Stated that "actual or potential conflict exists between the implementation of TRIPS Agreement and the realization of economic, social and cultural rights, in particular the rights to self-determination, food, housing, work, health and education, and in relation to transfers of technology to developing countries." See also Holger Hestermeyer, *Human Rights and the WTO: The case of Patents and Access to Medicines*. (Oxford: Oxford University Press, 2007) (hereinafter Hestermeyer, Human Rights and the WTO); Elangi Botoy Ituku, *Propriété Intellectuelle et Droits de L'homme: L'impact des brevets pharmaceutiques sur le droit à la santé dans le contexte du VIH/SIDA en Afrique*. (Bruxelles: Bruylant, 2007) (hereinafter Botoy Ituku, Propriété intellectuelle).

22 Hestermeyer, Human Rights and the WTO, *supra*; Botoy Ituku, Propriété Intellectuelle, *supra*,

23 Divvya Vorburger-Rajagopalan, *A Human Rights perspective on Farmers' Rights and the World Trade Organization*. (Ph.D Thesis, Graduate Institute of International and Development Studies, Geneva, 2009).

24 For the influence of human rights on WTO, see Ernst-Ulrich Petersmann, "Time for a United Nations 'Global Compact' for integrating human rights into the law of worldwide organizations: lessons from European integration." *European Journal of International Law*, vol. 13, no. 3, (2002): 621–650; "Human rights and international economic law in the 21st century – need for clarifying their interrelationships." *Journal of International Economic Law*, vol. 1 no. 1, (2001): 3–39; "From 'Negative' to 'Positive integration in the WTO: Time for 'mainstreaming' human rights into WTO law?." *Common Market Law Review*, vol.37, no.6. (December 2000): 1363–1382; and "The WTO Constitution and Human Rights," *Journal of International Economic Law*, vol.3, no.1, (2000): 19–25.

on the WTO and the right to health. Various suggestions have been advanced to resolve the conflict between protection of and access to IP from a human rights perspective. Most studies have concluded that interpretation of IP from a human rights perspective before a WTO dispute settlement panel,[25] or amendment of the TRIPS Agreement[26] could resolve the conflict between the two regimes. A comprehensive study on intellectual property and development[27] gives an overview of various types of IP from a development perspective. But there is no specific focus on education and copyright, let alone copyright in printed form. In most studies, there has been much emphasis on the TRIPS but almost total neglect of other treaties governing intellectual property such as the Berne Convention for the protection of literary and artistic works.[28] As concerns copyright in particular, scholars have taken a general view of access to protected IP works and argued for the application of 'fundamental rights' theory,[29] or use of human rights in general.[30] Recent literature focuses on access challenges in the digital environment,[31] issues which are most urgent for developed rather than developing countries.[32] A recent study by the African

---

25 Hestermeyer, Human Rights and the WTO, *supra;*

26 Botoy Ituku, Propriété Intellectuelle, *supra*

27 Commission on Intellectual Property Rights. *Integrating Intellectual Property Rights and Development Policy.* Report of the Commission on intellectual Property Rights. (London, September 2002). available at http://www.iprcommission.org.

28 Berne Convention, *supra.*

29 Christophe Geiger, "Fundamental rights, a safeguard for the coherence of intellectual property law?." *International Review of Intellectual Property and Competition Law (IIC)* vol. 35 no. 3, (2004): 268–280, (hereinafter Geiger, Fundamental rights).

30 Paul, L.C. Torremans (ed.) *Copyright and Human Rights: Freedom of Expression, Intellectual Property, Privacy,* The Hague, Kluwer Law International, 2004; Paul, L.C. Torremans (ed.) *Intellectual Property and Human Rights: Enhanced edition of Copyright and Human Right,* The Hague, Kluwer Law International, 2008

31 Ruth L. Okediji, "Development in the Information Age: Issues in the Regulation of Intellectual Property Rights, Software and Electronic Commerce," ICTSD/UNCTAD Project on Intellectual Property and Sustainable Development. Issue Paper no.9, May 2004, (available at: www.ictsd.net) (hereinafter referred to as Okediji, Development in the Information Age); by the same author; "Sustainable Access to Copyrighted Digital Information Works in Developing Countries." in Jerome H. Reichman and Keith, Maskus, eds. *International Public Goods and Transfer of Technology Under a Globalized Intellectual Property Regime,* (Cambridge, Cambridge University Press, 2005). (hereinafter referred to as Okediji, Sustainable Access); "The International Copyright System: Limitations, Exceptions and Public Interest Considerations for Developing Countries in the Digital Environment," ICTSD/UNCTAD Project on Intellectual Property and Sustainable Development. Issue Paper no.9, September 2005. (available at: http://www.ictsd.net) (hereinafter referred to as Okediji, The international copyright system); Alan Story, "Study Paper on Intellectual Property Rights, the Internet, and Copyright," Study Paper 5, Prepared as a background paper for the Commission on Intellectual Property Rights, available at http://www.iprcommission.org/graphic/documents/study_papers.htm, (hereinafter referred to as Story, Study Paper 5); Christophe Geiger, "Droit d'auteur et droit du public à l'information: pour un rattachement du droit d'auteur aux droits fondamentaux," Recueil Dalloz, no. 38, 2005, 2686–2689 (hereafter referred to as Geiger, Droit d'auteur); by the same author, The private copy exception, an area of freedom (Temporarily) preserved in the digital environment," *International Review of Intellectual Property and Competition Law,* vol. 37, no.4, (2006): 371–406.

32 At best, developing countries are just beginning to explore the benefits of protecting digital and internet content. See Center for International Environmental Law (CIEL), "Intellectual Property

Copyright and Access to Knowledge Project on access to knowledge in eight African countries pays attention to printed material, among other things, but suffers from limited coverage and does not address developments in the international arena.[33] The question of access to printed copyrighted material for education in developing countries has received relatively little attention.[34] This study seeks to fill the aforementioned research gap. In particular, the focus is on copyright in the analogue environment[35] and the challenges of access to protected works for tertiary or higher educational purposes in developing countries. We endeavour to find solutions to these challenges within the international copyright system,[36] while simultaneously taking into account the special circumstances of developing countries.

Structure of the Research

International copyright law contains safeguards for the use of protected works, normally referred to as limitations and exceptions (or generally flexibilities). The focus of this research is on limitations and exceptions to the rights of reproduction and translation, as well as the distribution right, to the extent that it represents an obstacle to the reproduction or translation of copyrighted work. Chapter one is a short primer on copyright. It highlights the development of international copyright and the purposes behind its protection at the international level. The chapter also briefly outlines the content of the three rights which represent the focus of this study.

Chapter two demonstrates that developing countries have special needs when it comes to access to copyrighted works. It also illustrates how copyright can be a barrier to

---

in European Economic Partnership Agreements with Africa, Caribbean and Pacific countries: What way forward after the CARIFORUM EPA and the interim EPAs?" April 2008, p. 15.

33 Chris, Armstrong, Jeremy, de Beer, Dick, Kawooya, Achal, Prabhala and Tobias, Schonwetter Tobias, *et al* (eds.). *Access to Knowledge in Africa: the Role of Copyright.* Claremont. UCT Press. 2010.

34 Story Alan, "Burn Berne: why the leading international copyright Agreement must be repealed," *Houston Law Review*, vol. 40, no. 3, (2003): 763–801; Ruth L. Okediji, "Fostering Access to Education, Research and Dissemination of Knowledge through Copyright," UNCTAD-ICTSD Dialogue on Moving the pro-development IP agenda forward: Preserving Public Goods in health, education and learning, Bellagio, 29 November – 3 December 2004. (available at: www.ictsd.net) (hereinafter referred to as Okediji, Fostering Access to Education). This is the only article specifically dedicated to access to printed copyrighted material by developing countries. But there exists a recent article on copyright and access to educational materials generally. See Margaret Chon, "Copyright and Capability for Education: and Approach from Below." In *Intellectual Property and Human Development: Current Trends and Future Scenarios.* (Cambridge: Cambridge University Press, 2010), 1–29.

35 In this research, the phrase 'analogue environment' is used interchangeably with 'printed material' or 'hard copy'.

36 But some scholars have advanced the view that the solution in copyright will normatively rest on human rights. See for example, Torremans (ed.) *Intellectual Property and Human Rights, supra.* It is not the place of this book to debate this view, but it will suffice to say that the type of material (whether printed versus digital) and type of access in question (for example criticism versus bulk copying) matters.

access to education in developing countries. Chapter three examines some of the specific exceptions (quotations and use in illustrations) found in international copyright law. The chapter's purpose is to point out the extent to which such exceptions facilitate access to printed copyrighted materials in developing countries.

In chapter four, we examine the general exception, commonly referred to as the three-step test. As in chapter three, the purpose is to show the extent to which this exception facilitates access to education. Through case studies of different national legislation, the chapter also explores whether copyright owners or their national governments intended to have strong and uniform access standards at the international level.

Chapter five examines special regimes put in place for access to copyrighted material in hard copy by developing countries. The question we address is whether the system of compulsory licensing for reproduction and translation as prescribed in the Appendix to the Berne Convention facilitates access to copyrighted works by developing countries, especially considering the fact they have special access needs. Three tables illustrate how the mechanism under the Berne Appendix works and outline the current and past usage of the Appendix. For purposes of a background, the chapter highlights early attempts at providing access to copyrighted works for developing countries at the international level. The chapter thus contains an analysis of the Stockholm Protocol.[37] This is meant to caution the negotiators for international instruments of the possible risks of putting much hope in a treaty as a solution for access.

In chapter six, we explore possible models of practice for access to copyrighted material by developing countries. In particular, we examine the national legislation and judicial practice of developed countries. Can developing countries use flexibilities like fair use or fair dealing, compulsory licensing outside the Berne Appendix, and parallel importation, to facilitate access to printed material? The chapter emphasizes the role of national courts in devising case-by-case exceptions for educational purposes.

Chapter seven explores institutional and normative solutions for access to copyrighted works. There have been a number of developments in the WTO and the World Intellectual Property Organization (WIPO) concerning access to protected material. While the WTO Doha Declaration on TRIPS and Public Health[38] focuses on access to medicine, we use it to demonstrate possible lessons for copyright in the field of education. In the case of WIPO, our focus is on the WIPO Development Agenda and the work of the Standing Committee on Copyright and Related Rights (SCCR). The question we wish to answer is to what extent such developments can be an international solution, or at least represent a process towards that solution, for access to educational materials in developing countries. The study ends by providing a summary of the main points and some general conclusions.

---

37 Protocol Regarding Developing Countries, reproduced in Records of the Intellectual Property Conference of Stockholm, June 11 to July 14, 1967, vol. II, Report of the Work of Main Committee II, World Intellectual Property Organizations, Geneva, 1971, p.1197 (hereinafter referred to as the Stockholm Protocol).

38 Declaration on the TRIPS Agreement and Public Health, adopted on 14 November at the 4th WTO Ministerial Conference, Doha, 9–14 November 2001, document no. WT/MIN(01)/DEC/2, dated 20 November 2001. ((available at http://www.wto.org/english/thewto_e/minist_e/min01_e/mindecl_trips_e.pdf)

CHAPTER ONE

A SHORT PRIMER ON COPYRIGHT

1.1. Introduction

This short primer, as the name suggests, is a very brief introduction to international copyright law. The purpose is to help the reader to understand the basics of copyright as they relate to this research. For this reason, it does not cover everything there is to know about copyright. For more detailed information on copyright or intellectual property in general, the reader is advised to consult other works.[1] In particular, this chapter traces the development of copyright law and highlights the reasons behind the international protection of copyright. The chapter describes the rights of reproduction, translation and distribution.

1.2. What Are Intellectual Property Rights?

Intellectual property (IP) is a creation of the human or legal mind. Therefore, intellectual property rights are, broadly, legal rights, awarded to individuals or companies for their creative work or intellectual activity in the industrial, scientific, literary and artistic fields. Intellectual Property is broadly divided into literary and artistic works and industrial property. The Convention establishing the World Intellectual Property Organization[2] (WIPO), provides that "intellectual property" shall include rights relating to: literary, artistic and scientific works; performances of performing artists, phonograms, and broadcasts; inventions in all fields of human endeavour; scientific discoveries; industrial designs; trademarks, service marks, and commercial names and designations; protection against unfair competition; and all other rights resulting from *intellectual activity* in the industrial,

1 Examples of basic literature include: World Intellectual Property Organization, *WIPO Intellectual Property handbook: Policy, Law and Use*. 2nd edition, Geneva: WIPO Publication no. 489 (E), 2004; and Gregory G. Lettermann, *Basics of International Intellectual Property Law*. (Ardsley: Transnational Publishers, Ardsley, 2001).

2 World Intellectual Property Organization, Convention Establishing the World Intellectual Property Organization, signed at Stockholm on 14 July 1967 and as amended on 28 September 1979, Geneva: WIPO publication No. 250(E), (hereinafter referred to as WIPO Convention).

scientific, literary or artistic fields.[3] Admittedly, this definition is broad and open ended. For example, what is "intellectual activity"? The phrasing of the Article suggests that this definition is merely suggestive of what constitutes intellectual property. The list is, longer than what is indicated, and it is possible to add to it.[4] Indeed, the tendency is to add to items that are protected by IPRs. At the international level, for example, there is now provision for protection of computer programmes under the TRIPS Agreement and technological protection measures under the World Intellectual Property Organization (WIPO) Copyright Treaty (WCT). Let us now examine more closely the definition of copyright – the focus of our study.

Copyrights protect literary and artistic works in many forms, including literature, the authorship or composition of musical and performed works, and the graphic, dramatic, cinematic, performing and the plastic arts. Specific examples of literary works that may be protected can be deduced from the definition of literary and artistic works provided at the international level. Article 2 of the Berne Convention provides in part:

> The expression "literary and artistic works" shall *include every production* in the literary, scientific and artistic domain, whatever the mode of its expression, such as books, pamphlets and other writings; lectures, addresses, sermons and other works of the same nature; dramatic or dramatico-musical works; choreographic works and entertainments in dumb show; musical compositions with or without words; cinematographic works to which are assimilated works expressed by a process analogous to cinematography; works of drawing, painting, architecture, sculpture, engraving and lithography; photographic works to which are assimilated works expressed by a process analogous to photography; works of applied art; illustrations, geography, topography, architecture or science.

The TRIPS Agreement refers to the Berne Convention for the definition of literary and artistic works.[5] The Agreement expressly excludes moral rights,[6] provided for under article 6*bis* of the Berne Convention, from protection.[7] In this work, we limit our discussion to

---

3 *Ibid,* Article 2(viii), (emphasis added). What is referred to as literary, artistic and scientific works belong to the copyright branch of intellectual property. The areas mentioned as performances of performing artists, phonograms, and broadcasts are usually called "related rights" or "neighbouring rights," that is, rights related to or neighbouring copyright. The areas mentioned as inventions, industrial designs, trademarks, service marks, and commercial names and designations constitute the industrial property branch of intellectual property.

4 WIPO Copyright Treaty, adopted in Geneva on 20 December 1996, entered into force on 6 March 2002, WIPO Publication no. 226(E)).

5 Article 1(2) of the TRIPS Agreement provides that "for the purposes of this Agreement, the term "intellectual property" refers to all categories of intellectual property that are the subject of Sections 1 through 7 of Part II." Under article 9(1) of TRIPS, Members are to comply with article 2 of the Berne Convention.

6 Moral rights are defined under Article 6*bis*(1) of the Berne Convention as rights given 'independently of the author's economic rights.' It is a right to 'claim ownership of the work and to object to any distortion, mutilation or other modification of, or other derogatory action in relation to, the said work, which would be prejudicial to his honour or reputation.'

7 Article 9 of the TRIPS Agreement entitled "Relation to the Berne Convention" provides:
Members shall comply with Articles 1 through to 21 of the Berne Convention (1971) and the Appendix thereto. However, Member shall not have rights or obligations under this Agreement in respect of the rights conferred under Article 6*bis* of that Convention or of rights derived therefrom.

economic rights for two reasons. First, unlike moral rights, both TRIPS and the Berne Convention protect economic rights. Second, as we shall demonstrate, it is the protection of economic rights that presents the greatest challenges with respect to access to printed educational materials in developing countries.[8]

1.3. Intellectual Property and Development in General[9]

A discussion on IP and development demands a separate study of its own. Reference to IP and development in this section is only meant to lay foundation for addressing development-related IP issues at a later stage in this research. There are various studies that have attempted to define the relationship between IP and development. So we would kindly refer the reader to some of them.[10]

Analysis of the impact of IP regimes on developed or developing countries is complex. However, it is clear that the development of an indigenous scientific and technological capacity is indispensable for development. Development of the appropriate scientific and technological capacity depends on many factors. But it will at the minimum require an effective education system especially at the tertiary level.[11]

In many countries that are new to the intellectual property regime, the claims of strong intellectual property rights are claims to be able to save the lives of vast proportions of the community afflicted at a young stage with terminal illness, to raise large swathes of people from severe poverty through the stimulation of economic development, and to bring benefits such as literary to more socially isolated groups and thus enable a broader range of valuable human experience.[12]

Indeed, history shows that countries have used IP regimes to further what they perceive as their own economic interests. In the area of patents, for example, a major step in the development of patent law was the U.S, Constitution of 1789 under which, in Article I, Section 8, Congress was granted the power to promote the progress of science and useful arts by securing for limited times to authors and inventors the exclusive right to their respective writings and discoveries. On 10 April 1790, the U.S. enacted "An Act to promote the progress of useful arts," Acts of the First Congress, ch. 34(7). In 1836, the U.S enacted

---

8 Although moral rights can also be an access barrier since they include the right to object to modification or adaptation of a work. However, this is more of a problem in the case of access to works in digital form, music and performances than printed material.

9 Most of the information in this section is adapted from Commission on Intellectual Property Rights, *Integrating Intellectual Property Rights and Development Policy*, 2002, chapter one. Available at http://www.iprcommission.org/home.html.

10 Examples include: Commission on Intellectual Property Rights, *ibid*; UNCTAD-ICTSD, *Resource Book on TRIPS and Development*, (Cambridge: Cambridge University Press, 2005); Daniel Gervais (ed.), *Intellectual Property, trade and Development: Strategies to Optimize Economic Development in a TRIPS-Plus Era*. (Oxford. Oxford University Press, 2007).

11 See section 2.2.

12 Graeme B., Dinwoodie, "The International Intellectual Property System: Treaties, Norms, National Courts, and Private Ordering," in Daniel Gervais, ed. *Intellectual Property, trade and Development: Strategies to Optimize Economic Development in a TRIPS-Plus Era*. (Oxford. Oxford University Press, 2007): 61–114, at 80.

the United States Patent Act, which is arguably, the first modern patent law of the U.S. The Act required all applications to be examined by the government patent office for novelty and usefulness. Although this law did not discriminate between U.S. and foreign inventors with respect to the examination or the extent of rights granted, foreign applicants had to pay much higher fees, especially if they were British. Such discrimination was abolished in 1861 for nationals of countries whose laws were non-discriminatory towards Americans. It was then possible to discriminate against among nations for economic purposes.

The German Patent Act of 1977 was an examination system, as opposed to registration. The most important feature of the Act is that it was possible not to grant patents for inventions deemed contrary to public order or morality. Patenting of inventions regarding luxuries, medicines, articles of food, or chemical products was prohibited. So while it was deemed important to encourage creativity, public policy took into account public welfare as well. Some European countries managed without patent law for much of the 19th century. Switzerland, for example, had a patent system only from 1799 to 1802, not re-establishing it until 1888.[13] The Netherlands prohibited patents from 1869 until 1912.[14] This shows that while patents may be useful, they are not indispensable either.

Until the adoption of the Paris Convention in 1883, and the Berne Convention in 1886, countries' ability to tailor the nature of their regimes to their own circumstances was unconstrained. Even then, the rules of these two Conventions exhibited considerable flexibility. The Paris Convention allowed countries to exclude certain fields of technology from protection and to determine the length of protection afforded under patents. It also permitted revocation of patents, and compulsory licences[15] to remedy abuses.

Numerous countries have at times exempted various kinds of invention in certain sectors of industry from patent protection. Often the law has restricted patents on products confining protection to processes for their production. Typically these sectors have been foodstuffs, pharmaceuticals and chemicals, based on the judgement that no monopoly should be granted over essential goods, and that there is more to be gained by encouraging free access to foreign technology, than by potentially stimulating invention in domestic industry. This approach was adopted by many countries, which are now developed, in the 19th century and for some until late in the 20th Century, and also in the East Asian countries (such as Taiwan and Korea) until relatively recently. However, the Agreement on Trade Related Aspects of Intellectual Property Rights (TRIPS)[16] now forbids discrimination in the grant of patent protection in respect of different fields of technology.

In the recent history, countries in East Asia used weak forms of intellectual property protection designed to suit their particular circumstances depending on their level of

---

13 Francois, Dessemontet. *Intellectual Property Law in Switzerland.* The Hague: Kluwer Law International and Stämpli, 2000. 23.

14 UNCTAD-ICTSD, *Resource Book on TRIPS and Development*, (Cambridge: Cambridge University Press, 2005).

15 A license granted by government to a third party authorizing him to perform acts covered by the exclusive right against the will of the owner of the intellectual property right. It is compulsory because it is granted again the will of the holder of the exclusive right.

16 Agreement on Trade-Related Aspects of Intellectual Property Rights, in *The Results of the Uruguay Round of Multilateral Negotiations, The Legal Texts*. Geneva: World Trade Organization, 1995. Annex 1C (hereafter referred to as the TRIPS Agreement).

development. For example, between 1960 and 1980, during which the economies Taiwan and Korea were transformed, both countries emphasized the importance of imitation and reverse engineering[17] as an important element in developing their indigenous technological and innovative capacity. Korea adopted patent legislation in 1961,[18] but the scope of patenting excluded foodstuffs, chemicals and pharmaceuticals.[19] The patent term was only 12 years. It was only in the mid-1980s, particularly as a result of action by the US under Section 301 of its 1974 Trade Act,[20] hat patent laws were revised, although they did not yet reach the standards that were later set under TRIPS Agreement. A similar process took place in Taiwan.[21] In its 1970 Patent Act, India weakened intellectual property protection in pharmaceuticals. The Act provided, among others, for process protection, for a period of seven years, in food, drugs and chemicals.[22] This allowed patented drugs to be reverse engineered, provided a different process is used in manufacture. This is widely considered to have been an important factor in the subsequent rapid growth of India's pharmaceutical industry, as a producer and exporter of low cost generic medicines, (medicines having a chemical equivalent of a patented drug).[23]

What history demonstrates is that countries have been able to adapt IPR regimes to facilitate technological learning and promote their own industrial policy objectives. Because policies in one country infringe on the interests of others, there has always been an international dimension to debates on IP. The Paris and Berne Conventions recognised this dimension, and the desirability of reciprocity, but allowed considerable flexibility in the design of IP regimes. The standards of protection cannot compare to today under the TRIPS Agreement. With the advent of TRIPS, a large part of flexibility has been removed. It is no longer possible for countries to adopt the kind of measures Korea or Taiwan adopted in their own economic programmes.

---

17 Process of evaluating something to understand how it works in order to duplicate or enhance it. This is particularly relevant in the copyright field where reverse engineering of software may be necessary to ensure interoperability/compatibility with other programs. It is also relevant, for example, to semiconductors and the production of generic medicines.

18 Korea, the Patent Act, Law No. 950, Promulgated on Dec. 31, 1961 Article 31, entitled "unpatentable inventions" provides that inventions liable to contravene public order or morality or to injure public health shall not be patentable, notwithstanding the provisions of Article 29(1) or (2). (Article 29 provides the criteria for patentability).

19 N. Kumar, "Intellectual Property Rights, Technology and Economic Development: Experiences of Asian Countries", Commission on Intellectual Property Rights (CIPR) background paper 1b, CIPR, London, 2002, at 23. Source: http://www.iprcommission.org/graphics/documents/study_papers.htm

20 United States, Section 301 of the Trade Act of 1974, as amended (19 U.S.C. § 2411), is the principal statutory authority under which the United States may impose trade sanctions against foreign countries that maintain acts, policies and practices that violate, or deny U.S. rights or benefits under, trade agreements, or are unjustifiable, unreasonable or discriminatory and burden or restrict U.S. commerce.

21 Kumar, *ibid,* at 23–26

22 India, the Patents Act, 1970, (No. 39 of 1970). (Indian Patent Act 1970). Article 5(a) provides that in the case of inventions claiming substances intended for use, or capable of being used, as food or as medicine or drug, no patent shall be granted in respect of claims for the substances themselves, but claims for the methods or processes of manufacture shall be patentable.

23 Kumar, *supra,* at 27–28

1.4. Historical Development of Copyright Protection: A Brief Survey

The first modern copyright statute was that of England, the Statute of Queen Anne, in 1710.[24] The Statute, entitled "An Act for the Encouragement of Learning, by Vesting the Copies of Printed Books in the Authors or Purchasers of Such Copies," had learning as its main focus. Already, at the beginning of the eighteenth century, there existed a relationship between the protection of private interest in intellectual property and public interest in learning.[25]

In order to encourage the production of public goods or books for learning, the authors needed to be protected from unauthorized use of their works. Therefore, the Statute of Anne banned unauthorized reproduction and sale of literary works and granted monopolies to printers of such works for a limited period of 21 years.[26] Its intent was both to prevent unauthorized printing, reprinting and publishing of books and writings and to encourage 'learned men to compose and write useful books'. Nevertheless, the Statute of Anne was largely the result of a campaign by an association of printers (the Company of Stationers) to reassert control over the English book trade, rather than a law to uphold the rights of authors. Under the Statute, the author of a book or books had "the sole right and liberty of printing and reprinting such books for the term of one and twenty years". This applied to books whose titles were entered into the register of the Company of Stationers.[27]

The Statute of Anne imposed limitations upon the exclusive rights of authors, including allowing of parallel imports and a form of competition policy. For example, the Statute permitted the "importation, vending, or selling" of books in foreign languages

---

24 The Statute of Ann, found in The Founders' Constitution, Volume 3, Article 1, Section 8, Clause 8, Document 2 http://press-pubs.uchicago.edu/founders/documents/a1_8_8s2.html (hereinafter referred to as the Statute of Ann)

25 We acknowledge that education may not have been defined as such at the time, but the point here is that the purpose for copyright was to encourage learning or education, and not to simply to economically compensate the copyright holder.

26 The Statute provides in part:
Whereas printers, booksellers, and other persons have of late frequently taken the liberty of printing, reprinting, and publishing, or causing to be printed, reprinted, and published, books and other writings, without the consent of the authors or proprietors of such books and writings, to their very great detriment, and too often to the ruin of them and their families: for preventing therefore such practices for the future, and for the encouragement of learned men to compose and write useful books; [...] that it may be enacted [...] That [...] the author of any book or books already printed, who hath not transferred to any other the copy or copies of such book or books, share or shares thereof, or the bookseller or booksellers, printer or printers, or other person or persons, who hath or have purchased or acquired the copy or copies of any book or books, in order to print or reprint the same, shall have the sole right and liberty of printing such book and books for the term of one and twenty years, to commence from the said tenth day of April, and no longer; and that the author of any book or books already composed, and not printed and published, or that shall hereafter be composed, and his assignee or assigns, shall have the sole liberty of printing and reprinting such book and books for the term of fourteen years, to commence from the day of the first publishing the same, and no longer; (italics original).

27 Statute of Anne, *ibid*, para. V.

printed overseas. The Statute also granted authority to a wide number of judicial, governmental and academic officials to determine if the sales price of a book was too high or unreasonable. Whoever conducted the price review had wide discretion to determine whether a price was unreasonable and to fix one that seemed just and reasonable. In such cases, the offending bookseller or printer had to pay costs and give public notice of the newly imposed price.[28] In short, there was a kind of price control which made protected works affordable to the public, and in turn, this encouraged learning.

Under the United States Constitution of 1789, the Congress has the power "to promote the Progress of Science and Useful Arts, by securing for limited Times to Authors and Inventors the exclusive Right to their respective Writings and Discoveries."[29] As in the case of the Statute of Anne, authors were protected as a way of encouraging them to provide public goods. The Copyright Act of 1790[30] protected books, maps and charts for a term of 14 years, renewable once as long as the author was still alive. The Copyright Act was amended to conform to international standards,[31] but the aforesaid provision of the Constitution remains unchanged.

These few historical examples demonstrate that at the national level, particularly in developed countries, there was always a public interest in granting copyright protection. Examples of the public interest goals of copyright have included the encouragement of learning and promotion of the progress of science and useful arts.

1.5. Development of Multilateral Protection of Copyright: Copyright Law Becomes a Means to Protect One Country's Works in Another Country

Interest in international protection of copyrights developed early in the nineteenth century as a result of the development of larger national markets for potentially copyrighted works, resulting from the growth and prosperity of the middle class, as well as the increasing transnational nature of those markets.[32] As international trade and cultural exchanges expanded, it became clear that protecting only national creations and inventions could lead to unjust results: if a nation protected only domestic literary and artistic works, foreign works would become available in "pirate" form – usually at a much lower price. This is the basis for the concept of "national treatment," according to which foreign

28 Statute of Anne, *ibid,* para. IV

29 The Constitution of the United States of America (U.S. Constitution), Article 1, Section 8, Clause 8.

30 The Copyright Act of 1790, Act of May 31, 1790, ch. 15. Various Statutory Revisions expanded the scope and term of protection. The rights included: prints (1802): musical compositions, but not public performance, with a term of protection of 28 years renewable for 14 years (1831), dramatic compositions, including public performance rights (1856), photographs (1865) and paintings, drawings, sculpture (1870). In 1909, the term of protection was renewable for another 28 years.

31 Copyright Law of the United State of America and Related Laws, Title 17 of the United States Code, June 2003 (hereinafter referred to as U.S. Copyright Act).

32 Lettermann., *supra* p. 259.

nationals are to be treated in a manner no less favourable than national right holders.[33] To alleviate the effects of only protecting one's own creations/inventions, while also obtaining benefits in return for protecting foreign subject matter, countries started entering into bilateral agreements which mutually granted national treatment to the nationals of partner countries.[34] Here the protection of copyright took on a new role: it became a tool for the protection of one country's works in another country. France led the way in this effort, starting in 1840, by negotiating bilateral treaties regarding the reciprocal recognition of copyright rights. This culminated in a French Decree of 1852, which extended copyright protection to all works without regard to their place of publication or the nationality of the creator.[35]

With the passing of time, there was a proliferation of bilateral treaties which became administratively difficult to manage. Catalogues of such treaties had to be published to allow authors, inventors and users to determine the status of protection around the world.[36] It became apparent that having one international copyright instrument would be useful. A private organization, the International Literary and Artistic Association (ALAI),[37] initiated negotiations towards the first international copyright convention,[38] the Berne Convention of 1886.[39] With the Convention, national standards were harmonized and there were increased opportunities to secure protection of authors' rights in more countries. Significantly, one must bear in mind the reasons why countries agreed to international agreements on regulation of intellectual property. Primarily, states wished to ensure better protection of their intellectual products, such as copyrights, in other countries. As we shall demonstrate, the literature on flexibilities tends to emphasize the access side of the argument, but there is no evidence that this was the focus of the original parties to international conventions – nor is it the aim today. It is not surprising that the early efforts at negotiating an international copyright treaty were made by ALAI, an association representing authors' interests, as opposed to the interests of users of copyrighted material.[40]

---

33 International copyright treaties contain provisions on national treatment. See for example Berne Convention, *supra,* article 5, and the TRIPS Agreement, *supra,* article 3.

34 For a more detailed account of the bilateral phase in the development of international copyright standards, see Daniel J. Gervais, "The Internationalization of Intellectual Property: New challenges from the very old and the very new," *Fordham Intellectual Property and Entertainment Law Journal,* vol. 12, (Spring 2002): 929–990, at 935–939, (hereinafter referred to as Gervais, the internationalization of IP). Ruth L. Okediji, "Back to bilateralism? Pendulum swings in international intellectual property protection," *University of Ottawa Law and Technology Journal,* vol. 1, (2004): 125–147, at 131–137, (hereinafter referred to a Okediji, Back to bilaterailism).

35 Lettermann, *supra,* pp. 259–260; Sam Ricketson *The Berne Convention for the Protection of Literary and Artistic Works: 1886–1986.* (Centre for Commercial Law Studies, Queen Mary College, Kluwer, 1987) (hereinafter referred to as Ricketson, the Berne Convention). See especially pp. 27–36 for content of such bilateral agreements.

36 Gervais, The Internationalization of IP *supra,* p. 935.

37 Commonly known by its French name, "Association Littéraire et Artistique Internationale" (ALAI).

38 Lettermann, *supra,* p. 260.

39 Berne Convention, *supra.*

40 Users may not have had an interest in having an international instrument at that time, since some of the Berne negotiators had provided for public/user interests in their national statutes. (see discussion in section 4.2).

It is also important to note that, since the first multilateral copyright statute – the Berne Convention – was a harmonization of different national and bilateral agreements, it only contained "minimum" standards likely to be acceptable to a sufficiently large number of states, or at the least, a strong core of such states.[41] The original minimum standards of the Berne Convention consisted of both national norms and practices of the negotiating states, common elements of existing bilateral agreements, and principles of bilateral commercial treaties.[42] One aspect that merits particular notice for our purposes is that the majority of developing countries, as we know them today, were not among the negotiating countries.[43] This explains why their national realities[44] were not taken into account. We must bear this in mind, for as we demonstrate below, the conflict between intellectual property rights and education in developing countries is largely a product of differences in these 'national realities' between developed and developing countries.

1.6. Purpose of International Copyright Protection

Intellectual property (IP) law gives creators and other holders of intellectual goods and services, for a limited period of time,[45] a right to prevent others from making use of their creation without their consent. It is not the ability of the formulator of an idea to use that idea that constitutes the IP right. Even without the creation of a separate legal right, no one challenges the formulator's ability to use – or not use – his or her creation. Instead,

---

41 The goals of the ALAI conference were: "[...] (3) the drawing up of certain articles, clear and concise, setting forth the principles that are most likely to be accepted by the various powers and which should constitute the text of a universal convention." See also Solberg, "The International Copyright Union," quoted in Barbara A. Ringer, "The role of the United States in international copyright–past, present and future," *Geo. Law Journal,* vol. 56, (1968): 1050–1079, at 1052. The "minimum" standard principle has been maintained. In case of the Berne Convention, parties are permitted to provide greater copyright protection. Governments can "enter into special agreements among themselves in so far as such agreements grant authors more extensive rights than those granted by the Convention, or certain other provisions not contrary to the Convention." (The Berne Convention, articles 19 and 20.) The TRIPS Agreement equally provides minimum standards. Members can implement in their laws more extensive protection than is stipulated, provided that such protection does not contravene the provisions of the TRIPS Agreement. (TRIPS Agreement, article 1).

42 Okediji, Fostering Access, *supra.*

43 Nora Maija Tocups, "The development of special provisions in international copyright law for the benefit of developing countries," *Journal of the Copyright Society of the U.S.A.*, vol. 29, (1981/1982): 402–421; Irwin A. Olian Jr., "International Copyright and the needs of developing countries: the awakening at Stockholm and Paris," *Cornell International Law Journal,* vol. 7, no. 2, (1973/1974): 81–112.

44 Developing countries found out, after making declarations affirming their obligations under the Berne Convention that they had a great need for copyrighted materials, but that they lacked the financial resources to recognize the rights of authors as they had agreed to do under the Berne Convention. Tocups, *ibid,* p. 408. For special needs of developing countries, see *infra,* chapter 2.

45 In case of copyright, the minimum period of protection is the life of the author plus 50 years (article 7 of the Berne Convention), or for 50 years if not calculated on the basis of the life of a natural person (article 12 of TRIPS).

it is the ability of the formulator to limit the use by others of the idea that constitutes the legal property of IP.

Countries have laws to protect intellectual property for two main reasons. One reason is to give statutory expression to the moral and economic rights of creators to their creations.[46] The second is to promote, as a deliberate act of Government policy, creativity and the dissemination and application of its results.[47] The right of owners to exclude others from using IP without a license from them is generally the greatest economic benefit to IP owners of their IP. IP may also be sold or licensed to others in exchange for monetary payments or other benefits to the IP owner.[48]

According to the Convention Establishing the World Intellectual Property Organization, the promotion of protection of intellectual property throughout the world was seen by the members of the organization as a way to encourage creative activity.[49] It is argued that without copyright, there would be little incentive for creative individuals to write novels, paint pictures or compose music. Nor would there be any incentive for publishers, broadcasters and record companies to invest in the exploitations of those works. Creating a property right in these matters enables them to be traded and permits copyright owners to earn money from them.[50]

Various theories exist as to the purpose of the copyright system. For example, the natural rights argument posits that the purpose of copyright is to reward the author for his creative efforts.[51] The law concretises pre-existing rights of the author to which he is by nature entitled. It is the property in one's own person that is extended to the fruits of one's work and the personal rights, which protect the works as an illustration of the personality of the author.[52] On the other hand, the utilitarian argument posits that the purpose of copyright is to act as an incentive for the author to create, for the benefit of society. Thus, according to Lettermann:

> [...] an IP right was established by the state not to reward existing creators of commercially valuable ideas but to prospectively induce creative people to spend the time, effort, and funds necessary to invent or produce such things that will be of future benefit to all society. [...] there are some public benefits to permitting protection for the creators of some ideas – particularly those that are patentable – as an inducement for those creators to inform all others of their

46 WIPO Convention, *supra,* Preamble.

47 WIPO Handbook, *supra.*

48 Lettermann, *supra,* p. 1.

49 WIPO Convention *supra,* preamble.

50 Peter J. Groves, *Sourcebook on Intellectual Property Law,* (London, Cavendish Publishing Limited, 2003), p. 261.

51 Lucie M.C:R. Guibault, *Copyright Limitations and Contracts: An analysis of the contractual overridability of limitations on copyright,* (The Hague: Kluwer Law International, 2002); William Fisher William, "Theories of intellectual property," available at http://cyber.law.harvard.edu/people/tfisher/iptheory.pdf

52 Christophe Geiger, " "Constitutionalising" intellectual property? The influence of fundamental rights on intellectual property in the European Union," *International Review of Intellectual Property and Competition Law,* vol. 37, no. 4, (2006): 371–406, at 378, (hereinafter referred to as Geiger, Constitutionalising IP).

> ideas which will permit others to build on such innovative ideas to make further advances in commercial technology.[53]

According to the utilitarian theory, the author is to be motivated to create new works by the prospect of a reward in the form of a right, which he can make use of to receive remuneration. Copyright presents itself as a means of rewarding the investment the author must make to create the work and as a remuneration of his efforts.[54] While there may exist some divergence between the different theories, at the least it is agreed that they are concerned with the material interests of the author.[55]

It has been argued that "a lack of copyright protection would not cause creativeness to dry up altogether."[56] In other words, there would still be creativity without copyright protection or granting of statutory rights. For example, authors not induced by copyright include authors of Opensource or open access products. In this category, one can find online journals which are accessed at no cost and Opensource software like Linux's products.[57] These are issues beyond the scope of this research. What is important to highlight for our purposes is that most of the works needed for access to education in developing countries, such as textbooks, are under copyright. If not, these works may be available online, which excludes access to them by the majority of developing countries whose access to the internet is very limited.[58] Although it may be true that there will be authorship without copyright, it is important to distinguish the kind of works in question.

Accordingly, this research focuses on works under copyright protection. As the basis of this research, we use international norms as provided under the Berne Convention for the Protection of Literary and Artistic Works (the Berne Convention) and the Agreement on Trade Related Aspects of Intellectual Property (TRIPS). We refer to the Universal Copyright

---

53 Lettermann, *supra,* p. 6. See also discussion on the historical development on IP, section 1.3). The argument of reward for creative effort is mainly supported in common law countries while civil law countries support the view that copyright is granted as a natural right. In practice, the difference is little, if not insignificant.

54 Geiger, Constitutionalising IP, *supra,* p. 378.

55 A detailed discussion on the different theories on the objective of the copyright system is beyond the scope of this study. But for a summary on the issue, see Guibault, *supra,* pp. 7–15, and the authorities cited therein. The author admits that both the naturalist 'reward' argument and utilitarian 'incentive' argument are concerned with the material interest of the author, *ibid,* p. 11. For a criticism of the two theories, see Geiger, Constitutionalising IP *ibid,* p. 379–382; Kaushik Goburdhun, *Access to knowledge in Africa: how to free a continent from the shackles of copyright,* (LLM thesis, Kent Law School, University of Kent, 2006). 60–87.

56 Groves, *supra* p. 261. in the same sense, see Geiger, Constitutionalising IP, *ibid,* p. 279.

57 For a summary of free access software, see Story, Study Paper Five, *supra,*.

58 The majority of works which are not under copyright are not the kind that developing countries need for access to education. Most of the electronic journals are either very specific, which renders them incapable of serving as general educational resources. An example is the Indian open access educational material programme, where most of the material is not only written in different Indian languages but also focuses on Indian culture. Alternatively, the on-line material is not easily accessible to the majority of developing countries' students who cannot access the internet. See discussion on special access needs of developing countries, in chapter 2.

Convention (UCC)[59] and other multilateral Copyright instruments only when necessary. The purpose of copyright as evidenced in the international instruments is to protect the economic interests of the author or right holder.[60] We illustrate this in more detail as we discuss the different flexibilities or limitations and exceptions to copyrights.

1.7. Rights Conferred by a Copyright

International copyright law grants a number of exclusive rights to authors or copyright holders.[61] Since the focus of this study is not on the rights as such but rather on the exceptions to such rights, we mention them only briefly here, although this does not prevent us from elaborating on their nature where needed to illustrate a point relating to an exception. Authors of literary and artistic works enjoy a number of exclusive rights, including the right to make, distribute and authorize the *reproduction or translation* of their works throughout the term of protection of their rights in the original works,[62] which is normally the life of the author plus 50 years after his death.[63] The rights granted under the TRIPS Agreement include the rights provided for under the Berne Convention[64] as well as the rental right provided for under article 11 of the Agreement.

This research puts emphasis on the reproduction and translation rights, because they are directly relevant for access to printed educational material in developing countries. For developing countries, which mainly depend on textbooks as a source of learning or educational material,[65] their major interest is in being able to reproduce protected textbooks or any learning material in hard copy form. Considering the fact that most protected works in developing countries are imported, and taking into account the multiplicity of languages in developing countries, translations of protected works are a necessity.[66] Our research also focuses on the distribution right, because if developing countries were allowed to reproduce and/or translate protected material but not permitted to distribute it, then few people would have access to the protected work.

---

59 Universal Copyright Convention, concluded at Geneva on 6 September 1952, entered into force on 16 September 1955, and as revised at Paris on 24 July 1971, entered into force on 24 July 1974, *U.N.T.S* 13444 (hereinafter referred to as UCC).

60 With the exception of moral rights, which do not form part of this discussion.

61 There is a subtle yet significant difference in the wording of article 9(2) of the Berne Convention and article 13 of the TRIPS Agreement. While the former refers to legitimate interests of the author the latter refers to legitimate interests of the right holder. For the discussion on use of author/right holder in international copyright law, see *infra,* section 4.3.6. However, in this work, unless specifically indicated, 'author' includes 'right holder'.

62 Berne Convention, *ibid,* Articles 8 and 9 (emphasis added).

63 Berne Convention, *ibid,* article 7(1). Where the term of protection is not equated to a natural person, then it is 50 years, (TRIPS Agreement, article 12).

64 Under the TRIPS Agreement, Members are supposed to comply with their obligations under the Berne Convention (article 2(2) of TRIPS) and they shall apply articles 1 through 21 of the Berne Convention and the Appendix thereto.

65 UNESCO, "Basic Learning Materials Initiative," Chapter 6, Available at http://www.unesco.org/education/blm/chap6_en.php.

66 See explanation in section 2.4.

1.7.1. *Reproduction Right*

The reproduction right is of special significance for both developed and developing countries, whether the material is in hard copy or in electronic form. Indeed, the right of the owner to prevent others from making copies (reproduction) of his work is the most basic right that copyright bestows. For example, the reproduction of copies of a protected work is the act performed by a publisher that wishes to distribute copies of a text-based work to the public, whether in the form of printed copies or digital media such as CD-ROMs. Likewise, the right of a phonogram producer to manufacture and distribute compact discs containing recorded performances of musical works requires, in part, the authorization by the composers of such works of the reproduction of their compositions on the recording. Hence, the right to control the act of reproduction is "the legal basis for many forms of exploitation of protected works."[67]

Article 9(1) of the Berne Convention provides for a general right of reproduction. This article stipulates:

> Authors of literary and artistic works protected by this Convention shall have the exclusive right of authorizing the reproduction of these works, in any manner or form.

A general right of reproduction was not recognized under the Berne Convention until the Stockholm Act of 1967.[68] The current text of the Convention is similar to the one discussed at Stockholm. During the Stockholm Conference, differences between the owners of copyrighted works and users were perceptible with respect to the definition of this right. India, one of the largest importers of English literature from the United Kingdom at the time,[69] contested the principle of the current text, which gave a general reproduction right, and instead preferred to either retain the previous text as presented at the Brussels Revision Conference, which was narrower in scope than the current text,[70] or to permit

67 WIPO Handbook, *supra*, p. 44.

68 Article 9 was inserted in the Berne Convention at the Stockholm Revision Conference. Article 24 of the Berne Convention provides for revision of the substantive provisions of the Convention. The revision conferences are named after the place where the revision took place. Thus, the Stockholm Revision Conference refers to a meeting revising the Berne Convention which took place in Stockholm. For more information on the subsequent development of the Convention between 1886 and 1971, see Ricketson, The Berne Convention, *supra*, chapter 3.

69 Ricketson, The Berne Convention *supra*, p. 620. It is reported that the reason the UK did not veto the Stockholm Protocol was the fear that countries such as India and Pakistan would withdraw from the Berne Convention on copyright, and that Britain would isolate herself from the underdeveloped countries who benefit from the Protocol, *ibid*, p. 620, quoting Sacks, Howard D., "Crisis in international copyright – the protocol regarding developing countries," *Journal of Business Law*, 1967, p.26.

70 The Brussels Text read:
"Serial novels, short stories and all other works, whether literary, scientific or artistic, whatever their purpose, and which are published in the newspapers or periodicals of one of the countries of the Union shall not be reproduced in the other countries without the consent of the authors."
The provision is reproduced in Records of the Intellectual Property Conference of Stockholm, 1967, vol. I, Preparatory Documents, S/1 (Berne Convention), World Intellectual Property Organization, Geneva, 1971, p.113. The Brussels text dealt with some aspects of the author's right of reproduction, but a general right of reproduction was not explicitly conferred on the author under the Convention.

the countries of the Berne Union to introduce a compulsory general licence subject to remuneration.[71] On the other hand, the UK, the largest exporter of English literature to India and many developing countries at the time,[72] preferred an even wider scope for the right of reproduction. It thus recommended that the Convention should expressly state that the right of reproducing a work also included the right to reproduce "substantial parts" of the work.[73] Therefore, the quantity or amount of the work reproduced has always been an important element of the general limitations on the right of reproduction or the three-step test.[74]

1.7.2. *Translation Right*

The discussions relating to the inclusion of the translation right in the first Acts of the Berne Convention mainly focused on the duration of such a right. The first text on translation to be included in the Convention provided for duration of protection of 10 years.[75] Translation rights were the subject of lengthy deliberations with regard to the needs of developing countries. As a result a special regime was created for developing countries, which we shall discuss later along with the Berne Appendix. At this point, it is important to bear in mind the fact that from the early stages of the Berne Convention, there were already tensions between developed and developing countries in relation to translation rights. It is reported that the provision on translation rights in the Brussels Act was the result of compromises between producers and users of copyrighted works. Countries like France, a major owner of copyrighted works, favoured the complete assimilation of the translation right into reproduction rights in general. The translation right was conceived as a form of reproduction. In contradiction, those countries with less developed literary and artistic traditions of their own, like Norway, wanted to have ready access to foreign works and therefore wished to limit the duration of the right.[76] The result was that countries that wished to have ready access either became parties to the different revision Acts while maintaining reservations to the provision on translation or they did not join the Convention at all.[77]

---

71 Records of the Intellectual Property Conference of Stockholm, 1967, vol. I, Conference Documents (Document S/86), World Intellectual Property Organization, Geneva, 1971, p.692. India proposed a compulsory licence where remuneration if not agreed upon would have to be fixed by the competent authority.

72 Martin Senftleben, *Copyright, limitations and the Three-Step Test*, (The Hague: Kluwer Law International, 2004); Ricketson, The Berne Convention, *supra*, p. 620.

73 World Intellectual Property Organization, Records of the Intellectual Property Conference of Stockholm, 1967, vol. I, Conference Documents (Document S/42), (Geneva: WIPO, 1971), p. 687.

74 See discussion in chapter 4.

75 *Bulletin de l'Association littéraire et artistique internationale,* Paris, July 1883, p.3, quoted in Jean Cavalli, *La genèse de la Convention de Berne pour la protection des oeuvres littéraires et artistiques du 9 septembre 1886,* (PhD thesis, University of Lausanne, Imprimeries Réunies, Lauanne, 1986), p. 185. For an account of the discussion surrounding the right to translation before its inclusion in the 1886 Berne Convention, see Cavalli, *ibid,* pp. 185–186.

76 Ricketson, The Berne Convention, *supra,* p.385.

77 Countries that joined with reservations include: the Netherlands, Japan (which was a major user of European works at the time), Estonia, Ireland, Italy, Iceland, Yugoslavia and Thailand.

1.7.3. *Distribution Right*

The Berne Convention does not expressly provide for a right of distribution other than in relation to cinematographic and related rights. According to article 14, authors of literary or artistic works have the exclusive right of authorizing the cinematographic adaptation and reproduction of these works, and the distribution of the works thus adapted or reproduced. However, according to article 6 of the WIPO Copyright Treaty (WCT),[78] authors of literary or artistic works enjoy the exclusive right of authorizing the making available to the public of the original and copies of their works through sale or other transfer of ownership. In other words, copyright grants the right of distribution of protected works to the copyright holder.[79] According to the agreed statement to article 6 of the WCT, the expressions "copies" and "original and copies," being subject to the right of distribution, refer exclusively to fixed copies that can be put into circulation as tangible objects. This means that textbook or printed material fall under this category. The WCT is a special agreement within the meaning of article 20 of the Berne Convention.[80]

1.8. Conclusions

History shows that at the national level, particularly in developed countries, there was always a development or public interest goal in granting copyright protection. Examples of the public interest goals of copyright have included the encouragement of learning and promotion of the progress of science and useful arts. However, this is not the case for the international protection of copyright. The protection of copyright at international level was motivated by the need to ensure better protection of one country's copyrighted works in another country. Developing countries, as we know them today, were not among the negotiating parties of the first multilateral copyright instrument. As such, their national realities and development interests were not taken into account. Copyright law confers a number of rights to a copyright holder. However, the reproduction and translation rights are most pertinent for access to printed copyrighted educational material in developing countries. The effectiveness of an exception to these two rights can be limited by a stringent distribution right.

Those that did not join include Russia and Turkey. For a summary of accession to the different revision conferences see Ricketson, The Berne Convention, *supra*, pp. 384–389.

78 WIPO Copyright Treaty (WCT), *supra*.

79 In some national jurisdiction like the United States, 'making available' is different from 'distribution', see for example *London-Sire Records, Inc et al* v. Doe 1 *et al*, 542 F.Supp.2d 153 (2008), and *Capitol Records, Inc v. Jammie Thomas* 579 F.Supp.2d 1210 (2008).

80 WCT, article 1. Article 20 of the Berne Convention allows contracting parties to enter into special agreements between them provided such agreements grant to authors more extensive rights than those granted under the Convention.

CHAPTER TWO

SPECIAL ACCESS NEEDS OF DEVELOPING COUNTRIES AND THE IMPACT OF COPYRIGHT ON ACCESS TO EDUCATION

2.1. Introduction

To better appreciate the usefulness of copyright limitations and exceptions (flexibilities) for access to education, it is essential to understand the access needs of developing countries. In this chapter, we outline the different kinds of needs and demonstrate why developing countries have special access needs that require special exceptions. We also illustrate the role of copyright in access to education in developing countries. However, an understanding of the basic elements of education can help in appreciating the concerns of developing countries. We thus begin this chapter by outlining the pertinent elements of education and the importance of such elements in attaining quality education which can lead to development. The chapter highlights the relationship between intellectual proeprty and development.

2.2. Understanding the Pertinent Elements of Education

There are various ways of defining education: by level, type or what it achieves. But it is difficult to capture what "education" encompasses in just a few words. In this study we are guided by definitions provided by human rights bodies. In doing so, we do not intend to address IP and education from a human rights perspective, but rather to demonstrate the grave implications of lack of access to education for an individual's life.

The Committee on Economic, Social and Cultural Rights (CESCR), defines education in different ways. For example, education is defined in terms of what functional aim it serves or what it can help an individual accomplish. Accordingly, education is both a human right in itself and an indispensable means to realizing other human rights.[1] Katarina Tomaševski, former Special Rapporteur on the right to education, has described

[1] General Comment No. 13, The right to education (art. 13 of the Covenant) in UN Doc. E/2000/22, Report of the Committee on Economic, Social and Cultural Rights, Twenty-first session, 1999, pp 111–127 (hereafter referred to as CESCR General Comment 13) paragraph 1 (hereinafter referred to as General Comment 13).

education as a multiplier. "[I]t is a multiplier in relation to other rights. It enhances all other human rights when guaranteed and forecloses the enjoyment of most, if not all, when denied."[2] Education enhances the realization of other human rights such as the right to food, the right to development, the right to health or the right to work. It overlaps with other human rights such as freedom of religion and the right to privacy.[3] Education is an empowerment right because it provides the individual with the ability to claim one's rights against the state.[4]

From a development perspective, education is key to achieving many development goals. Indeed, developing countries have argued that because education is the key to achievements in other fields, it must be given priority in development programs.[5] These elements serve to highlight the significance of education.

However, for education to have a multiplier impact, its quality is highly important. Indeed, the CESCR states, in relation to the child, that the education offered must be adequate in quality, relevant to the child and must promote the realization of the child's other rights.[6] Article 1 of the Convention on the Rights of the Child (CRC)[7] defines a 'child' as every human being below the age of 18 years unless, under the law applicable to the child, majority is attained earlier. Unfortunately, the CESCR and CRC definitions exclude students at the university level in many developing countries, where university or tertiary education starts at the age of 19.[8] It is the present author's view that for education to achieve its aims, it should be relevant to the person learning at all levels of education, regardless of whether or not the person is considered a child or not. In this connection, it is relevant to inquire as to the aims and objectives of education. We provide a response to this below.

2.2.1. *Aims and Objectives of Education*

According to article 13(1) of the International Covenant on Economic, Social and Cultural Rights (ICESCR), the main objective is to direct education to the full development of the human personality and sense of dignity.[9] In relation to children, the Convention on the Rights of the Child outlines the aims of education as to develop the child's personality, talents and mental and physical abilities to their fullest potential.[10] Article 26(2) of the

---

2 Katarina Tomaševski, *Education Denied: Costs and Remedies.* (London: Zed Books, 2003). 1.

3 Fons Coomans, "In Search of the Core Content of the Right to Education," in Audrey, Chapman, and Sage, Russell, eds, *Core Obligations: Building a Framework for Economic, Social and Cultural Rights*, (Oxford: Intersentia, 2002). 217–246 at p.220.

4 J. Donnelly and R.E. Howard, "Assessing National Human Rights Performance: A Theoretical Framework," *10 Human Rights Quarterly*, (1988): 214–248, p.214.

5 Tocups, *supra*, p. 410.

6 General Comment 13, *supra*, para. 1.

7 Convention on the Rights of the Child, adopted by General Assembly resolution A/RES/44/25 of 12 December 1989, entered into force on 2 September 1990, 1577 *U.N.T.S*, No..3. (hereafter referred to as Convention on the Rights of the Child).

8 This is mainly the case in countries with a British background.

9 International Covenant on Economic, Social and Cultural Rights, (1966), 993 *U.N.T.S* no. 3.

10 Convention on the Rights of the Child, *supra*, article 29(1)(a). The CESCR reiterates this position in General Comment 13, paragraph 4.

Universal Declaration of Human Rights (UDHR) provides, *inter alia,* that education shall be directed to the full development of the human personality.[11] The CESCR[12] takes the view that States parties are required to ensure that education conforms to the aims and objectives identified in article 13(1), as interpreted in the light of article 1 of the World Declaration on Education for All,[13] article 29(1) of the Convention on the Rights of the Child, the Vienna Declaration and Programme of Action,[14] and the Plan of Action for the United Nations Decade for Human Rights Education.[15]

What is missing in these definitions is precise reference to education at the tertiary level or higher institutions of learning. While there is no upper limit on education, there is at least a required minimum level of education at a given point in time and in a given environment. Whether defined as a human right or a development tool, access to higher education is essential, especially in the knowledge economy. As the Commission on Intellectual Property Rights summarized:

> Developing countries need educated people such as doctors, nurses, lawyers, scientists, researchers, engineers, economists, teachers and accountants. Without people skilled in these professions and a system of life-long learning and education, developing countries will be less able to absorb new technologies, generate innovation, and compete in the global knowledge economy. For example, even if developing countries can obtain cheap medicines they will still need trained doctors and nurses to administer them properly in order to save lives.[16]

In this case, access to educational material is not just a choice, but rather a necessity in order to enable an individual to integrate and compete in society. The scope of basic learning needs and how they should be met varies across individual countries and cultures, and inevitably, evolves with the passage of time.[17] Indeed, basic learning needs include both essential learning tools (such as literacy, oral expression, numeracy and problem solving) and basic learning content (such as knowledge, skills, values and attitudes) required by human beings to be able to survive, develop to their full capacities, live and work in dignity, participate fully in development, improve the quality of their lives, make informed decisions, and continue learning.[18] This means that the methods of satisfying these needs also inevitably change. Such methods range from simply having an instructor (at home or in some organized structure like a classroom), reading and

---

11 Universal Declaration of Human Rights, adopted by the General Assembly resolution 217 A (III) of 10 December 1948.

12 CESCR General Comment 13, para. 5.

13 Final Report of the World Conference on Education for All: Meeting Basic Learning Needs, Jomtiem, Thailand, 5–9 March 1990, Inter-Agency Commission (UNDP, UNESCO, UNICEF, World Bank) for the World Conference on Education for All, New York 1990, Appendix 1 Article 1.

14 UN Doc. A/CONF.157/23, World Conference on Human Rights, Vienna, 14–25 June 1993, Declaration and Programme of Action.

15 United Nations Decade for Human Rights: Human Rights Questions including alternative approaches for improving the effective enjoyment of human rights and fundamental freedoms, Document A/51/506/Add.1, appendix.

16 Commission on Intellectual Property Rights, *supra,* p. 114.

17 World Declaration of Education for All, *supra,* art. I(1)

18 World Declaration of Education for All, *supra,* article I(1).

teaching materials, to having access to a computer, the Internet and Internet-based material, databases and information technology. In other words, there are minimum features of any education process. We outline some of them below.

2.2.2. *Essential Features of Education*

The CESCR identifies the essential features of the right to education as availability, accessibility, acceptability and adaptability. *Availability* means that functioning educational institutions and programs must be available in sufficient quantity within the jurisdiction of the State party. What they require to function depends upon numerous factors, including the developmental context within which they operate. For example, all institutions and programs are likely to require teaching materials, while some will also require facilities such as a library, computer facilities and information technology.[19] The *basic element of a* functional *educational institution is the availability of reading and teaching materials.*[20]

Accessibility means that educational institutions and programs must be accessible to everyone, without discrimination, within the jurisdiction of the State party. Physical accessibility means that education must be within safe physical reach, either by attendance at some reasonably convenient geographic location, like a neighbourhood school, or via modern technology such as access to "distance learning" programs.[21] The central factor is that the institutions are functioning. Therefore, for some students,[22] easy access to computer and related programs and internet is a necessity, as in the case of on-line learning.

This leads us to another element of accessibility, that of economic accessibility. It means that education must be affordable for all. This dimension of accessibility is subject to the differential wording of article 13(2) in relation to primary, secondary and higher education: whereas primary education shall be available "free to all", States parties are required to progressively introduce free secondary and higher education.[23] Here one has in mind the cost of items such as educational materials in hard copy like textbooks and the cost of subscribing to educational resources like databases, journals, special electronic libraries, and computer programs. This dimension of accessibility applies to primary as well as other levels of education, and whether or not it is free, meaning whether or not the State pays for it. How then does this relate to intellectual property in general and copyright in particular? We provide an answer below with illustrative examples.

2.3. The Role of Copyright As an Access Barrier to Education in Developing Countries

Copyright protection is a barrier to access to educational materials since the copyright owner has the exclusive right of making, distributing and authorizing the reproduction or

---

19 General Comment 13 *supra,* para. 6(a).
20 Emphasis added.
21 General Comment 13, *ibid,* para. 6(b).
22 The word 'student' is used in a very general sense to include pupils and anyone involved in a learning process.
23 General Comment 13, *supra,* para. 6.

translation of his work. As far as developing countries are concerned, the materials most affected by copyright are textbooks, journals, course packs and any information found in libraries. Since the copyright gives right holders the monopoly right to control the sale, reproduction or translation of their works, right holders not only dictate the price of their work but also how it should be used. With regard to how the work should be used, the right holder controls activities like photocopying, reprinting, distributing or parallel importation of one's works. Normally, publishers do not grant licences for reprinting of books. If they do, the terms are so strict that in the end the reprinted books become very expensive.[24] At the same time, publishers also prohibit parallel importation of educational material from cheaper sources. For example, foreign publishers supplying the Thai book market prohibit the parallel importation of cheaper books from India or China. Similarly, books translated in Thailand cannot be exported to other countries.[25] Above all, they set prohibitive prices that developing countries or even well established developed country universities cannot afford.[26] For example, Cornell University cancelled its journal subscription with Elsevier, the world's leading publisher on scientific, medical and legal issues,[27] when negotiations for better journal prices failed.[28] Harvard University had to decrease the number of scientific journals it purchased from Elsevier because the publisher's practice of 'bundling' journals[29] strained the library's budget.[30] Stuart Shieber, Harvard's James O. Welch and Virginia B. Welch Professor of Computer Science, are reported to have concluded that "[m]ore and more, faculty members realise that the current system for dissemination of scholarly information is unsustainable. Commercial publishers act in the best interests of their shareholders rather than the

---

24 This is for example the case in Thailand and Indonesia. See Consumers International, Project on Access to Knowledge in Thailand, p.17, and Consumers International, Project on Access to Knowledge in Indonesia, p.20. Both projects are available at www.consumersinternational.org.

25 See Consumers International, Project on access to knowledge in Thailand, *ibid,* p.17.

26 In a recent survey Turner provides examples of highly priced journals as: A single title of the Journal of comparative neurology costs $15,294; Brain Research $16,634; Journal of Chromatography A-B $11,109 and Nuclear Physics A-B $19,396. See Turner, Scott, "Library sees red over rising journal price," available at www.brown.edu/Administration/George_Journal/vol24/24GSJ19c.html.

27 In 2005, Reed Elsevier Group Plc reported sales worth $8,887 million and a net income of $798 million. See www.hoovers.com/reed-elsevier-group-plc/--ID_41830--/free-co-factsheet-xhtml. In 2004, Elsevier commanded 18 percent of the market for science, technology and medicine journals, while non-profit publishers combined represented only 21 percent. See Harvard University, "Libraries take a stand: Journals present rising costs to libraries – and to scholarship," *Harvard Gazette Archives,* February 5, 2004, available at www.news.harvard.edu/gazette/2004/02.05/10-libraries.html

28 Cornell University, "After failed negotiations, CU library cancels Elsevier Journal Package," *Cornell Chronicle,* vol. 35 no. 17, December 11, 2003, available at www.news.cornell.edu/Chronicle/03/12/.11.03/CULElsevier.html.

29 'Bundling' refers to a practice where large number of journals are classified into a single subscription. In order to buy one set of journals, the subscriber, such as Harvard University library, has no alternative but to acquire other journals without the possibility of ending the subscription.

30 Harvard University, Libraries take a stand, *supra.* The library decreased subscription from 131 to 35 journals.

scholarly community."[31] There is no doubt, in Harvard's case, that reducing its subscriptions from 131 to only 35 journals[32] had a negative impact on access to scholarly information. Indeed, Marc Kirschner, the Carl W. Walter Professor of Systems Biology in the Harvard Medical School, lamented that "the behaviour of commercial publishers like Elsevier stands as an obstacle to science."[33]

If exorbitant pricing acts as a barrier to access to educational material in developed countries, the situation is much worse when it comes to developing countries. This is because developing country libraries have more limited financial resources and less bargaining power vis-à-vis established publishers than developed countries. Specifically, the Universities of Addis-Ababa (Ethiopia), Nigeria and Yaoundé (Cameroon) had to cancel subscriptions for 1200, 824 and 107 journals respectively.[34]

Restrictions on making copies of copyrighted material and the high costs of royalties for reproducing such material affect the educational goals of developing countries. For example, in South Africa, nursing teachers, public health nurses and other medical personnel who wish to distribute copyrighted materials about HIV/AIDS to students and patients are required to pay copyright royalty fees. As a result, circulation of information is seriously restricted.[35] An interview with a librarian in one of the most advanced academic libraries in South Africa revealed that "material on AIDS may be available in various journals but before nursing sisters can use it in training workshops to teach others about AIDS, copyright permission has to be sought and royalties paid for use. If the permission is denied, the material cannot be used and the information is therefore lost to those who need it urgently."[36] Most such fees are paid to publishers in developed countries since developing countries are net importers of copyrighted educational material from the developed world.[37]

In particular, prohibitive textbook prices are a major obstacle to access to educational material in developing countries. An average income household can pay up to six percent

---

31 Harvard University, Libraries take a stand, *ibid.*

32 Harvard University, Libraries take a stand, *ibid.*

33 Harvard University, Libraries take a stand, *ibid.*

34 Teferra Damtew, "Knowledge creation and dissemination in African Universities with special reference to information and communications technology," quoted in Goburdhun, *supra,* p. 30, footnote 87.

35 Story, Study Paper 5, *supra,* Appendix 2. Note that South Africa is categorized as a developed country by WTO (information available at http://www.wto.org/english/thewto:e/acc_e/acc:e.htm). The point is that if South Africa which is certainly much more developed than most developing countries is not able to fulfil its country's educational needs and its IPR rights obligations at the same time it is much more difficult for least developed countries.

36 See interview with Ms Denise Nicholson, Copyright Services Librarian, University of Witwatersrand, Johannesburg, South African, in Story, Study Paper 5, *supra,* Appendix 2. It is not difficult to see the impact of copyright protection on health as well, but here we focus on copyright and education.

37 On the amount and cost of books imported from the United Kingdom to Mauritius, see Goburdhun, *supra,* pp. 34–36.

of its monthly income for just one textbook.[38] Indeed, studies have shown that textbooks cost more in developing countries than in developed countries.[39]

What is the impact of copyright on the price of educational materials? Many factors determine the price of a book, but prices largely depend on market forces and competition. As an example, the price of a book in Thailand typically consists of: direct costs like paper and ink – 30%; royalty – 10% to 15%; labour cost – 15% and distribution costs – 25% to 40%.[40] Such prices would be much lower if the books were reproduced and distributed in Thailand instead of being imported. As mentioned above, obtaining a licence to reproduce textbooks is not common in Thailand, just like in many other developing countries. Even where a licensing agreement could be obtained, the terms do not favour making reprints in Thailand. At the same time, publishers impose conditions prohibiting the importation of books from cheaper sources like India or China.[41] In Thailand's case, between 10% and 60% of the price of a book results from copyright protection.[42]

Copyright, when enforced, has negative impact on access to educational materials. The use of copyrighted works without the permission of the right holder or royalty being paid incurs the risk of being sued. Copyright disputes in developing countries are not well documented, unlike in developed countries.[43] This gives a false impression of the gravity of the tension between copyright and access to copyrighted works, especially if such tension is measured by the number of decided cases. There are some cases worth referring to. In Uganda, in the case of *John Murray (Publishers) Ltd and others v George William Senkindu and another,*[44] the defendants were charged with copyright infringement when the first defendant sold counterfeit copies of the book *Introduction to Biology* in his Kampala Newstyles bookshop causing a decline in the plaintiff's sales. Ntabgoba, J.; found that the books sold by the first defendant were counterfeit. The plaintiffs were awarded

38 This has been the case in for example Mauritius. See Goburdhun, *supra,* p.36.

39 Goburdhun, *ibid,* pp. 35 and 36. The author calculates the cost of a book by comparing book prices in Mauritius and the UK in terms of percentage of GDP (Appendix 3) and by comparing sale prices of books to the average household earning in Mauritius. See also Consumers International, Project on access to knowledge in Thailand, 2006 and Consumers International, Project on access to knowledge in Indonesia, 2006, *supra.* For example, a student in Indonesia paying $81.70 for "Goodman & Gilman's – The Pharmacological basis of therapeutics" is equal to a student in the US paying $3,170.97 for the same book!

40 Interview with Ms Risuan Aramcharoen, Vice President of the Publisher and Booksellers Association of Thailand, reported in Consumers International Project on Access to knowledge in Thailand, *supra,* p. 17.

41 Due to regional pricing policy, books in China and India are much cheaper than say in the United States or United Kingdom. Consumers International Project on access to knowledge in Thailand, *supra,* p. 17.

42 10% represents the minimum amount of royalty while 60% represents the distribution cost that could be avoided, if a book that is already sold in Thailand was reprinted instead of importing a new one.

43 See for example chapter 6 on models of practice.

44 *John Murray (Publishers) Ltd and others v George William Senkindu and another,* Misc. Application HCCS 1018 of 1997 (unreported).

UGX10 710 000 (USD4 593) in lieu of actual loss incurred by the plaintiffs. In addition, they were awarded UGX6 000 000 (USD2 573) in damages. The court granted a permanent injunction restraining the defendant from committing further infringements against the plaintiff's copyright. Kampala Newstyles, which was one of the largest bookshops in Uganda, collapsed as a result of the case.

In Thailand, in the case of *Public Prosecutor v. Somsak Thanasarasenee,*[45] the defendant was charged with copyright infringement when he copied some or all of the chapters of five books without the permission of the publishers (co-plaintiffs). The defendant was ordered to give the co-plaintiffs all documents which infringed their copyrights and the defendant's four photocopy machines were forfeited. Similarly, in the case of *Public Prosecutor v. Ganokchai Petchdawong,*[46] the defendant was charged with copyright infringement when he copied excerpts from five books, all copyrighted under U.S. law, and produced 43 packs of compiled excerpts without the permission of the copyright owners.[47] In both cases, the defendants argued that the copies were used for educational purposes by the nearby university (Assumption University) and that the reproductions were made on the request of students or professors. The Copyright Act of Thailand allows the use of a protected work for educational purposes (such as research or study) which are not for profit subject to the three-step test.[48] Disregarding at this point whether or not these specific instances were covered by the exception for research or study, a significant point is that since it is up to the courts to decide whether or not copying is permitted under the law, any use of copyrighted material without the permission of the copyright holder is, *prima facie,* regarded as infringement. The possibility of being sued for copyright infringement discourages potential users.

If the risk of being sued for use of copyrighted material without permission does not discourage users of copyrighted work, at least the risk of being subjected to trade sanctions will. A large number of intellectual property holders are watch dogs for their governments in enforcing their rights, or at least reporting perceived infringement. This is for

---

45 *Public Prosecutor v. Somsak Thanasarasenee,* Supreme Court of Thailand, case No. 1732/2000, Judgement of April 4, 2000.

46 *Public Prosecutor v. Ganokchai Petchdawong,* The Supreme Court of Thailand, case No. 5843/2543 (2000) J.S.C., decided on September 18, 2000.

47 The copyright owners were publishers; Prentice Hall, Inc., The Mcgraw – Hill Companies, Inc., and International Thomson Publishing, Inc.

48 Thailand, Copyright Act, B.E. 2537 (1994) as amended, section 32(7). The three-step test in international copyright law allows the use of a protected work in certain special cases (step 1) provided the use does not conflict with the normal exploitation of the work (step 2) and does not unreasonably prejudice the legitimate interests of the copyright holder (step 3). See Article 9(2) of the Berne Convention and article 13 of the TRIPS Agreement. (We discuss the three-step test in chapter 4.) Section 31(1) of the Thai Copyright Act 1994 provides:
An act against a copyright work under this Act of another person which does not conflict with normal exploitation of the copyright work by the owner of copyright and does not unreasonably prejudice the legitimate rights of the owner of copyright shall not be deemed an infringement of copyright.
Subject to the provisions of the first paragraph, the following acts in relation to a copyright work shall not be deemed an infringement of copyright:
(1) research or study of the work which is not for profit;

example the case with the U.S. where the International Intellectual Property Alliance[49] collects information on actual or perceived copyright infringement in the world and advises the U.S. Trade Representative (USTR) on which countries should be put on the Special 301 Watch list. Special 301, as the name suggests, is a procedure set up under section 301 of the U.S. Code. It includes an annual review process led by the Office of the USTR. The U.S. trade law (Special 301) requires an annual review of intellectual property protection and market access practices in foreign countries. Special 301 and its leverage are a full-time process for the copyright industries which work with local private sector representatives, U.S. government officials, and U.S. Embassy officials to address and "resolve copyright problems in scores of countries."[50] If a country is placed on the Watch List, it becomes a candidate for trade sanctions if it does not amend its IP laws to conform to recommendations of the USTR for copyright legal or policy reforms.[51]

It is rightly lamented that if people cannot afford to buy books and educational materials, nor pay for photocopied extracts or copyright royalties, then they will not be able to obtain the information that they need and this will prevent them from receiving a reasonable education or even a basic one, in some instances.[52] Indeed, empirical evidence, based on interviews with relevant officials, students, educational community, shows that most students and libraries cannot afford to buy educational materials. Photocopying remains a major means of access to learning material.[53]

As mentioned above, this study excludes access issues relating to the Internet and technology in general. This is because, although these issues are important for both developed and developing countries, developing countries exhibit more pressing needs. Explication of the special access needs of developing countries helps us appreciate this position.

---

49 The International Intellectual Property Alliance (IIPA) is a private sector coalition formed in 1984 to represent the U.S. copyright-based industries in bilateral and multilateral efforts to improve international protection of copyrighted materials. IIPA is comprised of seven trade associations, each representing a significant segment of the U.S. copyright community. These member associations represent 1,900 U.S. companies producing and distributing materials protected by copyright laws throughout the world. See information on http://www.iipa.com/aboutiipa.html

50 See summary on Special 301 for copyright on http://www.iipa.com/special301.html.

51 In 2009, the IIPA proposed 39, (among whom 4 developed), countries for the Watch List for reasons of copyright piracy. See International Intellectual Property Alliance, "IIPA's 2009 Special 301 Report, on copyright protection and enforcement, submitted to the U.S. Trade Representative on February 17, 2009 by the International Intellectual Property Alliance," available at http://www.iipa.com/special301.html. This is to emphasize the fact that copyright has become a tool for international trade. For example, one of the recommendations to the USTR is that Indonesia takes "actions against book piracy, to protect local and foreign publishers from illegal photocopying on and near university campuses, print piracy, and unauthorized translations." This is the case regardless of the fact that no estimated trade losses were recorded due to book piracy for the previous year 2008. It was recommended that Indonesia be placed on the Priority Watch List, *ibid*, Appendix C.

52 Interview with Ms Denise R. Nicholson, in Story, Study Paper 5, *supra*, Appendix 2.

53 Chris Armstrong, Jeremy de Beer, Dick Kawooya, Achal Prabhala and Tobias Schonwetter, eds. *Access to knowledge in Africa: the Role of Copyright*. (Claremont: UCT Press, 2010).

2.4. Understanding the Special Access Needs of Developing Countries

When it comes to access to educational materials, developing countries have special needs that are not identical to those of developed countries. The main types of access to copyrighted material can be summarized in two categories. 1) consumptive access, which facilitates freedom of information or freedom of the press and cultural exchange.[54] This kind of access can be well served by exceptions such as quotations for criticism, review or news reporting.[55] 2) bulk access, which is most important for developing countries in which education is a top development priority. For such countries, the freedom to quote from copyrighted materials, or make ephemeral recordings, while important, is secondary to the need for affordable access to educational texts, scientific journals and other learning materials.[56]

Issues of access to information in electronic form or on the Internet are also of lesser interest to developing countries than affordable access to printed texts. One may easily assume that the global information society has become ubiquitous, but in fact, most of the world's population continues to have little to no access to the Internet.[57] Thus, for many people in developing countries, the types of copyright barriers that make access to knowledge or educational materials difficult on the Internet are irrelevant because access to the Internet is simply not an option. For example, for students in Kenya, the principal issue is not access to the Internet, but access to textbooks which are in short supply.[58] The whole of East Africa has an internet penetration rate of only 3 percent, the lowest rate in the world, while individuals pay on average between U.S. $250 and $300 per month for access, the highest cost in the world.[59] The developing world does not even come close to universal access to the Internet. A recent study conducted by the World Science Project found that lack of Internet access for African scholars was an important barrier to scholarly productivity. While computers and bandwidth do exist on university campuses in Africa, there are not enough resources to make a positive impact.[60] Doubtless, increasing

54 Ruth Okediji, "Africa and the Global Intellectual Property System: Beyond the Agency Model," in Abdulqawi A. Yusuf, ed. *African Yearbook of International Law,* vol. 12 (2004), (Leiden: Martinus Nijhoff Publishers, Leiden, 2006). 207–251 at 230 (footnote omitted) (hereinafter referred to as Okediji, Africa and the Global Intellectual Property System).

55 Article 10(1) of the Berne Convention.

56 Okediji, Africa and the Global Intellectual Property System, *supra,* p. 230.

57 In relation to access to education, a recent study on Africa demonstrates that limited access to internet is a barrier to distance learning and access to material on the internet. See Chris Armstrong *et al, supra.* This makes the textbook or printed material the more pertinent learning material in developing countries.

58 Alan, Story, Colin, Darch and Debora, Halbert, Debora, eds, *The Copy/South Dossier: Issues in economics, politics and ideology of copyright in the global south,* The Copy/South Research Group, 2006, p.115, available at http://www.copysouth.org, (hereinafter referred to as Story *et al,* the Copy/South Dossier).

59 The whole of Africa, with 14.3% of the total world population, has an internet penetration of only 5.3%. see Internet World Statistics, available at www.Internetworldstats.com.

60 Gisele Dodji Dovi, "More Internet Access Needed for Science to go Global," Science and Development Network, November 25, 2005. Available at: http://www.scidev.net/News/index.cfm?fuseaction=readNews&itemid=2502&language=1.

bandwidth and access to electronic communication is crucial to further advancement in African universities.[61] However, what is more urgent is bulk access to printed material. I explain why.

2.5. Why Developing Countries Need Bulk Access to Printed Copyrighted Material

If developing countries were to design copyright limitations and exceptions, they would be interested in providing exceptions to the reproduction and translation rights, both of which are provided for under the Berne Appendix.[62] This is because developing countries need bulk access to photocopied and translated works. Let me elaborate.

First, it should be noted that the extent of book publishing in developing countries is negligible;[63] the number of books in circulation and for sale is low and unaffordable for the average person.[64] Developing countries are essentially users and not producers of copyrighted materials. Therefore, many textbooks and other educational materials in

61 Steve Song, 'Viewpoint: Bandwidth Can Bring African Universities up to Speed,' IDRC Reports available at: http://www.idrc.ca/es/ev-84498-201-1-DO_TOPIC.html.

62 Discussed in detail in chapter 5.

63 Olian Jr., *supra,* pp. 81–112, p. 90 (stating that of the new books distributed in developing countries, sometimes as many as ninety-five percent are translations from foreign works, the majority of which are imported rather than published within the developing countries); UNCTAD/ICTSD, "Intellectual Property Rights: Implications for Development," Policy discussion paper, August 2003, p.129. Two recent studies on access to knowledge in Indonesia and Thailand revealed the same situation – most of the books, for tertiary education, especially technical education are imported. Even then, the imported books are mainly supplied to a small fraction of the population in the major cities. See Consumers International, Project on copyright and access to knowledge in Indonesia, 2006, *supra,* pp. 12–13; and Consumers International, Project on access to knowledge, Thailand, 2006, *supra,* pp. 12–13 and 18 (available at consumersinternational.org.). This emphasizes the need for reproduction of imported books.

64 United Nations Development Programme, News Bulletin, 18 October 2004, (http://www.undp.org/dpa/pressrelease/releases/2004/october/pr18oct04.html), reporting that every other person in the sub-Saharan region of Africa lives on less than one US dollar a day. This situation applies even to South Africa, the most developed country in Africa. On this point, see Francois Hendrikz, "The Book Chain in South Africa," in Roger, Stringer, ed. *The Book Chain in Anglophone Africa, International Network for the Availability of Scientific Publications.* (Oxford: Oxford University Press, 2002). 72–82. Hendrikz reports that the South African book market is relatively small. It is estimated that only 5% of the population could be regarded as a book-buying market. This may be due to illiteracy, leading to the lack of a reading culture, as well as the high cost of books, (p.77.) see also Denise Rosemary Nicholson, "Free Trade Agreements and TRIPS-plus: implications for developing countries in Africa," a paper presented at the World Library and Information Congress: 71th IFLA General Conference and Council under the theme "Libraries – A voyage of discovery," Oslo, Norway, August 14–18 2005, pp.2 and 5, (available at www.ifla.org/IV/ifla71/Programme.htm. The author uses the example of South Arica, the most developed country in Africa, to demonstrate the illiteracy crisis and how 'restrictive' copyright laws affect access to information. See also Andrew Rens, Achal Prabhala, and Dick Kawooya, "Intellectual property, Education and Access to Knowledge in Southern Africa," ICTSD, UNCTAD and Trade Law Centre for Southern Africa (TRALAC), 2006, 14–15 (hereinafter referred to as Rens *et al* IP, education and access to knowledge in Africa). It is reported that textbooks, particularly for tertiary education are routinely unavailable. They cite the example of Zambia.

developing countries contain material which is reprinted or adapted from books published in industrialized countries.[65] This requires that one obtains permission to use the protected materials. The administrative costs involved in obtaining this permission from the rights owners, who are mainly multinational companies from developed countries,[66] are high.

Second, developing countries depend mostly on printed copies of copyrighted works, as opposed to electronic works, for educational purposes. Furthermore, there are not many trained teachers to transmit the information. As UNESCO has explained, "In poor countries, with untrained teachers, the textbook becomes the most important, if not the only vehicle for the curriculum."[67] The textbook therefore assumes great significance for two main reasons: the lack of sufficient trained teachers and inadequate access to electronic literature. As one librarian at the University of Witwatersrand, South Africa testified:

> Even in more affluent parts of the country, the traditional hard copy/printed version is still the most used form of information. Even in many tertiary institutions which are fortunate to have state-of-the art technology, not all their students have access to computers at home and have to depend on the library's facilities for their information. Many of their students are from historically-disadvantaged backgrounds and they very often do not have the funds to purchase textbooks, let alone other educational material. Many of them depend entirely on photocopied course-packs and access to information in their institutions' libraries. The hard copy is therefore critical to the educational process in South Africa.[68]

---

65 UNESCO, "Basic Learning Materials Initiative," Chapter 6, Available at http://www.unesco.org/education/blm/chap6_en.php; Olian Jr., *supra,* pp. 81–112, p. 90.

66 UNESCO, *World Information Report 1997/98,* UNESCO, Paris, 1998, available at http://www.unesco.org/webworld/com_info_reports/wirenglish/chap23.pdf; Commission on Intellectual Property Rights, *Integrating Intellectual Property Rights and Development Policy,* 2002, p.114, available at http://www.iprcommission.org/home.html

67 UNESCO, "Basic Learning Materials Initiative," *supra,* Chapter 6.

68 Interview with Ms D. R. Nicholson, in Story, Study Paper 5, *supra,* Appendix 2., adding, that "An example, material on AIDS may be available in various journals but before nursing sisters can use the material in training workshops to teach others about AIDS, etc., copyright permission has to be sought and royalties paid for. If the permission is refused, the material cannot be used and the information is therefore lost to those who need it urgently. In such circumstances, where the information is for the public good in a critical situation (as is the AIDS pandemic in South Africa), surely this material should be available for non-commercial educational purposes, without having to get permission and pay high costs for it. Also, for educational purposes, there are many restrictions because of copyright [...]. Many educational institutions pay thousands of rands to copyright proprietors annually for copyright royalties and others do not have the resources to do so. This is affecting the flow of information and the type of information being provided to students. Ultimately, this will affect the whole educational system as the divide between the "haves" and the "have-nots" will widen. Rural educational institutions will provide a far inferior product to their students than more affluent urban institutions. Those needing the most assistance in accessing information will be the most hindered as they will only be able to get their information if they pay large sums of money to reproduce it. I do not believe that all copying should be free, but certain exemptions are necessary for educational purposes, especially in countries where education is in crisis."

For this reason, what is needed is bulk access to printed material for purposes of education and not simply a few copies. Developing countries need to be able to access copyrighted material at affordable prices but without discouraging creativity.[69]

Third, in relation to translation, developing countries need a lot of freedom to translate protected works. This is more so owing to the fact that, in developing countries, the language of instruction in school is not necessarily the language in which the teaching or reading material was written. Since most of the educational material is imported, it requires translation from the language of publication into the local language of instruction. In the case of Africa, which comprises most of the developing countries,[70] it is estimated that there are between 2000 and 3000 languages spoken on the continent, and about 8000 dialects.[71] Basic education is conducted in the native language.[72] To take another example from Asia, tertiary institutions in Indonesia depend on translated books for courses in sciences and technology because most of the instruction is in national languages.[73] As Chandler points out, the preferred way to transmit knowledge is via language, oral or written, in formal or informal settings.[74] Of crucial significance, this language must be understood by those to whom knowledge is to be transmitted. Consequently, translation is a very important element of access to copyrighted educational material in developing countries.

Lastly, imported books are more expensive than locally reproduced or translated books. This is due to a number of factors including foreign exchange limitations, the cost of transportation and the administrative costs involved.[75]

For the above reasons, bulk reproduction and translation become the most pertinent mechanism for access to printed works in developing countries. Yet, it is not possible to copy and/or translate protected works in bulk without violating the author's right to control the reproduction or translation of his work. One would have to get permission,

---

69 In another context, Professor Okediji refers to use of copyrighted material on terms that "do not erode downstream creativity". See Okediji, Sustainable Access, *supra*, p.149.

70 For example, 34 out of the 50 countries designated as LDCs are found in Africa. See UNCTAD, Statistical Profiles of LDCs, *supra*.

71 Information is available at http://africanlanguages.com/.

72 For example, in South Africa alone, there are 11 official languages. The *National Education Policy Act* (Act 27 of 1996) empowers the Minister of Education to determine a national policy for language in education. Subsequently the *Language-in-Education Policy* was adopted in 1997. According to paragraph 1 of the Policy, all the official languages should be used as languages of instruction in school. (Information available at http://www.cyberserv.co.za/users/~jako/lang/xho.htm.) For Africa language instruction in general and mother tongue instruction in particular, see Katrien Beeckman, "Mother tongue instruction in Africa: human rights treaty bodies and the language problem in education," *African Yearbook of International Law*, (2005): 163–192.

73 Consumers International, Project on access to knowledge in Indonesia, *supra*, p. 12.

74 Martin Trent Chandler, *Toward a context-specific language policy for developing countries with an emphasis on language-in-education*, (A thesis presented to the Faculty of the School of International Studies, Department of TESOL and applied linguistics, Biola University, May 1992): p. 63 (available at www.eric.ed.gov).

75 Olian Jr., *supra*, p. 89; see also Consumers International; Project on access to knowledge, Thailand, 2006, p. 12; and Consumers International, Project on access to knowledge, Indonesia, 2006, p.12. Consumers International compares prices between different imported and translated textbooks.

whether on a voluntary basis or by compulsory licensing, for every book that needs to be copied or translated. Clearly, such processes are not only slow, but also expensive. While copyright protection is not the predominant barrier to the access and use of printed materials, it reinforces other problems like cost of materials, overall economic conditions within poor countries and the scarcity of photocopying machines to reproduce and assist in the wider distribution of existing materials.

2.6 Conclusion

Education is an important tool for development. It is even more so for developing than developed countries. The quality of education, especially at tertiary and higher institutions of learning is a very important element in achieving development goals of developing countries. Access to quality educational material is key to ensuring quality education, which is a top development priority. Unfortunately, IP in general and copyright in particular are barriers to development by being an obstacle to achieving quality education in developing countries. Limitations on bulk access to copyrighted material through bulk reproduction and translation as well as parallel importation, coupled with high prices of copyrighted material, requirements for permission or licence to use copyrighted material as well as high licensing requirements, makes copyright an access barrier to education and thus development. Special circumstances in developing countries dictate the need for bulk access to printed copyrighted material through reproduction, translation and parallel importation. First, book publishing in developing countries is negligible and the number of books in circulation and for sale is low and unaffordable. As a result, many of the books in use are imported, which necessitates obtaining permission to use the protected works. Second, developing countries depend heavily on printed copyrighted works as opposed to electronic versions. Third, there is need for bulk translation of copyrighted works because the language of instruction is not the same as the language of publication of the learning material. Last, imported books are more expensive than locally reproduced or translated books.

CHAPTER THREE

THE EFFECT OF LIMITATIONS ON AND SPECIFIC EXCEPTIONS TO COPYRIGHT ON ACCESS TO EDUCATION IN DEVELOPING COUNTRIES

3.1. Introduction

It is often asserted that there is great flexibility under international copyright law for countries to realize national goals like literacy and education.[1] While it is not denied that flexibilities exist, what is not certain is whether these flexibilities can be effectively utilised by developing countries to achieve public interest goals like access to education. In this chapter, we examine limitations on and specific exceptions to the rights of reproduction and translation as they relate to printed material (analogue environment), with a view to demonstrating the extent to which they can be used to facilitate access to education in developing countries.

3.2. Limitations on Copyright Protection Do Not Promote Access to Educational Materials in Developing Countries

Limitations and exceptions as embodied in international copyright law can be broadly broken down into two categories. The first category entails limitations on copyright protection which expressly remove particular categories of works or material from the field of protection. The second category entails limitations on the rights of copyright holders. These two categories are now discussed in turn.

With respect to the first category, once a work is not protected, then there exists no challenge as to access to that work. Such limitations are inherent in the copyright system. They deny protection of a work, and thus preclude the granting of any rights to authors. Briefly, limitations under this category include the duration of protection, the requirement of originality and the idea-expression dichotomy. As regards duration, at the international level a work is protected for the life of the author plus 50 years.[2] Practice at the

---

1 See for example Common Wealth of Learning Copyright Audit on Copyright Law and Education, prepared by Achal Prabhala and Tobias Schonwetter, December 2006, p.1, (available at http://www.col.org/colweb/site/pid/4198) (hereafter referred to as COL Copyright Audit).

2 Berne Convention, article 7(1).

regional and national levels shows a tendency to increase the term of protection to the life of the author plus 70 or 75 years.[3] In respect of originality, copyright protects works that are original or contain a creative element.[4] As regards the idea-expression dichotomy, copyright protects the expression of ideas and not the idea itself.[5]

Exceptions relating to the subject matter of protection wholly exclude protection in the case of particular categories of works such as news of the day[6] or provisions that do not require protection to be given to particular categories, leaving this to national legislators to decide for themselves. Examples include official texts[7] and speeches delivered in the course of legal proceedings.[8] The legal justification for this kind of limitation is the assumption that there are clear reasons of public policy which dictate that copyright protection for the works in question might not be required. For example, it may be necessary in the public interest of free flow of information that these works should be readily and widely available.[9]

Limitations arising from criteria for protection are not expressly stated in the Berne Convention, but include the originality and fixation requirements. We briefly discuss them below.

3.2.1. *Creativity or Originality Requirement*

For a work to be protected, it must be considered an intellectual creation. Article 2(1) of the Berne Convention refers to literary and artistic works which are "productions in the literary, scientific and artistic domain". While these terms are not clarified, the negotiating history of this provision shows that the original parties to the Berne Convention agreed that there should be some element of creativity.[10] Accordingly, the terms depend on how

3 See for example the Council Directive 93/98/EEC of 29 May 1993 on harmonizing the term of protection of copyright and certain related rights, *Official Journal L 290, 24/11/1993 P. 0009–00.* The European Parliament has recently approved the extension of copyright protection for music recordings to 95 years. See "Music copyright to be extended to 95 years," available at http://www.europarl.europa.eu/news/expert/infopress_page/058-48812-040-02-07-909-20090209IPR48791-09-02-2009-2009-false/default_en.htm. Under Free Trade Agreements, some developing countries provide a term of protection longer than in TRIPS. For example Brazil, Ecuador and Peru provide for the life of the author plus 70 years, while Mexico provides for the life of the author plus 75 years, see discussion in Roffe, Pedro, "Bilateral Agreements and a TRIPS-plus world: the Chile – USA Free Trade Agreement," TRIPS Issues Papers, No. 4, Quaker International Affairs Programme (QIAP), Ottawa, 2004, section 3.3.1 (available at www.quno.org) (hereinafter Roffe, Bilateral Agreements). The text of the Chile – USA FTA is available at http://www.ustr.gov/Trade_Agreements/Bilateral/Chile_FTA/Final_Texts/Section_Index.html.

4 Berne Convention, *supra,* article 2(1).

5 TRIPS Agreement, article 9(2). At national level, see for example section 102(b) of the USA Copyright Act.

6 Berne Convention, *ibid,* article 2(8).

7 Berne Convention, *ibid,* article 2(4).

8 Berne Convention, *ibid,* Article 2*bis*(1).

9 Sam Ricketson and Jane C. Ginsburg, *International Copyright and Neighbouring Rights: the Berne Convention and Beyond.* 2nd ed. (volume I), (Oxford: Oxford University Press, 2006). p. 757, (hereinafter referred to as Ricketson *et al,* International Copyright, volume I).

10 Sam Ricketson, *The Berne Convention for the Protection of Literary and Artistic Works: 1886–1986.* (Centre for Commercial Law Studies, Queen Mary College, Kluwer, 1987), pp. 229–230.

national authorities define terms like creativity or originality. There must be creativity or originality. Yet, variations exist from country to country. In Japan, for example, the level of originality required is high. Articles 1 and 2(1)(i) and (ii) of the Japanese Copyright Law[11] require that "thoughts and sentiments are expressed in a creative way." In the United States the originality requirement is lower than in Japan, requiring that 'the work was independently created by the author and that it possesses at least a minimal degree of creativity.'[12] In the case of *Feist Pupl'ns Inc. v. Rural Tele. Serv Co.,* the U.S. Supreme Court held that originality in the case of works based primarily on factual materials requires some modicum of creativity.[13] This decision was followed by the Canadian Court of Appeal in *Tele-direct (Publ'ns) Inc. v. American Bus. Infor. Inc.,*[14] in which the Court held that the basis of copyright is the originality of the work in question. As long as work and discretion have entered into the composition, originality is established. This means that the likelihood of acquiring a copyright is lower in Japan than in the United States or Canada.

3.2.2. *Fixation Requirement*

A further requirement for copyright protection is that the work is fixed in some material form. This requirement is, however, optional for the parties to the Berne Convention.[15] Some countries, especially common law jurisdictions require that a work to be fixed in some form for it to be protected. Under U.S. Copyright law, a literary or artistic work must be 'fixed in a tangible medium of expression'[16] in order to qualify for protection. A work satisfies the fixation requirement if its embodiment in a copy or phonorecord, by or under the authority of the author, is sufficiently permanent or stable to permit it to be perceived, reproduced, or otherwise communicated for a period of more than transitory duration.[17] Under Kenya's Copyright law, literary, artistic and musical works are not eligible for copyright protection unless they are original and *have been written down, recorded or otherwise*

11 Japan, Copyright Law. (Law No.48 of May 6, 1970, as amended by Laws No.49 of May 18, 1978, No. 45 of May 19, 1981, No.78 of December 2, 1983, No. 23 of May 1, 1984, No. 46 of May 25, 1984, No. 62 of June 14, 1985, No.64 of May 23, 1986, No. 65 of May 23, 1986, No. 87 of November 1, 1988, No. 43 of June 28, 1989, No. 63 of May 2, 1991, No. 106 of December 16, 1992, No. 89 of November 12, 1993, No. 112 of December 14, 1994, and No. 91 of May 12, 1995), (Japan Copyright law). Article 2(1)(i) defines "work" as a production in which thoughts or sentiments are expressed in a creative way and which falls within the literary, scientific, artistic or musical domain; and article 2(1)(ii) defines an "author" as a person who creates a work.

12 *Feist Publications v. Rural Telephone Service Co.*, 499 U.S. 340 (1991), U.S. Supreme Court.

13 *Feist Publications, ibid,* The Court referred to the Constitution and concluded that Article I, 8, cl. 8, of the Constitution mandates originality as a prerequisite for copyright protection. It went on to say that the constitutional requirement necessitates independent creation plus a modicum of creativity. *Feist, ibid,* pp. 344–351.

14 *Tele-Direct (Publications) Inc. v. American Business Information, Inc.* (C.A.) 79 C.P.R. 3d 296 (1997), Court of Appeal, October 27, 1997.

15 Berne Convention, *supra,* article 2(2).

16 U.S. Copyright Act, 17 U.S.C. par. 102(a).

17 U.S Copyright Act, *supra.*

expressed in material form.[18] The terminology used is subjective and can only be decided on a case by case basis. On the other hand, civil law jurisdictions do not require fixation. A work is eligible for copyright protection as long as it is in such a form that others can perceive it, regardless of whether or not it is 'fixed' in a tangible medium of expression.[19] Requiring that the work be written, recorded or expressed in some material form minimizes the chances of protecting works that are already covered by copyright, since it is easier to prove that the work is not original.

3.2.3. *Usefulness of Limitations on Copyright Protection for Access to Education in Developing Countries*

Limitations or flexibilities relating to the criteria for protection of a work reduce the number of works that are protected. If works are not protected then, at least in theory, there is no need to ask for permission to access them. In reality, however, it is difficult to envisage a situation in which a work that is greatly needed by the public, such as a school textbook, would not be found as original or would not be fixed in some form. In fact, the likely scenario for a textbook that is not protected for lack of originality or fixation is that it will not find its way to the market. In such a case, no issue of access without permission arises. Furthermore, if a literary work is found not to be original, this means that an alternative work exists to the one that cannot be protected; an earlier or similar version of the work in question. Unfortunately, such scenarios do not exist in relation to much-needed school textbooks in developing countries. In effect, limitations in relation to the criteria of protection do not contribute to solving the problem of access to educational material in developing countries. For this reason, the present study focuses on limitations and exceptions to the rights conferred by a copyright. The second reason we do not focus on limitations on protection is that most developing countries already offer copyright protection for the kinds of works relevant to education. Hence, their challenge is in gaining access to protected works rather than deciding whether and how to protect such works. We will now turn to the second category of limitations: those that would apply when a literary work has been protected and thus the author has been granted rights to the work.

3.3. Limitations on Rights Conferred by a Copyright: General

There exist limitations upon the rights conferred by a copyright. The effect of such limitations or flexibilities is to limit the enjoyment of rights granted by a copyright. Once a work is protected, then the owner has the right to prevent use of the work unless there is an exception to the enjoyment of that right. These kinds of limitations on the rights

---

18 Kenya, the Copyright Act, 2001, Act no. 12 of 2001, section 22(1)(a) and (c) read together with 22(3)(b), (emphasis added).

19 See for example the French Law on the Intellectual Property Code (Legislative Part), (No. 92–597 of July 1, 1992, as last amended by Laws Nos. 94–361 of May 10, 1994, and 95–4 of January 3, 1995), article L.111-1. For a commentary on the French IP Code in general and on this article in particular, see Jean-Luc Piotraut, *Droit de la propriété intellectuelle,* (Paris: Ellipses, 2004). p. 34.

conferred by a copyright are the focus of our discussion. There exist three kinds of exceptions under this category: a) Exceptions to copyright protection which allow for specific uses of protected works without the permission of the copyright owner and without the user incurring any liability for copyright infringement. Within this category are (i) "specific" exceptions, where the permissible acts are specifically stated in international law, and (ii) "general" exceptions, which simply lay down guidelines for determining permissible acts. The latter category is commonly referred to as the "three-step test" and; b) Compulsory licensing mechanisms, which permit certain uses of protected works provided the right holder is remunerated. Under this category are general provisions addressed to all state parties and special provisions addressed to developing countries under the Appendix to the Berne Convention. Different legal justifications exist for each kind of provision. Category (a) represents a limited concession that certain kinds of uses of works that are otherwise protected should be allowed – there is a public interest that justifies overriding the private rights of authors to their works in these particular circumstances. In category (b), the author's rights continue to be protected but are significantly abridged. Public interest justifies the continuance of the use, regardless of the author's consent, but subject to the payment of appropriate remuneration.[20]

The need to strike a balance between the protection of copyright and the public interest cannot be ignored. This point has been emphasized in doctrine[21] as well as by courts.[22] Ever since the early revisions of the Berne Convention, it has been recognized that a need exists for restrictions or limitations upon the rights of authors in particular cases in the public interest. As has been reported by professor Ricketson, an expert on the negotiating history of the Berne Convention, the need for restrictions or limitations upon rights in particular cases was acknowledged in national laws at an early stage and at the outset of the negotiations that led to the Berne Convention. Numa Droz, the president of the 1884 Diplomatic Conference, reminded delegates that 'limits to absolute protection are rightly set by the public interest.'[23] The questions thus arise: what is the 'public interest' and 'whose public interest' is to be taken into consideration? Professors Ricketson and Ginsburg caution that the term 'public interest' is not internationally defined and understandings vary from country to country. Indeed, 'public interest' is a shifting concept that requires a careful balancing of competing claims in each case and one that is frequently

20 Ricketson, the Berne Convention, *supra*, p. 478.

21 For example, Christophe Geiger, "The three step test, a threat to a balanced copyright law?" *International Review of Intellectual Property and Competition Law*, vol. 37, no. 5, (2006): 683–699, (hereinafter referred to as Geiger, the three-step test); Hestermeyer, Human Rights and the WTO, *supra;* Botoy Ituku, Propriété Intellectuelle et Droits de L'homme, *supra*; Tawfik, *supra,* p. 8; Guibault, *supra.*

22 For example, in *Théberge v. Galerie d'Art du Petit Champlain inc.*, [2002] 2 S.C.R. 336, 2002 SCC 34, the Supreme Court of Canada, in justifying limitations on the right of reproduction stated: "The proper balance among these and other public policy objectives lies not only in recognizing the creator's rights but in giving due weight to their limited nature. In crassly economic terms it would be as inefficient to overcompensate artists and authors for the right of reproduction as it would be self-defeating to under compensate them," para. 31.

23 Ricketson, the Berne Convention, *supra*, p. 477. For a summary of the diplomatic conference of 1884 and other conferences leading up to the Berne Convention, see Ricketson *et al*, International Copyright, volume I, chapter 1.

interpreted in different ways at the national level depending upon historical, cultural and social circumstances.[24] With regard to copyright, the public interest of copyright owners is not always the same as that of developing countries,[25] who are mainly users of copyrighted works.[26]

There are a number of *permissible* limitations to the exclusive rights of copyright owners under international intellectual property law.[27] It is not within the scope of this study to discuss all of them in detail. In the following paragraphs, we discuss limitations on the rights of authors and copyright holders which are directly relevant to education or use of educational materials.[28] The question we seek to answer is whether such limitations or flexibilities can be used by developing countries to promote public interests such as access to educational materials in these countries. This necessitates an understanding of the content of these limitations and exceptions and their practical applicability for developing countries, especially as they relate to access to educational materials in the analogue environment.

In the following section we examine specific exceptions to copyrights. We reserve the analysis of general exceptions or the three-step test and exceptions under compulsory licensing or special regimes for developing countries to other chapters.

---

24 Ricketson *et al*, International Copyright, volume I, *ibid*, 2006, p. 756.

25 See discussion in section 3.5.1, *infra*, (national limitations at the time of Stockholm).

26 For example Africa, which comprises the majority of the world's developing countries is a net importer of intellectual property. See for example Yinka Otunba Lawal-Solarin, "Copyright and Education – A publisher's perspective from a developing world," (November 2005), available at http://www.wipo.int/edocs/mdocs/copyright/en/educ_cr_im_05/educ_cr_im_05_www_53637.doc. (Stating that both production and distribution [of books] to the francophone countries [of Africa] are still essentially from France.'

27 As we demonstrate later, there is no obligation under any international treaty on members to provide limitations or exceptions; it is only permissible to do so. On the contrary, there is an obligation to protect the rights. Also in this sense, see Carlos Correa, *Trade related aspects of intellectual property rights: a commentary on the TRIPS Agreement*, (Oxford: Oxford University Press, 2007). p. 135, (hereinafter referred to as Correa, TRIPS); see also Okediji, the International Copyright System, *supra*,. p. 14 (pointing out that the minimum rights provided under the [Berne] Convention are *mandatory*, while limitations and exceptions are *discretionary*) (emphasis added). But consider the view that flexibilities are a sovereign right and a sovereign decision. See Achal Prabhala, and Tobias Schonwetter, Common Wealth of Learning Copyright Audit on Copyright Law and Education, (December 2006), p. 2, (available at http://www.col.org/colweb/site/pid/4198). This assertion is misleading. As we demonstrate with the three-step test and the Berne Appendix, in practice, even the 'sovereign decision' is nonexistent for developing countries.

28 There is a wealth of literature on limitations and exceptions in international copyright law focusing on various issues. See for example: Ricketson, the Berne Convention, *supra*, chapter 9; Ricketson *et al*, International Copyright, volume I, *supra*, chapter 13; Sam Ricketson and Jane C. Ginsburg, *International Copyright and Neighbouring Rights: the Berne Convention and Beyond*, 2nd edition, (volume II), (Oxford: Oxford University Press, 2006). (hereinafter referred to as Ricketson *et al*, International Copyright, volume II), chapter 14 (on exceptions specifically addressed to developing countries under the Appendix to Berne Convention); Ruth L. Okediji, "Toward an international fair use doctrine," *Columbia Journal of Transnational Law*, vol. 39, (2000): (hereinafter referred to as Okediji, international fair use); Okediji, Development in the Information Age, *supra;* Okediji, Fostering Access to Education; *supra*; and Senftleben, *supra*.

3.4. Specific Exceptions to the Rights of Reproduction and Translation Relating to Education

While there are no provisions expressly providing copyright limitations for education, there are two specific exceptions that can directly impact education. These are the *lawful* rights of quotation[29] and utilization of a work by way of *illustration for teaching purposes.*[30]

3.4.1. *Quotations*

We mentioned above that limitations and exceptions in international intellectual property law are of a permission nature and not mandatory. However, the situation is different with respect to quotations. States are under an obligation to make exceptions for quotations.[31] Thus it is provided in article 10(1) of the Berne Convention that:

> It shall be permissible to make quotations from a work which has already been lawfully made available to the public, provided that their making is compatible with fair practice, and their extent does not exceed that justified by the purpose, including quotations from newspaper articles and periodicals in the form of press summaries.

The use of the word 'shall' creates an obligation on the part of the states to allow quotations. There is no equivalent provision in the TRIPS Agreement. However, since Members to the TRIPS Agreement are required to comply with articles 1–21 of the Berne Convention,[32] there is a specific exception for quotations as provided under article 10(1) of the Convention. Indeed, several commentators agree on this view.[33]

What is the scope of this exception? There are several conditions attached to the use of this exception: the work to be quoted must be lawfully available to the public; the making of the quotations must be compatible with fair practice; and the extent of the quotation should not exceed that justified by the purpose.[34] Let us analyse each of these elements in detail in order to elucidate their content.

---

29 The Berne Convention, *supra,* article 10(1) (emphasis added).

30 The Berne Convention, *ibid,* article 10(2) (emphasis added).

31 In the same sense, see Paul Goldstein, *International Copyright: Principles, Law and Practice,* (Oxford: Oxford University Press, 2001). p.304; Sam Ricketson, "WIPO Study on limitations and exceptions of copyright and related rights in the digital environment," Standing Committee on Copyright and Related Rights, 9th Session, Geneva, June 23 to 27, 2003, WIPO document SCCR/9/7 (E) dated April 5, 2003, p.4 (hereinafter referred to as Ricketson, WIPO study); and JamesLove, "Risks and Opportunities for access to knowledge," available at www.wsispapers.choike.org, (hereinafter referred to as Love, Risks and opportunities).

32 TRIPS Agreement, *supra,* article 9(1).

33 Also in this sense, see commentaries by Ricketson, the Berne Convention, *supra,* p. 489; W. Nordemann, K. Vinck, and P. Hertin, Internationales Urherrecht und Leistungsschutzrecht der deutschaprachigen län der unter Berũcksichtigung auch der Staaten der Europäischen Gemeinschaft, Kommentar, Werner, Dusseldorf, 1977, quoted in Ricketson, WIPO Study, *supra,* p. 48 and Nic Garnett, "Automated Rights Management Systems and Copyright Limitations and Exceptions," WIPO Standing Committee on Copyright and Related Rights, Fourteenth Session, Geneva, May 1 to 5, 2006, WIPO document SCCR/14/5, dated April 27, 2006, p. 12.

34 Berne Convention, *supra,* article 10(1).

3.4.1.1. Lawfully Made Available to the Public

The requirement that the work be lawfully available to the public includes work that has been made publicly available by the author or his consent and work that has been made available without his consent under a compulsory licence. It also applies to works made available by any means and is not limited to, for example, making of copies by the author. This can include the making of quotations by a critic or reviewer who takes down passages verbatim for use in his review.[35] Furthermore, there exists no limit on the kinds of works that can be quoted,[36] although the quoting must comply with other conditions such as compatibility with fair practice.

3.4.1.2. Compatible with Fair Practice

Article 10(1) of the Berne Convention requires that the making of the quotation must be compatible with fair practice. Whether a quotation is fair will be determined on a case by case basis. Indeed, it has been argued that "it is a question of proportion and there are cases where quite large numbers of extracts from articles or speeches fail to be quoted".[37] This was stated to imply that "the use in question can only be accepted after an objective appreciation".[38] However, in practice, the length of the quotation matters in deciding whether a use is fair practice or not. This conclusion can be supported by State practice. For example, the French Intellectual Property Code exempts the use of *short* quotations from published works where they are "justified by the critical, polemic, educational, scientific or informational nature of the work in which they are incorporated", as long as the author and source are clearly stated.[39]

It has been opined that the criteria referred to in the general exception of article 9(2)[40] of the Berne Convention would appear equally applicable in determining whether a particular quotation is 'fair': does it conflict with the normal exploitation of the work and unreasonably prejudice the legitimate interests of the author?[41] This argument begs the question whether the exception under article 9(2) of the Berne Convention, or the three-step test, applies to specific exceptions like article 10. The answer would appear to be in the negative considering the fact that article 10(1) of the Berne Convention is a specific provision in contrast to the article 9(2) (which we discuss in detail below under general exceptions). In this case, the *lex specialis* rule applies.[42] Article 10(1), which is more

---

35 Ricketson, the Berne Convention, *supra,* p. 491.

36 *Ibid.*

37 WIPO Guide to the Berne Convention, *supra,* pp. 58–59.

38 Records of the Intellectual Property Conference of Stockholm, 1967, *supra,* Vol. I, (Document S/I), p.117.

39 French Law on the Intellectual Property Code (Legislative Part), (No.92–597 of July1, 1992 (as amended) article L122-5(3)(a) (emphasis added).

40 Article 9(2) of the Berne Convention, or the three-step test, provides:
It shall be a matter for legislation in the countries of the Union to permit the reproduction of such works in certain special cases, provided that such reproduction does not conflict with the normal exploitation of the work and does not unreasonably prejudice the legitimate interests of the author.

41 Ricketson, the Berne Convention, *supra,* p. 492.

42 In this sense, see for example, Correa, TRIPS, *supra,* p. 140.

specific to quotations, should be used as the test instead of article 9(2), which applies to limitations on the right of reproduction in general. Indeed, it was the wish of some delegations at the Stockholm Conference that the exceptions to the right of reproduction provided by article 9 in no way affected the exceptions stipulated in other articles of the Convention.[43] This would apply to the TRIPS Agreement as well, since the exception for quotations is an obligation under TRIPS.

However, the general exception under article 9(2), or the three-step test, applies to article 10 to the extent that it is used as a means to define the scope of the exception. Specific exceptions must be read in the context of the whole Berne Convention and in light of its object and purpose.[44] Article 9(2) or the three-step test forms part of the context of the Berne Convention. The purpose of the Berne Convention is to protect authors' rights in an effective manner.[45] Article 9 fulfils this purpose better than article 10. Under article 9(2), the use of a copyrighted work that conflicts with the normal exploitation of that work will not be accepted. To that extent, 'fairness' is equated to absence of competition with means of exploiting the work in question. In this case, article 9(2) does not affect the exception under article 10 only to the extent that uses under the latter article do not conflict with the normal exploitation of the work. In this sense, article 9(2) is more specific in defining fairness than article 10.

Seen in the light of the TRIPS Agreement, the general exception or three-step test under article 13[46] applies to the interpretation of any limitations and exceptions under the Agreement. Most provisions of the Berne Convention (BC) form part of the context of the TRIPS Agreement,[47] including provisions on limitations and exceptions. The three-step test under article 13 applies to all limitations and exceptions provided for in the TRIPS Agreement and the Berne Convention.[48] Like article 9(2) BC, article 13 of TRIPS is more specific in defining the scope of limitations[49] than article 10 of BC.

3.4.1.3. Must Not Exceed That Justified by the Purpose

At the Stockholm Conference, the length of the quotation was not defined, although conditions for its use were introduced as reflected in the current text of article 10(1) of the

---

43 See comments of Mr Straschnov, the delegate of Monaco, in Records of the Intellectual Property Conference of Stockholm, 1967, *supra,* Summary Minutes (Main Committee I), p.885, para. 1071.

44 The Vienna Convention on the Law of Treaties, 1969, 1155 U.N.T.S, no. 331, article 31.

45 Berne Convention, *supra,* preamble.

46 Article 13 or the three-step test under the TRIPS Agreement which is worded in a way similar to article 9(2) of the Berne Convention stipulates:
Members shall confine limitations and exceptions to exclusive rights to certain special cases which do not conflict with a normal exploitation of the work and do not unreasonably prejudice the legitimate interest of the right holder.

47 With respect to copyright, Members to the TRIPS Agreement are to comply with articles 1 to 21 of the Berne Convention, with the exception of article 6*bis* providing for protection of moral rights. (See TRIPS Agreement, article 9(1)).

48 While the three-step test under the Berne Convention applies only to the reproduction right, the one under the TRIPS Agreement applies to all rights. See discussion in 4.3.1.

49 As a text and through judicial interpretation. While there has been judicial interpretation of article 13 of TRIPS and thus article 9(2) of BC (*United States – Section 110(5) of the US Copyright*

Berne Convention. It was agreed not to limit the quotations by length, but instead to allow quotations on the condition that the work is already lawfully available to the public, the quotations are compatible with fair practice and that they are made only to the extent justified by the purpose. France and Switzerland were opposed to having a text that did not define the length of the quotation. They proposed a reintroduction of the condition that the quotation be short.[50] It would seem that whether or not a quotation is justified by the purpose has to be decided on the facts of each case. In any case, it must be consistent with fair practice.

3.4.2. *Utilization of a Work by Way of Illustration in Teaching*

The relevant provision here is Article 10(2) of the Berne Convention, which provides as follows:

> "(2) It shall be a matter for legislation in the countries of the Union, and for special agreements existing to be concluded between them, to permit the *utilization, to the extent justified by the purpose*, of literary or artistic works *by way of illustration* in publications, broadcasts or sound or visual recordings for teaching, provided that such *utilization is compatible with fair practice.*"[51]

3.4.2.1. The Meaning of "Illustration in Teaching"

Seemingly, this exception is directly relevant to education, as it opens up a possibility of using a literary work for teaching. However, since the use must be by way of illustration, this implies an automatic limitation on the quantity allowed.[52] It has been argued that even if the phrase "by way of illustration" imposes some limitation, one cannot exclude the use of the whole of a work in appropriate circumstances, for example, in the case of an artistic work or short literary work.[53] Nevertheless, the examples presented (use in an artistic or short literary work) reinforce our point: the type and amount of work used in illustration are important. Consider the use of a school textbook in a developing country. What is needed is not illustration of a short literary work, but rather reproduction of the whole book. This sort of reproduction cannot be regarded as simply use by illustration since it will conflict with the normal exploitation of the work.[54]

Act, Report of the Panel, WT/DS160/R, Geneva, 15 June 2000), there is yet to be one on article 10 BC.

50 Records of the Intellectual Property Conference of Stockholm, 1967, *supra*, vol. II, Report of the Main Committee 1 (Substantive provision of the Berne Convention), p. 1146–1147, Documents S/45 and S/68, respectively. Again, we see the producers of copyrighted works protecting their interests by preferring restricted exceptions.

51 Emphasis added.

52 Also in this sense, see Correa, TRIPS, *supra*, p. 141, footnote 121.

53 Ricketson, WIPO Study, *supra*, p. 14.

54 The three-step test applies to article 10(2) BC as a means of defining the different elements of the article.

3.4.2.2. Use Must Not Exceed the Extent Justified by the Purpose

No quantitative limitations are contained in Article 10(2), apart from the general qualification that the utilization of works should only be "to the extent justified by the purpose (...) for teaching." According to the Report of the Main Committee, there was an indication as to the scope of the word "teaching". It was reported:

> "The wish was expressed that it should be made clear in this Report that the word 'teaching' was to include teaching at all levels–in educational institutions and universities, municipal and State schools, and private schools. Education outside these institutions, for instance general teaching available to the general public but not included in the above categories, should be excluded."[55]

Regardless of the definition of teaching, it would appear any illustration is allowed as long as it is limited to the purpose of teaching and compatible with fair practice.[56] Limiting the use to "teaching" excludes other means of learning that extend beyond formal settings, such as self study, post graduate research and peer group learning.[57] What constitutes 'fair practice' in relation to copyright in the analogue environment? We now explore this condition of article 10(2).

3.4.2.3. Compatible with Fair Practice

Whether an illustration is compatible with fair practice must be judged on a case by case basis. Nevertheless, the effect of use on the market of the protected work will determine whether an illustration is fair or not. As in the case of quotations, the three-step test applies to illustrations in teaching, or article 10(2). First and foremost, this is true because article 13 of TRIPS applies to all exceptions in copyright law.[58] The three-step test, whether under article 9(2) BC or article 13 of TRIPS is more specific in defining the limits of illustrations than article 10 BC.[59] Use in illustrations in a way that conflicts with the normal exploitation of the work, or cause a loss of revenue will not be fair practice.[60] How much revenue one loses depends on the kind of work. For example, an illustration in a publication, broadcast or recording for teaching may not cause a large loss in revenue as such. If a passage from a famous pop song were included, it appears safe to assume that the

55 Records of the Intellectual Property Conference of Stockholm, 1967, *supra*, vol. II, Report of the Main Committee I, p. 1148.

56 Okediji, the International Copyright System, *supra*, p.21.

57 Andres Rens, "Implementing the WIPO Development Agenda: treaty provisions on minimum limitations and exceptions for education," Shuttle Foundation Working Paper on Intellectual Property, 2008, p.7 (hereinafter referred to as Rens, Implementing the WIPO Development Agenda).

58 With the exception of article 10(1), since permitting quotations is an obligation. But this is only to the extent that it does not conflict with the normal exploitation of the work, as defined under article 9(2).

59 See discussion in 3.4.1.2.

60 In the same sense, see Ricketson, WIPO Study *supra*, p. 15; and Senftleben, *supra*, p. 197; and See also Ricketson *et al*, International Copyright and Neighbouring Rights, volume I, *supra*, p. 757.

potential royalty revenue would be negligible in comparison to the income accruing from the sale of CDs and the broadcasting of song on the radio. Similarly, a major source of income need not be anticipated when passages are taken from a novel, play or symphony. In such instances, the sale of copies, scores and the work's public performance occupy centre stage.[61] Yet, when the work is used in teaching, it might deeply impact on the exploitation of certain works. If, for instance, paintings or poems that are well known only among experts are included in school books, this may divest the author of a potential major source of royalty revenue. The poem can be reproduced more often than in the original publication. The painting only needs to be reproduced for the first time.[62] In other words, whether an illustration in teaching is fair practice depends on the type of work and the effect of its use on the market of that work.

It has been argued that the use of a work for the purpose of teaching can hardly be regarded as a pillar of the work's exploitation that in general forms part of its *overall commercialization.*[63] Article 10(2) BC, by and large, is

> [U]nlikely to conflict with normal exploitation for two reasons: first, the utilization of a work for teaching will often not constitute a potential major source of income when compared with other possibilities of exploiting the relevant work. Second, even if the use for teaching theoretically ranks among the circle of potential major sources of income, a conflict with a normal exploitation nevertheless does not arise because it does not constitute a *typical source of royalty revenue.*[64]

This argument is difficult to accept. First of all, the impact of a use on the market has to be measured with respect to a particular segment of the market and not on the basis of "overall commercialization". Each portion of the market has to be examined as such. The WTO Panel, in deciding normal exploitation stated that: "the essential question to ask is whether there *are areas of the market* in which the copyright owner would ordinarily expect to exploit the work, but which are not available for exploitation because of this exemption."[65] As regards illustration in teaching, the impact of use in the developed world will not be the same as that in a developing country. While developing countries rely significantly on textbooks and printed material for information, developed countries often obtain the same information from other sources like CDs or the Internet. Thus, for the right holder the particular textbook in the developing country is his typical source of revenue.[66] Since that textbook is the only source of information, illustrations from it are bound to be substantial in order to fulfil the purpose of 'teaching'. But, at the same time,

61 Senftleben, *supra,* p. 197.
62 Senftleben, *supra.*
63 *Ibid,* pp. 197–198, (emphasis added).
64 *Ibid.*
65 United States – Section 110(5) of the US Copyright Act, supra, para. 6.177 (emphasis added).
66 It is possible to think that if people are too poor to buy a book, then there is no market for it. However, whether a market exists for a work depends on the type of work. When it comes to textbooks, especially those of a scientific or technical nature, which are the only source of information, the choice is not so much as whether to buy the book or not, but rather of which other essential needs the family should give up so as to buy that book.

they will not constitute fair practice because they will lead to loss of revenue for the particular book in question.

Length or quantity of illustration is a determining factor. For example, under section 33(1) (a) of the UK Copyright Act, the inclusion of *a short passage* from a published literary or dramatic work in a collection which is intended for use in educational establishments and is so described in its title, and in any advertisements issued by or on behalf of the publisher does not infringe the copyright in the work if the work itself is not intended for use in such establishments and the inclusion is accompanied by a sufficient acknowledgement.[67]

3.4.3. *Conclusions on Effect of Specific Exceptions and Limitations on Access to Education in Developing Countries*

In this chapter we have demonstrated that specific exceptions and limitations cannot be used for access to educational materials in developing countries. Once a work is subject to a limitation, such as limited duration of protection, subject matter that cannot be protected, creativity, originality, etc, then the question of access does not arise (at least in theory). But quite often, works that are not protected, such as news of the day, are not crucial to the advancement of educational goals of developing countries. Likewise, in the case of duration of protection, theoretically, the works will be accessible after the duration elapses. But since this duration is long, there is need to go beyond limitations and apply exceptions to access. In the case of exceptions, the exceptions of quotations or illustrations in teaching apply only to limited quantities; otherwise use must be subjected to the three-step test. As we shall demonstrate below, the main impact of the three-step test is to limit the quantity of what can be used for free. Uncompensated exceptions are permitted only as long as the quantity is negligible. Accordingly, the use of a work as quotations or by way of illustration amounts to fair practice only as long as the amount of text used is short. But this is not the kind of access developing countries need. As demonstrated in chapter two, developing countries need bulk access to copyrighted works. We shall now turn to another form of uncompensated exception – the general exception under article 9(2) of the Berne Convention and article 13 of TRIPS (or the three-step test).

67 United Kingdom, Copyright, Designs and Patents Act 1988 (emphasis added)

CHAPTER FOUR

IMPACT OF THE THREE-STEP TEST UNDER THE BERNE CONVENTION AND THE TRIPS AGREEMENT ON ACCESS TO EDUCATION IN DEVELOPING COUNTRIES

4.1. Introduction

This chapter explores the general exception to copyright, or commonly referred to as the three-step test. In particular, this chapter examines whether the three-step test can be used to promote bulk access to printed educational material. To this end, the chapter traces the origins of the three-step test and reasons for its introduction in the Berne Convention at the Stockholm Conference (and later in the TRIPS Agreement). The chapter also examines the existing national limitations at the time of the Stockholm Conference, analyses the nature and meaning of the three-step test as it relates to access to educational material and its implication on the amount of works that can be used without the permission of the copyright owner. The chapter provides a detailed analysis of intention of the drafters of the three-step test and the judicial practice relating to the test before the WTO dispute settlement panel. Finally, the chapter makes a synthesis of the usefulness of the three-step test for access to educational materials in developing countries.

4.2. The Introduction of General Exception to Copyright in International Copyright Law

Article 9(2), which was added to the Berne Convention during the 1967 revision Conference at Stockholm,[1] was intended to institute a general exception to the reproduction right. Prior to the Stockholm Conference, the Berne Convention did not contain a general provision recognizing reproduction rights. Union Members were free to impose whatever restrictions they wished on reproduction rights, or even deny the protection altogether. In practice, reproduction rights were universally recognised under national legislation, but exceptions to these rights varied considerably from country to country.

[1] All documents relating to the revision of the Berne Convention in 1967 are found in Records of the Intellectual Property Conference of Stockholm, 1967, *supra*.

Some were quite widely drawn, particularly in those countries which were less culturally developed,[2] while other countries like France and Germany which were more culturally developed provided narrower exceptions.[3] Consideration of recognition of the right of reproduction in the Berne Convention started well before the Stockholm Conference. However, it was acknowledged that if a reproduction right was recognized in the Berne Convention, there existed a need for exceptions to that right. It was reported that the Study Group:[4]

> [R]eached the conclusion in its 1964 report that a provision on the right of reproduction should be proposed. This prerogative has a fundamental place in the legislation of countries of the Union; the fact that it is not recognized in the Convention would therefore appear an anomaly. The Study Group noted, however, that if a provision on the subject was to be incorporated in the text of the Convention, a *satisfactory formula would have to be found for the inevitable exceptions to this right.*[5]

The challenge at the time was (and, as we shall demonstrate, still is) how to find a satisfactory formula for copyright limitations and exceptions. The differences in levels of protection served to caution that, in the event the Convention contained a general right of reproduction, then it was important this right does not encroach upon the exceptions already embodied in national law. In this connection, the Study Group observed:

> On the one hand, it was obvious that all the forms of exploiting a work which had, or were likely to acquire, considerable economic or practical importance must in principle be reserved

---

2 For example the Finnish law of 8 July 1961, articles 11-21; the Maltese Copyright Act 1967, sections 7, 9 and 10; the Indian Copyright Act 1957, section 52.

3 Article 41 of the French Copyright Law of 1957; Article 53 and 54 of the German Law on Copyright and Neighbouring Rights (Copyright Law) of September 9, 1965, which entered into force on January 1, 1966, shortly before the Stockholm Revision Conference, restricted reproductions to strictly personal use. Only small parts of the work or single articles from a newspaper or periodical could be reproduced. Copying of large quantities could only be done against payment of remuneration to the copyright holder. (For the influence of German courts on this provision of the German Act, see Senftleben, *supra,* p. 54). It is not surprising that at the Stockholm Conference, the Federal Republic of Germany (FRG) proposed that the wording of the three-step test should include a direct reference to the author's right to remuneration. (See Records of the Intellectual Property Conference of Stockholm, 1967, *supra,* vol. I, Minutes of the Main Committee I, p. 618.) The German proposal was not approved. However, Ulmer, the German Chairman of the Main Committee I explained the rational of paying equitable remuneration. 'In the case of photocopies made by industrial firms, it could be assumed that there would be no "unreasonable" prejudice to the legitimate interests of the author if the national legislation stipulated that adequate remuneration should be paid.' Records of the Intellectual Property Conference of Stockholm, 1967, vol. I, Minutes of the Main Committee I, World Intellectual Property Organization, Geneva, 1971, p. 883.

4 The "Study Group" refers to the group set up to prepare for the Stockholm Conference. The Study Group was composed of the Swedish Government and the BIRPI.

5 Records of the Intellectual Property Conference of Stockholm, 1967, *supra,* Vol. I, Conference Documents, (Document S/1), p. 111 (emphasis added). What was not clear at the time of the proposal is what would be the measure of a satisfactory formula. The logical understanding of this would be that it would have to be satisfactory from the point of view of the authors, after all, this is the objective of the Berne Convention; to protect the rights of authors in as effective and uniform a manner as possible. (See Berne Convention, Preamble.)

> to the authors; exceptions that might restrict the possibilities open to authors in these respects were unacceptable. On the other hand, it should not be forgotten that domestic laws already contained a series of exceptions in favour of *various public and cultural interests* and that it would be vain to suppose that countries would be ready at this stage to abolish these exceptions to any appreciable extent.[6]

It is doubtful whether this observation by the Study Group represented widespread policy acceptable to the Berne Members at the time. Countries were ready to abolish exceptions if doing so was in their public interest. This included preventing those exceptions accepted at the national level from becoming international standards. While there may have been exceptions at national level, they were never intended to become widespread practice that would be considered a model for international legislation. This is more so considering the fact that circumstances in 1886, when the Berne Convention was concluded differed from those in 1967, when the Stockholm revision took place. The major difference was the level of technological advancement, which posed a major threat to copyright protection. Let me illustrate.

The exceptions most frequently recognized in domestic law related to the following works or methods of use: (1) public speeches; (2) quotations; (3) school books and chrestomathies; (4) newspaper articles; (5) reporting of current events; (6) ephemeral recordings; (7) private use; (8) reproduction by photocopying in libraries; (9) reproduction in special characters for use by the blind; (10) sound recordings of literary works for the use of the blind; (11) texts of songs; (12) sculptures on permanent display in public places; etc.; (13) artistic works used as a background in films and television programs; and (14) reproduction in the interest of public safety. However, the text discussed at the Stockholm Conference contained provisions relating solely to exceptions (1) through (6), with a proposal to delete exception (4).[7] This is clear evidence that the exceptions were not all acceptable to all Members. Indeed, as Ginsburg posits, not all the exceptions quoted represent "persuasive policy underpinnings."[8] This is more questionable when it comes to allowing exceptions for access by developing countries. At the time of the Stockholm Conference, there were 58 states party to the Berne Convention, and over one third were developing countries. However, one must consider that most of the developing countries joined the Convention by virtue of their status as colonies.[9] In this sense, they did not have domestic laws of their own, let alone the kind that would reflect their public interests. As we shall demonstrate below, the only country that had developed copyright laws, independent of those of copyright owners, was India. However, India's domestic policy on access to educational materials was not accepted at the Stockholm Conference. Therefore, while there were exceptions for the public interest, they were not intended to be applied

---

6 Records of the Intellectual Property Conference of Stockholm, 1967, *supra,* Vol. I, Conference Documents (Document S/1), pp. 111-112 (emphasis added).

7 Records of the Intellectual Property Conference of Stockholm, 1967, Vol. I, Conference Documents (Document S/1), *supra,* p. 112, footnote 1.

8 Jane C. Ginsburg, "Toward supranational copyright law? The WTO Panel decision and the "three-step test" for copyright exceptions," *Revue Internationale du droit d'auteur,* (2001): 3–65, at 39.

9 Ricketson, the Berne Convention, *supra,* p.592; Lazar, "Developing Countries and authors' rights in international copyright," *Copyright law Symposium,* vol. 19, no. 8 (1971), quoted in Tocups, *supra,* p. 406. The only country that was asked if it wanted to join was India.

beyond national borders. Their inclusion in an international instrument like the Berne Convention would empower consumers of copyrighted works to have easy access to such works. A comparison of the national limitations before the Stockholm Conference and the discussions during the Conference clarifies this point.

4.2. National Limitations at the Time of the Stockholm Conference

In the case of the Federal Republic of Germany (FRG), a new copyright law entered into force on the eve of the Stockholm Conference on January 1, 1966. It was not meant to facilitate access to protected works, but rather to ensure stronger copyright protection. "Its drafters aimed at paving the way for accession to the 1948 Brussels Act of the Berne Convention, *so that German authors could profit from the advanced level of protection granted therein*."[10] At the Stockholm Conference, a German copyright specialist, Mr Ulmer, chaired Main Committee I, which discussed limitations and exceptions. The FRG delegation proposed that the wording of the three-step test should include a direct reference to the author's right to remuneration.[11] Mr Ulmer elaborated the rationale of paying equitable remuneration: "[i]n the case of photocopies made by industrial firms, it could be assumed that there would be no 'unreasonable' prejudice to the legitimate interests of the author if the national legislation stipulated that adequate remuneration should be paid."[12] The German proposal was not approved. However, there is no doubt that the notion that copying of large quantities must be remunerated was embraced by a number of states, including the Netherlands.

In the case of the Netherlands, the Dutch copyright law[13] was being amended at the time of the Stockholm Conference. It came into force in 1972, after the Conference.[14] However, article 16(a) already contained an exception permitting the inclusion of already published works or parts thereof in anthologies and other works for educational or scientific ends, *on the condition that equitable remuneration is paid*.[15] Article 17, which had allowed making a few copies of literary or artistic works provided that the copies served personal practice, study or use, was amended.[16] The rule was intended for copying by hand rather than vast numbers of photomechanical reproductions. It was feared that new copying practices could enter into economic competition with a work's normal exploitation.[17] On 5 November 1964, a proposal for the amendment of the Copyright Act was

---

10 Senftleben, *supra*, p. 53 (emphasis added).

11 See Records of the Intellectual Property Conference of Stockholm, 1967, *supra*, vol. I, Minutes of the Main Committee I, p. 618.

12 Records of the Intellectual Property Conference of Stockholm, 1967, *supra*, vol. I, Minutes of the Main Committee I, p. 883.

13 Netherlands, the Copyright Act 1912 of September 23, 1912, as amended on May 22, 1958.

14 Ibid.

15 The Dutch legislation allowed more limited access than that of the FRG. While under the latter remuneration was for use by industrial firms, the Dutch legislation required remuneration even for educational or scientific use.

16 Netherlands, Copyright Act 1912, *supra*, article 17.

17 N. Van Lingen, "Opus ex Machina – Iets over de problematische verhouding tussen fotokopie en auteursrecht," *Nederlandnse Jurisprudentie*, (1969), 1115, quoted in Senftleben, *supra*, p. 59.

submitted to the Dutch parliament. The amendment sought to ensure that authors, to a great extent, could exert control over reproductions of their work. The new legislation permitted the making of few copies of literary and artistic works for personal practice, study or use. However, in the case of literary works, the quantity reproduced was important. Only reproduction of part of the work was allowed. Copying of the entire work was only possible with the permission of the author.[18]

At the Stockholm Conference, the Dutch position on exceptions was more conservative than what was proposed by the Study Group. For example, in the case of exceptions for 'private use', the Netherlands wanted to allow reproduction only for 'individual or family use'.[19] Similarly, the Netherlands was opposed to an abstract three-step test, as this would give "too much freedom of action to national legislations at the expense of the Convention".[20] The position of the Dutch delegation at the Stockholm Conference is reflected in the final legislation. Unremunerated reproduction is allowed only for solely personal practice, study or use. In such situations, only small parts of literary or artistic works can be copied. Copying by non-profit educational institutions for their students or pupils, provided that such reproductions are necessary for complementing the prescribed or recommended textbooks or non-profit libraries, is allowed *upon remuneration* of the author.[21] According to article 17 of the 1972 legislation, Organizations, institutions (other than non-profit educational institutions) or industrial undertakings can reproduce newspaper or periodical articles or small parts of books. Two conditions are attached to the use of a work under this article: the work copied must be of a scientific nature and the author must receive equitable remuneration.[22]

France's main focus at the time of the Stockholm Conference was the problem of private use. The French Copyright Code of 1957[23] provided only a few exceptions contained in one single article 41. According to this provision, from the moment a work has been disseminated, the author cannot forbid copying for *strictly private use*.[24] The wording of the article connotes a stricter standard than simply 'private use'. Thus, unlike the German and Dutch legislation where 'private use' included use by industrial undertakings and educational institutions,[25] the French legislation can only be understood as limiting the

18 Netherlands, Copyright Act 1912, article 17 of the proposed amendment of 5 November 1964.

19 Records of the Intellectual Property Conference of Stockholm, 1967, *supra,* vol. I, Conference Documents (Document S/1), p. 113.

20 Records of the Intellectual Property Conference of Stockholm, 1967, *ibid,* vol. I, Minutes of the Main Committee I, p. 885 (comments of Gerbrandy, speaking on behalf of the Netherlands).

21 Article 16(b) of the Dutch Copyright Act 1912 as amended on October 27, 1972, stb. 579 read together with the Royal Decree of June 20, 1974, stb. 251, as amended on 23 August 1985, stb. 471. The Royal Decree contains rules on reproduction of written materials by governmental institutions, libraries and for personal use. Levies for this use are paid to a separate Copyright Foundation, the "Stichting Reprorecht".

22 It makes sense that copying by such institutions is remunerated, since it is hard to ensure that the quantities copied are minimal. If large quantities were copied without remuneration, then there would be a conflict with the economic interests of the author.

23 France, Copyright Code, 1957, Law No. 57-298 of March 11, 1957.

24 France, Copyright Code, *ibid,* article 41-2 (emphasis added).

25 Although with a requirement of remuneration for large quantities.

exception to individual or family use.[26] Indeed, at the Stockholm Conference, the French delegation tabled a proposal to replace 'private use' as proposed by the Conference Programme with the wording 'for individual or family use'.[27]

In the case of the United Kingdom, the legislation in force at the time of the Stockholm Conference was the Copyright Act 1956. The Act permitted fair dealing with a work for the purposes of research or private study, criticism or review and for reporting current events.[28] These exceptions touch upon the specific exceptions in the Berne Convention (article 10). A general exception did not exist in the UK legislation. Yet at Stockholm, the UK was strongly opposed to listing specific exceptions to the right of reproduction and instead preferred a general formulation.[29] In fact, the final wording of the three-step test largely reflects the UK proposal, with slight modifications. The formulation proposed by the UK read:

> (2) It shall be a matter for legislation in the countries of the Union to permit the reproduction of such works or substantial parts thereof in certain special cases where the reproduction does not unreasonably prejudice the legitimate interests of the author and does not conflict with a normal exploitation of the work".[30]

In the view of the UK, a general formulation was preferred to specific examples of exceptions because:

> mention [...] of "private use" and "administrative purposes" goes too far and carries many dangers for authors and publishers. Most books are intended for private use, and these expressions could allow the wholesale use of copyright material, without payment, by large industrial organizations or for *governmental educational systems*. On the other hand, the formula we propose can take care of legitimate cases of private use and judicial and administrative purposes.[31]

With regard to developing countries, their practice was dramatically different from that quoted by the Study Group. For example, Article 31 of the Indian Copyright Act of 1957[32] provided for compulsory licensing. Hence, at the Stockholm Conference, India favoured a provision on compulsory licensing, in addition to possibilities listed by the Study Group. The Indian proposal called for payment of such remuneration which, in the absence of agreement, would be fixed by a competent authority.[33] At the Plenary session of the Berne

---

26 For a commentary on the French Copyright law at the time of Stockholm Conference, see Henri Desbois, *Le droit d'auteur en France,* 2nd edition, (Paris: Dalloz, 1966).

27 Records of the Intellectual Property Conference of Stockholm, 1967, vol. I, Conference Documents, (Document S/70), *supra,* p. 690.

28 United Kingdom, the Copyright Act 1956, sections 6(1), 6(2) and 6(3) respectively.

29 The UK was opposed to the mention of 'private use' and administrative purposes'. See Records of the Intellectual Property Conference of Stockholm, 1967, *supra,* vol. I, Minutes of the Main Committee one, p. 857.

30 Records of the Intellectual Property Conference of Stockholm, 1967, *ibid,* vol. I, Conference Documents (Document 42), Geneva, 1971, p. 687.

31 Records of the Intellectual Property Conference of Stockholm, 1967, *supra,* vol. I, Conference Documents (Document 13), p. 630 (emphasis added). Even governmental educational systems did not qualify for free use of copyrighted material.

32 United Kingdom, the Copyright Act 1957, Act No. 14 of June 4, 1957.

33 Records of the Intellectual Property Conference of Stockholm, 1967, *ibid,* vol. I, Conference Documents (Document S/86), p. 692. The following exceptions in the proposal of the Study

Union, the delegation of India contended that the protection of authors' rights could not be considered separately from the rights of users.[34] India suggested that the approach of the Berne Union to the Convention "should be reoriented as soon as possible, treating it less as a trade matter and more as a question of improving the educational and cultural needs of less fortunate users and making their existence felt in the fast-changing world."[35] India argued that Union members should be entitled to limit the exclusive right of reproduction in the public interest.[36]

The foregoing examples show that the Study Group's proposal did not represent acceptable policy underpinnings. It is not surprising that the positions expressed during the discussions on general exceptions often departed from those recommended. However, one cannot deny that some exceptions to exclusive rights existed in national laws. However, national practice was by no means uniform with respect to acceptable exception. What is clear is that countries with a strong interest in copyright protection such as France and UK favoured narrow exceptions. In contradiction, those with a strong interest in public access to copyrighted material, like India, favoured generous exceptions. This pattern underscores the nature of copyright: it is not intended to protect the public interest, but rather to promote the economic interests of authors. As mentioned earlier, where producer countries sought international copyright regulation, the aim was to ensure effective protection of their copyrighted works[37] and not to create rules that would facilitate access to those works. We shall now discuss the three-step test in greater detail.

4.3. The Nature of the Three-Step Test

The final provision of article 9(2) of the Berne Convention reads as follows:

> (2) It shall be a matter for legislation in the countries of the Union to permit the reproduction of such works in certain special cases, provided that such reproduction does not conflict with a

Group were supported by India, in addition to compulsory licensing: a) private use; b) for judicial or administrative purpose; and c) in certain particular cases where the reproduction is not contrary to the legitimate interests of the author and does not conflict with a normal exploitation of the work.

34 For developing countries or users of copyrighted works like India, users have rights [freedom to access protected works] just like holders of copyrighted works. This perception is very different from that of developed countries, like the UK, which view rights as only those of copyright holders. It is not surprising that the two groups of countries have different policies towards copyright protection, with developed countries preferring stronger protection while developing countries prefer stronger access to protected works.

35 Records of the Intellectual Property Conference of Stockholm, 1967, *supra,* vol. I, Plenary of the Berne Union, p. 807 (comments by Singh, speaking on behalf of India).

36 Records of the Intellectual Property Conference of Stockholm, 1967, *ibid,* vol. I, Minutes of Main Committee I, p. 884, (comments by Gae, speaking on behalf of India).

37 This fact is further emphasized during the Stockholm revision of the Berne Convention. See for example, the reasons for German copyright law of 1966 (see discussion in section 4.2.). It is strongly reflected in the objective of the Berne Convention as stated in the preamble. See also Frederick M. Abbott, "Protecting First World Assets in the Third World: Intellectual Property Negotiations in the GATT Multilateral Framework," *Vanderbilt Journal of Transnational Law,* vol. 22 (1989). 689–745, (hereinafter referred to as Abbott, protecting first world assets).

> normal exploitation of the work and does not unreasonably prejudice the legitimate interests of the author.

A similar provision, article 13 of the TRIPS Agreement provides that:

> Members shall confine limitations or exceptions to exclusive rights to certain special cases which do not conflict with a normal exploitation of the work and do not unreasonably prejudice the legitimate interests of the right holder.

These two provisions determine the circumstances under which Member States can provide exceptions to exclusive rights under the three-step test. There is a large amount of literature on the interpretation and scope of these two provisions.[38] It is not the intention of this study to add to that literature. Instead our purpose is to understand what the provisions, or the three-step test, in international intellectual property law in general and international copyright law in particular mean for developing countries and access to education. Consequently, our discussion below is limited to addressing this question.

Article 9(2) of the Berne Convention and article 13 of TRIPS stipulate three distinct conditions that must be complied with before a limitation or an exception can be justified under national law. These are that the limitation or exception: (a) must be granted in "certain special cases"; (b) must not conflict with the normal exploitation of the work"; and (c) should not unreasonably prejudice the legitimate interests of the author (or right holder). Before attempting to understand the meanings of these phrases as they relate to access to education in developing countries, we shall highlight the differences between the two provisions.

Admittedly, the TRIPS Agreement employs the same wording as the Berne Convention. Indeed, it has been argued that article 13 of TRIPS is inspired by article 9(2) of Berne.[39] However, there exist important differences, which affect the applicability of limitations and exceptions under these two treaties.

4.3.1. *The Three-Step Test under the Berne Convention Is Limited to the Reproduction Right While TRIPS Applies to All Rights*

The first difference is that while providing limitations and exceptions is optional under the two treaties, the Berne Convention permits limitations and exceptions only to the reproduction right while the TRIPS Agreement covers all exclusive rights. The WTO Panel in *United States – Section 110(5) of the US Copyright Act*,[40] the first international case to deal directly with the interpretation of the three-step test, acknowledged this difference.[41]

---

38 See for example Correa, TRIPS, *supra*; Ricketson, *et al*, International Copyright and Neighbouring Rights, *supra*, volume I,; Senftleben, *supra*; Ricketson, WIPO Study, *supra*; Sam Ricketson, "The Three-Step Test, Deemed Quantities, Libraries and Closed Exceptions," Advice prepared for the Centre for Copyright Studies Ltd, 2002, (available at www.copyright.com.au/reports%20&%20papers/CCS0202Berne.pdf.) (hereinafter referred to as Ricketson, the three-step test); Ginsburg, *supra*; Ricketson, the Berne Convention, *supra*.

39 See for example Correa, TRIPS *supra*, p. 135.

40 United States – Section 110(5) of the US Copyright Act, *supra*, para. 6.74.

41 United States – Section 110(5) of the US Copyright Act, *ibid*, para. 6.72, the panel stated "The language used in Article 13 of the TRIPS Agreement has its origins in the similar language

In this sense, it appears that the scope of limitations under TRIPS is wider than under the Berne Convention.[42] Indeed, it has rightly been suggested that the logical meaning of the TRIPS provision is such that it allows for the establishment of exceptions not present in the Berne Convention.[43] As one author has put it, article 13 of TRIPS is "a normative framework within which to assess every limitation or exception to all of the exclusive rights conferred either under the Berne Convention or under the WTO/TRIPS itself."[44] The question thus arises whether TRIPS narrows the scope of rights under the Berne Convention, since it seems to provide a wider scope of exceptions. In other words, is TRIPS a "Berne-minus" – diminishing the rights granted under the Berne Convention? Let us explore this question in the following paragraph.

4.3.2. *TRIPS Does Not Restrict the Enjoyment of Rights Granted under the Berne Convention*

Second, if the three-step test under the Berne Convention only applies to the exclusive right of reproduction under article 9(1), this means that under the Berne Convention specific exceptions such as use in illustrations for teaching or exceptions subject to payment of remuneration are not affected as such. On the other hand, article 13 of TRIPS applies to all rights under the TRIPS and Berne Convention, except moral rights.[45] TRIPS provides for "limitations and exceptions to *exclusive rights*" and not only to the right of reproduction. It would seem that TRIPS expands the scope of flexibilities, and as a consequence, restricts the enjoyment of the rights by authors. In this sense, it is arguable that article 13 of TRIPS is a "Berne-minus".[46] Is there a conflict between TRIPS and Berne, since TRIPS Members are under obligation to comply with their obligations under the Berne Convention? In fact, a conflict cannot arise because limitations and exceptions under the Berne Convention are not obligations. They are permissible acts. As Professor Okediji elucidates, "where a country does not establish any limits or exceptions, the international

used in Article 9(2) of the Berne Convention (1971), although the latter only applies in the case of the reproduction right." (Footnotes omitted.) See also Ricketson, WIPO Study, *supra*, p. 44.

42 In the same sense, see also Tawfik, *supra*, p. 10 (in relation to the Berne Convention and TRIPS); and Bruno Fairchild de Vuyst, M. Alea and Gunther Meyer, "Exceptions to intellectual property rights: lessons from WTO-TRIPS panels," *Murdoch University Electronic Journal of Law*, volume 10, No. 4, (December 2003), p. 6, (comparing TRIPS, WCT and the Berne Convention). The latter authors assert that the WCT and TRIPS extend the three-step test to *all economic rights* in the Berne Convention. This view is also supported by J.A.L. Sterling, *World Copyright Law: Protection of authors' works, performances, phonograms, films, video, broadcasts and published editions in national, international and regional law*, (London: Sweet & Maxwell, 2003), p. 440. This is certainly true of TRIPS which explicitly excludes moral rights from its protection, but there is no indication in the WCT that this is the case.

43 Correa, TRIPS, *supra*, p. 144.

44 Tawfik, *supra*, p. 10.

45 The rights under the Berne Convention include translation under article 8, public performance under article 11, broadcasting and other communications under 11*bis*, public recitation under article 11*ter*, and adaptation under article 12. In addition, TRIPS provides rental right under article 11.

46 Senftleben, *supra*, p. 88.

system does not consider this to be a violation of the treaty.[47] Yet, one aspect requires clarification. The exceptions under TRIPS apply to rights under the Berne Convention as incorporated into TRIPS plus rights in TRIPS not found in Berne.[48] Those (extra) limitations and exceptions cannot extend to the rights under the Berne Convention, like moral rights, which are not incorporated under TRIPS; otherwise Members will be violating their obligations under the Berne Convention.[49] Under article 2(2) of TRIPS Members may not invoke TRIPS to justify more expansive limitations and exceptions than those already founding Berne. This means that "any narrower limitations and exceptions clauses that exist in the Berne Convention should continue to serve as a floor below which domestic limitations and exceptions laws may not follow."[50] As emphasized by Ricketson, any exceptions or limitations in relation to the exclusive rights granted under the TRIPS Agreement will need to be consistent with what is already allowed under Articles 1-21 of the Berne Convention.[51] In other words, TRIPS is not and cannot be a 'Berne-minus'.[52] If this were the case, it would place Berne members who are also parties to the TRIPS Agreement in breach of their obligations.[53] We shall illustrate this further by clarifying the scope of the limitations and exceptions under the Berne Convention.

4.3.4. *The Scope of Limitations and Exceptions under the Berne Convention are Considerably Narrow*

Article 20 of BC permits governments to enter into special agreements among themselves. While this is not an obligation, there are obligations if Members choose to conclude such special agreements, which are: a) the special agreements grant authors more extensive rights than those granted by the Berne Convention; and b) the special agreement should

---

47 Okediji, fostering Access to Education, *supra,*.

48 See *United States – Section 110(5) of the US Copyright Act, supra,* para. 6.94; Ricketson, the Three-Step Test, *supra,* p. 42, Limitations and exceptions relate to rights of authors. The only right in the TRIPS agreement that is not found in the Berne Convention is the rental right under article 8 of TRIPS.

49 Under articles 2(2) and 9 of the TRIPS Agreement, nothing in parts I to VI shall derogate from existing obligations that Members have to each other under the Berne Convention, and Members shall comply with the Berne Convention. If the exceptions under TRIPS cover more rights than are provided for under the Berne Convention, it means reducing the rights to the authors and thus not complying with the obligations under the Convention. Providing exceptions is not an obligation under the Berne Convention but protecting the rights of authors is.

50 Laurence R. Helfer, "World Music on a U.S. Stage: An Analysis of the Section 110(5) WTO Dispute," in H. Hansen, ed., *International Intellectual Property law & policy*, vol. 6, (Huntington: Juris Publishing, 2001), Chapter 48, p. 48–5.

51 Ricketson, WIPO Study, *supra,* p. 50.

52 Also on this point, Senftleben, *supra,* p. 88. The author argues that "It would appear schizophrenic to allege that the TRIPS Agreement, by means of a reference to Article 20 BC (Berne Convention), places the obligation on its parties to vest authors with more extensive rights when entering into an additional agreement, while at the same time not meeting the standard of protection reached in the Berne Convention itself". Article 20 BC allows Members to enter into agreements between themselves provided they grant more protection to authors than is provided for under the Convention.

53 Ricketson, WIPO Study, *supra,* p. 51.

not contain provisions that are contrary to the Berne Convention. In other words, the scope of limitations and exceptions is the sum of under the Berne Convention and the provisions of a special agreement, if concluded. Since the special agreement must provide more extensive rights, then it provides less limitations.

In theory, it is possible to imagine a new set of rights for authors not covered by the Berne Convention with limitations which might be greater than those allowed under Berne, but because the limitations are not contradicting the rights acquired under Berne, they could legitimately be more extensive. But the practice of states does not reflect acceptance of this possibility. The special agreements concluded after Berne – the TRIPS Agreement, the WCT, the WPPT, regional agreements like the EU information technology Directive,[54] and the various bilateral and multilateral free trade agreements[55] – all provide more extensive protection but not more limitations. This reflects the intention of copyright owners, who are also the framers of the Berne Convention, which was intended to "exert a maximalist force over multilateral copyright regulation"[56] by, in effect, defining legitimate treaty activities in the copyright realm as only those that unambiguously enhance the rights of authors and owners.[57]

The limitations and exceptions under the Berne Convention are the difference between the Convention and the special agreement (where the latter exists). This means that the scope of exceptions is narrower than it appears in the Convention. We now turn to the third difference between the wording of the three-step test under TRIPS and under the Berne Convention.

4.3.5. *Article 13 of TRIPS Restricts the Use of Exceptions*

The third difference between the three-step test under TRIPS and that under the BC is that the TRIPS provision limits the use of exceptions. Under the Berne Convention, it is permissible for countries to allow, limitations and exceptions, while under the TRIPS, if such limitations or exceptions are allowed there is an obligation to limit them. Thus, the TRIPS Agreement provides that "[m]embers shall confine [limit] limitations or exceptions," before they are even subjected to the Three-Step Test.[58] This means the conditions under TRIPS are stricter than those under the Berne Convention, limiting the limitations.

---

54 Directive 2001/29/EC of the European Parliament and of the Council of 22 May 2001 on the harmonization of certain aspects of copyright and related rights in the information society, Official Journal L 167, 22/06/2001 P. 0010–0019.

55 See for example Pedro Roffe, "Bilateral agreements and the TRIPS-plus world: the Chile-USA Free Trade Agreement," TRIPS Issues Papers, No. 4, Quaker International Affairs Programme, Ottawa, 2004, (available at www.quno.org).

56 Ruth L. Okediji, The International Copyright System, *supra,* 4–9.

57 For more comments on article 20 of the Berne Convention, see Sam Ricketson, The Berne Convention, *supra,* pp. 684–686; Sam Ricketson, and Jane C. Ginsburg, International Copyright and Neighbouring Rights: the Berne Convention and Beyond, 2nd edition, (volume I), *supra,* p. 347–350, Ruth L. Okediji, "The regulation of creativity under the WIPO Internet Treaties," *Fordham Law Review,* vol. 77, (2009), 2379–2410, at 2388–2392.

58 See also the argument of Australia that TRIPS confines limitations and exceptions. *United States – Section 110 (5) of the US Copyright Act, supra,* Annex 1, written submission of Australia, (1 November 1999), para 2.3.

In this sense and contrary to what has been asserted, article 13 of TRIPS is not merely a restatement of article 9 of the Berne Convention.[59] It actually narrows the scope of exceptions. On this point, the WTO Panel has stated:

> It should be noted [...] that Article 13 cannot have more than a narrow or limited operation. Its tenor, consistent as it is with the provisions of Article 9(2) of the Berne Convention (1971), discloses that it was not intended to provide for exceptions or limitations except *for those of a limited nature.*[60]

This interpretation is consistent with article 20 of the Berne Convention, which allows parties "to enter into special agreements among themselves, in so far as such agreements grant more extensive rights than those granted by the Convention, or contain other provisions not contrary to this Convention." TRIPS is such an agreement. In the same sense, Senftleben refers to article 13 as a 'Berne-plus'.[61] However, Helfer contends that the 'Berne-plus' interpretation "would significantly constrain the ability of national governments to preserve balanced intellectual property regimes tailored to their local needs and conditions."[62] The 'Berne-plus' view has been further criticized by Professor Correa as defeating those who have argued for keeping (if not expanding) the room for socially valuable acts, such as "fair use". It has been argued that despite its narrow wording, Article 13, is the only window left in Section 1 of the TRIPS Agreement for allowing Members certain flexibility in recognizing and enforcing the rights covered (through incorporation of the Berne Convention) in the Agreement and the capacity to balance private and public interests.[63] In brief, Prof. Correa has reiterated the widely expressed position that the purpose of copyright is not to ensure its holder maximum economic return, but to balance authors' rights to obtain a fair return and society's interest in access to and use of information,[64] even if he concedes that the framers of the Berne Convention did not seem extremely concerned about this balance between authors and the public but were rather anxious to proclaim authors' rights.[65]

59 For a contrary view, see for example Correa, TRIPS, *supra,* p. 139. The wording may be similar, but not the same. It is the subtle differences in this wording that make the two articles different in both scope and impact.

60 *United States – Section 110(5) of the US Copyright Act, supra,* para. 6.97 (emphasis added).

61 Senftleben, *supra,* p. 90. See also Ricketson, Sam, "The boundaries of copyright: Its proper limitations and exceptions: International Conventions and Treaties," *Intellectual Property Quarterly,* 1999, pp. 56–94 (hereinafter referred to as Ricketson, the boundaries of copyright).

62 Laurence Helfer, "World music on a U.S. stage: a Berne/TRIPS and economic analysis of the Fairness in Music licensing Act," *Boston university law review,* vol. 80, issue 1, (2000). 93–204.

63 Correa, TRIPS, *supra,* p. 139. The author reminds of the important public policies that are at stake in the areas of copyright, such as access to information and education and the promotion of scientific research.

64 Correa, TRIPS, *ibid,* p. 140; In a July 2008 Declaration by the Max Planck Institute for Intellectual Property, Competition and Tax law "on a balanced interpretation of the "three-step test" in copyright law," one of the considerations for the Declaration is the belief that copyright law aims to benefit the public interest. The Declaration is available at http://www.ip.mpg.de/ww/de/pub/aktuelles/declaration_on_the_three_step_.cfm.

65 Correa, TRIPS, *supra,* p. 140, quoting Dworkin, G., "Exceptions to copyright exclusivity: Is fair use consistent with article 9(2) Berne and the new international order?," in Hansen, H., ed., *International Intellectual Property law & policy,* vol. 6, Juris Publishing, Huntington, 2001, pp. 66-3.

These arguments beg the question: do TRIPS and the Berne Convention provide a balanced regime? Is the purpose of copyright to ensure a balance between the author's private interests and the public interest of the society in access to protected works? Whether such a balance exists depends on the country and the particular copyright item being considered. For developing countries, especially with respect to the need to access printed material for education, such balance is absent for several reasons. First, the Berne Convention and the TRIPS Agreement are meant to ensure effective protection of the rights of authors.[66] If such protection is to be effective, then one has to limit the exceptions. This is one explanation why the provision of exceptions is only discretionary while protecting rights is compulsory. Second, the negotiating history of the revised Berne Convention demonstrates that only developing countries, which are not authors but users of copyrighted works, supported the use of exceptions specifically for educational purposes.[67] The Stockholm Protocol, which was opposed by developed countries, did not come into force due to lack of signatures.[68] This was a clear way for developed countries to oppose the provisions of the protocol. Third, the Appendix to the Berne Convention is so plagued with procedural complications that it is difficult to imagine that it was intended to be used by developing countries, which desperately need exceptions for reproduction and translation. Fourth, the TRIPS Agreement does not have express exceptions to copyright, save for the three-step test. Fifth, the TRIPS agreement does not have a social objective, at least for copyright.[69] We shall develop each of these points below.

It is important to clarify that this limitation by TRIPS on the ability of Members to craft limitations applies (at least in theory) only to TRIPS Members, and not to parties to the Berne Convention.[70] The question is: what is the practical importance of this relationship? We answer this further below. But first, we shall examine other differences between article 13 of TRIPS and article 9(2) of the Berne Convention.

4.3.6. *Of Authors and Right Holders: No Place for Social Interests Like Education in TRIPS*

The fourth difference between article 9(2) of the Berne Convention and article 13 of the TRIPS Agreement is that the former talks of prejudice to interest of the author, while the

66 Berne Convention, *supra,* preamble and the TRIPS Agreement, *supra,* preamble.

67 For example, during the Stockholm Conference, India argued for exceptions to the right of reproduction in public interest. See Records of the Intellectual Property Conference of Stockholm, 1967, vol. I, Minutes of Main Committee I, *supra,* p. 884, (comments by Gae, speaking on behalf of India).

68 See discussion under chapter 5.

69 On the absence of protection of social interest in the TRIPS Agreement, with emphasis on patents and access to medicines, see Botoy Ituku, Propriété Intellectuelle et Droits de L'homme, *supra,* especially part III.

70 It is for this same reason that the general limitations under the TRIPS Agreement cannot apply to all rights under the Berne Convention. It would amount to not complying with obligations under the Convention. Also in this sense, see Correa, TRIPS, *supra,* p. 145; see also the argument of the EC in that Article 13 only applies to rights newly introduced into TRIPS and does not apply to the Berne Convention rights incorporated by Article 9(1) of TRIPS. See *United States – Section 110 (5) of the US Copyright Act, supra,* p. 139. Although the Panel rejected this reasoning (para. 6.75), it shows the possible interpretation of the provision.

TRIPS Agreement refers to prejudice to the interest of the right holder. In effect, TRIPS broadens the interests to be taken into account (and correspondingly narrows the scope of potential exceptions) by referring to the interests of 'the right holder' – who is not the author (for example, a juridical person that has been assigned rights to a work).[71] This interpretation is consistent with the context of the TRIPS Agreement for the following reasons.

First, IP protection is to be granted to nationals of other Members. Nationals are defined in TRIPS as natural or legal persons that would meet the criteria for protection.[72] The interests of authors and those of right holders are different. 'Author' refers to individuals or small groups of individuals while the 'right holder' includes multinational corporations, collecting societies, publishers or film publishers. These are not the intellectual creators, but in reality economically exploit the copyrighted works. In the economic field, such people have contractual rights. Authors and contractual holders of rights have different interests in the work which affects the extent of limitations and exceptions.

Second, and more importantly, the use of the term 'right holders' as opposed to simply 'authors' or 'composers' reflects the trade orientation of international copyright law, which TRIPS clearly embodies.[73] Indeed, copyright is an essential element in the business model of publishers, television and record companies, and software producers because they grant their owners exclusive rights, *inter alia,* over the reproduction and distribution of protected works.[74] Reading the Agreement in context reveals that the protection of copyright is subjected to its primary objective, which is to foster international trade. To this end, Members of TRIPS desire to "reduce distortions and impediments to international trade" taking into account the need *to promote effective and adequate protection of intellectual property rights*.[75] Intellectual property protection is not an end in itself, but is a means to promote international trade. It thus makes sense, in an agreement dealing with *trade-related aspects of intellectual property rights*, to talk of right holders instead of authors.

Third and related to the second reason, is that the reference to the interests of a 'right holder' instead of 'author' excludes the possibility of reading the enforcement of moral rights of authors into TRIPS, thus reinforcing the trade character of the Agreement. Protection of moral rights or *droit moral* is a characteristic of continental Europe.

---

71 Correa, TRIPS, *ibid,* p. 136, see also Story, Alan, "Don't ignore copyright, the 'Sleeping Giant' on the TRIPS and International education agenda," in Drahos, Peter and Mayne, Ruth, eds., *Global Intellectual Property Rights: Knowledge, Access and Development*, Palgrave Macmillan and Oxfam, New York, 2002, pp. 125–143 at p. 131 (saying that the owner of copyright is often not the composer or author), (hereinafter, Story, Don't ignore copyright). See also the Max Planck Declaration "on a balanced interpretation of the "three-step test" in copyright law," *supra*. The Declaration, endorsed by a number of academic experts, differentiates between creators and right holders, defining the latter as those who require rights as a consequence of marketing or commercial exploitation of the work. The Declaration is available at http://www.ip.mpg.de/ww/de/pub/aktuelles/declaration_on_the_three_step_.cfm.

72 TRIPS Agreement, *supra,* article 1(3).

73 TRIPS does not protect moral rights. See TRIPS Agreement, article 9(1).

74 Commission on Intellectual Property Rights, *supra,* p. 105.

75 TRIPS Agreement, preamble.

According to Dietz, moral rights are linked to the author; a work is regarded as a materialization of its creator's personality. The author himself cannot assign or licence moral rights (which is not the case with economic rights).[76] As Senftleben has rightly concluded, the neutral mention of the right holder in article 13 of TRIPS cannot be understood as a reference to the author insofar as moral rights are concerned.[77] The moral rights in the Berne Convention are not only placed beyond the scope of TRIPS, but are also prevented from indirectly influencing its framework. Article 13 of TRIPS is rendered incapable of serving as a means of lending weight to non-economic interests.[78] My contention is the following: since the TRIPS Agreement is concerned with economic[79] or trade interests in copyright,[80] it is not equipped to defend non-economic interests such as education.

4.3.7. *Importance of Differences between Article 9(2) BC and Article 13 TRIPS*

The practical importance of the difference between the two provisions is minimal. There are 165 parties to the Berne Convention[81] and 153 Members of the TRIPS Agreement.[82] Besides, Members of the WTO, which are automatically parties to the TRIPS agreement, are automatically obliged to comply with articles 1–21 of the Berne Convention and its Appendix. We shall now analyse the different elements of the three-step test. What does it mean and what are the implications for access to education in developing countries?

4.4. The Meaning of the Three-Step Test and Its Implications for Access to Printed Copyrighted Material for Educational Purposes in Developing Countries

Since there is no definition of the different elements in the multilateral treaties, one must rely only on judicial interpretation. The first and so far the only such interpretation on this issue is by the WTO Panel in *United States – Section 110(5) of the US Copyright Act.*[83]

In June 2000, the World Trade Organization (WTO) ruled on a dispute initiated by the European Communities (EC) on behalf of the Irish performing rights organization against the United States. The EC alleged that section 110(5) of the US Copyright Act,[84] as amended

76 A. Dietz, "The moral rights of the author: moral rights and the civil law countries," *Columbia-VLA Journal of Law and Arts*, vol. 19(1995). 199–228, at .217–225.

77 Senftleben, *supra,* p. 225.

78 Ricketson, The boundaries of copyright, *supra.* p. 81.

79 As emphasis to this point, Geiger says that TRIPS has an economic logic, see Geiger, the three-step test, *supra,* p. 692.

80 The reasons for the inclusion of TRIPS in the GATT was the shared belief by developed countries, mainly the USA and OECD, that IP was an increasingly important component of national wealth and article of international trade, and thus it was properly the subject of trade protection, regardless of whether that was originally contemplated by the GATT. See Abbott, protecting First World Assets, *supra,* p. 692.

81 Information as of March 2012, available at www.wipo.int.

82 Information available as of 10 February 2012 at www.wto.org

83 *United States – Section 110(5) of the US Copyright Act, supra.*

84 United States Copyright Act of 1976, Act of 19 October 1976, Pub.L. 94-553, 90 Stat. 2541 (as amended).

by the Fairness in Music Licensing Act of 1998,[85] was in violation of the United States' obligations under the TRIPS Agreement. In the view of the EC, the measures under section 110(5) caused prejudice to the legitimate rights of copyright owners, thus nullifying and impairing the rights of the European Communities.[86] Briefly, section 110(5), as amended purported to exclude a broad range of retail and restaurant establishments from the need to obtain authorization from copyright holders for the public performance of musical works on their premises via radio and television transmissions. More precisely, section 110(5) (A), commonly referred to as the "home style exemption", allowed transmission on a single receiving apparatus of a kind commonly used in private homes. Section 110(5) (B), known as the "business exemption", allowed the transmission or retransmission by businesses of performances or displays to the public using loud speakers within a defined area.

As mentioned earlier, there is an enormous amount of literature analysing the Panel Decision, or at least elements of it. The present study's intention here is not to add to this literature, but to show what the three-step test means for developing countries and access to educational material in the analogue environment. To this end, the discussion on the Panel decision does not delve into the alleged violations as such, but rather focuses on the Panel's interpretation of specific conditions of articles 9(2) of the BC and 13 of TRIPS.[87]

4.4.1. *Certain Special Cases*

As to the definition of "certain", the WTO Panel, after consulting dictionary definitions, stated that:

> The ordinary meaning of "certain" is "known and particularised, but not explicitly identified", "determined, fixed, not variable; definitive, precise, exact".[88] In other words, this term means that, under the first condition, *an exception or limitation in national legislation must be clearly defined.* However, there is no need to identify explicitly each and every possible situation to which the exception could apply, provided that the scope of the exception is known and particularised. This guarantees a sufficient degree of legal certainty.[89]

This interpretation is consistent with the intention of the drafters of article 9(2). During the Stockholm Conference, the Netherlands made a proposal that the exceptions should apply only if they were expressly provided for in the Convention itself and in the national legislation concerned as well.[90] As regards the term "special", the Panel, again relying on dictionary meaning, stated:

---

85 Fairness in Music Licensing Act of 27 October 1998, Pub.L. 105-298, 112 Stat. 2830, 105th Cong., 2nd Session (1998).

86 *United States – Section 110(5) of the US Copyright Act, supra*, paras 2.1, 2.2 and 3.1 read together.

87 The reader will recall that the two provisions permit Members to provide exceptions to exclusive rights in (1) certain special cases which (2) do not conflict with a normal exploitation of the work and (3) do not unreasonably prejudice the legitimate interests of the author or right holder.

88 The New Shorter Oxford English Dictionary ("Oxford English Dictionary"), Oxford (1993), p. 364.

89 *United States – Section 110(5) of the US Copyright Act, supra*, para. 6.108 (emphasis added).

90 Records of the Intellectual Property Conference of Stockholm, 1967, *supra*, Report of the Main Committee I, (document S/81), p. 1144.

> The term "special" connotes "having an individual or limited application or purpose", "containing details; precise, specific", "exceptional in quality or degree; unusual; out of the ordinary" or "distinctive in some way". This term means that more is needed than a clear definition in order to meet the standard of the first condition. *In addition, an exception or limitation must be limited in its field of application or exceptional in its scope. In other words, an exception or limitation should be narrow in quantitative as well as a qualitative sense.* This suggests a narrow scope as well as an exceptional or distinctive objective. To put this aspect of the first condition into the context of the second condition ("no conflict with a normal exploitation"), an exception or limitation should be the opposite of a non-special, i.e., a normal case.[91]

Let us pause here and reflect on these two conditions: an exception or limitation should be "narrow in quantitative" and "in a qualitative sense."

4.4.1.1. Exceptions Must Be Narrow in Quantitative and Qualitative Sense

We wish to emphasize that both the quantitative and qualitative senses of "special" are important and useful in delimiting the scope of the three-step test. While there seems to be a de facto acceptance of the qualitative sense of "special", Senftleben has criticized the quantitative sense for difficulties in determining its scope; yet at the same time he concedes (although indirectly) that whether or not the test applies depends on the type of work at issue.[92] This is the nature of the three-step test. It has to be applied on a case by case. As Professor Ricketson rightly observes;

> [i]n any given case, this [the determination of the special character] will involve the consideration of all aspects of a proposed exception, including such matters as the rights and works involved, the persons who may take advantage of it and the purpose of the exception.[93]

The interpretation that exceptions should be narrow in a quantitative and qualitative sense is also consistent with the drafting history of the Berne Convention. Let me explain. During the Stockholm revision conference, Main Committee I adopted a proposal by the Drafting Committee that the second condition, "not conflict with the normal exploitation of the work", should be placed before the first, as this would afford a more logical order for the interpretation of the rule. If it is considered that reproduction conflicts with the normal exploitation of the work, then reproduction is not permitted at all. If it is considered that reproduction does not conflict with the normal exploitation of the work, the next step would be to consider whether it does not unreasonably prejudice the legitimate interests of the author. Only if such is not the case would it be possible in certain special cases to introduce a compulsory license, or to provide for use without payment.[94] The Committee went ahead to illustrate with the example of photocopying for various purposes.[95] If photocopying consists of reproducing a *very large number of copies*, then it may

91 *United States – Section 110(5) of the US Copyright Act, supra,* para. 6.109 (emphasis added, footnote omitted).

92 Senftleben, *supra,* pp. 138–144.

93 Ricketson, WIPO Study, p. 22.

94 Records of the Intellectual Property Conference of Stockholm, 1967, *supra,* vol. II, Report of Main Committee I, p. 1145.

95 Photocopying exception is directly relevant to access to educational materials in developing countries, see *infra,* chapter 2.

not be permitted because it conflicts with normal exploitation of the work (step 2). If it implies a *rather large number of copies* for use in industrial undertakings, it may not unreasonably prejudice the legitimate interests of the author provided that, according to national legislation, an equitable remuneration is paid (step 3). If *a small number of copies are made*, photocopying may be permitted without payment, particularly for *individual or scientific use* (step 1).[96] There is a quantitative element in all three steps. It is important to emphasize here that the only situation where photocopying (reproduction) is allowed for free is when the quantity is small. In other words, a small number is equivalent to a special case. It is this author's opinion that this interpretation is consistent with the understanding that states attach to this provision as expressed in their practice. In most national legislation, exceptions under the three-step test define the quantities or percentage of the whole that is allowed under free use. For example, in the case of reproduction from a textbook, the special character of the reproduction is determined on the basis of the percentage of the whole book that is reproduced.[97] Thus, the Panel's interpretation is not only consistent with the object and purpose of the Berne Convention, which is to protect the rights of authors to their literary and artistic works,[98] but is also consistent with the drafting history of the three-step test and state practice.

The Panel found that the 'business' exemption did not qualify as "certain special cases" because a substantial majority of eating and drinking establishments and close to half of retail establishments were covered by the exemption.[99] The 'home style' exemption was well defined and limited in scope, so it fulfilled the first test.[100] This serves to emphasize that quantity plays a significant role in determining "certain special cases".

4.4.1.2. Exceptions Are Not Justified by Reasons of Public Policy

Professor Ricketson has suggested that 'certain special cases' requires the existence of some 'special purpose' or justification underlying the exceptions that are made in a national law. It is argued that some such justification is required; not only should the case in question be for 'a quite specific purpose', but that there must also be "something 'special' about this purpose, 'special' here meaning that it is justified by some clear reason of *public policy* or some other exceptional circumstances".[101] For her part, Professor Ginsburg

---

96 Records of the Intellectual Property Conference of Stockholm, 1967, *supra*, vol. II, Report of Main Committee I, p. 1146 (emphasis added). Let us remember that quantity was an important element for producers of copyright works like France and the UK. (See discussion on exceptions in domestic law).

97 For example, the Copyright Act of Australia, Act No. 63 of 1968 as amended, Part VB, Division 2, Section 135ZG. Reproduction by educational institutions is limited to one percent of the total number of pages. Otherwise, multiple reproductions of works for educational institutions are allowed under statutory licenses, administered by a collecting society, the Copyright Agency Limited. Remuneration has to be paid.

98 The Berne Convention, *supra*, preamble.

99 *United States – Section 110(5) of the US Copyright Act, supra*, para 6.133.

100 *Ibid*, para 6.159.

101 Ricketson, The Berne Convention, *supra*, p. 482 (emphasis added), see also Mihály Ficsor, *The Law of Copyright and the Internet – The WIPO Copyright Treaties, their interpretation and implementation*, (Oxford: Oxford University Press, 2002), p.284.

has argued that certain special cases should not be interpreted as requiring that there should be some special purpose underlying it, because the purpose behind any given exception will fall to be tested by the second and third steps of the test.[102] It should be noted that subsequent to the Panel, Professor Ricketson changed his opinion and concurred with Professor Ginsburg.[103]

The WTO Panel addressed the question of whether an underlying public policy purpose can qualify an exception as being a special case. The U.S. argued before the WTO panel that the specific policy objective pursued by the exemption is the fostering of small businesses and preventing abusive practices.[104] In response to written questions posed by the Panel, to justify the submission that the exemption is a special case, the U.S. stated:

> important *public policy* concerns underlie both Sections [...] the record is clear that Congress was concerned with small "mom and pop" businesses. Small businesses play a particularly important role in the American social fabric. They foster local values and innovation and experimentation in the economy. Small businesses also create a disproportionately greater number of economic opportunities for women, minorities, immigrants, and those formerly on public assistance, and thus are an essential mechanism by which millions enter the economic and social mainstream.[105]

Disregarding the details of whether or not the U.S. exemption can be qualified as a clear reason of public policy,[106] we shall now focus on the question of whether an exception granted to achieve a public policy objective can qualify as a "special case" within the meaning of the three-step test. For example, can massive reproduction of a textbook for use by an educational institution be allowed under the three-step test? The WTO Panel answered this question in the negative. Instead, stated that the term "certain special cases" should not be equated lightly with "special purpose".[107] While noting the interpretation given by Ricketson in relation to article 9(2) of the Berne Convention, the Panel was hesitant to use the interpretation of a term developed in the context of an exception for the reproduction right for interpreting the same terms in the context of a similarly worded exception for other exclusive rights conferred by copyrights.[108] The question that arises at this point is whether the Panel would have come to a different conclusion if the right involved was a reproduction right. The present author holds that this would not be so. The Panel gave additional reasons for not accepting the interpretation: it is not in line with either the wording of article 13 or the interpretation of other WTO rules. Thus, the Panel found it difficult to reconcile the wording of Article 13 with the proposition that an exception or limitation must be justified in terms of a legitimate public policy purpose in order

102 Ginsburg, *supra*, pp. 39–41.

103 Ricketson, WIPO Study, p. 22.

104 *United States – Section 110(5) of the US Copyright Act*, *supra*, para 6.115.

105 *United States – Section 110(5) of the US Copyright Act*, *ibid*, attachment 2.3, replies of the United States to written questions from the Panel – first meeting (19 November 1999), Q.17 (emphasis added).

106 For a detailed argument on this, see Senftleben, *supra*, 150–151.

107 *United States – Section 110(5) of the US Copyright Act*, *supra*, para 6.111. (footnote omitted).

108 *Ibid*, para 6.111, footnote 114. In the case at hand, the panel was dealing with the rights of public performance, communication to the public of performances and broadcasting.

to fulfil the first condition of the Article. The Panel recalled in this respect that in interpreting other WTO rules, such as the national treatment clauses of the GATT and the GATS, the Appellate Body has rejected interpretative tests which were based on the subjective aim or objective pursued by national legislation.[109]

Furthermore, there exists a risk in justifying 'special' cases using reasons of public policy. This would leave it up to each country to decide the scope of this condition based on its own public policy. First of all, 'public policy' is an unstable term whose meaning depends on the definition given by each country in a particular circumstance. Indeed, Professors Ricketson and Ginsburg agree when they state that public interest is a shifting concept that is frequently interpreted in different ways at the national level.[110] Such terminology would accord uncertain and restricted protection of the authors, which would be contrary to the object and purpose of the Berne Convention. The Convention has as its purpose the 'protection of rights of authors in their literary and artistic works' in as effective and uniform a manner as possible.[111] The above interpretation is also in line with the desires of the TRIPS Members to take into account the need to promote effective and adequate protection of intellectual property rights.[112] To conclude, the Panel stated:

> In our view, the first condition of Article 13 requires that a limitation or *exception in national legislation should be clearly defined and should be narrow in its scope and reach.* [...] public policy purposes stated by law-makers when enacting a limitation or exception *may be* useful from a *factual* [not normative] perspective for making inferences about the scope of a limitation or exception or the clarity of its definition.[113]

This is in line with article 20 of the Berne Convention, which requires that special agreements, like TRIPS, entered into by Members of the Convention should grant more rights, but without providing for expansion of limitations. It is not surprising then that the TRIPS Agreement requires Members to "confine" limitations or exceptions. This interpretation reflects the intention of the drafters of article 9(2) of the Berne Convention. For example, the Netherlands proposed that it should be clarified that the limitations should be defined in national legislation.[114]

4.4.1.3. Certain Special Cases and Access to Education in Developing Countries

With respect to developing countries, the test of "certain special cases" means that they can copy only a few pages (limited quantitatively) otherwise they must pay remuneration. In terms of quality (limited qualitatively), "certain special cases" excludes copying from technical or scientific textbooks. Let us consider the example of the textbook, "Introduction to the Mathematical and Statistical Foundations of Econometrics."[115]

---

109 *Ibid,* (footnote omitted).

110 Ricketson, *et al* International Copyright and Neighbouring Rights, volume I, *supra,* p. 756.

111 Berne Convention, *supra,* preamble and article 1.

112 TRIPS Agreement, *supra,* preamble, first paragraph.

113 *United States – Section 110(5) of the US Copyright Act, supra,* para 6.112 (emphasis added).

114 See Records of the Intellectual Property Conference of Stockholm, 1967, *supra,* vol. I, Conference Documents (Document S/81), p. 691.

115 Herman J. Bierens, Introduction to Mathematical and Statistical Foundations of Econometrics, (Cambridge: Cambridge University Press, 2004).

Each paragraph of the book is intended for the reader to understand the next. Much of the work is explained through formulae and figures. For such a book, copying a page of it amounts to copying a very important part of the book – each formula or page is important in itself. Applying the "qualitative" test of "limited" would make it impossible to copy from such a book.[116]

Furthermore, developing countries cannot use their education policy as a reason for granting an exception since "certain special cases" are not determined by reason of public policy.

Let us now explore the second step of the three-step test, which requires that the exception should not conflict with a normal exploitation of the work.

4.4.2. *"Does Not Conflict with a Normal Exploitation of the Work"*

Again relying on the dictionary definition, the WTO dispute settlement Panel concluded that "exploit" or "exploitation," in the context of "works," can be taken as referring to the activity by which copyright owners employ the exclusive rights given to them, including the reproduction right, to "extract economic value from their rights to those works."[117] In the view of the WTO Panel, there are two possible connotations of the phrase "normal exploitation": the first being of an empirical nature, that is, what is regular, usual, typical or ordinary in a factual sense, and the second reflecting a "somewhat more normative, if not dynamic, approach, i.e., conforming to a type or standard."[118]

Under the empirical approach, the question to ask would be whether the exempted use would otherwise fall within the range of activities from which the copyright owner would *usually expect* to receive compensation.[119] However, according to Professor Goldstein, an obvious circularity underlies this requirement. At least historically, Goldstein argues, an author will normally exploit a work only in those markets where he is assured of legal rights; by definition, markets for exempted uses fall outside the range of normal exploitation. Consequently, it might be thought that to expand an exemption is to shrink the "normal market," while to expand the definition of "normal market" is to shrink the permitted exception.[120] It is difficult to identify any difference between the reasoning of the Panel and that of Goldstein. Let us illustrate with the example of reproduction or copying of a textbook. If we apply the Panel's definition of 'exploit', a copyright owner would usually extract economic value from the textbook if he makes the photocopies himself and sells them or authorizes another person through a license to do so and receives compensation. This is the 'usual' or 'ordinary way of extracting economic value from the textbook. This is what the reproduction right grants the copyright owner. An exception to the right of reproduction does not, contrary to the inference by Goldstein, take away this right,

116 A case in point, although in another context, is the case of *Harper & Row, Publishers, Inc. v. Nation Enterprises,* 471 U.S 539 (1985), where the defence of fair use was denied even when a small amount was copied because, according to the court, the text copied was substantial as it represented the heart of the book. We discuss this case in detail at a later stage.

117 *United States – Section 110(5) of the US Copyright Act, supra,* para. 6.165.

118 *Ibid,* para. 6.166.

119 *Ibid.*

120 Goldstein, *supra,* pp. 295–296.

but only places a constraint on the extent to which it can be enjoyed. It is not each instance of photocopying or reproduction that prevents the right holder from exploiting the work; for example, copying one page from a text.[121] In this sense, expanding the exception would not imply shrinking the market.

The "normative" or dynamic approach, on the other hand, would look beyond this purely quantitative assessment and would seek to take into account prospective technological and market developments, although all the details thereof might not presently be fully known. It is also conceivable that uses presently not controlled by copyright owners might subsequently become so, as the result of technological change. An example might be private copying, where the transaction costs involved in monitoring such uses might now be reduced because of new technologies.[122] This remains true even for copyright in the analogue environment. As illustrated above, the discussions at Stockholm reflect cautiousness by states that technological changes, such as the existence of modern photocopiers, could make copying for private use, for example, conflict with the normal exploitation of the work.[123] In other words, the term 'normal exploitation' in the Berne Convention and the TRIPS agreement has to be interpreted in an evolutive manner,[124] bearing in mind their object and purpose.[125]

Accordingly, the phrase "normal exploitation" should be interpreted as including "in addition to those forms of exploitation that currently generate significant or tangible revenue, those forms of exploitation which, with a certain degree of likelihood and plausibility, could acquire considerable economic or practical importance."[126]

This interpretation is supported by the drafting history of article 9(2). In its interpretation, the Panel was guided by the report of the Study Group, composed of representatives of the Swedish Government and the *Bureaux Internationaux réunis pour la protection de la propriété intellectuelle* (BIRPI),[127] which was set up to prepare for the Revision Conference at Stockholm in 1967. The Panel found persuasive guidance[128] in the suggestion of the Study Group that:

> [a]ll forms of exploiting a work, which have, or are likely to acquire, considerable economic or practical importance, must be reserved to the authors.[129]

---

121 Except for a technical or scientific book.

122 Ricketson, WIPO Study, *supra*, p. 23.

123 See discussion on national limitations at the time of Stockholm Conference, section 3.2..

124 On the use of this concept, see Susan Isiko Štrba, *Dispute Settlement Under the TRIPS Agreement in Relation to Human Rights*, (Mémoire of Master Degree at the Graduate Institute of International Studies, Geneva, 2001), 44–45.

125 "To protect, in as effective and uniform a manner as possible, the rights of authors in their literary and artistic works" and "to promote effective and adequate protection of intellectual property rights," Preamble of the Berne Convention and the TRIPS Agreement, respectively.

126 *United States – Section 110(5) of the US Copyright Act, supra*, para. 6.180.

127 The *Bureaux Internationaux réunis pour la protection de la propriété intellectuelle* or United International Bureau for the Protection of Intellectual Property (BIRPI) is the predecessor of the World Intellectual Property Organization.

128 *United States – Section 110(5) of the US Copyright Act, supra*, paras. 6.179 and 6.181.

129 Records of the Intellectual Property Conference of Stockholm, 1967, *supra*, (Document S/1: Berne Convention; Proposals for Revising the Substantive Copyright Provisions (Articles 1-20).) Prepared by the Government of Sweden with the assistance of BIPRI.

This interpretation reflects the wish of some delegations, such as the Federal Republic of Germany (FRG), that provision clearly indicate that reproduction should not conflict with the author's right to obtain equitable remuneration.[130] This is the accepted view among some scholars as well. For example, according to Ricketson and Ginsburg, exceptions under national law that do not enter into economic competition (present or potential) with non-exempted uses should therefore not be contrary to the second condition of article 9(2).[131]

The Panel concluded:

> We believe that an exception or limitation to an exclusive right in domestic legislation rises to the level of a conflict with a normal exploitation of the work (i.e., the copyright or rather the whole bundle of exclusive rights conferred by the ownership of the copyright), if uses, that in principle are covered by that right but exempted under the exception or limitation, enter into economic competition with the ways that rights-holders *normally* extract economic value from that right to the work (i.e., the copyright) and thereby deprive them of *significant or tangible commercial gains*.[132]

4.4.2.1. Conflict with Normal Exploitation and Access to Educational Materials in Developing Countries

With respect to exceptions that facilitate access to education, such as private copying for personal use or by an educational institution, library or archives, what is a "normal exploitation"? Again, the answer would depend on the particular work in question and the user involved. If we consider the example of academic publishers who are directly connected with our examples of uses listed, how do they *normally* extract economic value from a textbook? Academic publishers like Elsevier mainly publish for profit. Developing countries are major importers of textbooks from the UK and the USA. In particular, the most imported books are those on technical or scientific subjects.[133] These are not locally produced – imported versions are the only ones on the market. Extensive copying of academic works or textbooks is certain to conflict with 'normal exploitation' of these works in developing country markets.

4.4.3. *"And That Do Not Unreasonably Prejudice the Legitimate Interests of the Author/ Right Holder"*

Given that any limitation would cause some degree of prejudice to the right holder, the key question here is whether that prejudice is unreasonable.[134] With regard to tolerable

---

130 Records of the Intellectual Property Conference of Stockholm, 1967, *ibid,* vol. I, Conference Documents, (document S/67), p. 690. The FRG wished to add another paragraph which read, "in certain particular cases where permission does not conflict with a normal exploitation of the work or with the author's right to obtain equitable remuneration which, in the absence of agreement, shall be fixed by competent authority, and where permission is not contrary to the legitimate interests of the author."

131 Ricketson, *et al,* International Copyright and Neighbouring Rights, volume I, *supra,* p. 770.

132 *United States – Section 110(5) of the US Copyright Act, supra,* para. 6.183, (emphasis added).

133 See Consumers International, *supra.*

134 WIPO Guide to the Berne Convention, *supra,* para.9.8.

levels of "prejudice," the Panel noted that the text's formulation, "not unreasonably prejudice," "connotes a slightly stricter standard" than "reasonable." While acknowledging that the treaty text permits copyright owners' interests to undergo some prejudice, the Panel determined that the prejudice would reach an "unreasonable" level "if an exception or limitation causes or has the potential to cause an unreasonable loss of income to the copyright owner."[135] Indeed, as Senftleben summarizes, "the circle of interests that must be taken into account in the context of the third criterion can be circumscribed as follows: the economic interest of the authors in the exploitation of the exclusive rights recognized in international copyright law always plays a decisive role."[136]

As far as copyright is concerned, there is always an economic element to be considered. Public policy interests are not taken into account. But first, we must clarify that this is not the case with patents. "Legitimate interests" under patent law, as demonstrated by the WTO Panel and supported by the TRIPS Agreement, can refer to social or public interests. We shall now explain.

4.4.3.1. Legitimate Interests for Patents Are Different Than Those for Copyright

As noted above, the Panel on section 13 of TRIPS takes an economic view in determining what amounts to "legitimate interests" in copyright. The panel expressed the view that one way of looking at legitimate interests is the economic value of the exclusive rights conferred by copyright on their holders. It argued that it is possible to estimate in economic terms the value of exercising, for example, by licensing, such rights.[137] However, with regard to patents, legitimate interests are not limited to economic interests. This is because article 30 of TRIPS, the only provision in either the Paris Convention[138] or TRIPS that provides for a general exception to the rights of a patent owner, also takes into account the legitimate interests of third parties.[139] Indeed, WTO jurisprudence distinguishes between the three-step test under copyright and that under patents, (articles 13 and 30 of TRIPS respectively).[140] In a previous decision on article 30, the Panel rejected

---

135 *United States – Section 110(5) of the US Copyright Act, supra*, para. 6.229.

136 Senftleben, *supra*, p. 225.

137 *United States – Section 110(5) of the US Copyright Act, supra*, para. 6.226.

138 Paris Convention for the Protection of Industrial Property, (20 March 1883), Stockholm Act (1967), modified in 1979, Publication of the World Intellectual Property Organization no. 201(E) (hereinafter referred to as Paris Convention).

139 Article 30 of the TRIPS Agreement entitle "Exceptions to reads:
Members may provide limited exceptions to the exclusive rights conferred by a patent, provided that such exception do not unreasonably conflict with a normal exploitation of the patent and do not unreasonably prejudice the legitimate interests of the patent owner, taking account of the legitimate interests of third parties.

140 Article 30 of the TRIPS Agreement, entitled "Exceptions to Rights Conferred" provides:
Members may provide limited exceptions to the exclusive rights conferred by a patent, provided that such exceptions do not unreasonably conflict with a normal exploitation of the patent and do not unreasonably prejudice the legitimate interests of the patent owner, taking account of the legitimate interests of third parties.

the reasoning that legitimate interests are necessarily limited to economic value.[141] The panel reasoned that "[l]egitimate interests of third parties" makes sense only if 'legitimate interests' is construed as a concept broader than legal interests.[142] With regard to the definition of "third party," referred to in the last phrase of article 30, Canada took the position that *general societal interests*, and particularly interests connected with *health policy*, were within the ambit of the term "third parties" and thus were entitled to consideration. In support of this position, Canada, together with several of the third party participants in the proceedings, relied most heavily on the statements of objectives and principles stated in Articles 7[143] and 8.1[144] of the TRIPS Agreement.[145] The Panel aligned itself with the reasoning of Canada. It stated that:

> [t]o make sense of the term "legitimate interests" in this context, that term must be defined in the way that it is often used in legal discourse – as a normative claim calling for protection of interests that are "justifiable" in the sense that they are supported by relevant *public policies or other social norms*. We may take as an illustration one of the most widely adopted Article 30-type exceptions in national patent laws – the exception under which use of the patented product for scientific experimentation, during the term of the patent and without consent,

---

141 *Canada – Patent Protection of Pharmaceutical Products*, Report of the Panel, WT/DS114/R, 17 March 2000, paras 7.60ff. The Panel noted the difference in wording between Articles 13 and 30 of the TRIPS Agreement. The latter also refers to "taking account of the legitimate interests of third parties".

142 *Canada – Patent Protection of Pharmaceutical Products, ibid*, para 7.71.

143 Article 7 of the TRIPS Agreement entitled "objectives" stipulates:
The protection and enforcement of intellectual property should contribute to the promotion of technological innovation and to the transfer and dissemination of technology, to the mutual advantage of producers and users of technological knowledge and in a manner conducive to social and economic welfare, and to a balance of rights and obligations.

144 Article 8 of the TRIPS Agreement entitled 'Principles' reads.
1. Members *may* in formulating or amending their laws and regulations, adopt measures necessary to protect public health and nutrition, and to promote the public interests in sectors of vital importance to their social economic and technological developments, *provided that such measures are consistent with the provisions of this Agreement,* (emphasis added).

145 *Canada – Patent Protection of Pharmaceutical Products, supra*. Submissions of third parties are found in part V, Arguments of third parties. Third parties that took the same argument are: Australia, which argued that "Patent rights had been developed, enforced and bounded with the intention of serving the broader public interest through the provision of effective private rights. Exceptions to patent rights needed to be justified by reference to the overall public interest and should seek to maintain the fundamental balance of interests and mutual advantage at the core of the patent system, so as to serve the overall public benefit. The TRIPS Agreement set this balance of interests into an international trade context." (Australia, para. 5.3); Brazil, which argued that "intellectual property rights do not exist in a vacuum. They are granted taking into account other social and economic welfare policy interests and values," (Brazil, para, 5.12); Colombia, which argued for public policy objectives (Colombia, para. 5.17); Cuba, relied on articles 7 and 8 of TRIPS (Cuba, para 5.18); India, relied on article 8 and argued for balance between rights and obligations of producers of technical knowledge and users of the knowledge (India, para. 5.20); Japan's main argument was based on 'underlying policy objectives' (Japan, para. 5.24); and the USA which defined 'third parties' as the generic manufacturing industry and the consumers of patented medicines (USA, para. 5.32).

> is not an infringement. It is often argued that this exception is based on the notion that a key public policy purpose underlying patent laws is to facilitate the *dissemination and advancement of technical knowledge and that allowing* the patent owner to prevent experimental use during the term of the patent would frustrate part of the purpose of the requirement that the nature of the invention be disclosed to the public.[146]

With regard to copyright, the panel rejected the United States' argument for an exception based on public policy consideration.[147] In the *Canada – Pharmaceutical Patents*, Canada and the panel apply the principle of 'effective interpretation' to give meaning to the provision of article 30 of TRIPS.[148] To do otherwise, as the Panel explains in the quoted paragraph, would render the phrase 'legitimate interests of third parties' redundant.

Understanding this difference between copyright and patents is essential as it highlights the fact that, while TRIPS may contain built-in public interest provisions, this is only true where patents are concerned.[149] It is not the case with copyright. It must be emphasized that there is no such built-in balance between rights of copyright holders and the public interest of access to protected works. Reference to articles 7 and 8.1 of the TRIPS Agreement clearly underscores our argument. The Agreement refers to technological knowledge, which excludes copyrights, especially in the analogue environment.[150]

4.5. Exceptions to the Right of Translation

Under the Berne Convention, there exists no explicit provision for exceptions to the exclusive right of translation.[151] However, there is an implied exception. According to the Report of the Stockholm Conference, "it was fairly obvious that exceptions to other exclusive rights such as the right of reproduction, implied corresponding exceptions in respect of the right of translation and that the Convention had generally been applied in this way".[152] For example, the right to reproduce press articles also includes the right to

---

146 *Canada – Patent Protection of Pharmaceutical Products, supra*, paras 7.69.

147 See discussion in section 4.4.1.2 (exceptions are not justified by reason of public policy).

148 On the use of this principle in previous IP related WTO decisions, see for example *India – Patent Protection for Pharmaceutical and Agricultural Chemical Products*, (complaint by the European Communities), WT/DS79/R, 24 August 1998, para. 7.39. And on the use of the principle generally, see *Ambatielos* (*Greece v. United Kingdom*), (Preliminary objection), Judgement of 1 July 1952, I.C.J Reports 1952, p.28; and generally, Susan Isiko Strba, *Dispute Settlement Under the TRIPS Agreement in Relation to Human Rights, supra*, 53–62.

149 For the view that TRIPS does not contain in-built public interest goals like access to health, see generally Botoy Ituku, Propriété Intellectuelle et Droits de L'homme, *supra*.

150 In the same sense, see also Correa, TRIPS, *supra*, p. 92, (stating that reference to technological knowledge implies patents. Although at the same time the author argues for a reading of flexibilities for copyright into TRIPS through article 13). See also Florian Kebler, "Article 7: Objectives," in Peter-Tobias Stoll, Jan Busche, and Katrin Arend, eds *WTO-trade-related aspects of intellectual property rights*, Max Planck Institute for Comparative Public Law and International Law, (Leiden: Martinus Nijhoff Publishers, 2009). 179–187 at 181.

151 The only express exception to the right of translation is that under the Berne Appendix, which is addressed to developing countries. We discuss this later.

152 Records of the Intellectual Property Conference of Stockholm, 1967, *supra*, vol. II, Report of the Main Committee I, p. 1165.

reproduce them in the form of translation.[153] It was generally agreed that articles 2*bis* (2), 9(2), 10(1) and (2) and 10*bis* (1) and (2) essential imply the possibility of using the work not only in the original form but also in translation, subject to the same conditions, in particular that the use conforms with fair practice and that, here too, as in the cases of all uses of the work, the moral rights are reserved.[154]

What remains unclear is whether an implied exception to the translation right under article 9(2) also implies that the exception is subject to the three step test. The logical interpretation would be that it does, as to interpret otherwise would be to grant fewer translation rights – which would be contrary to the object and purpose of the Convention.

4.6. The Usefulness of the Three-Step Test for Access to Educational Materials in Developing Countries

If one considers the three-step test as merely providing guidelines which facilitate the task of striking a proper balance,[155] then one can argue that states in general, and developing countries in particular, can use it to strike a balance between the protection of the rights of authors/right holders and access to educational materials. This would make sense if we assumed that the three-step test under the Berne Convention and the TRIPS Agreement provided mere guidelines. Unfortunately, this is not the case. The three-step test, at least in relation to copyright, provides strict guidelines from which it is not easy to derogate. This is more so if considered in relation to the rights of reproduction and translation, exceptions to which are particularly important for developing countries. Ultimately, the three-step test cannot be used by developing countries to facilitate access to educational materials in the analogue environment. As one author summarizes:

> The three-step test is not a public interest limitation to exclusive rights. Instead, it is a limitation on the *scope of limitations* that member states can implement to promote access and dissemination of works domestically.[156]

As demonstrated above, the text of the TRIPS Agreement limits 'limitations' to exclusive rights.[157]

---

153 Records of the Intellectual Property Conference of Stockholm, 1967, *supra,* vol. II, Report of the Main Committee I, p. 1165.

154 *Ibid.* Article 2*bis*(2) of the Berne Convention grants Members the freedom to decide by legislation the conditions under which lectures, addresses and other works of the same nature which are delivered in public may be reproduced by the press, broadcast, communicated to the public by wire and made subject to public communication. Article 10*bis*(1) deals with possible reproduction by the press, broadcasting or the communication to the public by wire of articles published in the newspapers on periodicals of current economic, political or religious topics. Article 10*bis*(2) allows reproduction and making available to the public of certain works to the extent justified by the informatory purpose. The two articles do not form part of the focus of our discussion.

155 Senftleben, *supra,* p. 212.

156 Okediji, Fostering Access, *supra.*

157 See discussion under 4.3.5 (Article 13 of TRIPS restricts use of exceptions).

Some authors have advocated for "a new or reverse reading of the three-step test".[158] According to Geiger, this entails a reverse reading, where the third step is analysed before the second one. It is argued that since the third step foresees some prejudice to the interests of the right holder, the judge should consider the justification behind the limitation and make a differentiated analysis in light of the many interests and fundamental rights at stake.[159] It is important to adopt an extremely restrictive approach to the notion of "normal exploitation" in order to place the third step in the centre.[160] Then the judge should examine the second step. The psychological effect would not be negligible: after balancing the interests, the judge will certainly be less inclined to censor the use by adopting a purely economic approach and would therefore use the second step to "knock it into shape".[161] The second stage should only be used as a "corrective measure to avoid the grossest conflict with the normal exploitation of the work."[162] According to Gervais, the author has a right in respect of any commercially significant use; use that would normally be the subject of a commercial transaction. "Any situation not covered by this right would be one that is not subject to normal commercial exploitation and is justified by a valid public interest purpose."[163]

However, a reverse reading of the test will not solve the problem of bulk access by developing countries as bulk copying will very likely lead to gross conflict with normal exploitation or commercially significant use of the work which will require remuneration of the right holder. The three conditions of the three-step test apply cumulatively; a limitation or an exception is consistent with the three-step test only if it fulfils each of the three conditions.[164] Consequently, changing the order will not make the test less restrictive. Finding that an exception does not prejudice the legitimate interests of the right holder (condition three) does not prevent an inquiry into the compatibility of that exception with the second condition (does not conflict with the normal exploitation of the work). The three conditions represent separate and independent requirements that must each be satisfied.[165]

The proposal for "a new reading of the three-step test" also overlooks another important element – the sociological element on the panellists. As we demonstrate in various

158 Geiger, Right to copy, *supra,* p. 7. Also by the same author, The three-step test, *supra,* at 697; "The role of the three-step test in the adaptation of copyright law to the information society," UNESCO e-Copyright Bulletin, January – March 2007, 1–21, p. 18 (hereinafter referred to as Geiger, adaptation of copyright law to the information society); Daniel Gervais, "Towards a New Core International Copyright Norm: the Reverse Three-Step Test," *Marquette Intellectual Property Law Review,* vol. 9 no. 1, (2005): 1–35, p. 32.

159 Christophe Geiger, "The role of the three-step test in the adaptation of copyright law to the information society," UNESCO e-Copyright Bulletin, (January – March 2007). 1–21, p. 18 (hereinafter referred to as Geiger, adaptation of copyright law to the information society).

160 Geiger, adaptation of copyright law to the information society, *ibid,* p. 18.

161 Geiger, *ibid,* 18–19.

162 Geiger, Right to copy, *supra,* p. 7. Also by the same author, The three-step test, *supra,* at 697; adaptation of copyright law to the information society, *supra,* 1–21, p. 18.

163 Gervais, Towards a New Core International Copyright Norm: the Reverse Three-Step Test, *supra,* p. 30.

164 *United States – Section 110(5) of the US Copyright Act, supra,* para. 6.74.

165 *United States – Section 110(5) of the US Copyright Act, supra,* para. 6.97.

parts of this study,[166] the TRIPS Agreement is concerned with trade-related aspects of intellectual property rights, or precisely, protection of economic interests of right holders. As such it is not equipped to cater for social interests like access to educational materials. Thus a panellist interpreting the TRIPS Agreement will to a large extent be influenced by the fact that he has to resolve an issue within a trade environment. Therefore the likelihood of interpreting the Agreement to cater for social interests like education is very narrow.[167] This is more likely in relation to copyright and education since the Agreement does not contain exceptions to copyright – except for the general three-step test.[168] On the whole, one should be cautious not to put hope in the WTO dispute settlement system to solve the conflict between protection of economic interests and promotion of public interest needs, especially access to educational materials. This study is premised on the fact that developing countries have very limited resources. For such countries resorting to the expensive dispute settlement system of the WTO is not the first option. That said, even for a national judge, the psychological effect hoped for in a reverse reading may work to favour the right holder. If the judge is sitting in a commercial court (as is often the case in developing countries) and not a court that caters for national social policies, he might come to the same result as the WTO panel.

We therefore reach the conclusion that the three-step test cannot be used by developing countries to provide bulk access to educational materials because it focuses on the market effect of the use, and only a small amount of copying is allowed. Even in such cases, the use should not result in competition with the market of the protected work. In summary, the general exception or the three-step test, cannot facilitate bulk access to printed copyrighted materials by developing countries.

We shall now explore the special international regimes for access to copyrighted material by developing countries.

---

166 See for example sections 4.3.6 and 4.4.3.1.

167 But see Graeme B. Dinwoodie and Rochelle C. Dreyfuss, "Designing a Global Intellectual Property System Responsive to Change: the WTO, WIPO and Beyond," *Houston Law Review,* vol. 46 no. 4 (2009). 1187–1234, at 1219, (saying that if panels considered overall effect of a violation or infringement on trade on the world market and not on the domestic market, then panels are less inclined to find violation by small economies that have modest or no impact on the world market). See also, Graeme B. Dinwoodie and Rochelle C. Dreyfuss, *A Neofederalist Vision of TRIPs: Building a Resilient International Intellectual Property System,* Oxford University Press, Oxford, (2012 Forthcoming), chapter 3, page 22 (arguing that if adjudicators "paid closer attention to impacts on world market -rather than on rotely counting rights – they would have left states with more room to manoeuvre. In particular, emerging economies would benefit from such an approach. If complaints about activities with only local effects were regarded sceptically, developing countries would have more leeway to provide their populations with easier access to educational materials and training opportunities").

168 There are limits on relying on interpretation as such. See for example Pauwelyn, *supra,* p.272, and Andrew Clapham, *Human Rights Obligations of Non-Sate Actors,* (Oxford: Oxford University, Oxford, 2006), p. 171 (concurring with Pauwelyn).

CHAPTER FIVE

SPECIAL LEGAL REGIMES FOR ACCESS TO EDUCATION IN DEVELOPING COUNTRIES

5.1. Introduction

The preceding chapter demonstrated that general exceptions, or the three-step test, under international copyright law cannot be effectively used by developing countries to provide bulk access to copyrighted educational materials. However, international copyright law provides a special regime for access to copyrighted works by developing countries. This regime, the Appendix to the Berne Convention (Paris Act), or the Berne Appendix, forms the focus of our analysis in this chapter. The purpose is to demonstrate the extent to which the provisions of the Berne Appendix promote or facilitate access to copyrighted educational materials in developing countries. But before getting into the details of the Appendix, it is essential to understand the preceding events to be able to appreciate the Appendix. For this reason, we shall discuss the Stockholm Protocol prior to the Appendix.

5.2. The Stockholm Protocol: A Sign of Lack of Interest in Access Problems of Developing Countries

5.2.1. *Background*

In the course of the preparatory work for the Stockholm Conference, one of the most important tasks of the Revision Conference[1] was considered to be the establishment of rules for the benefit of developing countries. In 1964, the Swedish/BIRPI Study Group, organized to prepare for the Stockholm Conference, proposed provisions to that effect. It proposed an additional article to the Berne Convention, giving developing countries the right to make reservations with respect to provisions of the Convention on certain points.[2] A number of events triggered this new focus on the problems of access by developing countries.

1 Intellectual Property Conference of Stockholm, 1967, *supra.*
2 Records of the Intellectual Property Conference of Stockholm, 1967, *supra,* (vol. I), Preparatory Documents: S/1 (Berne Convention), p. 137.

5.2.2. *History of the Preparatory Work and Studies*

The first event spurring the emerging focus on the problems of developing country access was the African Study Meeting on Copyright, held at Brazzaville in August 1963. It recommended, among other things, that in the course of the preparations for the Stockholm Conference, the following should be considered: (a) a review of article 7 of the BC concerning the term of protection, with a view to the reduction of this term; (b) amendment of article 20 of the BC, with the objective of making possible bilateral agreements promoting exchanges; and (c) inclusion of special provisions safeguarding, on the one hand, the interests of African countries in respect of their folklore, and permitting, on other hand, the *free use of protected works for educational and scholastic purposes.*[3]

The second event was the joint session in New Delhi of the Permanent Committee and the Intergovernmental Copyright Committee, (the governing bodies of the Berne Union and the Universal Copyright Convention) in December 1963. It is reported that India, a developing country, proposed the study of the possibility of introducing into the Berne Convention (a) the right of member countries to grant *compulsory licenses for the reproduction of copyrighted works for educational purposes,* and (b) provisions relating to translation, similar to those in the Universal Copyright Convention.[4] India's then Minister of Education had emphasized the need for special provisions to ensure that copyright conventions did not impede the free flow of information and education.[5] The two Committees invited their Secretariats to conduct a study of these matters and report on them to the next joint session of the Committees.

The above two meetings highlighted the concerns relating to access to copyrighted materials by developing countries and were the first efforts at the international level aimed at addressing the access problem. It would appear that the concerns expressed by developing countries attracted the attention of the Sweden/BIRPI Study Group. The latter Study Group proposed to include in the BC a new Article 25*bis,* which would allow for exceptions to the Berne Convention in 'favour' of developing countries. It was stated in the Programme of the Stockholm Conference that the desire for special rules for the benefit of developing countries was grounded in the need to allow exceptions to copyright

---

3 Records of the Intellectual Property Conference of Stockholm, 1967, *supra,* (vol. I), Preparatory Documents: S/1 (Berne Convention), p.137 (emphasis added).

4 Records of the Intellectual Property Conference of Stockholm, 1967, *supra,* (vol. I), Preparatory Documents: S/1 (Berne Convention), p.137. The Universal Copyright Convention (UCC) of 1952 permitted the granting of compulsory licenses for the translation of writings which had not been published in a country's national language within seven years from the date of first publication. The grant of such nonexclusive licenses was conditioned upon compliance with prescribed administrative procedures, and the assurance that the owner of the right of translation would receive a compensation which was just and conformed to international standards. (Universal Copyright Convention, concluded at Geneva on 6 September 1952, entered into force on16 September 1955, article V(2)). Even if CL under the UCC was subject to a number of conditions, the mere presence of a provision on CL was considered to render the UCC more favourable to the needs of developing countries than the BC.

5 Records of the Intellectual Property Conference of Stockholm, 1967, *supra,* (vol. II), Summary Minutes, Main Committee II, (comment by Mr Krishinamurti of India), p. 947.

protection – at least for an interim period – to facilitate *cultural, social and educational expansion* in these countries.[6] Draft article 25*bis* provided in part as follows:

(1) Any country which desires to accede to this Convention but which, *with regard to its economic situation and its social needs*, does not consider itself immediately in a position to make provision for the protection of all the rights forming the object of this Convention, may, by a notification deposited with …… at the time of accession, declare that it will, for a period of ten years from the accession,

[…]

(d) reserve for itself to determine the regulations for the protection of works covered by this Convention when such works are used for *exclusively educational or scholastic purposes;*

(e) reserve the right to make arrangements in derogation of Article 20 of this Convention. […]."[7]

This proposal does not expressly refer to compulsory licensing as requested by India, although it is arguable that this could be covered under the phrase "determine the regulations."

The role of developing countries in clarifying their access needs did not end with the two conferences mentioned above. Not satisfied with the draft presented by the Study Group, ten developing countries[8] submitted a new draft of the Protocol further clarifying the needs of developing countries. Led by India, they argued for a general exception for use of copyrighted works for educational purposes without financial compensation to the author. A joint proposal by six developing countries sought to avail themselves of; (a) reservations to the right of translation, (b) reservations o the term of protection, (c) right to the protected works for educational or scholastic purposes, and (d) "the right to permit reproduction of literary and artistic works for exclusive use in its territory on payment of just remuneration to be fixed, failing agreement with the author, by its competent authority."[9] Below, we shall discuss some of the provisions of the Protocol and evaluate their usefulness for access to education in developing countries.

5.2.3. *Substantive and Procedural Provisions of the Protocol*

As it could be expected, the proposal for reservations to article 20 BC was rejected. Allowing developing countries to derogate from article 20 would have meant giving them a chance to conclude special agreements without providing increased protection for the rights of authors. This would go against the intention of the drafters of the Berne

6 Records of the Intellectual Property Conference of Stockholm, 1967, *supra,* vol. I, Preparatory Documents: S/1 (Berne Convention), p.142 (emphasis added).

7 *Ibid,* p. 137–138 (emphasis added).

8 These included Congo (Brazzaville), Congo (Kinshasa), Gabon, Ivory Cost, Madagascar, Morocco, Niger, Senegal and Tunisia. See *ibid,* Conference Documents (Document S/160), p. 702.

9 Records of the Intellectual Property Conference of Stockholm, *supra,* vol. I, Preparatory Documents: S/1 (Berne Convention), p. 140. Two delegations were categorically opposed to introduction of such a reservation.

Convention, who were the owners of copyrighted works.[10] Nevertheless, the Protocol allowed developing countries to make a number of reservations that were directly relevant to access to protected literary works. These reservations, all contained in article 1 of the Protocol, related to: duration of protection, translation, reproduction, broadcasting and general educational uses. In this discussion, we shall focus on translation, reproduction and general educational uses.

First, in relation to translation, a compulsory license for translation could be applied for if, after three years from the date of a works' first publication, or any longer period determined by the legislation of the developing country concerned, a translation of this work had not been published in that country in the 'national or official or regional language or languages of that country' by the owner of the translation right, or with his authorization. Any national of such country could obtain a non-exclusive license from the 'competent authority' to translate and publish the translation into a language in which the work was not published.[11] Translation rights were to cease to exist ten years from the date of publication of the original work if within that time the copyright owner had not published, in one of the countries of the Union, a translation in the language for which protection was claimed.[12]

There were a number of conditions for granting a compulsory license for translation:

a). The national seeking the license had to prove that he had requested and been denied authorization to make a translation, or that after due diligence on his part he had been unable to locate the owner of the right. Under the same conditions, a license could also be granted where all previous editions of a translation in that language in that country were out of print.[13] The Protocol did not define 'due diligence,' but it would seem that the next paragraph describes what it would entail.

b). Where the owner could not be found, appropriate notice was to be sent to the publisher whose name appeared on the work and, where the author's nationality was known, to the diplomatic or consular representative of the country of which he was a national.[14] The exercise of 'due diligence' on the part of the intending applicant for a CL included sending notice to the publisher or the diplomatic or consular representative. In other words, the intending applicant would have to bear the cost of issuing the service notice before depositing the application. This would serve to discourage would-be applicants.

c). Through national legislation, the country granting the compulsory license had to "assure the payment of the holder of the translation right a just compensation, to assure payment and transmittal of such compensation, subject to national currency regulations, and to assure correct translations of the work".[15] The advantage of subjecting payment of

10 At least at the time, since the original Berne Convention had been negotiated by developed countries who were the owners of protected works.

11 Protocol Regarding Developing Countries, article 1(b)(ii)-(ix), reproduced in Records of the Intellectual Property Conference of Stockholm, 1967, *supra,* vol. II, Report of the Work of Main Committee II, p. 1197.

12 Stockholm Protocol, *supra,* article 1(b)(i).

13 Stockholm Protocol, *supra* article 1(b)(ii).

14 *Ibid,* article 1(b)(iii).

15 *Ibid,* article 1(b)(iv).

royalties to national currency regulations is minimization of the challenges posed by foreign exchange.

d). Of particular interest, the Protocol provided for compulsory licensing for export. Copies of works translated or reproduced under a compulsory license could be exported and sold to another country availing itself of the reservation. In addition, it was possible to export and sell to a country that could not avail itself of the Protocol, if the legislation of the latter allowed importation of products made under compulsory licensing.[16] Only copies of work published in a country for the said educational purposes could be imported and sold in other countries availing themselves of the reservations. An example was that of a translation made in India which could be imported into Ceylon (Sri Lanka) but not into Japan.[17] The effect, therefore, was that such copies would be in a language relevant to the educational needs of that country. The rationale for the provision was that no harm was done in such a case, as the work would have been subject to an identical license in the second country.[18]

e). Where the author failed to publish a translation within a period of ten years, at the end of this time the obligation of the licensee to pay compensation came to an end.[19] As would be expected, developed countries were opposed to such a provision.[20] Yet the waiting period of ten years was already too long. Very few textbooks, especially of a technical or scientific nature, would still be valuable even if they were translated.

Second, in the case of reproduction, the Protocol provided for a nonexclusive compulsory license to reproduce and publish a work for educational or cultural purposes if the work had not been published in a country in its original form during a period of three years from the date of first publication.[21] It was understood that this wording was not to be interpreted in a restrictive manner.[22] On the other hand, restriction of the right of reproduction for educational or cultural purposes excluded from the field of application of the reservation all works whose educational or cultural purpose was not evident, such as detective and adventure stories.[23]

Finally, it was possible to issue a compulsory license for uses destined *exclusively for teaching, study and research in all fields of education,* provided that due provision was made to assure to the author a compensation which conformed *to standards of payment made to national authors.*[24] It would seem that exceptions for distance education could

16 *Ibid,* article 1(b)(v).

17 Records of the Intellectual Property Conference of Stockholm, 1967, *supra,* vol. II, Report of the Work of Main Committee II, (Protocol Regarding Developing Countries), World Intellectual Property Organizations, Geneva, 1971, pp.1197–1198.

18 Records of the Intellectual Property Conference of Stockholm, 1967, *supra,* vol. II, Report of the Work of Main Committee II, (Protocol Regarding Developing Countries), p. 1197.

19 Stockholm Protocol, *supra,* article 1(b)(viii).

20 This was the case, for example, with, Italy and the Netherlands. See Records of the Intellectual Property Conference of Stockholm, 1967, *supra,* vol. II, Report of the Work of Main Committee II, (Protocol Regarding Developing Countries), pp. 976–978.

21 Stockholm Protocol, supra, article 1(c).

22 Records of the Intellectual Property Conference of Stockholm, 1967, *supra,* vol. II, Report of the Work of Main Committee II, (Protocol Regarding Developing Countries), p. 1196.

23 *Ibid.*

24 Stockholm Protocol, *supra,* article 1(e) (emphasis added).

fall within this provision, although at the time this would make little sense since information communications technology was not developed so as to facilitate distance learning. This reservation did not apply solely to the rights of translation and reproduction, but could be invoked for other uses of literary and artistic works.[25] The advantage of paying compensation according to standards applied to national authors would be to minimize losses related to currency conversion.

5.2.4. *Evaluation of the Protocol*

The Protocol represented an important development in the history of the Berne Convention and international copyright law. Considering the fact that there was a complete absence of provisions for access to printed material by developing countries, the discussion and drafting of such a Protocol was remarkable. If it had been implemented, the Protocol would have been a landmark as a model of international cooperation in copyright issues.

At the same time, it would be misleading to assume that the interests of developing countries were the driving force behind the proposed protocol. As was explained during the Stockholm Conference, the protection of authors' rights in countries that had recently gained independence was one of the problems that solicited the attention of the Swedish Government as the host country of the Revision Conference and that of the BIRPI for several years.[26] While it was admitted that exceptional measures for the benefit of developing countries were in principle justified, it was objected that if those countries found themselves unable to organize protection as effective as accession to the Berne Convention would imply then they ought to become parties to the Universal Copyright Convention[27] instead of the Berne Convention.[28] There was no doubt, however, that the adoption by developing countries of copyright legislation within the framework of the Berne Convention would be of considerable advantage to the authors from developed countries:

---

25 Records of the Intellectual Property Conference of Stockholm, 1967, *supra,* vol. II, Report of the Work of Main Committee II, (Protocol Regarding Developing Countries), p. 1197.

26 *Ibid,* p. 1193.

27 Universal Copyright Convention (UCC), concluded at Geneva on 6 September 1952, entered into force on 16 September 1955, and as revised at Paris on 24 July 1971, entered into force on 24 July 1974. Unlike the Berne Convention, the UCC was concluded under the auspices of UNESCO.

28 France and the United Kingdom were particularly opposed to the Protocol as it would weaken the level of copyright protection. Authors in those two countries were willing to help developing countries in their 'development', but did not understand why the assistance should be entirely at their expense. See Records of the Intellectual Property Conference of Stockholm, 1967, *supra,* (vol. II), Summary Minutes, Main Committee II, pp. 949–950. The Universal Copyright Convention (UCC) offered less protection than the Berne Convention. It offered a minimum level of international copyright protection accommodating countries which had not acceded to the Berne Convention, either because their legislation did not conform to Berne standards, or because fundamental differences existed between their systems of protection and that of the Berne Union. (For a summary of the pertinent provisions of the then UCC, see Olian Jr., *supra,* p. 84–86.) This explains why developed countries advised developing countries that were unable to provide the high standards of protection of the Berne Convention to join the UCC. In other words, if developed country authors were to help developing countries with access problems, it would not be at the cost of their copyrights.

"[c]onditions in several of these countries would certainly improve and one of the consequences of this development would be the *increasing exploitation of literary and artistic works*. In these circumstances, it would naturally be to the authors' advantage if the protection granted to them had been organized from the start on the pattern of the Berne Convention."[29]

It is not surprising that there existed no obligation on the part of developed countries to facilitate access to their protected works in developing countries. Any developed country which chose to accede to the substantive provisions of the Stockholm Act would necessarily be bound to the Protocol. Conversely, a country that did not accede to the substantive provisions did not have to apply the Protocol. However, the most significant loophole was that a nation could voluntarily bind itself to the Protocol despite rejecting the substantive provisions.[30] The result was that a Member of the Berne Union which did not accede to either the substantive provisions of the BC or the Protocol was in a position not to grant any of the exceptions in favour of developing countries as laid down in the Protocol.

For developing countries, most of the provisions intended for their benefit were useless. As highlighted above, the procedural requirements of notification make the application process for a CL too expensive for developing countries. Waiting periods of three or ten years are excessive for a country that is in desperate need of reading or teaching material. Even if the waiting period for application for a CL were three years, the lengthy procedure for such an application works to make this period too long.[31]

For developed countries, the Protocol signified a substantial threat to the existence of copyright protection as it had evolved over a period of several hundred years, as well as a confiscation of the rights of individual authors, composers, and publishers. Provisions with open-ended terminology like "teaching, study and research in all fields of education" or "educational and cultural purposes" aroused fear of substantial abuse. This was magnified by the prospect that developing countries would attain a majority position in the Berne Union if the Protocol were enacted.[32] The result of the lack of satisfaction by developing and developed countries concerning the Protocol was the Berne Appendix, which we shall discuss below.

5.3. A Special Legal Regime for Developing Countries: The Berne Appendix

We have demonstrated that the specific exceptions to the rights conferred to an author do not serve the purpose of allowing the sort of access to educational materials that developing countries need. In particular, allowing the use of work in illustration for teaching

29 Records of the Intellectual Property Conference of Stockholm, 1967, *supra*, vol. I, Preparatory Documents: S/1 (Berne Convention), p.138. This is further evidence that if developed countries, and in particular owners of copyrighted material joined the international copyright Conventions, it was not to facilitate access to their IP works, but instead to ensure their better protection at international level.

30 The Berne Convention, *supra*, article 28.

31 See also Olian Jr., *supra*, p. 102.

32 Olian Jr., *supra*, p. 102.

purposes does not solve the problem of bulk access. Using a literary work only for illustration means that students and teachers will not have the full texts of the works. In other words, the quantity allowed is too little to serve the purpose. Developing countries require bulk copying, not just illustration.

Concerning the general exceptions, we already demonstrated that the three-step test is not the kind of limitation developing countries need either. The quantities that can be allowed without compensation are very limited, having the effect of use for illustration. Second, copying of large quantities can only comply with the three-step test if compensation is paid. Having to pay compensation for large quantities of works discourages the use of such an exception by developing countries that are already financially constrained.

One additional type of flexibility merits our analysis: the Appendix to the Berne Convention. This is a special legal regime designed for developing countries (although not expressly closed to developed countries) for access to literary works in printed form through compulsory licensing. The question we shall seek to answer is whether such a regime indeed facilitates such access, and if not, what it reveals about the international copyright system.

5.3.1. *The Link between the Stockholm Protocol and the Appendix to the Berne Convention*

While it was considered important to maintain the stability and credibility of the BC by admitting the newly independent states,[33] developed countries were not prepared to do so at any cost. The Stockholm Protocol was designed to attract and keep developing countries within the Berne Union[34] but not at the cost of the original purpose of the Berne Convention, which was to "constitute a Union for the protection of the rights of authors in their literary and artistic works."[35] So by 1970, the Protocol had not entered into force, and there were clear signs that this would not happen since developed countries were becoming increasingly reluctant to commit themselves to the special regime proposed for developing nations.[36] The result was a call for a revision of the Protocol mainly by developed countries (which were strongly influenced by their own authors and publishing industries). The risk of a Union mainly comprised of developed countries was obvious. On the other hand, developing countries were aware that they might gain nothing at all if a solution more acceptable to the developed countries could not be found. Thus both sides

---

33 On this point see Okediji, sustainable Access, *supra*, p. 156. (Stating that the preservation of the Berne Convention's self-image as a dominant multilateral copyright agreement was an important factor in considering changes that would encourage the newly independent countries to become members.)

34 See discussion above and Olian Jr., *supra*, p. 103 (saying that the Protocol was signed out of political pressure).

35 The Berne Convention, *supra*, article 1.

36 Authors' and publishers' Associations in developed countries, particularly the UK were opposed to the Protocol. Their governments were certainly influenced. The UK, for example clearly stated that it would not ratify the Protocol. For a detailed narrative of the events immediately following the adoption of the Protocol and reaction of developed countries see Ricketson, The Berne Convention pp. 621–622, 624. This is reminiscent of the Protocol Amending the TRIPS Agreement (see *infra*, Section 7.2).

"accepted the need for some kind of salvage operation."[37] This 'salvage solution' was the revision of the Berne Convention, with a focus on the provisions for access by developing countries.[38] To minimize the chances of developing countries joining the Universal Copyright Convention (UCC), the latter was revised at the same time as the Berne Convention. The major effect of the revision of the UCC was to afford more protection to authors and make it less attractive for developing countries to leave the Berne Convention and join the UCC. The result of the revision of the Berne Convention was the Appendix.[39]

Unlike the Stockholm Protocol, which never became a legal instrument due to lack of signatures, the Berne Appendix is a recognized legal instrument specifically addressing access to copyrighted works in printed or analogue form by developing countries. Whether such an instrument is, in practical terms, effective in allowing such access is the subject of our inquiry. To this end, in the following paragraphs, we discuss the various substantive and procedural provisions of the Appendix to the Berne Convention. Table 1 in the Appendix summarizes both the procedural and substantive requirements of the Berne Appendix.

5.3.2. *Substantive Provisions of the Appendix*

The Appendix allows developing countries to issue compulsory licenses for the *translation* of works in printed or analogue form only for the purpose of teaching, scholarship or research.[40] Compare this with the Stockholm Protocol, which allowed compulsory licensing for reproduction and translation for teaching, study and research in all fields of education. In relation to the mentioned activities, compulsory licensing under the Appendix is only for translation and not reproduction. With regard to *reproduction and publication*, a compulsory license under the Appendix can be issued for use in systematic instructional activities. This provision would seem to exclude private study, research and distance education. The Appendix is more restricted than the Protocol.

The compulsory licensing system under the Berne Appendix requires compensation of the copyright holder.[41] Ironically, research or study is not a compensated exception in a number of developed countries. For example, fair dealing with a literary work for research or study or fair use of a work for these purposes is not an infringement of a copyright. No compensation is required for the use of a work if it is proved that the use is fair.[42]

---

37 Ricketson, The Berne Convention, *supra* p. 124.

38 The discussions were concerned essentially with reservations in relation to the rights of translation and of reproduction. See Records of the Diplomatic Conference for the Revision of the Berne Convention, Paris, July 5 to 24, 1971, (Conference Documents), World Intellectual Property Organization, Geneva, 1974, WIPO Publications No. 385 (E), p. 45.

39 For detailed discussions of the events leading to the revision and the revision processes for the two Conventions, see Olian Jr., *supra*, p. 107; Tocups, *supra*, pp. 414–416; Ricketson, the Berne Convention, *supra*, pp. 624–632; and Okediji, Sustainable Access, *supra*, pp. 142–187.

40 The Berne Convention, *supra*, Appendix, article II(5).

41 The Berne Convention, *ibid*, Appendix, article IV(6).

42 See for example fair dealing with a work for research or study is allowed under the Australian Copyright Act 1968 Act no.63 of 1968 (as amended), Part III, Division 3, section 40; the U.S. Copyright Act allows the fair use of a work for teaching (including multiple copies for classroom use), scholarship, or research, (Copyright Act of 1976, Act of 19 October 19976, as amended

Disregarding, at this point the question of whether such provisions fall under the Berne Convention, they at least reflect the importance attached to access to printed text for educational purposes in these countries. However, the same importance was not attached for developing countries. The inevitable conclusion is that there existed no intention to facilitate free access to developed countries' works by developing countries. This conclusion is reinforced by the stringent procedural requirements for implementing the already narrow exception.[43]

What also appears peculiar is the difference in uses for translation and reproduction licenses. For exceptions to the reproduction right under article 9(2) BC, there are implied exceptions to the translation right.[44] This is not the case under the Appendix. One has to submit a different application for a CL for translation and another for reproduction.

Of particular interest to this discussion are the procedural conditions for making use of the Appendix. Below, we shall analyse these conditions.

5.3.3. *Procedural Requirements of the Appendix*

First of all, to be able to use the Appendix, a developing country must make a declaration to the Director General of WIPO at the time of ratification or accession indicating that it will avail itself of the Appendix.[45] The Declaration is renewable for a period of ten years by depositing notification with the Director General of WIPO not more than 15, and not less than 3, months before the expiration of the ten-year period then running.[46] The periodic notifications, while they may serve to give sufficient notice to other Members as to when the ten-year period will expire,[47] are cumbersome, adding more work for already understaffed developing country IP offices. The result is to discourage the use of the system.

5.3.3.1. Waiting Period for Translation License

There is a waiting period within which to apply for a translation license. An application for a compulsory license for translation can be made three years after the first publication of a work, upon the further condition that no translation of the work has been published in the language of general use in the country where the application is to be made or if all the translated editions are out of print.[48] If the language in general use in the developing country is not in general use in one or more of the developed countries, the waiting period

---

through to 13 December 2003, Title 17 United states Code (USC), section 107); in Canada, fair dealing with a work for purpose of research or private study is not an infringement of a copyright (Copyright Act, 1985 (R.S., c. C-30, s.1) as amended, section 29). At the time of the Paris Conference which discussed the Appendix, the cited provisions were in force for the mentioned developed countries.

43 We discuss these requirements below.

44 Records of the Intellectual Property Conference of Stockholm, 1967, *supra,* vol. II, Report of the Main Committee I, p. 1165.

45 The Berne Convention, *supra,* Appendix, article I(1).

46 The Berne Convention, *ibid,* Appendix, article I(2).

47 Ricketson, *et al,* International Copyright and Neighbouring Rights, volume II, *supra,* p. 928.

48 The Berne Convention, *supra,* Appendix, article II(2)(a) and (b).

of three years can be reduced to one year.[49] The period of three years can also be reduced if there is unanimous agreement by the developed countries which are members of the Union and in which the language is in general use.[50] Originally, the Appendix did not define the phrase "general use". However, the joint UNESCO/WIPO Guidelines on the implementation of the Berne Appendix define "language in general use" as English, Spanish and French.[51] In such a case, the translation license can only be applied for after three years. This requirement excludes translation to a mother tongue which is not an official language or 'language in general' use – but which is in fact the language of instruction of many educational institutions in developing countries.[52] The result is that the minimum waiting period for applying for a compulsory license for translation is three years.

If an application for a translation license is made after three years, the applicant must wait six months before the license is granted. In the case of an application made after one year of publication, the license cannot be granted before a period of nine months expires. Before an application is considered valid, there exists a long procedure which the applicant must follow (we shall outline it below). It is only after that procedure has been fulfilled that the six or nine months start to be counted.[53]

In addition, if within the six or nine month period the owner of the translation right makes the translation, the compulsory license will not be granted. In other words, one cannot be certain about receiving the CL. This is the situation even after going through a lengthy process of application. The provision, at minimum, works to discourage potential applicants who would not want to risk spending time and money without being assured they will receive the license. The provision also works to shield the copyright owner from being subjected to compulsory licensing. Three years is long enough to amount to a non-working of the copyright. Thus, failure to provide the translation within this period should be sanctioned by a CL for failure to work or abuse of IP rights, and not shielded. In the case of patents, for example, a CL for failure to work can be applied for three years from the grant of a patent.[54] But unlike in the case of the Appendix, the patent owner is not shielded by a grace period of six or nine months.

---

49 The Berne Convention, *ibid*, Appendix, article II(3)(a).

50 *Ibid*, Appendix, article II(3)(b).

51 Guidelines on the system of translation and reproduction licenses for developing countries under the copyright conventions prepared by the Secretariat and adopted by the Working Group on the Formulation of Guiding Principles covering the problems posed by the practical implementation of the licensing procedures for translation and reproduction under the copyright conventions, Geneva, November 17 to 21, 1980, UNESCO/WIPO Doc UNESCO/WIPO/WG.II/CWA/4, dated November 21, 1980, Annex A, para. 36, (hereafter referred to as UNESCO/WIPO Guidelines).

52 For example in South Africa all the eleven official languages are also languages of instruction in schools (information available at http://www.cyberserv.co.za/users/~jako/lang/xho.htm). On mother tongue in Africa in general, see Beeckman, "Mother tongue instruction in Africa: human rights treaty bodies and the language problem in education, *supra*, pp. 163–192.

53 The Berne Convention, *supra*, Appendix, article II(4)(a).

54 The Paris Convention, *supra*, article 5(A).

The long waiting period essentially means that by the time a CL is granted, books in the scientific and technical field will be outdated.[55] Yet, these are the kinds of books for which a CL would be most needed, (as opposed to books of fiction) and which will have to be imported. In effect, the only way a developing country will use protected works that require translation is through the owner of the copyright, with all its implications for the price.

5.3.3.2. Waiting Period for Reproduction License

In the case of CL for a reproduction, the waiting period depends upon the type of work. An application for a CL for works of the natural and physical sciences including mathematics and technology can only be made three years after the first publication of the work and cannot be granted before six months after the application. In the case of works of fiction, poetry, drama and music, and for art, the waiting period is five years. For all other works, the waiting period is seven years.[56] The baseline is that an overpriced book – the price of which is not reasonably related to that normally charged in the country for comparable works – will be the only book on the market for a period of between three and a half and seven years.[57] What is striking is the fact that a license cannot be issued to reproduce and publish a translated work where the translation was not published by the owner of the translation right or with his authorization, or where the translation is not in a language in general use in the country in which the license is applied for.[58] The effect is that translations made under compulsory licenses cannot be the subject of a CL for reproduction. Each license has to be applied for separately, which means going through the rigorous procedural requirements twice. This is more so owing to the fact that in many developing countries, especially in Africa, there are a multiplicity of languages. Reproduced or photocopied works will often need to be translated.

5.3.3.3. Requirements Applying to both Translation and Reproduction Licence

In both cases of compulsory licensing, the applicant has to prove that he requested and was denied a voluntary license or that he has done everything possible and still failed to find the right holder.[59] At the time of request for a CL, the applicant must inform any national or international information centre. If the owner of the copyright cannot be found, the applicant must send, by registered mail, copies of his application to the publisher whose name appears on the work and to any national or international information centre which may have been designated, in a notification to that effect deposited with the Director General, by the Government of the country in which the publisher is believed to have his principal place of business.[60] All this must be done before an application is considered. The applicant incurs the cost of the application even while he is not sure of

55 See also Okediji, Sustainable Access, *supra,* p. 156.
56 Berne Convention, *supra,* Appendix, article III(3) and (4).
57 *Ibid,* Appendix, article III(1), (2) and (3)(i) and (ii) read together.
58 The Berne Convention, *supra,* Appendix, article II(5)(i) and (ii).
59 *Ibid,* Appendix, article IV(1)
60 *Ibid,* article IV(1) and (2).

receiving the license. This uncertainty is compounded by the fact that the applicant has to wait for at least six months before getting the CL, and within that period his application may be cancelled if the copyright owner decides to make the translation or supply the market with copies at a reasonable price.[61]

Copies made under a CL must be labelled, indicating the title of the work on all copies. In the case of translation, the original title of the work must appear on the copies.[62] Unlike the Protocol, the Appendix does not allow granting of compulsory licenses for export, the only exception being if the translation is into a language other than English, French or Spanish and the translated copies are sent to a national of the country granting the CL living in another country. Even then, this is limited to the government use of the work.[63] In the case of patents, where a CL is issued to remedy an anti-competitive practice such as fixing high prices, as is the case in the Appendix,[64] there is the possibility of exporting regardless of whether or not the CL is for government use or for use by a private person.[65]

There must be just compensation which is consistent with *standards of royalties for freely negotiated licenses*. Should national currency regulations intervene, the competent authority must make all efforts, by the use of international machinery, to ensure transmittal of the compensation in internationally convertible currency or its equivalent.[66] This provision raises a number of issues. It assumes that the competent authority has the means to determine the amount of the royalty for the books in question. If the owner of the copyright has not been found after due diligence on the part of the applicant, then the competent authority or applicant would have to carry out some sort of market research for a similar book to establish the amount of the royalty for negotiated licenses. This defeats the purpose of CL, especially for reproduction.

According to the Appendix, a CL for reproduction should be applied for if copies of the published work are not distributed *at a price reasonably related to that normally charged in the country for comparable works*.[67] This means the CL is intended to remedy an anti-competitive practice, manifested by the charging of high prices. In the case of patents, where a CL is granted as a measure against an anti competitive practice, the amount of remuneration is not regulated by the patent holder, but by the competent authority.[68] In the case of the Berne Appendix, the copyright owner, who performs an anti-competitive

61 *Ibid*, Appendix, articles II(6) and III(6).
62 *Ibid*, Appendix, article IV(3).
63 The Berne Convention, *supra*, Appendix, article IV(4)(c).
64 *Ibid*, Appendix, article III(2).
65 TRIPS Agreement, article 31(f) and (k) read together.
66 Berne Convention 1971, Appendix, article IV(6)(a).
67 *Ibid*, Appendix, article III(2) (emphasis added).
68 The TRIPS Agreement, article 31(k). The Egyptian legislation provides for CL for abuse of rights or exercise of rights in a manner contrary to fair competition, including: fixing exorbitant prices or preferential treatment of agents with regard to prices or sales conditions; failure to supply local market or supplying under prohibitive terms; stopping production of patented items etc; undertaking acts or practices which have adverse effect on free competition etc. (Egyptian law on the protection of intellectual property rights, Law no. 82 of 2002, article 35(5)). Likewise, the legislation of Argentina provides for CL for anti-competitive practices (Law no. 24, 481 on Patents and Utility Models, 1996, article 44).

act, has the liberty to decide the royalty amount without the government or competent authority intervening. Furthermore, the Appendix assumes that there is a 'competent authority' that can issue the license, which is not always the case. In the end, this procedure is lengthy and expensive, which defeats the purpose of the Appendix – to afford access to protected works to developing countries at affordable prices.

Again, it is important to bear in mind that articles 1 to 21 of the Berne Convention apply to the TRIPS Agreement by virtue of article 9(1) of the TRIPS Agreement. This means that the general and specific exceptions in the Berne Convention apply to TRIPS as well.

5.3.4. *Assessment of the Berne Appendix*

In legal terms, what does the Appendix signify? In terms of the Convention's overall development as a major instrument regulating private rights in the area of international law, the form of the Appendix may be regretted. It is an extremely detailed set of provisions which exceeds the original Berne Act in length. Professor Ricketson rightly questions the need for such detail, particularly in a Convention which had traditionally been concerned with the prescription of general principles of protection.[69] The logical explanation is that there was no intention on the part of the developed countries to come up with a document that could be implemented. Making the Appendix procedurally complicated was an obvious way of achieving this. This lack of intention by developed countries to cooperate with developing countries in facilitating access to copyrighted works for educational purposes is not new to the Berne system. The discussions at Stockholm on the content of the three-step test and the Stockholm Protocol reflect this situation as well.[70] It was therefore important for developed countries that the Appendix is procedurally complicated, so as to make its implementation impossible.

5.3.5. *The Practical Consequences of the Appendix*

While it is difficult to point to any obvious benefits that have directly flowed to developing countries due to the adoption of the Appendix, there are real consequences of the Appendix.[71] Its substantive provisions represent a delicate compromise between widely differing conceptions of the role of copyright.[72] The developing countries never

---

69 Ricketson, The Berne Convention, *supra,* p. 663.

70 At Stockholm, developed countries showed a lack of willingness to allow the same exceptions that existed in their national law to be elevated to the international level. That is why they were opposed to making a list of exceptions and in the end a general provision on exceptions to the reproduction right (see discussion in section 4.2.). As regards the Protocol, it is enough to mention that the UK abstained from voting for it, the USA threatened not to join the Berne Convention if the Protocol was adopted and France, after voting for it, campaigned against it and in the end did not sign. See Ricketson, 1987, 621–623. As Professor Okediji summarizes, the Stockholm Protocol was an unsuccessful model for international cooperation. See Okediji, Sustainable Access, *supra,* p. 156.

71 Ricketson, The Berne Convention, *supra,* p. 663.

72 Developing countries support the view that the best copyright laws are those which serve the community rather than the individual interest; that copyright protection should facilitate access by as many people as possible so as to promote the development of education, science and culture. See Lazara, "Developing countries and authors' rights in international copyright," *Copyright Law Symposium,* vol. 1, 1971, quoted in Tocups, *supra,* p. 408. In developed countries,

argued for the abolition of copyright, but they did urge that its prescriptions be lowered in certain circumstances so as to assist their economic development in the areas of education and training.[73] The developed countries, or rather the authors' and publishers' organizations of those countries, argued in turn that their rights should not be used as a means of providing economic assistance to developing countries. This illustrates a major challenge of international copyright law. The emphasis is on economic rights and not on facilitating access to copyrighted works,[74] hence allowing access to copyrighted products is viewed as ceding economic rights rather than fulfilment of a public interest of users. Unsurprisingly, a request for access to copyrighted works to fulfil an educational purpose is considered by copyright owners as asking for economic subsidization.[75]

The Appendix, it is argued, can be seen as an incentive to authors and publishers in the developed countries to cooperate in making voluntary licensing arrangements: the compulsory licenses remain in the background both as a reminder of the needs of developing countries and as a threat to be brought into operation if there is a reluctance to cooperate.[76] However, as we have demonstrated, the procedural requirements shield copyright holders by discouraging would-be applicants for a CL. The right holders know this, so they do not have any incentive to cooperate. The fact that developing countries have not invoked the Appendix acts, in our view, to assure copyright owners that it is an instrument that cannot be implemented. Ultimately, they do not feel threatened by its existence and thus they do not feel 'coerced' to cooperate.

The fact that few developing countries have invoked the Appendix has been interpreted to mean that authors and publishers in developed countries have been far more willing to license their works than was previously the case.[77] However, the reasons for

---

copyright has different purposes at national and international level. At national level, it can be a means to achieve certain public interests like learning and promotion of science. At international level, or precisely in international relations, copyright is a tool of trade.

73 Developing countries were consistent in indicating that they acknowledge the importance of copyright. For this reason, they did not ask for blanket exceptions, but for specific safeguards to allow them achieve certain social goals, mainly educational. Requests to that effect did not start with the Appendix, but are manifest in the discussions on limitations to the general right of reproduction at Stockholm and on the Stockholm Protocol.

74 See discussion under the three-step test for example (chapter 4). The compliance of an exception with a test is judged on the basis of its economic effect.

75 At its 18th Congress held in Amsterdam from June 9–25, 1968, the International Publishers' Association (IPA) had called upon its member associations to "urge their governments to provide such technical and economic aid as would eliminate any need to ratify or implement the Stockholm Protocol, and together with the publishing, to facilitate the local distribution of needed books in developing countries., reported in Ricketson, the Berne Convention, *supra,* p. 622.

76 V. de Sanctis, "L'avenir du droit d'auteur international a la lumière des conferences de revision de juillet 1971," 1972 *Interauteurs*, 39, p.42ff, quoted in Ricketson, the Berne Convention, *supra,* p. 663.

77 Ricketson, Berne Convention, *ibid*, p.663. However, there is no evidence to show that publishers in developed countries have been willing to licence, or to increase supply of their works in developing countries. Indeed, three recent studies on access to knowledge in developing countries show that despite strong protection of copyrighted works, there has not been a

which the Appendix is not invoked is simply that the procedural requirements make it impossible to use. Either the application process for a CL is expensive or the waiting periods and conditions attached make it useless to apply for a CL since the subject matter of application will be outdated by the time a CL is granted.[78] Furthermore, high levels of protection adopted by many developing countries, especially African countries, have been interpreted as a sign that developing countries are relatively more concerned with the protection of authors' rights. To support this argument, one author refers to the several national laws which are patterned on the *Tunis Model Law on Copyright which was prepared under the auspices of WIPO.*[79] This argument is not very tenable. First, WIPO's role is not to promote the needs of developing countries, but the protection and enforcement of intellectual property rights.[80] Therefore, the technical assistance offered by WIPO to developing countries has been aimed at achieving these goals. For this reason, WIPO's technical assistance has in the past focused on helping developing countries in drafting or implementing their laws according to international IP conventions and not to promote access to protected works.[81] The fact that many developing countries copied the model laws of WIPO can better be explained by the fact that they lacked the technical expertise and personnel to draft complicated IP laws and thus ignorantly welcomed the technical assistance of WIPO.[82] Our point here is that if developing countries provide high levels of

---

corresponding increase in supply of those works. See for example Consumers International, Project on copyright and access to knowledge in Indonesia, (2006) and Consumers International, Project on access to knowledge in Indonesia, (2006) (both available at www.consumersinternational.org); and the African Copyright and Access to Knowledge Project (2009), (available at www.aca2k.org).

78 On this point, see Okediji, Sustainable Access, *supra,* p.163.

79 Ricketson, the Berne Convention, *supra,* p. 663 (footnote omitted) (emphasis added). An example of country that drafted its law using the WIPO model law is Swaziland.

80 This trend might be changing in light of current developments like the WIPO development Agenda. We discuss this at a later stage.

81 The first technical assistance offered to developing countries in relation to the Appendix was the joint UNESCO/WIPO Guidelines on providing "Guiding Principles covering the problems posed by the practical implementation of the licensing procedures for translation and reproduction under the copyright conventions." The lengthy Guidelines, like the Appendix, only strengthen the position of copyright holders. They reiterate the provisions of the Appendix and clarify those provisions that are not clear, like 'language in common use' but in favour of copyright holders. A more recent example of author-centred assistance from WIPO can be found in the Report on technical assistance from 2000 to 2005. In the Report, it is clear that assistance given in terms of legislative assistance, includes comments on a country's draft IP law, providing a model law and revision of national IP legislation. See "Information on WIPO's Development Cooperation Activities, January 2000–June 2005," World Intellectual Property Organization, Geneva, WIO Document WIPO/EDS/INF/1 Rev (E) dated September 23, 2005 (available at www.wipo.int/ip-development). To give more concrete examples, the Botswana Copyright and Neighbouring Rights Act of 2000 (Act no. 8 of 2000), which is intended to help Botswana comply with its obligations under the TRIPS Agreement was drafted with the technical assistance of WIPO. Likewise, WIPO Assisted Namibia in updating its 1994 Copyright Act to make it TRIPS compliant (see Statement by the Ministry of Foreign Affairs of Namibia, available at www.op.gov.na/Decade_peace/mfa.htm).

82 In an interview with an officer of WIPO working on technical assistance (TA) on 27/02/08, he explained that developing countries approached WIPO for TA in bringing their laws into

protection, it is because the model laws given by way of technical or legislative assistance contain provisions requiring such levels of protection. Minimum input was provided by developing countries in the design of domestic copyright laws.[83]

The Appendix reinforces the position of authors and publishers in deciding upon the use of information and knowledge, but does not alleviate access issues such as those relating to research, distance learning, use in libraries or more precisely, bulk access to printed material. As Story has written,

> [a]lthough the Berne Appendix is labelled as a set of "special provisions regarding developing countries," it is, in reality, a distraction from the real struggle to win better access rights for the South; it is a mere table scrap, a tactical cul de sac, a legal nightmare. The 'special' situation found across many parts of the South is *not* addressed and, not surprisingly, its provisions have seldom been used by countries of the South in the 35 years since it came into existence.[84]

Indeed, the provisions of the Appendix have seldom been used. Only a handful of countries have made a declaration of intention to use the Appendix, fewer have legislation similar to it and none has used the provision. Other countries include provisions similar to the Appendix in their national legislation without making the required Declaration or even being party to the BC. We shall examine the use of the Appendix in detail below.

---

compliance with international treaties. When the deadline for applying the TRIPS Agreement was approaching, there were many such requests (WIPO and WTO have an Agreement to cooperate in providing Legal-Technical Assistance to developing countries that are Members of one organization, even if they may not be Members of the other. See Agreement Between the World Intellectual Property Organization and the World Trade Organization, concluded 22 December 1995, entered into force on 1 January 1996, World Intellectual Property Organization, Geneva 1997. Publication of the World Intellectual Property Organization no. 223, article 4).

83 For support of the idea that national laws in developing countries are not their own models, James Love emphasizes the fact that the laws are either modelled after European and US system, "often based upon colonial statutes, or the modern-day equivalent: laws informed by WIPO technical assistance". See James Love, "Access to medicine and compliance with the WTO TRIPS accord: models for state practice in developing countries," in Peter Drahos, and Ruth Mayne, eds, *Global Intellectual Property Rights: Knowledge, Access and Development,* Palgrave Macmillan and Oxfam, New York, 2002, pp.74–89, p.76. Davis argues that the lack of domestic input in the design of domestic copyright regulation is a reflection of low level of institutional capacity in developing countries. See Kevin E. Davis, "Regulation of Technology Transfer to Developing Countries: The Relevance of Institutional Capacity," *Law and Policy,* vol. 27(2005), quoted in Ruth L., Okediji, "Africa and the Global Intellectual Property System: Beyond the Agency Model," in Abdulqawi A.Yusuf, ed. *African Yearbook of International Law,* vol. 12 (2004), (Leiden: Martinus Nijhoff Publishers, 2006). 207–251, p.241 (hereinafter referred to as Okediji, Africa and the global IP system). On the contrary, professor Okediji explains the lack of domestic input as a result of the harmonizing effect. (*ibid*). Whatever the reason, the fact is that in the end the domestic laws of developing countries contain highest international standards of protection, which are not their choice.

84 Story *et al,* The Copy/South Dossier, *supra,* (emphasis original). In the same sense, Prof Okediji has stated that the Appendix has been a complete failure. See Okediji, The International Copyright System, *supra,* p. 25.

5.4. Practice on Compulsory Licensing for Translation and Reproduction (Berne Appendix)

The lack of legislative expertise and absence of input in drafting legislation of developing countries is clearly reflected in the use of the Berne Appendix. At the time of writing (January 2012), out of the 165 contracting parties to the Berne Convention,[85] only 34 countries (Algeria, Argentina, Bahrain, Bangladesh, China, Cuba, Egypt, Guinea, India, Jamaica, Jordan, Korea, Lesotho, Liberia, Mauritius, Malaysia, Mexico, Mongolia, Niger, Oman, the Philippines, Samoa, Singapore, Sri Lanka, Sudan, Surinam, Syrian Arab Republic, Tanzania, Thailand, Tunisia, United Arab Emirates, Uzbekistan, Vietnam and Yemen) have, by notifying the Director General of WIPO, availed themselves of the facilities of the Berne Appendix.[86] Tables 2 and 3 in the Appendix summarize the past and current notifications under the Berne Appendix. The tables also indicate which of the countries with valid or past notifications have included the provisions of the Appendix or some imitation thereof in their national laws.

All the 34 countries availed themselves of both articles II and III, except Samoa and Thailand which availed themselves of only article II, which allows compulsory licensing for translation. The choice made by Samoa and Thailand may be explained by the fact that CL for translation can only be issued at least three years after the publication of a work. There is the possibility of issuing a CL after one year of publication into a language that is not in general use in one of the developed countries which are members of the Berne Union if the language in question is not English, French, or Spanish. However, limiting themselves to the possibility of granting compulsory licenses for translation only is unnecessary restriction for countries like Samoa and Thailand (or any developing country) which are in dire need of access to copyrighted material.

Of the 34 countries, only 16 (Bangladesh, Cuba, Jordan, Korea, Mongolia, Oman, the Philippines, Samoa, Sri Lanka, Sudan, Syrian Arab Republic, Thailand, United Arab Emirates, Uzbekistan, Vietnam and Yemen)[87] have valid notifications.[88] The remaining 18 countries have not renewed their notifications. (Tables 2 and 3 summarize the situation on notifications.) Only a handful of countries incorporate the Appendix into or have provisions similar to it in their national legislation. We highlight the main features of national legislation below.

Of the 16 countries with valid notifications, only 9 countries (Bangladesh, Cuba, Jordan, Sri Lanka, Sudan, Syria, Thailand, United Arab Emirates and Vietnam) have legislation making reference to the Berne Appendix.

Cuban legislation contains detailed provisions on compulsory licensing. For national works, any government institution, body, company or social organization can receive a compulsory licence for use of a scientific, technical, literary, artistic or educational work for non-profit purposes.[89] The licence is non-transferable, but there is no mention of compensation. For the purpose of public interest, Cuban legislation permits, without

85 World Intellectual Property Organization, www.wipo.int/treaties/en
86 See World Intellectual Property Organization, www.wipo.int/treaties/en/notifications/Berne
87 Information available on the WIPO website at www.wipo.int/treaties/en/notifications/Berne
88 Information available on the WIPO website at www.wipo.int/treaties/en/notifications/Berne
89 Cuba, Law No.14 of 1977 on Copyright, article 36.

compensation, the translation or reproduction of a copyrighted work for reasons of social interest provided that: the work is needed for the development of science, technology, education or professional advancement; the work is used for non-profit purposes; and it is used within the Cuban State.[90] The Berne Appendix requires payment of compensation and public interest is not a permitted use.

In relation to compulsory licensing for translation, the Copyright law of Jordan provides that any Jordanian citizen has the right to obtain a compulsory license (permit) from the Minister of Culture to translate any foreign product published in a printed or any other form to the Arabic language, and to publish this translation in a printed and any other similar form, provided that three years have elapsed since the first publication date of this work and that no translation thereof has been published in Jordan by the owner of the translation right or with his approval or in the case the translated copies have been consumed.[91] This provision simply reproduces article II(a) and (b) of the Appendix to the Berne Convention. Nevertheless, Jordan has the option to use the flexibility relating to the waiting period to promote education. The waiting period of three years before a CL for translation can be issued weakens the effectiveness of the provision. Jordan, being an Arabic speaking country, has the option to shorten this period to one year, but it did not take advantage of this possibility.[92]

With respect to CL for reproduction, any Jordanian citizen can obtain a compulsory license from the Minister of Culture for reproduction of a copyrighted work, provided that no copies thereof were distributed in the Kingdom to meet the needs of the *public or for school or university education* through the copyright owner or with his consent, for a price proportionate to the prices of products similar thereto in the Kingdom.[93] The Berne Appendix uses the phrase "general public or in connection with systematic instructional activities."[94] Therefore the Jordan provision is broader than the Appendix. As in the case of translation, the waiting period is three years.[95] However, unlike for translation, this period cannot be reduced. This goes to show the effect of procedural requirements on the effective application of the Berne Appendix.

A copy reproduced and published under CL license should be sold at a price less than or equal to a price proportionate to the prices of products similar thereto in the Kingdom.[96] In all cases of CL, the author of the original work is entitled to fair compensation, "proportionate to the copyright standards accredited in the optional contracts, between people in the kingdom and the people in the author's country."[97] The wording of the legislation does not specify the exact amount of compensation. This leads to legal and

90 Cuba, Law No.14 of 1977 on Copyright, article 37.

91 Jordan, the Copyright Law, Law No. 22 of 1992 (as amended by laws No.14 of 1998, No. 29 of 1999 and 52 of 2001), article 11(a).

92 The Berne Convention, *supra*. Article II(3)(b) of the Appendix stipulates that application of a shorter period of one year instead of three years is possible where the language in question is not English, French or Spanish. Arabic is none of the three languages that is excluded.

93 Jordan, the Copyright Law, Law No. 22 of 1992, *supra* article 11(b)(2) and (c), (emphasis added).

94 The Berne Convention, article III(2)(a)(iii) and (b) of the Appendix.

95 Jordan, the Copyright Law, Law No. 22 of 1992, *supra,* article 11(b)(1).

96 *Ibid,* article 11(d).

97 *Ibid,* article 11(b)(3).

practical difficulties. Legally, there is lack of certainty. The practical implications are that in the end the copyright users either pay a high price for the works or do not use them at all. Voluntary licenses (optional contracts) are by their very nature contractual relations between the users and owners of copyrighted work. If the amount of compensation is left to be decided on contractual terms, then the party with the better bargaining position, who is the author in most cases, will decide the amount. In the end, the works are expensive.

The conditions and procedure for granting compulsory licenses are to be determined by regulations issued for that purpose.[98] At the time of writing, no regulation had been issued to this effect, which leads to the conclusion that the provision has not been used.

Sri Lanka, like Cuba, appears to provide more than what is stipulated in the Appendix, allowing compulsory licensing for translation without compensation.[99] The implementing legislation does not mention the procedural requirements which have to precede the grant of a compulsory licence for translation. But it is hard to draw any meaningful conclusions from this provision since there is no evidence it has been used.

Similarly, Sudanese law contains more liberal provisions than in the Appendix. There are exceptions for reproduction, translation or adaptation of a published work for personal and private use,[100] without mention of compensation. This might be understood as use of exceptions but the uses mentioned in the legislation are not provided for under article 10 of the BC. It also permits the publication of a work if public interest so requires, upon payment of compensation to the right holder.[101] "Public interest" is not defined, which arguably, allows use of compulsory licences for purposes not stipulated under the Appendix.

Syrian law also provides for compulsory licenses but without following the strict requirements of the Appendix. The Government may in public interest request, via mail, the right holder to publish a work within six months. The waiting period is shorter than under the Appendix. If the work is not published within the stipulated period, the Government can do so, against payment of compensation.[102] The provision does not conform to the detailed procedural requirements of the Appendix. The law contains several exceptions for translation or reproduction of a work for private or personal use, use by a public library, scientific organization or educational institution.[103]

The provisions relating to compulsory licensing in the United Arab Emirates are contained in article 21 of the law of copyright.[104] The article stipulates:

> [a]ny person may ask the ministry of information for a compulsory license for either copying or translation or for both of *any work protected by the provisions of this law* only after three years from the date of publication of the work in case of translation license. The license shall be

98 Jordan, the Copyright Law, Law No. 22 of 1992, *supra,* article 11(e).
99 Sri Lanka, Code of Intellectual Property, s. 15.
100 Sudan, Copyright and Neighbouring Rights Act 1996, section 14.
101 Sudan, Copyright and Neighbouring Rights Act 1996, section 20(1).
102 The Arab Republic of Syria, Copyright Law No 12 of 2001, section 21.
103 The Arab Republic of Syria, Copyright Law No. 12 of 2001 section 37.
104 United Arab Emirates, Federal Law No. 7 of 2002 concerning copyrights and neighbouring rights.

> issued supported with reasons determining the time and place of exploitation, and the fair reward due to the author provided that the purpose of such grant of license always be exclusive to meet the needs of *education in all its types, levels and to the needs of public libraries and archives* in accordance with specifications, conditions and restrictions of the implementing regulations and this law for granting this license in a way to secure non-occurrence of unjustifiable damage to the legitimate interests of the author or his successors in title or affect ordinary exploitation of the work. The council of ministers shall issue a decision specifying the fees to be charged in this regard.[105]

The mechanism stipulated under the quoted provision significantly differs from the one provided under the Berne Appendix. First, the legislation refers to "any work protected by the provisions of this law." In effect, this includes computer programs, databases or any other work that is not in hard copy form. The Berne Appendix permits CL for works in hard copy format only. Second, the waiting period of three years before asking for a compulsory license for translation is too long. The UAE, like Jordan, has the possibility of reducing this period to one year. The UAE does not take advantage of this flexibility.

Third, the requirement that the license be issued supported by reasons determining the time and place of exploitation represents an unnecessary extra work on the part of the relevant authorities since it is not required under international IP law. Furthermore, the requirement places a limitation upon the choice of where to exploit the work, which again is not required by under international copyright law but also poses unnecessary restrictions on the licensee.

Fourth, it would seem that the provision creates more space for the use of copyrighted works for education. The purpose of the CL is to meet the "needs of education in all its types, levels and to the needs of public libraries and archives". The list is longer than in the Berne Convention. The provision allows for various types of education, such as long distance, adult or home education as well as traditional classroom education. However, since CL is subject to the three-step test, its scope in allowing access to protected works is very limited.

Fifth, CL is subject to the three-step test. The exploitation should not harm the legitimate interests of not only the author, but also the successor in title. This is not a requirement under the Berne Convention. Most worrisome, however, is the fact that the legislation adds more restrictions to the already cumbersome procedure laid down under the Berne Convention.

Sixth, the remuneration is to be determined by a council of ministers, providing the chance to decide the remuneration on a case-by-case basis. Finally, CL is to be granted in accordance with the specifications, conditions and restrictions of the implementing regulations. As in the case of Jordan, there were no implementing regulations at the time of writing. This might mean the provisions have not been applied.

Thailand provides very detailed laws and rules closely related to the Appendix, but with some flexibility. Where a compulsory license for translation is granted, the amount of remuneration can be determined by the Director General (of the copyright office) if the

105 United Arab Emirates, Federal Law No. 7 of 2002 concerning copyrights and neighbouring rights, article 21 (emphasis added).

parties fail to reach an agreement.[106] This in a way protects the applicant for a compulsory licence.

Vietnam, like Cuba, provides for a general compulsory licence on grounds of public interest. The law stipulates that in the circumstances where the achievement of defence, security, people's livelihood objectives and other interests of the State and society specified in this Law needs to be guaranteed, the State may prohibit or restrict the exercise of intellectual property rights by the holders or compel the licensing by the holders of one or several of their rights to other organizations or individuals under appropriate terms. The limitation on rights to inventions classified as state secrets complies with regulations of the Government.[107] There is no mention of compensation or any procedural requirements outlined in the appendix. It is not clear how this provision reconciles with Vietnam's obligations under the US-Vietnam Free Trade Agreement, which restricts the use of the Appendix.[108]

Some countries that have issued notifications to use the Appendix have not incorporated the Appendix into their national laws. This is the case with, the Philippines and Mongolia.

A number of countries have not renewed their notification to use the Appendix but nevertheless have provisions on compulsory licensing in a way similar to the Appendix. For example Algerian law contains detailed Appendix-like provisions on compulsory licensing for translation and reproduction.[109] Some countries allow translation and/reproduction in ways that are broader than the Berne Appendix. For example, China permits translation or reproduction of few copies of a published work by teachers or scientific researchers for use in classroom teaching or scientific research if the works are not published for distribution.[110] This exception extends to works in the digital environment[111] and e-learning,[112] which are not provided for in the Berne Appendix.[113] Indian law contains detailed provisions on compulsory licensing for translation and reproduction in a way prescribed by the Appendix, but payment of "royalties is calculated at such rate as the Copyright Board may in the circumstances of each determine in a prescribed manner".[114]

---

106 Thailand, Copyright Act of B.E. 2537 of 1994, Articles 54 and 55.

107 Vietnam, Law No. 50/2005/QH11 of 29 November 2005 on Intellectual Property, as amended by Law No. 36/2009/QH12, article 7 (3).

108 Agreement between the United States of America and the Socialist Republic of Vietnam on Trade Relations. Chapter II, Article 4(5).

109 Algeria, Copyright and Neighbouring Rights Act of July 19, 2003, Articles 33 to 40.

110 Copyright Law of the People's Republic of China, 7 September 1990, as amended in 2010, article 22(6).

111 Decree of the State Council of the People's Republic of China, no. 468: Regulations on Protection of the Right of Communication through Information Network, adopted at the 135 Executive Meeting of the State Council on 10 May, 2006, article 6.3.

112 *Ibid*, article 8.

113 Alberto Cerda Silva, "Beyond the Unrealistic Solution for Development provided by the Appendix to the Berne Convention on Copyright," *American University International Law Review*, (forthcoming 2012), p.37 (arguing that the Berne Appendix allows issuing compulsory licences for digital works).

114 India, Copyright Act No. 1 o 1957 as amended by Act No. 49 of 1999, articles 32(4)(i) and 32A(4)(i).

In other words, the amount of compensation does not have to be determined according to the rate for freely negotiated licences as required by the Appendix.

Egypt, presents an interesting case in relation to compulsory licensing for translation and reproduction even if it has not renewed its notification. Under article 148 of the Egyptian copyright law, the translation right in a work written in a foreign language terminates if that work has not been translated into Arabic within three years from the date of first publication.[115] After that, any interested party can obtain a licence for commercial and professional exploitation of the work against payment of a *fee specified by the executive implementing regulations, but the amount of compensation should not exceed one thousand Egyptian pounds.*[116] It would therefore seem that there is a possibility for a CL under the BA within three years. After that, if the right of translation is not exploited, the work falls into the public domain, and there can be a public domain kind of licence for translation, granted due to lack of timely translation.[117] The compatibility of this provision with international requirements is questionable. However, there is no proof that is it being applied in Egypt. On the contrary, the main public initiatives for translation of works into Arabic rely on voluntary licensing.[118] Furthermore article 170 provides that any person may request from the competent minister the granting of a personal licence for the reproduction or translation, or both, of any work protected under the law, without authorization of the author for the purpose of meeting teaching requirements of all kinds and levels, against equitable remuneration to the author or his successor, *to the extent that such is not in contradiction with the normal exploitation of or does not unduly prejudice the legitimate interests of the author or copyright holder.* This provision is not limited to literary works (as is the case with the Berne Appendix) and it would seem that it includes computer programs, since it refers to 'any work protected by this law'. The provision for grant of a compulsory licence does not refer to the cumbersome procedure requirements of the Appendix, but at the same time, it is limited by the general three-step test.[119]

---

115 Egypt, Law on the protection of intellectual property rights, Law No. 82 of 2002, Book three, (Copyright and related rights), Article 148. For comments on this article, see Ahmed Abdel Latif, "Egypt's Role in the A2K Movement: an Analysis of Positions and Policies," in Nagla, Rizk and Lea, Shaver (eds.), *Access to Knowledge in Egypt: New Research on Intellectual Property, innovation and Development,* London: Bloomsbury Academic, 2010. 16–55 at 59.

116 Egypt, Law on the protection of intellectual property rights, Law No. 82 of 2002, Book three, (Copyright and related rights), Article 183 (emphasis added).

117 Hossam A. El Saghir, "Intellectual Property in Egypt," Supplement 53 International Encyclopaedia of Laws, 2009, pp. 45–46, at p. 65, quoted in Alberto Cerda Silva, *supra,* p. 27.

118 Bassam Awad, Moatasem El-Gheriani and Perihan abou Zeid, "Egypt," in Chris Armstrong *et al* (eds.) *Access to Knowledge in Africa: the Role of Copyright,* (Claremont: UCT Press, 2010), 22–56 at 49.

119 Ironically, this provision was considered by some industries to be broad and needed to be deleted. See recommendations of the International Intellectual Property Alliance (IIPA) to the USTR for the 2007 Special 301 Report. It was recommended that Egypt deletes the provision on compulsory licensing. The IIPA also recommended that Egypt be placed on the Priority Watch List. Information available at http://www.iipa.com/2007_SPEC301_TOC.htm. This is an example of the role of industry in intellectual property enforcement and their impact in preventing public access to protected works.

Lesotho, like Egypt, has not renewed its Declaration to use the Appendix. However, Section 10 of the Copyright Order of 1989[120] allows a person other than the right holder to apply to the Minister for a licence to make a translation of a copyrighted work into English or Sesotho and publish the translation in Lesotho. The statutory licence allows translation for teaching, scholarship and research, and reproduction only by means of printing.[121] Compulsory licensing for reproduction or printing can be issued for systematic instructional activities.[122] By limiting reproduction to printing, the provision excludes other means of reproduction like photocopying or scanning. The procedural requirements are exactly the same as those laid down in the Berne Appendix, which does not facilitate access to learning material. Following the procedure under the Appendix is challenging particularly for an LDC country such as Lesotho, where communication channels are undeveloped, not to mention the overall desperate economic situation.

Tunisia would seem to conform to the Berne appendix as its legislation contains detailed provisions for compulsory licence for translation based the requirements of the Appendix,[123] but it has not renewed its notification for the WIPO Director General. Tunisia no longer avails itself of the facilities provided by the Appendix.

The third category includes countries that have never availed themselves of the Appendix but still provide for compulsory licensing. Bolivia had not availed itself of the mechanism provided by the Appendix, but it authorizes government to issue a compulsory licence for use of a work in the public interest, upon payment of royalty.[124] However, the Andean Community Common Regime on Copyright, to which Bolivia is a party, forbids any legal or compulsory licences that exceed the limits provided by the Berne Convention.[125] It is not clear whether a general provision on "public interest" exceeds to permitted uses under the Appendix.

Colombian law contains a general provision for translation of foreign works into Spanish for the purpose of teaching, scholarship or research, upon payment of just compensation. The legislation outlines in detail the procedural requirements for grant and use of the compulsory licence for translation, in a way similar to the Appendix.[126] The Colombian legislation contains detailed provisions on the grant and use of compulsory licences for reproduction in a way outlined in the Appendix.[127] Similarly, the laws of El Salvador,[128] Honduras,[129] Panama[130] and the Dominican Republic[131] contain general

120 Lesotho, Copyright Order of 1989, No. 13 of May 1989.

121 Lesotho, Copyright Order of 1989, *ibid,* section 10 read together with First Schedule, 4(a).

122 Lesotho, Copyright Order of 1989, *ibid,* section 11 read together with Second Schedule, 4(a).

123 Tunisia Law No. 2009-33 dated 23 June 2009 amending and completing Law No. 94-36 dated 24 February 1994 relating to Literary and Artistic Property, Articles 13 and 14.

124 Bolivia, Copyright Act No. 1322 of 1992, Article 25.

125 Andean Community Decision No. 351 Common Provisions on Copyright and Neighbouring Rights (of December 17 1993), Article 32.

126 Colombia, Copyright Law No. 23 of 1982 on Copyright, articles 45 to 57.

127 Colombia, Copyright Law No. 23 of 1982 on Copyright, articles 58 to 70.

128 El Salvador, Law on the Promotion and Protection of Intellectual Property, (Legislative Decree No 604 of 15 July 1993), Article 77.

129 Honduras, Decree No 4-99E, Copyright and Neighbouring Rights Law, Article 122.

130 Panama, Law No. 15 of 1994 on Copyright and Neighbouring Rights, Article 84.

131 Dominican Republic, Copyright Law No. 65 of 2000, Articles 45 to 47.

provisions for compulsory licensing for translation and reproduction accordance with the Berne Appendix. In addition, the Dominican Republic provides for a compulsory licensing for the use for the public necessity of the economic rights that are considered of high cultural, scientific and educational or social value for the country or in the public interest, upon payment of compensation.[132]

Equally, Djibouti has never availed itself of the facilities of the Appendix but it provides for compulsory licensing for translation, one year from the date of publication of the work, against payment of fair and equitable compensation.[133] There is no reference to the complex substantive and procedural requirements of the Appendix. Kuwait law contains a provision that is closely related to that of Egypt. A compulsory licence for translation of a foreign work can issue within one year after the publication of the work, against payment of fair compensation.[134] Again there is no mention of the procedural requirements outlined in the Appendix. The right of translation expires five years from the date of publication of the work, if the author does not exercise his right within that period.[135] This provision goes beyond the Appendix. In relation to national works, the Minister of Information can request, through registered mail, a right holder to publish work if he deems that the publication of such work is in the public interest. If the publication is not done within one year of the request, the Minister may obtain a Court Order to publish the work, and can carry out the translation, upon payment of fair remuneration.[136]

South Africa permits the translation of a work which is the subject of another exception.[137] In addition, the South African Copyright Tribunal can issue a compulsory licence when the right holder refuses to grant a voluntary licence on reasonable terms.[138] Furthermore, the Copyright law authorizes the government to adopt Regulations on circulation, presentation, exhibition of a work or production.[139] It would seem that in effect, the Regulations can allow "non-voluntary licence schemes."[140]

In the last category is Uganda, which is not a party to the Berne Convention, but has incorporated the provisions of the Berne Appendix into its national law.[141] It permits grant of non-exclusive compulsory licences for translation and reproduction in a way outlined

132 Dominican Republic, Copyright Law No. 65 of 2000, Article 48.

133 Djibouti, Law No. 154/AN/06 of 23 July, 2006 on Protection of Copyright and Neighbouring Rights, Article 55

134 Kuwait, Law No 64 of 1999 Concerning Intellectual Property Rights including Explanatory Memorandum, Article 16.

135 Kuwait, Law No 64 of 1999 Concerning Intellectual Property Rights including Explanatory Memorandum, *ibid.*

136 Kuwait, Law No 64 of 1999 Concerning Intellectual Property Rights including Explanatory Memorandum, *supra,* Article 14.

137 South Africa, Copyright Act 1978 as amended 18 June, 2002, Section 12(11).

138 South Africa, Copyright Act 1978, *ibid,* Sections 29 and 33.

139 South Africa, Copyright Act 1978, *ibid,* Section 45.

140 Tobias Schonwetter, Caroline Ncube and Pria Chetty, "South Africa", in Armstrong *et al,* (eds.), *Access to Knowledge in African: the Role of Copyright,*UCT Press, South Africa, 2010) 231–280, 243.

141 Uganda is a party to the TRIPS Agreement which incorporates many of the provisions of the Berne Convention, including the Appendix.

in the Appendix.[142] However, in the case of translation, the compulsory licence can issue within one year after publication of a work, even for translation into English[143] which is against the requirements under the Appendix.[144]

In summary, it is hard to identify a country that has used the Appendix. In terms of legislation, a number of countries have general compulsory licensing provisions on grounds of public interests. While others, in addition to the general provision, allow the use of compulsory licensing under the Berne Appendix. One would question the practical implications of the general provision for public interest on the provision outlined in the Berne Appendix. It would defeat reason if a country with both provisions (general compulsory licence for the public interest and a specific one under the Berne Appendix) uses the cumbersome Berne system when it can achieve a faster result with less procedural hurdles and costs. However, since there is no evidence of any compulsory licences having been issued, it is hard to evaluate the impact of having the two sets of provisions. Nevertheless, the fact that several countries provide for compulsory licences for public interest, even if this is not stipulated in the Appendix, as opposed to merely for systematic instructional activities or teaching, scholarship or research, might be an indication of how members have chosen to meet public interest needs. This fact cannot be ignored when considering an international solution for access to copyrighted material, as is happening under the WIPO Standing Committee on Copyright and Related Rights.[145]

In all of the cases where national legislation provides for compulsory licensing, there is no follow up. No licences have been granted. Contradicting legislation is evidence of lack of or little domestic input in its drafting. Most of these countries have received legislative advice from the WIPO secretariat. For example, Jordan received advice on the revision of its "copyright law to be compatible with Berne, TRIPS, WCT and WPPT" and model implementing provisions were sent by WIPO,[146] Egypt received draft laws and advice on the revision of its IP law[147] and the UAE received model implementing provisions.[148]

5.5. Conclusions on Special Legal Regimes for Access to Protected Works

In this chapter, we have explored the special regimes for access to copyrighted works by developing countries. While developed countries recognize the fact that developing countries have special access needs, the former are not willing to facilitate access by a developing country at the expense of their authors and publishing industries. For this reason, special legal regimes like the Stockholm Protocol were not accepted by developed

142 Uganda, Copyright and Neighbouring Rights Act 2006, Sections 17 and 18.
143 Uganda, Copyright and Neighbouring Rights Act 2006, sections 17(2)
144 The waiting period for a compulsory licence for translation into English is three years. See Berne Convention, Appendix, article II(3)(a).
145 See Chapter 7
146 Information on WIPO's Development Cooperation Activities, January 2000 – June 2005, World Intellectual Property Organization, Geneva, WIPO Document WIPO/EDS/INF/1 Rev (E) dated September 23, 2005, available at www.wipo.int/ip-development, p.304.
147 *Ibid*, p. 129.
148 *Ibid*, p.383.

countries. In particular, the Appendix to the Berne Convention, which provides "special provisions regarding developing countries" to permit compulsory licensing for translation and reproduction of copyrighted works in hard copies, cannot be used by developing countries. The complicated administrative and procedural requirements render the use of the Appendix overly expensive for developing countries.

In other words, none of the special regimes for developing countries serve the purpose of facilitating access to educational materials in printed form.

CHAPTER SIX

MODELS OF PRACTICE RELATING TO LIMITATIONS AND EXCEPTIONS TO COPYRIGHT FOR EDUCATIONAL PURPOSES

6.1. Introduction

The Berne Convention and the TRIPS Agreement grant states the discretion to determine the conditions under which certain copyrights can be exercised and to impose limitations on the enjoyment of those rights. It is important to remember that international law does not impose on states to provide limitations or exceptions, but rather grants *permission* to establish them at the national level. In other words, limitations and exceptions are permissive and not mandatory. Therefore, in general, how states take advantage of this 'permission' affects how they balance the enjoyment of copyrights and access to copyrighted works by the public, through limitations and exceptions. Inevitably, where the state is not able to effectively use the flexibility – in a developing country for example – it cannot achieve a balance between private interests in copyright and the public interest of education or access to knowledge.

In the preceding chapters, we demonstrated that developing countries cannot use the two major exceptions, the three-step test and compulsory licensing under the Berne Appendix, to promote access to copyrighted works for educational purposes. In this chapter, we shall explore possible models of practice for access to protected works beyond the specific exceptions provided under the Berne Convention, three-step test and the Berne Appendix.

National courts now contribute to the development of international intellectual property law.[1] Indeed, when compared with the traditional negotiation of treaties, national court development of 'international law' is more responsive to social conditions and hence more dynamic; and it is more readily subject to refinement by a range of national political institutions.[2] Therefore, in this chapter emphasis is placed on the role that courts,

---

1 Graeme B. Dinwoodie, "The International Intellectual Property System: Treaties, Norms, National Courts, and Private Ordering," in Daniel Gervais (ed.), *Intellectual Property, trade and Development: Strategies to Optimize Economic Development in a TRIPS-Plus Era.* (Oxford. Oxford University Press, 2007). 61–114, at 98 (hereafter referred to as Dinwoodie, The International Intellectual Property System).

2 Dinwoodie, The International Intellectual Property System, *ibid,* pp. 98–99.

and not just legislators, might play in crafting case-by-case educational exceptions in a way that makes WTO retaliation harder.

A survey of national legislation on limitations and exceptions reveals a mixture of the Anglo-American and the continental system in providing for flexibilities. The former system supplements statutory limitations and exemptions with the so-called "fair use" or "fair dealing" doctrine. These are close to, but not the same as, "fair practice" as it is used in the Berne Convention. On the other hand, the continental legal tradition essentially provides a number of statutory exemptions, allowing the use of the published copyrighted materials without the copyright owner's authorization.

In this chapter, we examine commonly used flexibilities, like fair use, fair dealing, compulsory licensing or quasi compulsory licensing outside the Berne Appendix and government use, in developed and some developing countries in an attempt to illustrate possible models of practice for developing countries for access to education. Although compatibility of fair use with the three-step test has been questioned,[3] our starting point is that there exists a *factual* acceptance by developing countries of the fair use or fair dealing principles. We, however, devise a "fairness" model that answers to the special needs and national realities of developing countries.

We believe that the flexibilities selected require minimum financial input for implementation. These respond better to the economic needs of developing countries described in chapter two.[4] At the same time, the use of fairness principles and compulsory licensing (outside the Berne Appendix) to facilitate access to copyrighted material are widely acceptable practices, especially among developed countries, who are the major producers of copyrighted material.

6.2. Factual Acceptance of Fair Use and Fair Dealing by Developing Countries

It may be observed that a number of states have either officially endorsed the concept of fair use/dealing by including it in their national legislation or relied on it for guidance in

---

3 We return to this at a later stage in this chapter.

4 There are other possible solutions which fall outside copyright. These include Open access to publicly funded research and granting of prizes instead of copyright for innovation. As an example of the former, the US National Institute of Health (NIH) makes public all publicly funded research. The NIH ensures that the public has access to all published results of NIH funded research to help advance science and improve human health. (see information on www.publiaccess.nih.gov). The EU has a similar programme. See Commission on the European Communities, Brussels, 20 August, 2008, document C(2008) 4408 final, available at http://ec.europa.eu/research/press/2008/pdf/decision_grant_agreement.pdf. On prizes to stimulate innovation, see a compilation of different projects on the website of Knowledge Ecology International, at: http://www.keionline.org/content/view/4/1/. In both cases, so far the focus is on medicine or science. These are good initiatives but they are hard to implement by developing countries. In the case of publicly funded research, the government has to fund the research or find means to do so (the EU has provisions for co-funding projects with a party outside the EU). This is economically not viable for developing countries. The same goes for prizes. There has to be a prize pool, money for paying those who win the prizes. In most cases, such pools are funded by donors who have interest in the projects for which there is competition. It is not possible to take into account the interest of developing countries.

defining other concepts like fair practice. A number of country legislation contains some type of fairness provision. Either they use the phrase "fair use" as such or "fair dealing". Some countries go a step further and define fair use or fair dealing according to section 107 of the US Copyright Act.[5] There is, therefore, a *factual* or *de facto* acceptance of the usefulness of fair use/dealing by developing countries. We shall illustrate this below.

Before proceeding, a caveat must be added. A number of developing countries provide for fair use or fair dealing for purposes of teaching, education, research or private use. Thus, it is not disputed that such exceptions are mentioned in legislation. However, we do not intend to list all of the legislation of developing countries. The focus of this study and this section in particular, is to explore the extent to which the exceptions mentioned in the legislation promote the public interest of access to teaching and reading material. The difference between a flexibility that promotes the public interest and one that does not lies in the conditions and procedure for using that flexibility, not in the mere fact that it is mentioned in national legislation. For this reason, the focus of this chapter's discussion is to show whether and how the conditions and procedure attached to the use of a particular flexibility provided for in national legislation promote in practice, a balance between copyright and access to copyrighted material by developing countries. The examples cited below represent the few countries where national legislation directly or by implication, provides for the public interest of education. One noteworthy aspect is that some fair use or fair dealing provisions are subject to the three-step test, or some of its elements. Such cases have been classified under fairness, in an effort to show what little existing practice there is. In what follows, we shall present a survey of developing country legislation in relation to fair use or dealing.

With respect to Kenya, section 26(1) of the copyright law allows *reproduction* in any material form of the original work or its translation or adaptation, *distribution* to the public of the work by way of sale, rental, lease, hire, loan, *importation* or similar arrangement and communication to the public and broadcasting of the whole work or a substantial part thereof, either in its original form or in any form recognizably derived from the original, by *way of fair dealing* for the purposes of *scientific research*, subject to acknowledgement of the source.[6] The legislation does not specify a definition of or guidelines on how to determine "fair dealing." In addition, the legislation permits only the copying of two short passages of a work, which is very little. The fair dealing provision does not apply to long distance learners, as indeed the provision is only applicable to institutions registered under the Education Act.[7] This effectively prevents the use of such materials in community learning centres without the payment of royalties or licence fees. These fees are unfortunately passed on to the user, making it more expensive for those in rural areas where such community centres play a pivotal role in adult education and vocational training.[8]

5 See infra, section 6.2.
6 Kenya, the Copyright Act 2001, Act No. 12 of 2001, section 26(1)(a)
7 Kenya, the Copyright Act 2001, *ibid*,
8 See Story, *et al* The Copy/South Dossier, *supra*, pp. 94–95.

The legislation of Botswana permits *dealing* with a work, for example by way of reproduction of a single copy for personal purposes, but subject to the three-step test.[9] The legislation also permits use of a work for illustration in 'face-to-face' teaching.[10] The provision therefore excludes the possibility of use in long distance education.

South Africa's legislation allows fair dealing with a literary or musical work: (a) for the purposes of research or private study, by the person or private use of the person using the work; and (b) for the purposes of criticism or review of that work.[11] Brunei and Darussalam, like South Africa, provides for fair dealing for purposes of research and study, although the conditions for determining fair dealing are not listed.

However, a number of countries outline the criteria for determining 'fairness' in a way similar to section 107 of the U.S. Copyright Act.[12] Examples include: the Dominican Republic,[13] Jamaica,[14] Antigua and Bermuda,[15] Belize,[16] St. Vincent and the Grenadines,[17] and Uganda.[18] The Philippines goes a step further and provides for fair use in exactly the same way as the United States. The Copyright law of the Philippines permits the *fair use* of a copyrighted work for teaching *including multiple copies* for classroom use, scholarship, research and *similar purposes*.[19] The criteria for determining "fair use" are defined in exactly a similar manner as under section 107 of the US Code.[20]

---

9 Botswana, Copyright and Neighbouring Rights Act 2000, Act no.8 of 2000, sections 12 and 13 read together.

10 Botswana, Copyright and Neighbouring Rights Act 2000, *ibid*, sections 15.

11 South Africa, Copyright Act 1978, Act no. 98 of 1978, as amended, section 12(1)(a). This provision is very similar to the US fair use or Canadian fair dealing provisions.

12 U.S. Copyright Act, *supra*. Section 107. Section 107 reads in part:
[...] the fair use of a copyrighted work, including such use by reproduction in copies or phonorecords or by any other means [...] for purposes such as criticism, comment, news reporting, teaching (including multiple copies for classroom use), scholarship, or research, is not an infringement of copyright. In determining whether the use made of a work in any particular case is a fair use the factors to be considered shall include—

(1) the purpose and character of the use, including whether such use is of a commercial nature or is for non-profit educational purposes;
(2) the nature of the copyrighted work; and
(3) the amount and substantiality of the portion used in relation to the copyrighted work as a whole;
(4) the effect of the use upon the potential market or value of the copyrighted work.

13 Dominican Republic, the Copyright Act, 2003, article 66.

14 Jamaica, Copyright Act 1993, Act no. 4 of 1993, section 53.

15 Antigua and Bermuda, Copyright Act 2002, section 54.

16 Belize, Copyright Act 2000, chapter 252, section 58.

17 St Vincent and the Grenadines, Copyright Act 2003, section 50(1).

18 Uganda, Copyright and Neighbouring Rights Act, 2006, Section 15.

19 Philippines, Intellectual Property Code, 1997, Republic Act No. 8293 of 6 June 1997, section 185.1 (emphasis added). The use of phrase like 'including' and 'similar purposes' is important as it leaves a lot of flexibility as to the scope of permitted uses. It means the list is only illustrative of possible uses. This makes it possible to accept other purposes whenever it is deemed necessary.

20 Section 185.1 of the Philippine Intellectual Property Code stipulates, in similar terms to section 107 of the US Code, that in determining whether the use made of a work in any particular case is fair, the factors to be considered shall include:

Israeli's legislation is particularly innovative in attempting to facilitate access to protected works. The Copyright Act has always allowed for fair dealing with any work for the purposes of private study, research, criticism, review or newspaper summary.[21] However, the recently amended legislation provides for fair use, in similar terms to Section 107 of the U.S. Copyright Act, but with modifications to suit the needs of a developing country. Section 19 of the new Copyright Act provides that "Fair use of a work is permitted for purposes *such as*: private study, research, criticism, review, journalistic reporting, quotation, or instruction and examination by an educational institution."[22] There is, however, one particular improvement: the first factor for determining fair use (the purpose of the use) omits any reference to the commercial or non-commercial nature of the use. This is an important development in terms of a provision on fair use. As we shall elaborate below, the commercial character of a 'use' normally leads to rejection of the defence of fair use in the United States. On the other hand, dealing with a work, even for profit, may be found as fair by Canadian courts if it serves the public interest.[23] Consequently, the new Israeli copyright Act contains a mixture of the US fair use and the Canadian 'new standard' of fair dealing.[24] Israeli's legislation has indeed been described as "the right copyright law".[25] However, its effect is yet to be tested. The Minister may issue regulations prescribing the circumstances under which the use of a copyrighted work can be deemed fair,[26] but no regulations have been issued yet.

(a) The purpose and character of the use, including whether such use is of a commercial nature or is for non-profit education purposes;
(b) The nature of the copyrighted work;
(c) The amount and substantiality of the portion used in relation to the copyrighted work as a whole; and
(d) The effect of the use upon the potential market for or value of the copyrighted work.

21 Israeli, Copyright Act 1911, as amended, on 19 November 2007, entered into force on May 25, 2008, Section 19 (found in Law Statutes of Israel, Issue 2199 of November 25, 2007, p. 34), article 2(1).

22 Israel, the Copyright Act 1911, *ibid*, (emphasis added).

23 See discussion on fair dealing in Canada, section 6.4.

24 On the new standard of fair dealing in Canada, see *infa*, section 6.4.3.

25 Jonathan Band, "The right copyright law," Jerusalem Post, 28 March 2008. Available at http://www.policybandwidth.com/doc/20080410-Israel-Fair-Use.pdf

26 Israel, Copyright Act, Section 19. The IIPA expressed its concern that by means of these regulations "potentially opens the door for even broader exceptions to be introduced in Israel" (See International Intellectual Property Alliance, "IIPA's 2009 Special 301 Report, on copyright protection and enforcement, submitted to the U.S. Trade Representative, on February 13, 2006 by the International Intellectual Property Alliance," available at http://www.iipa.com/special301.html.) In response, the Israeli Government stated that "to the extent that regulations can be promulgated under the new section 19 with regard to specifying fair uses, such regulations are always subordinate to the primary legislation and can not contradict it." See 2009 Submission of the Government of Israel to the US Trade Representative with respect to the 2009 "Special 301 Review," available at http://www.justice.gov.il/NR/rdonlyres/BD753811-E87A-4AB2-8ADD-DC9423DFC794/13684/2009special301submission.pdf

As concerns developed countries, Japan is in the process of amending its copyright law to include a fair use provision. The new stipulation will closely follow that of the United States.[27]

It may be concluded from the practice discussed above that there is an acceptance of fair use or fair dealing-type of provisions at the national level. But due to the lack of judicial practice in developing countries, it is difficult to point out whether there are any benefits for developing countries in imitating developed countries' fairness doctrines. We shall therefore discuss the U.S. fair use and the Canadian fair dealing below, in an attempt to assess to what extent they can serve, if at all, as models of practice in developing countries for access to educational materials in printed form.

6.3. United States: Fair Use under Section 107 of the US Copyright Act of 1976 and before the U.S. Courts

In 1976, the U.S. Congress codified the copyright and fair use case law in the Copyright Act.[28] Under section 107 of the U.S. Copyright Act, the fair use of a copyrighted work is not an infringement of copyright. The provision stipulates that the fair use of a copyrighted work, including use by reproduction in copies or phonorecords or by any other means [...] for purposes such as criticism, comment, news reporting, teaching (including multiple copies for classroom use), scholarship, or research, is not an infringement of copyright. In determining whether the use made of a work in any particular case is a fair use, the factors to be considered include: (1) the purpose and character of the use, including whether such use is of a commercial nature or is for non-profit educational purposes; (2) the nature of the copyrighted work; (3) the amount and substantiality of the portion used in relation to the copyrighted work as a whole; and (4) the effect of the use upon the potential market for, or value of the copyrighted work.[29]

The list of elements to be considered in determining fair use is not exhaustive. It is only a list of factors 'to be considered'.[30] The reason for the open-ended list, it is explained, is that the endless variety of situations and combinations of circumstances that can arise in any particular case precluded the formulation of exact rules.[31] "Fair use" is an "equitable rule of reason", each case raising the question of fair use has to be decided on its own facts.

---

27 Yasukazu Akada, "Fair use' stipulation planned for intellectual property," *The Asahi Shimbun*, 28 May 2008, available at http://www.asahi.com/english/Herald-asahi/TKY200805280068.html

28 *Folsom v. Marsh*, 9 F. Case 342 (C.C.D. Mass. 1841) (No 4, 901).

29 U.S. Copyright Act, section 107, (emphasis added). For a brief summary on judicial development of the four elements of fair use see Michael G. Anderson, Paul F. Brown, , and Andre P. Cores, "Market substitution and copyright: predicting fair use case law," *University of Miami Entertainment & Sports Law* Review, vol. 10 no. 33, (1993): 33–50, at 39 (hereinafter referred to as Anderson *et al*, Market substitution).

30 House of Representatives Report on the 1976 Copyright Bill, House Committee on the Judiciary, House Report No. 94-1476 to accompany s. 22, 94th Congress, 2nd Session, September 3 1976, p. 65. This fact was emphasized in *Sony Corp. v. Universal City Studios*, 464 U.S. (1984), para. 79.

31 House of Representatives Report on the 1976 Copyright Bill, *ibid*, p. 66, see also Lloyd L. Rich, "How much of someone else's work may I use without asking permission?: the fair use doctrine," Part I, The publishing Law Centre, (1996). available at http://www.publilaw.com/work.html.

Indeed, the general intention underlying the provision is explained in the legislative history of the 1976 Copyright Act as follows:

> The statement of the fair use doctrine in section 107 offers some guidance to users in determining when the principles of the doctrine apply. However, the endless variety of situations and combinations of circumstances that can arise in particular cases precludes the formulation of exact rules in the statute. The bill endorses the purpose and general scope of the judicial doctrine of fair use, but there is no disposition to freeze the doctrine in the statute, especially during a period of rapid technological change. Beyond a very broad statutory explanation of what fair use is and some of the criteria applicable to it, the courts must be free to adapt the doctrine to particular situations on a case by case basis."[32]

The fair use provision is open-ended, which allows a number of cases to be considered as conforming to fair use. Each use of the exception would have to be considered on a case by case basis. The disadvantage of such an open-ended system is that it opens space for litigation since what is fair use has to be determined by the courts. The result, as shall be illustrated below with specific cases, is legal uncertainty.

Some authors have posited that including classroom copying for educational use under fair use only brought confusion to the concept of fair use and that educational use should have been provided for under a separate limitation.[33] This argument leads us to question the boundaries of the fair use provision for education in the Statute. Should the limits of copying for educational or classroom use be defined by some kind of statute or should it be left to the interpretation of section 107 by the court? This question is pertinent, especially considering the fact that during the codification of fair use, clarifying the boundaries of fair use for education was a contentious issue.[34] The result was an agreement on guidelines for classroom copying, the purpose of which we shall clarify below.

6.3.1. *The Role of Industry in Defining Copying for Classroom Use: Clarifying the Purpose of the Agreement on Guidelines for Classroom Copying in Not-For-Profit Educational Institutions with Respect to Books and Periodicals*

As mentioned above, the fair use doctrine was codified in 1976. Most of the discussions centred on classroom reproduction, especially photocopying.[35] The result was an "Agreement on guidelines for classroom copying in not-for-profit educational institutions with respect to books and periodicals,"[36] signed between educational institutions on the

32 House of Representatives Report on the 1976 Copyright Bill, *supra*, p. 66.

33 L.E. Selzer, *Exceptions and fair use in copyright*, Harvard University Press, Cambridge (Mass.), 1998, p. 59, (quoted in Guibault, *supra*, p. 72), and G. K. Klingsporn, "The Conference on fair use (CONFU) and the future of fair use guidelines," *Columbia VLA – Journal of Law and the Arts*, (1999). 101–126, p. 108.

34 House of Representatives Report on the 1976 Copyright Bill, *supra*, p. 66.

35 House of Representatives Report on the 1976 Copyright Bill, *ibid*,

36 Agreement on Guidelines for classroom copying in not-for-profit educational institutions with respect to books and periodicals, in House of Representatives Report on the 1976 Copyright Bill, House Committee on the Judiciary, House Report No. 94-1476 to accompany s. 22, 94th Congress, 2nd Session, September 3 1976, pp. 68–70.

one hand and authors and publishers on the other.[37] As its name suggests, the agreement provided guidelines on quantities in case of (i) single copying for teachers; and (ii) multiple copying for classroom use.

Single copying for teachers: The guidelines permit the making of a single copy by or for a teacher at his or her individual request for his or her scholarly research or use in teaching or preparation for a class. The quantities allowed under the guidelines are; a chapter from a book, an article from a periodical or newspaper, a short story, short essay or short poem, or a chart, graph, diagram, drawing, cartoon or picture from a book, periodical or newspaper.[38]

Multiple copies for classroom use: This is provided for under paragraph II of the Guidelines. Multiple copies (not to exceed in any event more than one copy per pupil in a course) may be made by or for the teacher giving the course for classroom use or discussion, subject to a number of conditions. For example, copying must be for one course in the school and must be limited to only one short poem, article, story or essay if it is from the same author or to three from the same collective work or periodical volume during the same class term.

In both situations of copying, only a small part of the work can be copied; one article from a periodical or newspaper, a short story, short essay or short poem, or a chart, graph, diagram drawing, cartoon or picture from a book, periodical or newspaper. The guidelines do not permit the copying of whole textbooks for example. As the Agreement's name indicates, copying must be done for classroom use within an educational institution. In effect, the Guidelines preclude copying by home learners or distance learners who do not study in a formal classroom, since copying must be done within an educational institution and for classroom use within that institution, by or for its teacher. Copying under the Guidelines should not substitute for the purchase of books, publishers' reprints or periodicals.[39] This automatically excludes bulk copying, and thus access, which would have the effect of substituting for the purchase of the original publication.

According to scholars such as Guibault, the Guidelines clarified the boundaries of the fair use doctrine in the field of education.[40] Yet, other authors argue that, the Guidelines have no effect, as they 'do not have a force of law'.[41] What are these boundaries, if any?

---

37 Educational institutions were represented by the Ad Hoc Committee of Educational Institutions and Organizations on Copyright Law Revisions, while copyright owners were represented by the Authors League of America and the Association of American Publishers. See Agreement on Guidelines for classroom copying in not-for-profit educational institutions with respect to books and periodicals, in House of Representatives Report on the 1976 Copyright Bill, *supra,* p. 70.

38 Agreement on Guidelines for classroom copying in not-for-profit educational institutions with respect to books and periodicals, *supra,* para. I.

39 *Ibid,* para. III.

40 Guibault, *supra,* p.72.

41 Jonathan Band, "Educational fair use today," Association of research libraries, p. 2, available at http://www.policybandwidth.com/doc/20080203-educationalfairusetoday.pdf. (Band argues that the guideline have no force of law). Also in a similar tone, the Guidelines are said to be voluntary for interpreting 'multiple copies for classroom use". See Harris, Lesley Ellen,

What is the legal effect of the Guidelines? As our discussion on the judicial application of fair use shall reveal,[42] the Guidelines allow much more limited access compared to the fair use doctrine as applied by courts.[43] Is one limited to the Guidelines in deciding fair use for educational purposes? It is possible to argue that the Guidelines are a special regime applying to copying of books and periodicals for educational use. In this case, the general fair use doctrine would not apply because of *lex specialis*. However, we argue that this is not the case. The Guidelines specifically state their purpose as "to state the minimum standards of educational fair use under Section 107." They are not intended to limit the types of copying permitted under the standards of fair use under judicial decision and which are stated in Section 107.[44] Reading the Guidelines otherwise would render redundant Section 107. The Statute provides that "the fair use of a copyright work including such use as teaching (including multiple copies for classroom use) is not an infringement of copyright." The boundaries of such use for teaching and classroom use are left to be defined by the courts on a case by case basis. In short, the Guidelines do not set any boundaries for copying from books and periodicals for classroom use. Consequently, one is not limited to the Guidelines when determining fair use for teaching and classroom use.

What are the advantages, if any, for developing countries in adopting exceptions like fair use? Before answering this question, we shall examine the few cases that are of direct relevance to education. The analysis below summarises the relevant case law relating to fair use in copyright law, especially in the analogue environment.

6.3.2. *Judicial Practice on Fair Use and Access to Printed Educational Material*

The reader may recall that Section 107 of the U.S. Code permits fair use of a copyrighted work, including such use by reproduction in copies for purposes such as criticism, comment, teaching (including multiple copies for classroom use), scholarship, or research. In determining whether the use made of a work in any particular case is a fair use the factors to be considered include: (1) the purpose and character of the use, including whether such use is of a commercial nature or is for non-profit educational purposes; (2) the nature of the copyrighted work; (3) the amount and substantiality of the portion used in relation to the copyrighted work as a whole; and (4) the effect of the use upon the potential market or value of the copyrighted work. We examine how courts have interpreted these different factors, especially factors 1, 3 and 4 in relation to printed copyrighted material.

"Comparing fair dealing and fair use," *The Copyright & new media law newsletter*, volume 10, issue 4 (2006), p. 6.

42 See *infra*, section 6.3.2.

43 This is true only to the extent that the use of a work under the 'fair use' doctrine does not conflict with the economic interests of the author. The Guidelines define the quantity that can be copied, but under fair use, quantity alone is not decisive of whether the use is allowed or not. To that extent, the Guidelines allow much more limited access to protected works than fair use.

44 Agreement on Guidelines for classroom copying in not-for-profit educational institutions with respect to books and periodicals, *supra*, preamble.

6.3.2.1. Purpose and Character of the Use, Including Whether Such Use Is of a Commercial Nature or Is for Non-Profit Educational Purposes

The first factor in determining whether a use of a copyrighted work is fair use is the purpose and character of the use, including whether such use is of a commercial nature or is for non-profit educational purposes. In other words, if a use is of a commercial nature, it is more likely that fair use defence will be rejected. This has been confirmed in the case of *Sony Corp. v. Universal City Studios,* wherein the Court stated that, as a general rule, commercial use of copyrighted material is presumptively an unfair exploitation of the monopoly privilege that belongs to the owner of the copyright.[45] On the other hand, if the use is for a non-profit purpose, the defence of fair use might be accepted. We now illustrate this with reference to specific cases.

In *Basic Books, Inc. v. Kinko's Graphics Corporation,*[46] the plaintiffs[47] alleged that Kinko's infringed their copyrights when it copied excerpts from books, the rights to which were held by the plaintiffs, without permission and without payment of required fees, and sold the copies, to students of several universities for a profit. The United States District Court for the Southern District of New York rejected the defence of fair use. In examining the purpose of the use, it was found that the use of the copyrighted material by Kinko's was monetary gain.[48]

It is important to note that the court also considered "other factors" not listed in section 107 of the US Copyright code. These included the fact that the defendant had effectively created a new nationwide business allied to the publishing industry by usurping the plaintiffs' copyrights and profits. According to the court, "this could not be sustained as it would frustrate the intent of the copyright law which has been the protection of intellectual property and, more importantly, the encouragement of creative expression."[49]

Compare this case with *Princeton University Press et al v. Michigan Document Service et al,*[50] decided five years after *Basic Books, Inc. v. Kinko's.* In brief, the plaintiffs (appellees) brought a copyright infringement action against the defendants (appellants) alleging that the defendants infringed on copyrights held by the plaintiffs when Michigan Document Service (MDS) made multiple copies of excerpts from various materials provided by University of Michigan professors, compiled these copies into "coursepacks"[51] at the

45 *Sony Corp. v. Universal City Studios*, 464 U.S. 451, (1984)

46 *Basic Books, Inc. v. Kinko's Graphics Corporation,* 758 F. Supp. 1522, S.D.N.Y, (1991).

47 The plaintiffs were major publishers in New York city, i.e. Basic Books, Inc., Harper & Row Publishers, Inc., John Wiley & Sons, Inc., Mcgraw-Hill, Inc., Penguin Books USA, Inc., Prentice-Hall, Inc., Richard D. Irwin, Inc., and William Morrow & Co., Inc

48 The Court clarified that "The crux of the profit/non-profit distinction is not whether the sole motive of the use is monetary gain but whether the user stands to profit from exploitation of the copyrighted material without paying the customary price," *ibid,* para. IA(1), citing *Harper & Row, Publishers, Inc. v. Nations Enters*, 471 U.S. at 562.

49 *Basic Books, Inc. v. Kinko's Graphics Corporation, supra,* para. IA(5).

50 *Princeton University Press v. Michigan Document Service,* 1996 FED App. 0046P (6th Cir.)

51 Coursepacks are compilations of various copyrighted and uncopyrighted materials, which may include journal articles, newspaper articles, course notes or syllabi, sample test questions, and excerpts from books. Professors select the contents of the coursepacks and deliver the selected

request of professors, and sold the coursepacks to students for a profit. The district court for the Eastern District of Michigan granted summary judgment to the plaintiffs, finding that the defendants' infringement was "wilful," and issued an injunction against the defendants. The defendants appealed the district court's decision, defending their copying practices primarily on the ground that the coursepacks are a "fair use" of the copyrighted works and not an infringement.[52] The Court of Appeals upheld the defence of fair use.[53]

In examining "the purpose and character of the use, including whether such use is of a commercial nature or is for non-profit educational purposes", the Court of Appeals explained that there are two parts to this test: (1) the degree to which the challenged use has transformed the original, and (2) the profit or non-profit character of the use. Ordinarily, analysis under the first factor centres on "whether the new work merely 'supersede[s] the objects' of the original creation [...] or instead adds something new, with a further purpose or different character, altering the first with new expression, meaning, or message; it asks, in other words, whether and to what extent the new work is 'transformative.' "[54] The Court went on to explain that because works that are transformative are more likely to promote science and the arts, transformative works are likely to be found as fair use, whereas works that merely copy the original are likely to be found as infringements of the copyrighted work, with the exception of the straight reproduction of multiple copies for classroom distribution.[55] In *Kelly v. Arriba* the Court of Appeals affirmed that the fair use exemption "permits courts to avoid rigid application of the Copyright Statute when, on occasion, it would stifle the very creativity which that law is designed to foster."[56] This is no doubt based on the test of the transformative nature of the copying. The Court in *Princeton University Press v. MDS* concluded that, although the transformative value of the coursepacks is slight, the fact that the coursepacks are "multiple copies for classroom use" preserves MDS's claim of "fair use."[57] In other words, if the copying is for classroom use, making multiple copies is allowed even if there is no transformative element involved. But as we demonstrate further on, this does not include bulk or straight copying of the whole work.

As to the second part of the first element (the profit or non-profit character of the use), the Court found MDS's production and sale of the coursepacks to be a clear for-profit

materials to MDS with an estimate of the number of students expected in the course. The professors assign the material to students enrolled in a particular class and inform these students that they may purchase the required materials in coursepack form at MDS if they wish. *Princeton University Press v. Michigan Document Service, supra,* para. I.

52 *Princeton University Press v. Michigan Document Service, supra,* para III.

53 *Ibid,* para. VI.

54 *Ibid,* para. V(A).

55 Ibid.

56 *Kelly v. Arriba Soft Corporation,* 336F.3d 811, (9th Cir. 2002), para. II(A), quoting *Dr. Seuss Enters, L.P. v. Penguin Books USA. Inc* 109F. 3d 1399 (9th Cir 1997).

57 *Princeton University Press v. Michigan Document Service, supra,* para. V(A), quoting *Campbell v. Acuff-Rose Music, Inc.,* 114 S.Ct. 1164, 1171 (1994). A work is transformative if it adds something entirely new to the original copyrighted work. Important factors include whether the new work has a different purpose or different character than that of the copyrighted work.

"use"[58] yet it upheld the defence of fair use. This is counterintuitive, since in *Basic Books, Inc. v. Kinko's Graphics Corporation* selling coursepacks for profit was not fair use of the copyrighted material. Why this difference in conclusions? Let us analyse the case in more detail in order to appreciate the court's decision.

In the aforementioned case of *Princeton University Press v. MDS*, the Court found as significant the undisputed fact that MDS could produce "multiple copies for classroom use," at a profit, for less than it would cost the professors or students to produce them. The professors and students, who might otherwise have copied the materials themselves, had assigned the task of copying to a professional service that could perform the task more efficiently. On these facts, the for-profit provision of this service did not weigh against a finding of fair use. Here, *MDS obtained a profit by providing a service*. MDS charged on per-page basis for copyrighted materials. But MDS did not "exploit" copyrighted material because its fee did not turn on the content of the materials, copyrighted or not, that it copied.[59] The Court concluded:

> The business of producing and selling coursepacks is more properly viewed as the exploitation of professional copying technologies and the inability of academic parties to reproduce printed materials efficiently, not the exploitation of copyrighted, creative materials. We hold that the Copyright Act does not prohibit professors and students who may make copies themselves from using the photoreproduction services of a third party in order to obtain those same copies at less cost. Thus, the coursepacks fit within the exception to the "transformative" quality requirement, and the predominant character of the use of excerpts in coursepacks is not commercial but "non-profit educational".[60]

In other words, service provided by MDS was viewed as a necessity rather than an infringement, regardless of the fact that a profit was made in the process. Interestingly, this was not the case in *Basic Books v. Kinko's*. Was *Kinko's not* offering a service to professors and students just as MDS did? Surprisingly, the Court in *Basic Books, Inc. v. Kinko's* did not consider *Kinko's* photocopying activities as a service to professors and students, but rather a commercial activity because, according to the court, *Kinko's* had the intention of making profit.[61] *Kinko's* provided incentives to professors to choose their copy centre over others. This practice, according to the Court, was a clear indication that *Kinko's* recognized and sought a segment of a profitable market.[62] Such reasoning begs the question whether MDS set out to engage in the business of photocopying without the intention of making a profit. This was of course not the case. There was no indication whatsoever that MDS was a not-for-profit organization in its provision of photocopying services.

The difference in findings between the two cases, *Basic Books, Inc. v. Kinko's* and *Princeton University Press v. MDS* is difficult to appreciate without considering the other factors for fair use. In the *Princeton University Press* case, another factor, not listed in the Copyright Act and different from the one in *Basic Books, Inc. v. Kinko's,* was considered. The fact that incentives for producing higher educational materials may not revolve

58 *Princeton University Press v. Michigan Document Service, supra*, para V(A).
59 *Ibid*, para. V(A).
60 *Ibid*, (emphasis added).
61 *Basic Books, Inc. v. Kinko's Graphics Corporation, supra*, para. IA(1).
62 *Ibid*.

around monetary compensation, but may instead arise from the need for wide dissemination of the work, was considered to be highly relevant in determining fair use.[63] In the case, more than one hundred authors declared on record that they write for professional and personal reasons such as making a contribution to the discipline, providing an opportunity for colleagues to evaluate and critique the authors' ideas and theories, enhancing the authors' professional reputations and improving career opportunities. The declarants stated that their primary purpose in writing is *not for monetary compensation and that they advocate wide dissemination of excerpts from their works via coursepacks without imposition of permission fees.*[64] This highlights two things. First, it confirms the fact that the statutory list is not conclusive and courts have the liberty to consider other relevant factors, such as social interests like education. Developing country courts can take into account other factors based on the social economic conditions. Second, and more important, taking non-economic incentives for producing course work into consideration only serves to emphasize the importance of the economic interests of the author or right holder in determining a finding of fair use. The separation between transformative and 'not-for profit' use becomes superficial when the economic interests of the author are harmed. This explains the difference in the Courts' findings between the *Basic Books, Inc,* and *Princeton University* cases. In the former case, the economic interests of the right holders were stronger than in the latter case.

6.2.1.2. Amount and Substantiality of the Portion Used

As regards the third factor of fair use, the amount and substantiality of the portion used, the U.S. Supreme Court in *Sony Corp. v. Universal City Studios* found that copying of entire programs for viewing later at a convenient time ("time-shifting") was fair use.[65] The test in this case was the existence of actual or potential *commercial harm* for the copyright holder. It was found that no such harm existed.[66] Again, the Court attaches commercial consideration to another element, in this case the test of substantiality.

However, the use of a few words of a work has been found as contrary to fair use, not because of the amount of words used but because the words used represented a "substantial" part of the work. Thus, in the case of *Harper & Row Publishers, Inc. v. Nation Enterprises,* a political opinion magazine which used only 300 out of 7,500 words of an excerpt from the U.S. President Ford's memoirs was found guilty of copyright infringement.[67] We shall now discuss *Harper & Row* in some detail to help the reader appreciate how it relates to developing countries.

To recount the relevant facts of the case, in 1977, President Ford contracted with Harper & Row to publish his memoirs. Harper & Row then contracted with Time magazine for the exclusive right to publish, one week before the book was to be shipped, a 7,500-word excerpt from the book. In exchange, Time magazine agreed to pay US$ 25 000

63 *Princeton University Press v. Michigan Document Service, supra,* para. V(E).
64 *Ibid,* (emphasis added).
65 *Sony Corp. v. Universal City Studios,* 464 U.S. 417, (1984), para 52.
66 *Ibid,* para. 50 (emphasis added).
67 *Harper & Row, Publishers, Inc. v. Nation Enterprises, supra,* 471 U.S. 539 (1985).

(US$ 12 500 in advance, and the balance at the time of publication). However, an unauthorized source provided The Nation magazine with the unpublished Ford manuscript. An editor at The Nation magazine produced a 2,250-word article, at least 300 to 400 words of which consisted of verbatim quotes of copyrighted expressions taken from the manuscript. As a result of the publication of The Nation's article, Time magazine cancelled its article and refused to pay the remaining US$ 12 500 to the petitioners. The petitioners subsequently brought a suit in the District Court for the Southern District of New York against the respondent publishers of The Nation, alleging, *inter alia*, violation of the Copyright Act. The District Court found that an infringement had occurred under the Copyright Act and awarded damages of US$ 12 500. On appeal, the Second Circuit Court reversed the lower court's finding of infringement, holding that The Nation's publication of the 300 to 400 words was sanctioned as a "fair use" under section 107 of the Copyright Act. The case wound up in the Supreme Court, which concluded that all four factors of "fair use"[68] weighed against the defendants. On the question of substantiality, the court concluded that use of the 300 words was not fair use because those few words were substantial as they represented "*the heart of the book*".[69] Again, as in the case of *Basic Books, Inc. v. Kinko's*, substantiality is determined by the quality of the information.

The court in *Basic Books, Inc. v. Kinko's* found and concluded that the portions copied were critical parts of the books since this was the likely reason for which the college professors used them in their classes.[70] In other words, the portions copied were substantial. It was found that in almost every instance, Kinko's had copied an entire chapter of the plaintiffs' book. Copying an entire chapter of a book was found to be "substantial because they [the chapters] are obviously meant to stand alone, that is, as a complete representation of the concept explored in the chapter."[71]

The above cases present a number of challenges for access to educational material in developing countries. If substantiality is determined on the basis of the quality of the information copied, then any reading material assigned by a professor is substantial information and its use is likely to be unfair. As the Court of Appeals reasoned, professors assign readings containing useful information for their students, taking the best, or the "heart" of the works. Likewise, any person who copies portions of a textbook is likely to infringe copyright since they copy the information that they find relevant.[72]

---

68 Just to remind ourselves, the four factors of "fair use" as listed in section 107 of the US Code are: (1) the purpose and character of the use, including whether such use is of a commercial nature or is for non-profit educational purpose; (2) the nature of the copyrighted work; (3) the amount and substantiality of the portion used in relation to the copyrighted work as a whole; and (4) the effect of the use upon the potential market for, or value of the copyrighted work.

69 *Harper & Row, Publishers, Inc. v. Nation Enterprises, supra,* 471 U.S. 539 (1985), para. IV (emphasis added).

70 *Basic Books, Inc. v. Kinko's Graphics Corporation, supra,* para. IA(3), citing *Harper & Row, Publishers, Inc. v. Nations Enters, supra,* para IV, where the court stated that the fact that a substantial portion of the infringing work was copied verbatim is evidence of the qualitative value of the copied material."

71 *Basic Books, Inc. v. Kinko's Graphics Corporation, ibid,* para. IA(3).

72 *Basic Books, Inc. v. Kinko's Graphics Corporation, ibid,* para. IA(3).

Determining substantiality on the basis of the quality of information automatically militates against wholesale copying of books. For example, in the case of *Worldwide Church of God v. Philadelphia Church of God, Inc,*[73] verbatim copying of almost the entire book was found to be unfair use of the work. In the case, the appellant, Worldwide Church of God ("WCG"), was a non-profit religious organization whose late Pastor General, Herbert W. Armstrong, wrote a 380-page book entitled *Mystery of the Ages* (MOA), the copyright to which was held by WCG. After Armstrong's death, WCG retired MOA from distribution and use. The appellee, Philadelphia Church of God ("PCG"), also a non-profit religious organization, subsequently appropriated the MOA for use in its religious observance, copying it in its entirety and distributing large numbers of copies to its members and the public without permission from WCG. PCG advertised its version of MOA in newspapers and periodicals and received substantial contributions from persons who received its version of MOA. When PCG ignored WCG's demand that it cease infringing upon its copyright and continued distribution of its MOA, this action followed.

Concerning the third factor of fair use, amount and substantiality of the portion used, PCG's use of the MOA was found to be unfair. PCG copied the entire MOA verbatim, deleting only the "Suggested Readings" and the reference to "Worldwide Church of God" from the copyright page. Concerning the mount copied, the court stated that, "while wholesale copying does not preclude fair use *per se*, copying an entire work "militates against a finding of fair use."[74] As to the substantiality of the portions copied, the court concluded that "the fact that a substantial portion of the infringing work was copied verbatim is evidence of the qualitative value of the copied material, both to the originator and to the plagiarist ...."[75]

6.3.2.3. Effect of the Use upon the Potential Market or Value of the Copyrighted Work

With regards to the fourth factor, the effect on the market, the Court in *Harper & Row* called this "undoubtedly the most important element of fair use."[76] The loss of revenue is proof of an infringement if there is a causal link between the two. Thus, finding against the defendants, the Court stated that "Time's cancellation of its projected serialization and its refusal to pay the US$ 12 500 [to Harper and Row] were the direct effect of the infringement." This was "clear-cut evidence of damage."[77] The Court explained that once a copyright holder establishes a causal connection between the infringement and loss of revenue, the burden shifts to the infringer to show that the damage would have occurred even had there been no use of the copyrighted expression.[78] The causal connection was established. The Court's reasoning echoes a previous decision of *Sony Corp v. Universal City Studios.* The court had stated in respect to the adverse effect of a use on the market

73 *Worldwide Church of God v. Philadelphia Church of God, Inc,* 227 F 3d 1110 (9th Cir. 2000).
74 *Worldwide Church of God v. Philadelphia Church of God, Inc, sipra,* para. IIC(3) (footnote omitted).
75 *Ibid,* para. IIC(3), quoting *Harper & Row, Publishers, Inc. v. Nation Enterprises, supra,* para. IV.
76 *Harper & Row, Publishers, Inc. v. Nation Enterprises, supra,* para. IV, see also *Princeton University Press v. Michigan Document Service, supra,* para. II.
77 *Harper & Row, Publishers, Inc. v. Nation Enterprises, ibid.*
78 *Ibid.*

that "actual harm need not be shown [...]. Nor is it necessary to show with certainty that future harm will result. What is necessary is showing by a preponderance of the evidence that *some* meaningful likelihood of future harm exists."[79] In the case of *Harper & Row v. Nation Enterprises,* decided upon in the same year as *Sony Corp. v. Universal City Studios,* the Court stressed that:

> More importantly, to negate fair use one need only show that if the challenged use "should become widespread, it would adversely affect the potential market for the copyrighted work.[80]

The test of market effect explains why the Courts in *Basic Books, Inc. v. Kinko's* and *Princeton University Press v. Michigan Document Service,* both involving two photoreproduction shops selling course materials to students for profit, found the use of copyrighted material to be unfair in one case and fair in the other. In *Basic Books, Inc. v. Kinko's,* the defendant had several stores nationwide, servicing hundreds of colleges and universities enrolling thousands of students. While not denying that reading the packets could whet the appetite of students for more information from the authors, the Court was of the opinion that "it is more likely that the purchase of the packets obviates purchase of the full texts." The Court found that Kinko's copying unfavourably impacted upon the plaintiffs' sales of their books and collections of permissions fees.[81] On the other hand, while it was true that Michigan Document Service's purpose of the use (first factor) was for profit, there was no effect on the market for works belonging to Princeton University Press (PUP). The students who used the coursepacks were not a market for purchase of the original works; the professors would not otherwise have required students to purchase the original works. There was evidence that the professors would not have assigned the copyrighted works in the absence of available coursepack compilations of excerpts. For this reason, there was no damage to the market of the original.[82] Indeed, as the court pointed out, the economic consideration is the most important factor in determining "fair use".[83]

It is possible that in certain instances the court may find a use of a copyrighted material to be fair even when such use *seems* to have a negative impact on the market of the protected work, which gives the impression that a negative impact on the market may not necessarily lead to a finding of unfair use. This appears to be the message of *Campbell v. Acuff-Rose Music, Inc.,*[84] decided upon ten years after *Harper & Row*. While not denying the fact that parody can harm the market at all, the Supreme Court of the United States surprisingly made a finding of fair use. This has been interpreted as a clarification by the court that market impact is *not* always conclusive as to whether the use is unfair.[85] Examination of the Supreme Court's reasoning is necessary in order to appreciate its

79 *Sony Corp. v. Universal City Studios, supra,* para. V B (emphasis original).

80 *Harper & Row, Publishers, Inc. v. Nation Enterprises, supra,* para. IV, affirming *Sony Corp. v. Universal City Studios, supra.*

81 *Books, Inc. v. Kinko's Graphics Corporation, supra,* para. IA(4).

82 *Princeton University Press v. Michigan Document Service supra,* para. V(E).

83 *Harper & Row, Publishers, Inc. v. Nation Enterprises, supra,* para. IV.

84 *Campbell v. Acuff-Rose Music, Inc,* 510 U.S. 569 (1994).

85 See for example, Ruth L. Okediji, "Toward an international fair use doctrine," *Columbia Journal of Transnational Law,* vol. 39, (2000). 75–175, at 118 (hereafter referred to as Okediji, international fair use doctrine).

opinion and understand why a court would make a finding of fair use even where there *seems* to be adverse market effect. The Supreme Court explained that "when a lethal parody, like a scathing theatre review, kills demand for the original, it does not produce a harm recognized under the Copyright Act. [...] the role of the courts is to distinguish between biting criticism that merely suppresses demand and copyright infringement, which usurps it".[86] If a negative effect on the market for a work evolves *only indirectly* from the exempted use, (like a biting criticism of the original), the adverse market effect will not count as a factor in determining fair use.[87] In other words, there must be a direct causal link between the use and the market impact.[88] In this case, no causal link was established and thus the conclusion of fair use.

While the four elements are cumulative, the economic impact of the use is a strong determining factor. For example, in determining the purpose of use, a commercial as opposed to a non-profit use will not pass the test of fair use, even if the courts state that economic value is not the only determining factor. The situation in the *Princeton University* case represents the exception rather than the rule. The authors declared that they were not publishing for profit, but rather to be read.[89] They did not have a legitimate interest in the market. It is not surprising that this fact came as an additional element to the four listed in the statute.

6.3.3. *Compatibility of Fair Use Doctrine with the Three-Step Test: The Market Effect Test*

In fact, the compatibility of fair use with international law has come into question. Some scholars have argued that since the Berne Convention already accommodates 'fair practice' and its more liberal iteration, the U.S. fair use, its status should remain unchanged under TRIPS, given that the latter incorporates the substantive provisions of the former.[90] Others disagree and instead contend that the U.S. kind of fair use exception, which are open-ended and discretionary, would be in violation of the TRIPS Agreement. According to Professor Okediji;

> [...] the indeterminacy of the fair use doctrine violates the Berne Convention.[91]

While not ruling out the possibility that any specific judicial application of Section 107 of the U.S. Copyright Act will comply with the three-step test as a matter of fact, Professor Ricketson contends that:

---

86 *Campbell v. Acuff-Rose Music, Inc*, 510 U.S. 569 (1994), II D.

87 In the same line, see Senftleben, *supra*, p. 187.

88 See *Harper & Row, Publishers, Inc. v. Nation Enterprises, supra*, para. IV. See also Anderson *et al*, Market substitution, *supra* p. 47 (saying that the key to predicting fair use cases is determining whether the substitution effect was the cause of market impairment (or adverse market effect).

89 *Princeton University Press v. Michigan Document Service, supra*, para. V E.

90 See for example Tyler G. Newby, "What's fair here is not fair everywhere: Does the American fair use doctrine violate international copyright law," *Stanford Law Review*, vol. 51, (1999). 1633–1663, at 1633; and Willem Grosheide, "Copyright law from a user's perspective," *European Intellectual Property Review*, (2001). 321–325, at 321.

91 Okediji, toward an international fair use doctrine, *supra*, p.117.

> [...] the real problem is with a provision that is framed in such a general and open-ended way. At the very best, the statutory formulation here raises issues with respect to unspecified purposes (the first step) and with respect to the legitimate interests of the author (third step).[92]

In Ricketson's opinion, the fair dealing exception of Australia's Copyright legislation would conform to article 13 of TRIPS.[93] He argues further that;

> [...] in the case of section 40(2), compliance with the three-step test is established without any great difficulty. The factors listed in that section are directed specifically at the kinds of issues raised by the three-step test and allow, moreover, for a case by case determination of whether there will be a fair dealing for the purpose of research or study. This subsection, indeed, is a shining example of compliance with the three-step test.[94]

It is difficult to support Professor Ricketson's argument. First of all, there is hardly any noticeable difference between the "open-ended" U.S. provision on fair use and the "precise" Australian legislation.[95] The only difference is that the latter offers a longer list than the former. But even if article 40 of the Australian Copyright Act is more extensively elaborated than section 107 of the U.S. Copyright Act, this does not automatically make the latter incompatible with international law or the three-step test. First, it is the conduct of the U.S. in relation to section 107 that determines whether or not it complies with international law. A state does not violate an international obligation by simply passing national legislation that may seem contrary to the international treaty, but rather by its behaviour in relation to that national legislation.[96] Indeed, the U.S. has defended the compatibility

---

92 Ricketson, WIPO Study, *supra*, p. 69.

93 Section 40 of the Australian Copyright Act, entitled "Fair dealing for purpose of research or study" provides in part: (1) A fair dealing with a literary, dramatic, musical or artistic work, or with an adaptation of a literary, dramatic or musical work, for the purpose of research or study does not constitute an infringement of the copyright in the work.

(1A) A fair dealing with a literary work (other than lecture notes) does not constitute an infringement of the copyright in the work if it is for the purpose of, or associated with, an approved course of study or research by an enrolled external student of an educational institution.

(2) For the purposes of this Act, the matters to which regard shall be had, in determining whether a dealing [...] constitutes a fair dealing with the work or adaptation for the purpose of research or study include: (a) the purpose and character of the dealing; (b) the nature of the work or adaptation; (c) the possibility of obtaining the work or adaptation within a reasonable time at an ordinary commercial price; (d) the effect of the dealing upon the potential market for, or value of, the work or adaptation; and (e) in a case where part only of the work or adaptation is reproduced, the amount and substantiality of the part copied taken in relation to the whole work or adaptation.

94 Ricketson, WIPO Study, *supra*, p.69.

95 In support of this argument see Tawfik, *supra*, p.14. In her opinion, a comparison of the impugned U.S. provision and the compliant Australian one, read in light of Ricketson's conclusions, would indicate that there is only a very fine line between formulations that, in his opinion, would conform to Article 13 and those that would not.

96 *Applicability of the obligation to arbitrate under section 21 of the United Nations Headquarters Agreement of 26 June 1947*, Advisory Opinion of 26 April 1988, I.C.J. Reports, 1988, paras. 42–43. In 1987 the U.S. Congress passed the Anti-Terrorist Act which was aimed at closing certain entities including the Palestine Liberation Organization (PLO) Observer Mission in New York. However, the UN General Assembly received assurances that the Anti-Terrorist Act would not apply to

of fair use with the TRIPS Agreement relying on judicial practice.[97] Second, while international law requires that an exception or limitation in national legislation be clearly defined, there is no need to identify explicitly each and every possible situation to which the exception could apply, provided that the scope of the exception is known and particularised.[98]

Third and most importantly, emphasis upon 'market effect' by the U.S. courts places the fair use doctrine to the same level as the three-step test. In *Sony Corp v. Universal City Studio,* the only reason "time shifting"[99] was declared fair use was because "no likelihood of harm was shown on trial, and the plaintiffs admitted that there had been no actual harm to date".[100] This speculative anticipation of market harm will always disfavour a finding of fair use. Indeed, six years later, the Courts sought to create some space for flexibility, by providing a clearer test for market effect. Following the case of *Campbell v. Acuff-Rose Music, Inc,* only evidence of substantial harm would weigh against a finding of fair use.[101]

Scholars mostly agree that the magnitude and not likelihood of market impairment should be the determining factor. For example, in 1988 Fisher, commenting on *Harper & Row v. Nation Enterprises,* argued to be helpful, the market impact factor "must be modified. [...] a court confronted with a fair use defense must estimate the *magnitude* of the impairment caused by privileging the defendant's conduct; merely ascertaining the *existence* of adverse impact will not suffice."[102] Leval has argued that market impairment should not turn the fourth factor [the impact of the use on the market] in favour of the copyright holder unless it is reasonably substantial.[103]

---

the PLO offices in New York. There was also evidence that the Act was not being applied. Thus there was no breach by U.S. of its obligations under the UN Head Quarter Agreement. Although the court did not state it as such, the only understanding one gets is that if a state enacts national legislation that seems to violate international obligations, there is no violation simply by virtue of such an enactment. A violation only arises from the conduct of the state in relation to that legislation. This understanding of the Court's view is not supported by the separate opinions of JJ. Oda, Schwebel and Shahabuddeen, who instead think that the breach exists the moment the law is enacted.

97 See discussion below and also Jayashree Watal, *Intellectual Property Rights in the WTO and Developing Countries.* (The Hague: Kluwer Law International, 2001). p.288.

98 *United States – Section 110(5) of the US Copyright Act, supra,* para. 6.108 (while defining limited exceptions). For the U.S., this scope is defined by the courts, which are guided by the market effect of the use.

99 Recording a television program so as to watch it later at a time convenient to the viewer.

100 *Sony Corp. v. Universal City Studios, supra,* para. IV B. Likewise, the in the case of *Princeton University Press v. Michigan Document Service, supra,* the Court found fair use because the authors did not have an interest in the market. As such no market was hurt by the use.

101 *Campbell v. Acuff-Rose Music, Inc, supra,* para. II D. Not every negative impact on the market will weigh against fair use. But this does not mean that market effect is not an important factor in determining fair use. If the harm is substantial, then market effect will work against a finding of fair use.

102 William. W. Fisher III, "Reconstructing the Fair Use Doctrine," *Harvard Law Review,* vol. 101, 1988, 1659–1795, 1671–1672 (emphasis original).

103 Pierre N. Leval, "Towards a Fair Use Standard," *Harvard Law Review,* vol. 103, (1990). 1105–1136. The author argues that by definition, every fair use involves some loss of royalty revenue

Indeed, as a result of its focus on the market effect, the fair use doctrine mirrors the three-step test. One is inclined to surmise that this is the reason fair use has not attracted a dispute under the TRIPS Agreement for failure to comply with the three-step test. While there may be a difference in phraseology between the fair use provisions in the U.S. Copyright Act and article 13 of the TRIPS Agreement, both protect the economic interests of the author.

However, is the conclusion that the market effect test makes fair use compatible with international copyright law also true for parody? We shall answer this question in the following paragraphs.

6.3.4. *The Relationship between Market Effect, Parody and the Three-Step Test*

Does the market effect test, which raises the fair use doctrine to the level of the three-step test in relation to copying of printed works, equally apply for parody? In cases of parody, U.S. courts tend to make a finding of fair use, even when it seems that there is an adverse market effect.[104] In fact, U.S. judicial practice was criticized during the TRIPS Council review of U.S. legislation in 1996[105] as violating the three-step test. In particular, the European Communities (EC) asked the United States to explain how the fair use doctrine, "as it has been broadly applied and interpreted by U.S. courts, particularly in connection with 'parody' that diminished the value of the work, is consistent with TRIPS article 13, given the obligation to 'confine limitations or exceptions to exclusive rights to certain special cases which do not conflict with a normal exploitation of the work and do not unreasonably prejudice the legitimate interests of the right holder.' "[106]

The EC question conveys the message that every use that diminishes the value of a work is contrary to article 13 of the TRIPS Agreement. As the case of *Campbell v. Acuff-Rose* has shown, this is not the case. In response to the EC question, the U.S. argued that fair use embodies essentially the same goals as article 13 and that the doctrine protects only those types of uses which do not interfere with the copyright owner's normal exploitation of the work or unreasonably prejudice his or her rights.[107] The U.S. used the case of *Campbell v. Acuff-Rose* to explain that, for example a scathing book review certainly may diminish the value of the book but would not infringe the copyright unless it substituted for the purchases of the book in the market place.[108] In contrast, harm to the market for other adaptations of the copyrighted work will clearly weigh against a finding of fair use.[109] The U.S. government's response has been criticized for allegedly not depicting the reality of its

because the secondary user has not paid royalties. Therefore, if an insubstantial loss of revenue turned the fourth factor in favour of the copyright holder, this factor would never weigh in favour of the secondary user. Therefore, he suggests, market impairment should not turn the fourth factor in favour of the plaintiff unless it is reasonably substantial. *Ibid,* pp. 1124–1125.

104 For example in *Campbell v. Acuff-Rose, supra..*

105 Council for TRIPS, Review of Legislation on Copyright and Related Rights, WTO Doc. IP/Q/USA/1, dated October 30, 1996 (hereafter referred to at Council for TRIPS, Review of Legislation).

106 Council for TRIPS, Review of Legislation, *ibid,* para. IV(1).

107 Council for TRIPS, Review of Legislation, *supra,* para. IV(1).

108 *Ibid.*

109 *Ibid.*

judicial practice [on fair use], which, it is argued, does not reflect compliance with international law, or the three-step test.[110] We argue that the U.S. position reflects judicial practice on fair use, including parody. We have demonstrated that judicial practice on fair use places it at the level of the three-step test, which makes fair use compliant with international law. We shall now explain why parody is compliant with the three-step test and thus with international law.

In *Campbell v. Acuff-Rose*, the Supreme Court distinguished between "biting criticism that merely suppresses demand and copyright infringement which usurps it."[111] This distinction between potentially remediable displacement and irremediable disparagement is reflected in the rule that there is no protectable derivative market for criticism. The market for potential derivative uses includes only those that creators of original works would in general develop or licence others to develop. Yet, "the unlikelihood that creators of imaginative works will licence critical reviews or lampoons of their own productions removes such uses from the very notion of a potential licensing market."[112] In other words, the market served by a work of parody is not the kind that a right holder in the original work will normally exploit within the meaning of the three-step test. Hence, there is no conflict with the normal exploitation of the copyrighted work.

In addition, if the parody affects the market by merely suppressing the demand, then there is no substantial harm to the market.[113] In such a case, the parody does not have an adverse market effect, which leads to a finding of fair use. On the other hand, if the parody usurps the market for the original or derivatives thereof, then the market impact is substantial, leading to a copyright infringement and rejection of the fair use defence.[114]

The above distinction between a parody that has a direct market effect and one that does not is highly important if we are to appreciate the relationship between the market effect of a parody and a finding of fair use. The failure to make this distinction is at the root of the EC's discontent with the United States' fair use exception for parodies.[115] A parody that diminishes the value of the work does not necessarily prejudice the legitimate interest of the copyright holder, but rather it is a parody that usurps or substitutes the market for that work.[116] Indeed, as the U.S. rightly retorted, if article 13 [of TRIPS] were to forbid all value-diminishing uses, this would serve to quell all but "flattering commentary or benign parody".[117]

---

110 Okediji, toward an international fair use doctrine, *supra*, pp. 117–122.

111 *Campbell v. Acuff-Rose, supra*, para. II D.

112 *Ibid.*

113 A reasonable prejudice to the legitimate interest of the right holder is accepted under the three-step test. See article 9(2) of the Berne Convention and article 13 of the TRIPS Agreement.

114 *Basic Books, Inc. v. Kinko's Graphics Corporation, supra*, para. IA(4)

115 John C. Jr Knapp, "Laugh, and the whole world … scowls at you?: a defense of the United States' fair use exception for parody under TRIPS," *Denver Journal of International Law & Policy*, vol. 33, no. 2, (2005).347–366, at 352.

116 On market substitution as leading to an automatic refusal of a fair use defence, see Anderson *et al* Market substitution, *supra*, pp. 33–50. The authors agree that determining market substitution in parody cases is not the same as in copying printed material.

117 Council for TRIPS, Review of Legislation, *supra*, para. IV(1).

We conclude that the market effect test in determining fair use applies also to parody. This places parody on the same level as the three-step test[118] and thus in compliance with international copyright law.[119]

6.3.5. *Application of Fair Use to Developing Countries: The Case of Africa*

Are there any benefits for developing countries in using the fair use doctrine? A number of authors and advocates of access to IP works as a matter of public interest have argued that developing countries should emulate the examples set by developed countries in providing access. In the particular case of access to copyrighted material, fair use or fair dealing have emerged strongly as a principle that can be used by both developed and developing countries.[120] As demonstrated earlier, there exists an undeniable acceptance of fair use by developing countries, which is demonstrated by the inclusion of fair use provisions in national legislation. If fair use provisions were framed differently in developing country legislation—if for example, they were more precise and not subjected to the

---

118 The three-step test in article 9(2) of the Berne Convention and article 13 of the TRIPS Agreement require that a use of copyrighted work be confined to limited exceptions in a way that does not conflict with the normal exploitation of that work or prejudice the legitimate interests of the copyright holder. "Normal exploitation" of a work and "legitimate interests" have been interpreted by the WTO Panel to mean "economic interests." See discussion in section 4.4.2 and 4.4.3. Thus a use of a copyrighted work that negatively affects the market of that work conflicts with the normal exploitation of that work by the copyright holder and prejudices his legitimate interests. The fair use doctrine is similar to the three-step test because any use that negatively affects the market of the protected work is unfair use. Similarly, a parody that destroys the market of a copyrighted work is unfair use and equivalent to the three-step test. In another context, Spitz has demonstrated that the strict interpretation the fair use provision and the linkage to market effect, including in cases of parody, means that fair use is not as liberal as it is normally perceived to be. It resembles the three-step test and is the same as author-centred copyright systems such as France and the U.K. See Brad Spitz, "Droit d'auteur, copyright et parodie, ou le mythe de l'usage loyal," *Revue international du droit d'auteur,* vol. 204, (2005). 55–153.

119 In agreement see Spitz, Droit d'auteur, *ibid,* p. 119, (affirming that the rule that the parody "cannot be confused with the typical production of the parodied work or with any work of the author in question" (quoting Françon, André, "Questions de droit d'auteur relative aux parodies et productions similaires," *Le Droit d'auteur/Copyright,* June 1988) is similar to the requirement of fair use: respect for the original work's economic exploitation or market, which is similar to the three-step test.)

120 See for example Carys Craig, "The changing face of fair dealing in Canadian copyright law: a proposal for legislative reform," in Geist, Michael, ed. *In the public interest: the future of Canadian copyright law,* (Toronto: Irwin Law, 2005). 437–461, pp. 438–439 (arguing that the fair dealing provisions found in the Canadian Copyright Act be replaced with an open-ended defence similar in form to the U.S. fair use defence); Daniel Gervais, "Towards a new core international copyright norm: the reverse three-step test," *Marquette Intellectual Property Law Review,* vol. 9 no. 1, (2005). 1–36, p. 4. (advocating for creation of a new international copyright norm based on the Berne Convention's three-step test, in harmony with the U.S. fair use doctrine) (hereinafter referred to as Gervais, towards a new core international fair use norm). On use of fair use for the purpose of better protection of IP as opposed to allowing its use, see Ruth L. Okediji, "Toward an international fair use doctrine," *Columbia Journal of Transnational Law,* vol. 39, (2000). 75–175, at 150. The author advocates for an international standard of fair use, in order not to jeopardise the level and quality of protection that TRIPS offers.

three-step test—would they serve to promote access to education in the analogue environment? In this section, we shall analyse the appropriateness of transplanting the fair use doctrine of developed countries to the developing country context.

The case law provides guidance as to the application of the four elements listed as a checklist for fair use.[121] In all the cases cited, each element of fair use was proved or otherwise, by a detailed analysis of the facts of each case, supported by evidence. In this sense, the criteria for determining whether or not a use of a copyrighted work is fair use are not clear, as one must depend on different and sometimes unforeseeable factors. Whether the various elements are fulfilled has to be decided by courts on a case by case basis. To that extent, we can agree with Nimmer that it is a "fairy tale to conclude that the four factors determine resolution of concrete fair use cases."[122] This means that what is fair use is left to litigation. This implies not only legal uncertainty, but more importantly for developing countries, serious financial consequences. For developing countries, litigation is a very expensive endeavour. More specifically, since most of the copyrighted works of relevance to education are owned by foreign publishers, for whom litigation imposes a lesser financial burden, this is likely to become a common occurrence, albeit one which is very costly for developing countries. Many defendants in developing countries cannot afford the costs of litigation. Since most of the copyrighted material is imported, mainly from the U.S., this means that the litigation is between local user(s) and foreign owner(s) or their representative(s).

It may be recalled that fair use, as a justification for use of a copyrighted work, serves as an affirmative defence to a claim of copyright infringement and thus the party claiming that its use of the original copyrighted work constitutes a fair use typically carries the burden of proof as to all issues in the dispute.[123] Since the burden is on the defendant to prove fair use, instead of infringement, some copyright owners frequently make claims of infringement even in circumstances where the fair use defence would likely succeed in the hope that the user will refrain from the use rather than spending resources on his defence. Since in some cases paying royalty fees may be much less expensive than having a potential copyright suit threaten the publication of a completed work in which a

121 Although we must remember that the list of elements is not exhaustive.

122 David Nimmer, " 'Fairest of them all' And other fairy tales of fair use," *Law & Contemporary Problems,* vol. 66 No. 263, (Winter/Spring 2003). 263–287, at 282 and 287.

123 See *Campbell v. Acuff-Rose Music, Inc., supra*. This was reaffirmed by a number of decisions, such as *American Geophysical Union v. Texaco Inc.,* 60 F.3d 913, 918 (2d Cir. 1994), para. 23. On the bearer of burden of proof in particular, see *Columbia Pictures Inc. v. Miramax Films Corp.,* 11 F. Supp.2d 1179, 1187 (C.D. Cal. 1998). It would seem that the trend is changing especially in the digital environment. In a recent case of *Lenz v. Universal Music Corp. et al,* 572 F.Supp.2d 1150 (N.D. Cal. 2008), the Court stated that "[i]n order for a copyright owner to proceed under the DMCA with "a good faith belief that use of the material in the manner complained of is not authorized by the copyright owner, its agent, or the law," the owner must evaluate whether the material makes fair use of the copyright., *ibid,* III (A). This case cannot be of general application. First, Section 512(c)(3)(A)(v) of the U.S. Copyright Code, as amended by the Digital Millennium Copyright Act (DMCA), which was quoted by the Court, only applies to material on online environment and not printed material. Section 512 is entitled "Limitation on liability related to material on online". Secondly, this is so far the only case interpreting section 512 of the DMCA. It is too soon to say that it represents judicial practice of the US.

publisher has invested significant resources, many authors seek a licence even for uses copyright law ostensibly permits without liability.[124] In the case of publishers, there might be the option of publishing on time or later. But for someone in a developing country who needs access to copyrighted material for educational purposes, not using a work for fear of a lawsuit is not an option, but a deprivation; and is not fair.

If developing countries could afford the cost of litigation, there existed legal certainty, and they only had to determine the content of fair use, would it serve to allow access to educational material? Apart from the fact that fair use provisions are highly difficult to understand,[125] the major shortcoming is that the amount legally allowed under the doctrine cannot serve the access needs of developing countries.[126] As one author has stated;

> [t]he amount of material that can be used legally (that is, using the fair use exemptions) from any given copyrighted book or article is pitifully small. A person trying to learn to read on a literacy program in the South cannot learn to read if she or he can only have access to the odd sentence or a couple of paragraphs; this is the amount which typically is allowed at no charge under a fair use/fair dealing standard. Rather, they need access at no charge to complete books, many books, and other materials; fair dealing/fair use approaches forbid this.[127]

Admittedly, the amount of a work copied is not the sole determinant of whether a use is fair or not. However, in the case of a technical or mathematics textbook, the substantiality of the work copied does not need to be measured in terms of quantity but quality. Copying of formula or method from a book is copying the 'heart 'of the book according to *Harper & Row,* which makes the use unfair. Under such circumstances, developing country universities which depend heavily on imported technical or scientific books cannot rely on the defence of fair use.

As illustrated in chapter 2, developing countries need to have bulk access—to be able to copy large or whole portions of a textbook or periodical. As regards the character of the copying, whether it is transformative or not, one might presume that this would not be a problem for developing countries. After all, according to case law, multiple copying for

---

124 Example of a user of copyrighted material who had to pay to continue using the copyrighted work is Google for its book search project. A lawsuit was brought by authors and publishers, claiming that Google had violated their copyrights and those of other Right holders of Books and Inserts, by scanning their Books, creating an electronic database and displaying short excerpts without the permission of the copyright holders. (See *The Authors Guild, Inc., et al v. Google Inc.*, case no. 05 CV 8136 (S.D.N.Y), filed on September 20, 2005.) Google denied the claims, yet went ahead to make a settlement with the publishers and authors. See information on settlement on http://books.google.com/booksrightsholders/

125 See for example, the speech of Professor Julien Hoffman, Commonwealth of Learning, Department of Commercial Law, University of Cape Town, Cape Town, South Africa, at the Information Meeting on Educational Content and Copyright in the Digital Age, World Intellectual Property Organization, Geneva, Switzerland, 21 November 2005 http://www.eff.org/deeplinks/archives/004193.php#004193. He highlighted the fact that the technical terms like 'reasonable portion' have to be interpreted by the courts but the university cannot afford the cost of litigation.

126 *Basic Books, Inc. v. Kinko's Graphics Corporation, supra*, and *Worldwide Church of God v. Philadelphia Church of God, Inc, supra.*

127 Story *et al,* the Copy/South Dossier, *supra,* p. 139. We address the question of allowed quantities under fair dealing below.

classroom distribution, even if not transformative in nature, is fair use.[128] This is in line with section 107 of the US Copyright Act, which allows for fair use for teaching (including multiple copying for classroom use). However, this does not mean copying of whole volumes or textbooks. It refers to making many copies of a few pages from a textbook.[129] In the case of developing countries, it is important to differentiate between bulk access and making multiple copies of an article from a periodical, a chapter or a few pages of a book for classroom use. The provision on fair use and the case law cover the latter situation, which, although laudable, does not serve to allow access to copyrighted works by developing countries in need of bulk access.

Previously, we stated that there is inherent uncertainty in relying on the fair use doctrine, since each case must be decided based on its own facts. However, a noticeable trend does exist: the economic interests of the author or right holder weigh more heavily than social interests in the determination of fair use. Since developing countries need bulk access to protected works, it is difficult to imagine a situation where bulk copying of a textbook, for example, would not affect a very important element of fair use—the market of the original work. Mass copying or bulk access means that fewer people will buy the original book.[130] This inevitably affects the market of that book, and thus causes financial harm to the copyright holder. In such a case, the bulk copying constitutes not only unfair use but also causes unreasonable prejudice to the legitimate interests of the copyright holder.[131]

The debate on limitations and exceptions and in particular the narrower question of 'fairness' for public access in developing countries plays out with respect to economically deprived contexts and societies looking to education as a remedy to long-term development challenges. An overview of the education rank indices in Africa reveals that even the most developed countries on the continent rank among the least developed in the world record.[132] This underscores that developing countries need special copyright exceptions

---

128 *Princeton University Press v. Michigan Document Service, supra*, para. V(A).

129 It is true that the courts do not always indicate as how much copying is too much (see Fisher III, "Reconstructing the Fair Use Doctrine,", *supra*, p 1675). However, in the case of textbooks, precisely books on science or technology, it is difficult to imagine how multiple copying of whole textbook will not harm the market for such books. The photocopied versions and the original copyrighted textbooks serve the same purpose so there will be market substitution.

130 It is true that developing countries can not afford the cost of text book. So the logic is that if the book is so expensive that no one can afford it, then there will be no sales lost since there was no market for it in the first place. Unfortunately, because of income inequality there is at least one percent of the population in question that can afford the book. For example in Indonesia and Thailand, foreign or imported books sell in certain urban centres where the population is relatively better off than in semi urban or rural centres. (See Consumers international project of access to knowledge, *supra*.) The publishers know this well, otherwise they would not take the trouble to export books to developing countries if not even one person can buy them.

131 According to the WTO Panel, prejudice to the legitimate interests of the right holders reaches an unreasonable level if an exception or limitation causes or has the potential to cause an unreasonable loss of income of income to the copyright owner. See *United States – Section 110(5) of the US Copyright Act, supra*, para. 6.249. See *infra*, section 4.4.3.

132 According to the UNDP education ranking of 177 countries, South Africa ranks 121, Botswana 124, Namibia 125, Lesotho 138 and Swaziland 141. See UNDP, *Human Development Report*

that will respond to their special economic needs. Photocopying is a major access mechanism to protected works in developing countries. In their report, authors Rens, Prabhala and Kawooya note contributory factors other than copyright which either hinder or enhance access to knowledge for educational purposes. Contributory factors which enhance access to knowledge include informal activities involving reproduction for educational purposes mainly through petty photocopying enterprises in and around educational institutions.[133] Let us illustrate using the example of one African institution of higher learning, Makerere University, which is Uganda's leading public university. Photocopying businesses complement the efforts of higher education in that they serve as a mechanism for increasing access to learning materials.[134] In the case of Makerere University, the university's faculties cannot afford to use published scholarly materials because of either high cost or lack of availability. Therefore, the tendency is to make publications available through photocopying.[135] A total of 76 photocopying machines (mostly petty photocopying enterprises) produce an average of 43,400 copies every day.[136] An interpretation of fair use according to the U.S. standard would rule this to be an infringement of copyright.[137] Yet, the reality is that most students and faculty cannot afford to buy their own educational materials. Likewise, the under-funded libraries cannot afford to stock needed textbooks.[138] Does this mean that the U.S. fair use doctrine is completely irrelevant for access to copyrighted material in developing countries? We argue that this is not the case. We hold that there is a case for fair use in developing countries. We shall briefly discuss this question below, but it will be further developed after the discussion of fair dealing.

6.3.5.1. A Case for Fair Use in Developing Countries

In chapter four, we concluded that since the three-step test emphasizes the economic interests of the copyright holder, developing countries which are financially disadvantaged cannot benefit from it as an exception. We have demonstrated that the judicial application of fair use places it at the same level as the three-step test. This means it does

2007/2008: Fighting climate change: Human solidarity in a divided world, (New York: Palgrave Macmillan, 2007). 269–272. Note that South Africa and Namibia are among the most developed countries in Africa.

133 Rens *et al* IP, Education and Access to Knowledge in Southern Africa, *supra*. Contributory factors to access include; excessive pricing, unavailability of materials and unsuitability of contents, government resource constraints. *Ibid,* pp. 10–20.

134 For various accounts of the importance of photocopying for access to learning materials in Africa, see Chris, Armstrong, *et al* (eds.). *Access to Knowledge in Africa, supra.*

135 Rens *et al, supra,* section 3.

136 *Ibid.* Note that these figures were based on an informal scientific survey of photocopying at Makerere University.

137 See for example *Basic Books, Inc. v. Kinko's, supra,* para. IA (3). Copying of an entire chapter in a book was found to be unfair use.

138 Uganda is certainly not a unique example among developing countries in having under-funded libraries. See for example the detailed account of a Colombian academic who tries hard to do research with great difficulty due to under-funded university library in Bogotá. See the excellent narrative in Story *et al* the Copy/South Dossier, *supra,* p. 115; Chris, Armstrong, *et al* (eds.). *Access to Knowledge in Africa, supra.*

not serve to facilitate access to copyrighted educational works in developing countries. However, there is still reason to include a fair use provision in the national legislation of developing countries. This is because an open-ended provision leaves it to the courts of developing countries to interpret those provisions according to their economic circumstances and policy objectives. Leaving the courts to decide the scope of fairness certainly creates uncertainty as the outcome cannot be predicted. However, "unpredictability [of the outcome of the judicial process] is inherent in the judicial process".[139] The U.S. judicial interpretation of section 107 of the Copyright Act does not have to be copied by developing country courts. Developing countries should include a fairness provision in their legislation but interpret it in a broad manner, the way Canadian courts have done in certain cases. This leads us to a discussion on fair dealing in Canada.

6.4. Fair Dealing for the Purpose of Research or Private Study: The Case of Canada

Providing exceptions for research or private study is one way of allowing access to educational materials. Article 29 of the Canadian Copyright Act provides for fair dealing for the purpose of research or private study.[140] Unlike standard provisions such as the fair practice of the Berne Convention,[141] there is no requirement to acknowledge the source or any other condition attached. However, like the Berne Convention, the Statute does not provide any guidelines as to how to determine fair dealing—for example, the amount of reproduction that can be allowed under the provision. However, a recent unanimous decision of the Supreme Court of Canada, in *CCH Canadian Ltd v. Law Society of Upper Canada*[142] (hereafter referred to as *CCH Canadian*), represents a landmark in the development of Canadian Copyright law as it relates to exceptions. Throughout the decision, the Supreme Court settled several issues, ranging from the standard of originality to the scope of "fair dealing" and its relationship to fair use. The Court outlined elements to be considered when determining fair dealing. In addition, and more important for our discussion, the Court defined exceptions in very broad terms, including referring to fair dealing as a "user right", which if taken literally would have important legal implications for access to copyrighted works. We shall now discuss this case in some detail.

The relevant facts of the case are that the appellant, the Law Society of Upper Canada, maintains and operates the Great Library at Osgoode Hall in Toronto, a reference and research library. The Great Library provides, upon request, photocopy services for Law Society members, the judiciary and other authorized researchers. Under this "custom photocopy service", legal materials are reproduced by the Great Library staff and delivered in person, by mail or by facsimile transmission to the requesters. The Law Society also maintains self-service photocopiers in the Great Library for use by its patrons.

In 1993, the publisher, CCH Canadian Ltd (respondent) instituted an action for infringement against the Law Society before the Federal Court, Trial Division, seeking, *inter alia*,

139 Knapp, *supra*, p. 357.
140 Canadian Copyright Act, 1985, R.S., c. C–30, s. 1, section 29.
141 The Berne Convention, article 10.
142 *CCH Canadian Ltd v. Law Society of Upper Canada*, 2004 SCC 13.

a declaration that the Law Society had infringed upon copyright when the Great Library reproduced a copy of each of CCH Canadian's works. The respondent also sought a permanent injunction prohibiting the Law Society from reproducing these works as well as any other works they published. The Law Society denied liability and counterclaimed for a declaration that copyright is not infringed when a single copy of a reported decision, case summary, statute, regulation or a limited selection of text from a treatise is made by the Great Library staff, or one of its patrons on a self-service copier, for the purpose of research.

One of the issues before the Court was whether the photocopies made by the Law Society and sent to lawyers or the copies made directly by patrons of the Great Library infringe upon the reproduction right. If there was found to be *prima facie* infringement, then a subsequent question was whether the "fair dealing" exception for the purpose of research or private study under Section 29 of the Copyright Act applied in this case. On 4 March 2004, the Supreme Court of Canada found in favour of the publishers on the issue of infringement, but ruled in the same breath that all the copies made were permitted under section 29 of the Copyright Act. We shall analyse certain aspects of the case below.

6.4.1. *The Court Lists Factors for Determining Fair Dealing: Towards International Harmonization of the Fairness Principle*

The court listed and analysed the factors determining whether use of a work is fair dealing. It relied on a range of cases from Canada and the UK as well as taking examples from the U.S. doctrine of "fair use."[143] In the UK decision in *Hubbard v. Vosper,* the Court of Appeal had stated:

> It is impossible to define what is fair dealing. It must be a question of degree. You must consider first the number and extent of the quotations and extracts. Are they altogether too many and too long to be fair? Then you must consider the use made of them. If they are used as a basis for comment, criticism or review, that may be a fair dealing. If they are used to convey the same information as the author, for a rival purpose, that may be unfair. Next, you must consider the proportions. To take long extracts and attach short comments may be unfair. But, short extracts and long comments may be fair. Other considerations may come to mind also. But, after all is said and done, *it must be a matter of impression.* As with fair comment in the law of libel, so with fair dealing in the law of copyright. The tribunal of fact must decide.[144]

Persuaded by that decision and the U.S. doctrine on fair use, the Court outlined the factors to be considered in determining whether dealing is fair or not. These were: (1) the purpose of the dealing; (2) the character of the dealing; (3) the amount of the dealing; (4) alternatives to the dealing; (5) the nature of the work; and (6) the effect of the dealing on the work.[145] According to the Court, this list of factors provides a useful analytical framework

---

143 *CCH Canadian Ltd v. Law Society of Upper Canada,* 2004 SCC 13, paras. 53–60.

144 *Hubbard v. Vosper,* [1972] 1 All E.R. 1023 (C.A.), at p. 1027 (emphasis added). This case only outlines possible considerations, but the final decision will depend on the circumstances of each case.

145 *CCH Canadian Ltd v. Law Society of Upper Canada,* 2004 SCC 13, para. 53, confirming the list of the Federal Court of Appeal in *CCH Canadian Ltd v. Law Society of Upper Canada,* 2002 FCA 187, para. 150.

to govern determinations of fairness in future cases.[146] Section 29 of the Canadian copyright Act, unlike the U.S. section 107 on fair use, does not provide a checklist for determining fair dealing. However, in the *CCH Canadian* case, the Court, for the first time, elaborates such a list. This is an innovation on the part of the Court. However, relying on the UK and the U.S. to determine fair dealing is indicative of a move towards harmonization of the 'fairness' principle in international law.[147]

There are important differences between the fair use and fair dealing lists. First, while in the case of fair use all four factors listed in the statute must be tested, this is not the case with the Canadian list, although the number of elements to be proved is not indicated. In this case, it means that there is more certainty in relying on fair use than fair dealing. Second, while in the case of fair use the effect of the use of the work on the market for the copyrighted work is the most important factor in determining fair use,[148] this is not the case for fair dealing. The court in *CCH Canadian* stated that "Although the effect of the dealing on the market of the copyright owner is an important factor, it is neither the only factor nor the most important factor that a court must consider in deciding if the dealing is fair."[149] This means that the economic interest of the author is not the decisive element in determining fair dealing. Therefore, Canadian courts have more flexibility when determining fair use than U.S. courts.[150]

There are risks in relying on the U.S. method of determining fair use to decide fair dealing, the least of these being legal uncertainty. What is fair dealing will depend largely on the context and circumstances of each case. Indeed, the Supreme Court stated that, in some contexts, there may be factors other than those listed that may help a court decide whether the dealing was fair.[151] According to the Supreme Court, the purpose of the fair dealing exception is to ensure that users are not unduly restricted in their ability to use and disseminate copyrighted works.[152] Ironically, this restriction on use cannot be removed by general statements that have to be clarified in a court. Indeed, in the case of Canada, one would hope that after the CCH case there would be certainty or some kind of assurance, as the case seems to declare rights, which in essence should give security to users. However, after the decision, educators were not certain of the limits of copying for educational use. They sought additional assurance through an amendment of the Copyright Act "to create a safe harbour for all educational uses of publicly available

146 *CCH Canadian Ltd v. Law Society of Upper Canada*, 2004 SCC 13 para. 52 and 53 (emphasis added).

147 Although some scholars had made an analogy between the fair dealing provision of Canada and that of the UK and the U.S. fair use, there had not been a formal judicial listing of the factors that determine fair dealing. This, in my view, is a formal judicial acknowledgement of the influence of UK and US law on Canadian law. On the influence of UK jurisprudence on Canada see Victor Nabhan, "La photocopie et le droit d'auteur au Canada," *Revue Internationale du droit d'auteur*, vol. 99 (1979). 3–27, at.11.

148 *Harper & Row, Publishers, Inc. v. Nation Enterprises, supra*, quoting *Sony Corp. v. Universal City Studios, supra*, p. 451.

149 *CCH Canadian Ltd v. Law Society of Upper Canada*, 2004 SCC 13 para 59, quoting *Pro Sieben Media AG v. Carlton UK Television Ltd.*, [1999] F.S.R. 610 (C.A.), per Robert Walker L.J.

150 See also in the same line, Harris, *supra*, p. 7.

151 *CCH Canadian Ltd v. Law Society of Upper Canada*, 2004 SCC 13 para 60.

152 *Ibid*, para. 63.

Internet material".[153] Otherwise, "educational institutions and their students, teachers, and staff will remain in a most uncomfortable position – contorted in a legal limbo – awaiting some future court ruling to clarify more precisely the notion of "fair dealing."[154]

6.4.2. *The Court Restates the Purpose of Copyright: Towards a Balance between Interests of Copyright Owners and Users*

Canadian legislation does not define the purpose of copyright. Traditionally, Canadian courts considered the purpose of copyright as solely to protect the interests of copyright holders. For example, in a 1990 decision in the case of *Bishop v. Stevens*, the Court stated that the Copyright Act was passed with one single objective—to benefit authors of all kinds.[155]

Seven years later, in the case of *Compagnie Générale des Etablissements Michelin-Michelin & Cie v. National Automobile, Aerospace, Transportation and General Workers Union of Canada (CAW-Canada) et al*,[156] the Federal Court of Canada still considered the purpose of copyright to be the protection of authors. In brief, during their 1994 campaign to unionize the plaintiff's Canadian affiliate's plans in Nova Scotia, the defendants distributed a leaflet depicting Michelin's symbol, the "Michelin Tire Man", also known as "Bibendum". In the CAW's leaflet, a smiling, large Bibendum figure stood cross-armed, one foot raised over the head of a worker, whose companion warned him thus: "Bob, you better move before he squashes you!" Bob was depicted replying: "Naw, I'm going to wait and see what happens". The leaflet also bore the logo of CAW-Canada and a captain inviting workers to sign up with the union. Michelin took action alleging, inter alia, copyright infringement. At the outset, the defendants admitted the subsistence of copyright in Michelin's several Bibendum design, but pleaded that they had not substantially reproduced the copyright works. However, should they be found to have substantially reproduced Bibendum, the defendants argued that the design on their leaflet constituted a parody, i.e. a form of criticism of the work.

Justice Teitelbaum found that the defendant's parody of a corporate logo could not be included under the category of "criticism" within the meaning of section 29 of the Copyright Act.[157] This conclusion is not surprising, the court having previously defined

---

153 Council of Ministers of Education, Canada, "Educational use of the internet: "fair dealing" just may not be enough," *Copyright Bulletin 3*, March 14, 2008, available at http://www.cmec.ca/copyright/bulletins2008/bulletin-03.en.pdf.

154 *Ibid.* We realize that the Council of Ministers is concerned with access to works of the internet. However, the uncertainty relates to the amount of text that can be copied, something that is not only specific to works on internet. Reference was specifically made to the Supreme Court's statement that in some circumstances, using whole work may be fair dealing while in other circumstances it may not be fair dealing, and that making multiple copies and distributing them widely tends to be unfair.

155 *Bishop v. Stevens*, [1990] 2 S.C.R. 467, at 478–479, cited in Craig, *supra*, p. 452.

156 *Compagnie Générale des Etablissements Michelin-Michelin & Cie v. National Automobile, Aerospace, Transportation and General Workers Union of Canada (CAW-Canada) et al*, 1997, 71 C.P.R (3d) 348.

157 *Ibid*, para 381. Section 29 of the Canadian Copyright Act provides for fair dealing for the purpose of criticism, but "criticism" is not defined anywhere in the Act. This is a flexibility in itself,

the objective of copyright law as the protection of authors and ensuring that they are compensated for their creative energies and works.[158]

The author centred view of the Copyright Act visibly influenced the way the courts interpreted the Copyright Act in general and exceptions in particular. Exceptions like fair dealing tended to be interpreted in favour of the copyright owners. This approach is similar to that of continental Europe, which takes a naturalist approach to copyright. The naturalists view the purpose of copyright as protecting the author's interests.[159] Under this approach, limitations and exceptions are very strictly drafted by legislators and interpreted by courts.[160] For example, in France the free use of copyrighted material by educational institutions is limited to making analysis and short quotations which are justified by the educational character of the work in which they are incorporated. Multiple copying is only allowed under statutory licensing.[161] Under a system of mandatory collective administration of the reprographic right, schools and other educational institutions can reproduce works for classroom use upon equitable remuneration of the copyright owner. In Germany and the Netherlands, specific limitations allow parts of works or short works to be reproduced and assembled in anthologies or to be used in illustrations for the purpose of teaching. As in the case of France, multiple copying [not bulk copying] for classroom use is allowed under the statutory license, subject to equitable remuneration to the right holder through a reprographic regime.[162]

However, in recent years a shift has taken place, as the highest court of Canada has embraced the view that copyright law is about balancing competing interests of copyright owners on the one hand and those of users of copyrighted works on the other. This change in attitude from merely protecting the rights of copyright owners to balancing the interests of owners and users, was first manifest in the case of *Théberge v. Galerie d'Art du Petit Champlain Inc.*[163] In the case, the Supreme Court of Canada stated:

> The Copyright Act is usually presented as a balance between promoting the public interest in the encouragement and dissemination of works of the arts and intellect and obtaining a just reward for the creator (or, more accurately, to prevent someone other than the creator from appropriating whatever benefits may be generated). [...] The proper balance among these and other public policy objectives lies not only in recognizing the creator's rights but in giving due weight to their limited nature.[164]

---

which allows inclusion of different types of criticism like parody. However, if a court views the purpose of copyright in general or the Copyright Act in particular as to benefit the copyright owners, it will have a narrow view of the scope of fair dealing.

158 *Ibid,* para 115.

159 For a summary on the purpose of copyright in general, see Guibault, *supra,* pp. 7–15;

160 We illustrate court interpretation of limitations below when discussing 'user rights', (section 6.4.4.).

161 Law on the Intellectual Property Code (Legislative Part), as amended as last amended by Law No. 97-283 of March 27, 1997, article L 122-5, and article L 321-1 to article L 321-12, and Guibault, *supra,* p.70.

162 see Germany, Law on Copyright and Neighbouring Rights (Copyright Law) of September 9, 1965, as last amended by the Law of May 8, 1998, article 46 and 47 and the Dutch Copyright Act, 1912, as last amended by the Law of October 27, 1972, article 16.

163 *Théberge v. Galerie d'Art du Petit Champlain Inc.*, 2002 SCC 34.

164 *Théberge v. Galerie d'Art du Petit Champlain Inc., ibid,* paras 30–31.

Canada's legislation, unlike that of its neighbour the U.S., does not define the purpose of copyright.[165] However, in the case of *Théberge*, the Supreme Court of Canada outlined the purpose of copyright as to promote the public interest in the encouragement and dissemination of work of the arts and intellect and obtaining a just reward for the creator. This marks a visible move from the naturalist approach of continental Europe, where the purpose of copyright is viewed as to reward the creator, to a utilitarian approach, common to the U.S. The utilitarian approach views copyright as serving a public interest.[166] In the case of the U.S. the public interest in copyright is "to promote the progress of science and useful arts by securing for limited times to authors and inventors the exclusive right to their respective writings and discoveries."[167]

In the case of Canada, the new purpose of copyright as outlined in *Théberge*, is "promoting the public interest in the encouragement and dissemination of works of the arts."[168] This purpose has been emphasized in subsequent cases, like *CCH Canadian,*[169] *Society of Composers, Authors and Music Publishers of Canada v. Canadian Association of Internet Providers* (*SOCAN*)[170] and *Euro Excellency v. Kraft Canada Inc.*[171] The *SOCAN* case is particularly important, as it not only confirms this purposive interpretation of the Copyright Act by *Théberge*, but also explains that the purpose of exceptions such as temporary copying is to benefit the public good. Thus, "caching"[172] is dictated by the need to deliver faster and more economic service, and should not, when undertaken only for such technical reasons, attract copyright liability."[173] While "caching" is certainly an instance of substantial reproduction, it is a technical process only; as such, it does not consist of an attempt to appropriate the legitimate economic interests of the copyright holder, and therefore does not constitute infringement.[174]

---

165 According to the U.S. Constitution, the goal of copyright is to promote the progress of science and useful arts by securing for limited times to authors and inventors the exclusive right to their respective writings and discoveries. See United States Constitution, article 1, Section 8.

166 For more on the utilitarian approach to copyright, see Robert L. Ostergard, Jr., "Intellectual property: a universal human right?" *Human rights quarterly,* vol. 21, (1999). 156–178. He criticises this approach for being uncertain of the outcome (p. 163), but at least agrees that IP should not only emphasize the exclusive rights of producers but must also take care of the interests of consumers and national welfare. *Ibid,* at 157.

167 United States Constitution, article 1, Section 8.

168 *Théberge v. Galerie d'Art du Petit Champlain Inc., supra,* para 30.

169 *CCH Canadian Ltd v. Law Society of Upper Canada, supra,* 2004 SCC 13, para. 10, citing *Théberge,* and emphasizing that courts should strive to maintain an appropriate balance between the two goals.

170 *Society of Composers, Authors and Music Publishers of Canada v. Canadian Association of Internet Providers,* 2004 SCC 45, para. 132, (after referred to as *SOCAN*). The Supreme Court of Canada refers to copyright law as a balance between the interests of creators and users of works.

171 *Euro-Excellence Inc. v. Kraft Canada Inc.,* 2007 SCC 37, para. 76, (citing Théberge and CCH Canadian) para 81.

172 "Caching" is the storage of Web files for later re-use at a point more quickly accessed by the end user.

173 *SOCAN,* supra, para. 116, also in agreement, see Euro-Excellence Inc. v. Kraft Canada Inc., *supra,* para. 81.

174 *SOCAN,* para. 116, and *Euro-Excellence,* para. 81.

The *CCH Canadian* case is of particular interest for access to education in developing countries since it deals with fair dealing for research and private use, an exception that is directly relevant to access to printed educational material—the focus of our discussion. As mentioned above, Canadian legislation does not state the purpose of copyright. At the same time, there exists a lack of consensus among publicists as to the purpose of copyright in Canada.[175] Only courts have stated the purpose of copyright, through what they perceived to be an interpretation of the Copyright Act. The Court's statement on the purpose of copyright is timely in clarifying the legal position and breaking new ground in Canadian copyright law.

6.4.3. *CCH Canadian and the Transformation of Exceptions: Court Defines Exceptions in Very Broad Terms*

To emphasise and demonstrate its "copyright as a balance" approach stated in *Théberge*, the Supreme Court of Canada, in *CCH Canadian*, was more emphatic in stating the purpose of exceptions in general and "fair dealing" in particular. The true turning point in moving away from the traditionally narrow interpretation of exceptions came when the Federal Court of Appeal (FCA) rejected such an interpretation, arguing that it defeated the purpose of balance between copyright owners and public interests. The FCA stated:

> The Trial Judge erred in law when he stated that exceptions to infringement must be "strictly construed." There is no basis in law or in policy for such an approach. An overly restrictive interpretation of the exemptions contained in the Act would be inconsistent with the mandate of copyright law to harmonize owner's rights with legitimate public interests.[176]

The Supreme Court emphasized the need for a balanced reading of the phrase "fair dealing" for the benefit of owners and users of copyrighted works. It is important to recall that the prior practice was to define author's rights in broad terms but not exceptions or limitations. To start with, the Court provided a list of open-ended factors that could be used to guide a flexible and contextual fair dealing analysis,[177] as opposed to the closed list provided under section 29 of the Copyright Act.[178] In other words, the Court has gone a step further and defined 'balance' in a more abstract, expansive manner allowing it to generously interpret "fair dealing".[179]

---

175 On the purpose of copyright in Canada see Teresa Scassa, "Interests in the balance," in Michael Geist, ed. *In the public interest: the future of Canadian copyright law,* (Toronto: Irwin Law, 2005). 41–65, pp. 42 46. The author demonstrates the absence of a definition of the purpose of copyright in Canadian legislation and the lack of consensus by scholars on the possible purpose before 2004.

176 *CCH Canadian Ltd v. Law Society of Upper Canada*, 2002 FCA 187, para. 126.

177 *Ibid,* para. 150 and *CCH Canadian Ltd v. Law Society of Upper Canada,* 2004 SCC 13, para. 53.

178 Section 29 of the Canadian Copyright Act provides for fair dealing for the purpose of research or private study, criticism or review and news reporting. So the only test that determines fair dealing is its purpose; whether it falls within the purposes outlined by the Act. An open-ended list of factors to consider expands the chances of finding that the dealing with a work is fair.

179 The Court refers to balance in an abstract manner in that it does not refer to balance as provided by the Copyright Act. If it did then it would be restricted to protecting interests of copyright holders and owners as reflected in the Statute. This would not cater for users, who are not provided for in the statute except for the limited and restricted exceptions. This abstract

Prior to reviewing the scope of fair dealing under the Canadian Copyright Act, the Supreme Court clarified some general considerations related to exceptions to copyright infringement. Under the exception of "fair dealing", a defendant is normally required to prove that his or her dealing with a work has been fair. Yet, according to the Supreme Court of Canada, "fair dealing" is not simply a defence, but forms an integral part of the copyright Act. The Court stated:

> Procedurally, the defendant is required to prove that his or her dealing with a work has been fair; however, the fair dealing exception is perhaps more properly understood as an integral part of the *Copyright Act* than simply a defence. The fair dealing exception, like other exceptions in the *Copyright Act*, is a *user's right*. In order to maintain the proper balance between the rights of a copyright owner and users' interests, it must not be interpreted restrictively. [...] User rights are not just loopholes. Both owner rights and user rights should therefore be given the fair and balanced reading that befits remedial legislation."[180]

To demonstrate the 'balanced reading', the Court defined "research" in broad terms. It stated that "research" must be given a *large and liberal* interpretation, in order to ensure that users' rights are not unduly constrained, and it is not limited to a non-commercial or private context.[181] For example, lawyers carrying out the business of law for profit are conducting research within the meaning of section 29.[182] The Court thus concluded that the Law Society's dealings with the publishers' works through the Society's custom copying service were research-based and fair.

It may appear somewhat worrisome that when defining the 'purpose of the dealing' the Court said research done for commercial purposes may not be as fair as research done for charitable purposes.[183] Yet, lawyers doing research for business purposes are covered by fair dealing. What would amount to commercial use? Isn't law business not commercial in nature? It would appear that the Court did not consider the person doing research as an end, but rather looked at the motive for the research. Indeed, the court noted that "[r]esearch for the purpose of advising clients, giving opinions, arguing cases, preparing briefs and factums is nonetheless research."[184] Simply put, lawyers facilitate the legal system. Likewise, lawyers are professional people and not trading companies. Lawyers are not properly so-called commercial enterprises. As one author has stated, "lawyers are professional people and not trading companies, even if they work for profit".[185] In other words, the definition of 'research' by the Court has to be understood within the particular context of the end-use. The Court's finding that the lawyers' activities were research-based

---

concept of balance is reflected in the way the Court creates an open-ended list of factors for determining fair dealing, and its broad definition of fair dealing to amount to a 'user right'. This 'abstract' balance permits the court not to read the Copyright Act to the letter, but to interpret it according to the perceived purpose of copyright.

180 *CCH Canadian Ltd v. Law Society of Upper Canada*, 2004 SCC 13, para. 48 (emphasis added).

181 *Ibid*, para. 51 (emphasis added).

182 *Ibid*, para. 51.

183 *Ibid*, para. 54.

184 *Ibid*,, para. 51, in agreement with the Court of Appeal.

185 Daniel Gervais, "Le Droit d'auteur au Canada: le point après CCH," *Revue Internationale du droit d'auteur*, vol. 203 (2005). 3–61, p.45 (hereafter, Gervais, Le droit d'auteur).

is best explained by the fact that the copying was a necessary part of the research.[186] Indeed, the Court had cautioned that the allowable purposes should not be given a restrictive interpretation as this could result in undue restriction of users' rights.[187] Thus, "research and private study", for example, can and should be interpreted in a way that allows the achievement of the purpose of research. As an example, in order to facilitate research, it may be necessary to interpret another factor such as, the amount of the dealing, less restrictively. In fact, the Court explained that "for the purpose of research or private study, it may be essential to copy an entire academic article or an entire judicial decision. However, if a work of literature is copied for the purpose of criticism, it will not likely be fair to include a full copy of the work in the critique."[188] In a later decision, the Supreme Court explained that 'caching' is dictated by the need to deliver a faster and more economic service. As a result, caching is not an infringement of copyright, even if it is a form of substantial reproduction.[189]

It is the present author's opinion that the checklist of factors to be considered when determining fair dealing is subject to the "purposeful" interpretation of the Act. If lawyers' research benefits a public interest like facilitating the legal system then their dealing with the work is fair, regardless of the kind of research, including for profit. If copying by way of caching facilitates faster and more cost-effective delivery of information, then it is fair dealing even if substantial reproduction is involved.

The expansive definition of exceptions in general and "fair dealing" in particular represents an important development in Canadian copyright law. As mentioned above, the Canadian courts had been very conservative in interpreting exceptions to protected works, considering them as limited defences to copyright infringement rather than as entitlements in their own right.[190] The broader definition of an exception to accommodate the motive and purpose of its use is a praiseworthy development and can be considered a possible example for developing countries. An expansive definition of exceptions to copyrighted works allows policy makers and practitioners like teachers and educational institutions, whose primary function is to provide information for purposes of research or education, greater protection from liability for copyright infringement.

6.4.4. *A Rights Approach to Exceptions: Exceptions and User Rights*

The Court in *CCH Canadian* referred to exceptions in general and fair dealing in particular as 'user rights'. The practice of considering exceptions as rights is not new in international intellectual property law. For example, in the case of patents, the WTO Ministerial

---

186 *CCH Canadian Ltd v. Law Society of Upper Canada*, 2004 SCC 13, paras 63 and 73.

187 *CCH Canadian Ltd v. Law Society of Upper Canada*, 2004 SCC 13, para. 54.

188 *Ibid*, para 56, see also Abraham Drassinower, "Taking User Rights Seriously," in Michael Geist, ed., *In the Public Interest: supra*, 462–479, at 469.

189 *SOCAN, supra*, para. 116, also cited with approval in *Euro-Excellence Inc. v. Kraft Canada Inc., supra*, para. 81.

190 See discussion above in 6.4.4 and Tawfik, *supra*, pp. 2 and 5; Craig, *supra*, p. 438 and Daniel J. Gervais, "The purpose of copyright law in Canada," *University of Ottawa Law & Technology Journal (uoltj)*, vol. 2 no.2, (2005). 315–356, p. 317 (hereinafter referred to as Gervais, the purpose of copyright law in Canada).

Conference at Doha understood article 31 of the TRIPS Agreement, which allows for compulsory licensing, as granting rights to do so. Thus, according to the Doha Declaration on the TRIPS Agreement and Public Health, "Each Member has the right to grant compulsory licences" and "Each Member has the right to determine what constitutes national emergency or other circumstances of extreme urgency".[191] Indeed, the Declaration has been said to reiterate rights.[192]

However, it was not until the Decision of the Supreme Court of Canada in *CCH Canadian* that the notion of 'rights' in relation to copyright limitations and exceptions attracted particular attention.[193] The Supreme Court in the case of *CCH Canadian* referred to fair dealing as a user right three times.[194] In yet another decision on 26 July 2007, in the case of *Euro-Excellency Inc. v. Kraft Canada Inc,* case the Supreme Court of Canada again referred to fair dealing as a 'user right'. It thus stated that, once copyright is granted for a given work, the protection that it provides must not be extended beyond its natural limits and must take proper account of *user rights* such as the right to *deal fairly* with a copyrighted work.[195] There is, therefore, no doubt that the Court deliberately refers to 'user rights'.

However, is fair dealing for research or study a right for the user? Or, to pose a more general question, are exceptions 'user rights'? In continental Europe, the situation is clear: exceptions are not user's rights. At best, they represent immunities. Let me illustrate with reference to private copying, the most common exception available.

Article 6(4) of the EC Copyright Directive[196] provides that, in the absence of voluntary measures taken by right holders, Member states should take appropriate measures to ensure that right holders make available to the beneficiary of an exception or limitation provided for in national law the means of benefitting from that exception. The provision is compulsory for exceptions such as, illustrations in teaching or scientific research and reproduction by publicly accessible libraries, educational establishments, museums or archives but is optional for private copying.

---

191 Declaration on the TRIPS Agreement and Public Health, adopted on 14 November at the 4th WTO Ministerial Conference, Doha, 9–14 November 2001, document no. WT/MIN(01)/DEC/2, dated 20 November 2001. (available at http://www.wto.org/english/thewto_e/minist_e/min01_e/mindecl_trips_e.pdf), para. 5(a) and (b).

192 Phillip McCalmam, The Doha Declaration and Development: Prospects for intellectual property rights reform, Asian Development Bank, Manila, (2002). 3–5. I wound understand the Declaration as reiterating "freedom" to issue a compulsory license than as "right." This is more so considering the fact that the implementation of the Declaration is subject to a number of conditions, in the same way use of limitations and exceptions is subject to conditions protecting right holders.

193 see for example Gervais, le Droit d'auteur au Canada, *supra*. Tawfik, *supra;* Craig, *supra*; and Drassinower, *supra.*

194 *CCH Canadian Ltd v. Law Society of Upper Canada*, 2004 SCC 13, twice in para. 48 and once in para. 58.

195 *Euro-Excellence Inc. v. Kraft Canada Inc., supra,* para. 80.

196 Directive 2001/29/EC of the European Parliament and of the Council of 22 May 2001 on the harmonization of certain aspects of copyright and related rights in the information society, Official Journal L 167, 22/06/2001 P. 0010–0019.

In May 2005, Belgium amended its copyright law in order to transpose the Directive into Belgian law.[197] Article 79*bis* (2) requires that right holders take adequate voluntary measures, within a reasonable period, to provide beneficiaries of certain exceptions with the means to use those exceptions.[198] The obligation under this provision relates to exceptions such as the making of anthology, reprography, analogue and digital reproductions for the purpose of illustration for teaching or scientific research and exceptions for the benefit of the disabled. It excludes private copying.

The measures to be taken by the right holders are said to be voluntary in nature, but a beneficiary of an exception has the possibility to litigate in case such measures are not provided. Thus, under article 87*bis*, the president of the tribunal of first instance has the power to establish a violation of article 79*bis* (2) (i.e., the lack of adequate measures enabling the user to benefit from the exception concerned) and order the right holder to take the necessary action. Various persons, including the beneficiary of the exception, can request the president of the court to establish the violation in question.

Therefore, it would appear that there exists a kind of enforcement mechanism for exceptions in Belgium. Indeed, a study commissioned by the European Commission's Internal Market Directorate-General has referred to this mechanism as an enforcement of limitations.[199] Does this mean that exceptions as such are user rights under Belgian law? We do not believe that this is so.

This provision of the law is an implementation of Directive 2001/29/EC, which deals with copyright in the information society. Article 6(4) of the Directive is meant to respond to the challenges of technological measures,[200] but does not create rights for users as such. In fact, obligations arise under article 6(4) only when the right holder has put in place technological protection measures.[201] At best, the Belgian amendment is an attempt to balance the rights of copyright holders and specified public interests such as educational and scientific purposes and use in public institutions such as libraries and archives.[202] This balancing must be done in accordance with international law.

---

197 See Loi du 22 mai 2005 transposant en droit belge la Directive 2001/29/CE due 22 mai sur l'harmonisation de certains aspects du droit d'auteur et des droits voisins dans la société de l'information, (Published in the Moniteur Belge (Official Journal, 27/05/2005, p. 24997.))

198 The limitations covered under article 79*bis* include: the making of an anthology; reprography; analogue and digital reproductions for the purpose of illustrations for teaching or scientific research; exceptions for the preservation of cultural and scientific patrimony; ephemeral recordings made by broadcasters; exception for the benefit of disabled people; and the exception for social institutions. Like the Directive, article 79 does not include private copying.

199 Guido Westkamp, *Implementation of Directive 2001/29/EC in the Members States*, Queen Mary Intellectual Property Institute, Centre for Commercial Law Studies, (Queen Mary, University of London, February 2007). p. 133.

200 The Directive was meant to ensure that national law was adapted and supplemented "to respond adequately to economic realities such as new forms of exploitation." Directive 2001/29/EC, recital 5.

201 Article 6 of Directive 2001/29/EC is entitled "obligations as to technological measures".

202 Directive 2001/29/EC, recital 34. EU Member States are encouraged to promote voluntary measures taken by right holders, including the conclusion and implementation of agreements between right holders and other parties concerned, to accommodate *achieving the objectives of certain exceptions ad limitations* provided for in national law in accordance with the Directive. See Directive 2001/29/EC Recital 51.

Indeed, under the Directive, all limitations and exceptions are subject to the three-step test,[203] which means the right holders' economic interests have to be taken into account when implementing the exceptions. Furthermore, the exceptions in the Directive apply to lawful uses, which are defined as uses authorized by the right holder or not restricted by law.[204] It thus makes sense that the right holder has an obligation to enable the beneficiaries of the exceptions to enjoy them. Otherwise, it would be fraudulent for the right holder to allow the use of a work but then make such use impossible by installing a technological protection measure. There would be redundancy in a law creating such an exception. Accordingly, the exceptions are not rights in themselves. Indeed, jurisprudence does not support the idea that exceptions are user rights, even in the digital environment. A case decided upon five months after the implementation of the Directive supports this argument. This was a test case for articles 79bis and 87*bis*.

In the case of *Test Achats v. EMI Recorded Music Belgium et al,* the Brussels Court of Appeal stated that the private copying exception does not constitute an enforceable right.[205] To summarize the facts, the appellant, the *Association Belge des Consommateurs Test Achats* (Test Achats), is an association formed to defend interests of consumers. The defendants, EMI recorded Music Belgium, Sony Music Entertainment, Universal Music and Bertelsmann Music Group Belgium, distribute musical compact discs (CDs). Several consumers who had bought CDs distributed by the aforementioned companies could not make copies for private uses (like listening to the music in the car instead of in the house)[206] because the CDs had technological protection measures (TPMs). Test Achats logged a complaint before the tribunal de première instance of Brussels[207] demanding, *inter alia,* that the defendants stop using TPMs on CDs as this prevented the consumers from exercising their right to private copying. Test Achats also asked that the defendants remove the protected CDs from the market and acknowledge the violation of the right to private copying. Test Achats based its request mainly on two provisions of the Belgian Law on Copyright and Neighbouring Rights.[208] Article 22(1)(5) allows reproduction of sound and audiovisual works within the family circle.[209] Article 87 permits any interested party to request the tribunal de première instance to ascertain the existence and order the termination of an infringement of copyright or of a neighbouring right.

As to the issue of whether the private copying exception is a right, the tribunal de première instance of Brussels stated that:

---

203 Directive 2001/29/EC, article 5(5).

204 Directive 2001/29/EC, *supra,* Recital 33 and article 5(1).

205 *Test Achats v. EMI Recorded Music Belgium et al,* Brussels Court of Appeal, 9 September 2005, case 2004/AR/1649.

206 For example, one consumer made a copy of the CD so he could listen to it in his car, but the copy was rejected by the radio.

207 *Test Achats v. EMI Music Belgium et al,* Tribunal de Première Instance de Bruxelles, 25 May 2004, case 2004/46/A.

208 Belgium, Law on Copyright and Neighbouring Rights, 30 June 1994 (as amended).

209 Article 22(1)(5) provides that once a work has been published, its author may not prohibit reproductions of sound and audiovisual works made within the family circle and exclusively intended for that circle.

> [L]a copie privée n'est pas un droit mais une exception. [...] L'exception signifie uniquement (de manière négative) qu'il n'est pas nécessaire d'obtenir une autorisation du titulaire du droit voisin pour effectuer une copie privée. [...] En ce sens la copie privée est une simple cause d'immunité garantie par la loi.

Test Achats appealed this judgment.[210] However, the Court of Appeal confirmed the finding of the tribunal de première instance. Concerning the request to stop the distribution of right-protected CDs, the Court of Appeal clarified that Article 87 can only be invoked in case of an infringement of copyright or neighbouring right. An exception like private copying is not the same as a copyright or neighbouring right and cannot be a cause of action in cessation before the court. The Court stated that:

> *Une exception au droit d'auteur ne peut constituer en elle-même un droit d'auteur ni fonder une action en cessation.* [...] L'exception de copie privée n'a donc pas pour effet de transférer à la personne qui effectue une copie privée un droit d'auteur ou un droit voisin sur le CD dont elle tire une copie, ou sur la copie réalisée. Elle ne fait pas davantage naître un tel droit dans son chef. L'action de Test Achats ne se fonde donc sur un droit d'auteur ou un droit voisin. Par conséquent, elle ne peut avoir trait à une portée à un tel droit.[211]

The Court refers to "an exception" generally and not specifically to private copying. It is thus clear that under the Belgian copyright law, an exception to copyright such as private copying is not a user right. In other words, users do not get rights from exceptions. For this reason, one cannot claim the enforcement of an exception by court.[212]

A further example from France emphasizes the fact that exceptions are not rights for users. The French Copyright law allows private copying of a protected work.[213] In the case of *Studio Canal et al v. S. P and Union fédérale des consommateurs (UFC) Que choisir,*[214] Mr Parquin bought a DVD of David Lynch entitled "*Mulholland Drive.*" He wanted to copy the DVD onto a video cassette so that he could watch the film with his parents, who did not have a DVD player at their home. However, this was not possible because of a copy control mechanism or technological protection measures (TPMs). Together with the UFC, he sued Studio Canal, seeking an injunctive order to remove the TPMs because they constrained his "right" to engage in private copying. The claim of a "right" to private copying was rejected at every stage of the proceedings which led the parties as far as the Court of Cassation and then the Court of Appeal which heard the case on remand. The Court of

---

210 *Test Achats v. EMI Recorded Music Belgium et al,* Brussels Court of Appeal, supra.

211 *Ibid,* (emphasis added).

212 See also Séverine Dussolier, "Copie privée *versus* mesure techniques de protection: l'exception est-elle un droit?," *Auteurs & Media,* vol. 4, 2004, pp. 341–345, p. 345. Commenting on the decision of the tribunal de première instance, Dussollier posts that the exception for private copying is an interest (and not a right) so its protection cannot be a basis for an action in cessation.

213 Under the French Law on the Intellectual Property Code (Legislative Part), Article L 122-5(2) private copying is a permitted exception.

214 *Studio Canal et al v. S. Parquin and Union fédérale des consommateurs (UFC) Que choisir.* For a commentary on this case, see Valérie-Laure Benabou, "Chronique de France," in *Revue Internationale du droit d'auteur,* vol. 215, (January 2008). 154–259, pp. 222–226; and on the 2004 decision, see Geiger, The three-step test, *supra,* pp. 683–699.

Appeal held that private copying was not a right but a statutory exception.[215] The Court explained:

> [S]i la copie privée peut être, à supposer les conditions légales remplie, opposée pour se défendre à une action, notamment, en contrefaçon, elle ne saurait être invoquée, come étant constitutive d'un droit, au soutien d'une action formée à titre principal, peu important, au regard du principe *pas de droit pas d'action*, l'existence d'une rémunération pour copie privée acquittée par les consommateurs.[216]

In other words, the exception of private copying is not a right in and of itself. While it can be put forward as a defence in a legal action, notably for infringement, it cannot be invoked as constituting a right in support of a main action, regardless of the existence of remuneration for private copying paid by consumers. The Court of Appeal has been criticised for "[accepting] that it has jurisdiction to assess a defence based on the exception of private copying in the event of an action for infringement brought against a copier but refuses positively to enforce a claim of a right to engage in private copying where the right holder erected an obstacle preventing it."[217] However, as the Court rightly stated, the private copy exception is only a statutory exception and not a right that can be enforced in a court of law.

It is interesting to note that, while there are numerous commentaries on the *CCH Canadian case,*[218] only two authors, Gervais and Drassinower, have endeavoured to give their view of the meaning of 'user rights' as used by the Supreme Court of Canada. According to Professor Gervais, the view that fair dealing is a user right results from a "utilitarian policy". The utilitarian policy creates a contractual relationship between authors and the society, which, he argues, is represented by the public domain. In this case, the public domain must receive consideration in exchange for rights granted to authors. Understood in this sense, then, users as contractual partners should have rights.[219] This reasoning makes sense, considering the fact that the court has leaned toward a utilitarian approach to copyright. As demonstrated above, copyright is intended to serve the public interest, not only the interests of copyright owners.

For his part, Drassinower opines that users have rights when they are authors in themselves. If a user transforms a copied work, as opposed to straight copying, then he is an author and has rights.[220] This argument echoes the U.S.'s first test of fair use: the purpose and character of the use (of a copyrighted work). For a use to be fair under this test, the copying must be transformative.[221] Following the logic of Drassinower's argument, consumers or users who merely copy for study (as opposed to research) do not have rights

---

215 *Studio Canal et al v. S. P and Union fédérale des consommateurs (UFC) Que choisir*, Court of Appeal of Paris, Decision of 4 April 2007, p.9.

216 *Ibid.*

217 Benabou, *supra*, p. 224.

218 See for example Harris, *supra*; Tawfik, *supra*, Craig, *supra*.

219 Gervais, le Droit d'auteur au Canada, *supra*, p. 37.

220 Drassinower, *supra*, p. 470. This view is supported by the Supreme Court in *Euro-Excellence Inc. v. Kraft Canada Inc., supra*, para. 79.

221 *Princeton University Press v. Michigan Document Service, supra*, para. V (A), quoting *Campbell v. Acuff-Rose Music, Inc., supra.*

since they are not authors. Under the U.S. fair use doctrine, straight copying for classroom use is exempted from the transformative rule. But this does not seem to be the case under the 'new fair dealing' standard set by the court in *CCH Canadian*. However, Drassinower makes a distinction, and argues that those who do not copy for purposes of writing or authorial ends, can still be covered by 'user rights' (albeit in a different way). Relying on the example of temporary copying of files from the internet ('caching'), he explains that a distinction should be made between reproduction and infringement. A reproduction that does not harm the authorial right of the author, Drassinower argues, ought not to be treated as an infringement but rather as a legitimate use covered by user rights.[222] This reasoning is best understood if considered from the perspective of the Supreme Court. Supporting Drassinower's reasoning as consistent with the purpose of copyright, the Supreme Court in *Euro-Excellence* explained that "not every substantial reproduction of a copyrighted work counts as an infringement of copyright."[223] The Court further explained that [the exception of] 'caching' is justified by the *public interest* [not a right] of delivering faster and more economic services.[224] We can conclude that 'user rights' as used in this context can refer to the public interest in accessing the services provided through the Internet. In this sense, users have "rights" because they do not have to obtain a licence to access the work. But this is not the same as a right that can be claimed before a court of law.[225] Consequently, exceptions amount to immunities.[226]

The use of the phrase "user rights" should thus be understood as underlining the dual purpose of the Copyright Act, to balance interests of users and owners of copyrighted material. This view is further supported by the fact that the Supreme Court in *CCH Canadian* used the phrase "user rights" interchangeably with "interests". It thus stated: "The fair dealing exception, like other exceptions in the Copyright Act, is a *user's right*. In order to maintain the proper balance between the *rights of a copyright owner* and *user's interests*, it must not be interpreted restrictively."[227] This means that "user's rights" in paragraph 48 should be understood in light of the fact that "fair dealing is an integral part of the Copyright Act". Accordingly, the Act should be interpreted in a liberal and generous manner.[228] However, to state that exceptions in general or fair dealing in particular are user rights is unnecessarily misleading for users who cannot demand their enforcement before a court of law, let alone secure protection from infringement suits. A determination

---

222 Drassinower, *supra*, p. 474.

223 *Euro-Excellence Inc. v. Kraft Canada Inc., supra*, para. 79.

224 *Ibid*, para. 81 (emphasis added).

225 Such rights that can be enforced or claimed in a court of law or against someone have been referred to as claim-rights or rights "in its strict sense." See respectively, Peter Jones, *Rights*, (London: Macmillam, London, 1994), p. 12 and Wesley N Hohfeld, *Fundamental legal conceptions as applied in judicial reasoning*, (New Haven: Yale University Press, 1919), quoted in Jones, Peter, *ibid*.

226 This puts the status of exceptions in Canada at the same level as in Belgium or France. (see preceding discussion on the cases on *Test Achats* and *Mulholland Drive*).

227 *CCH Canadian Ltd v. Law Society of Upper Canada, supra*, 2004 SCC 13, para. 48 (emphasis added).

228 In the same line, see Drassinower, *supra*, p. 468.

of 'fairness' is made with regard to a checklist of factors to be tested against factual situations, which is not the same for the determination of rights of copyright owners.

This clarification is important for developing countries who mainly depend in imported copyrighted works for higher and tertiary education. It would be misleading to assert that exceptions, for example for teaching, are user rights when they cannot claim such "rights" before a court of law. This would only open the risks of more law suits resulting from unlawful massive use of copyrighted works.

6.4.5. *Broad Definition of Exceptions Does Not Conflict with the Three-Step Test*

Does the decision of the Supreme Court violate the three-step test? The broad interpretation of fair dealing in light of the purpose of the Copyright Act would seem to violate the three-step test, since it is not 'limited' and allows copying for profit, which may conflict with the legitimate interests of the copyright holders.[229] The three-step test allows for limited exceptions which should not conflict with the normal exploitation of the work or unreasonably prejudice the legitimate interest of right holders. In the case of large corporate users like the Law Society of the Great Library, a conflict with the legitimate interests of the copyright owners can only be avoided if the latter are remunerated. The Supreme Court did not order remuneration (which makes sense since it did not find that there was an infringement). Indeed, concern has been raised that the Court moved Canadian law dangerously close to a violation of the TRIPS Agreement and its three-step test.[230] The present author does not agree with such a position, because acts that can be done under fair dealing do not necessarily violate the three-step test. Let me elaborate with reference to the example of copying for research or private study.

Section 30 of the Canadian Copyright Act provides for general exceptions, within the meaning of the three-step test. In relation to library copying in particular, section 30(2) of the Copyright Act allows copying for research or study under very restrictive terms. It is permissible to make a single copy of an article contained in (a) a scholarly, scientific or technical periodical, or (b) a newspaper or periodical, other than a scholarly, scientific or technical periodical, if the newspaper or periodical was published more than one year before the copy is made for research or private study. There are fundamental differences between fair dealing for purposes of research and private study under section 29 and library copying for the same purpose (section 30). We shall mention only two that are of direct relevance to this discussion. First, the exemption under section 30 is limited to copying from scholarly, scientific or technical periodicals, allowing copying from other periodicals or newspapers only after they have been on the market for at least one year. Section 29 does not limit copying to periodicals, nor does it specify the kind of periodicals. Second, copying under section 30 is limited to one article in a periodical, while under section 29 there is no limitation on quantity as long as the dealing is fair. What is fair is

229 see discussion in section 4.4 (the meaning of the three-step test and its implication for access to printed copyrighted material for education in developing countries).

230 Gervais, the purpose of copyright law in Canada, *supra*, p. 322.

decided on the basis of a factual inquiry based on the criteria outlined by the Federal Court of Appeal in *CCH Canadian*.[231] The question then is what section should one apply? The Supreme Court in *CCH Canadian* specifically addressed the difference between the two provisions. The Court explained:

> As an integral part of copyright law, section 29 fair dealing exception is always available. Simply put, a library can always attempt to prove that its dealings with a copyrighted work are fair under section 29 of the Copyright Act. It is only if a library were unable to make out the fair dealing exception under s.29 that it would need to turn to s.30 of the Copyright Act to prove that it qualified for the library exemption.[232]

In other words, if a dealing with a work for purposes of research or private study is fair, then it falls under section 29 of the Act. If it is not fair, then it falls under section 30. It is incumbent upon the library to choose between taking advantage of the more liberal fair dealing exception and the general exception subject to the three-step test.[233] The three-step test (section 30) starts to apply where the fair dealing provision stops, and they do not operate at the same time.

Trosow has rightly observed that this reasoning of the court makes section 30(2) redundant except in situations where the defence of fair dealing is not available.[234] This is one of the merits of *CCH Canadian*. The Court moves far away from a mere specific exception, but not so far as to violate the three-step test (a general exception), through expansive interpretation of a specific exception.[235] Put differently, when the fair dealing exception applies, the application of the general exception under section 30 is suspended. In such a case, there is no possibility of violating the three-step test since it is not functional.

6.4.6. *Lessons for Access to Education in Developing Countries*

The Supreme Court of Canada, the country's highest court, has set a standard for Canadian courts to interpret the Copyright Act in such a way as to balance the competing interests of copyright holders and users. Indeed, some authors have described the precedent set by

---

231 *CCH Canadian Ltd v. Law Society of Upper Canada*, 2002 FCA 187, *supra*, para. 150 and 2004 SCC 13, para. 53. There are other differences, especially in relation to the digital environment, but which are not the focus of our research here. For a discussion of the difference between the two provisions in light of electronic access for research, see Samuel E Trosow, "The changing landscape of academic libraries and copyright policy: interlibrary loans, electronic reserves, and distance education," in Michael Geist, (ed.), *In the Public Interest: The Future of Canadian Copyright Law*, *supra*, 373–407, at 386.

232 *CCH Canadian Ltd v. Law Society of Upper Canada, 2004 SCC 13, supra*, para. 49.

233 The court does not expressly say that, but in stating that the fair dealing exception is always available, it is close to saying that.

234 Trosow, *supra*, p. 388.

235 We demonstrated in chapter three that specific exceptions under article 10 of the Berne Convention such as illustrations in teaching are so narrow and limited that they do no serve to facilitate access to protected works. The only way to give meaning to similar provision fair dealing is to interpret it broadly.

CCH Canadian as a long overdue change in the fortunes of fair dealing.[236] Yet, others have expressed doubts about the impact of 'utilitarianism' on author's rights.[237]

However, scholars agree with the purposeful interpretation of the Copyright Act to meet the public interest. It is agreed that protection is a means to an end, and its reach, especially when it is to stop or exclude uses, should be limited where this does not serve the underlying purpose or imposes too high a social cost.[238] There is also, agreement on the importance of following the open-ended "fair use" kind of provision. Indeed, scholars like Professor Craig recommend that the current "rigid and restrictive fair dealing provisions currently found in the [Copyright] Act be replaced with an open-ended defence similar in form to the United States' fair use defence."[239] Such statutory revision is deemed necessary to "support and cement the significance of *CCH* [*Canadian*] in the development of a robust fair dealing defence."[240] This kind of recommendation is not new, but it reiterates the significance of having an open-ended fair use style provision. In 1984, the Sub-Committee on the Revision of Copyright[241] rejected a similar proposal (to amend the Copyright Act along the lines of the U.S. fair use provision) put forth in a Canadian White Paper.[242] However, since 2002, the Supreme Court through its rulings has demonstrated the need for Canadian law to adopt more open-ended provisions in similar fashion to the U.S. fair use. Beyond Canada, scholars have advocated for an "international fair use doctrine" for different purposes.[243]

The Canadian jurisprudence presents more than just a duplication of the fair use doctrine and a contribution towards the international harmonization of the fairness principle. For developing countries, a flexible fair use/dealing model permits courts to address new challenges in a principled manner, guided by the policy concerns underlying the law. But such a model needs to be suited to developing countries. We contend that a model constructed along the lines of the one proposed below would serve this purpose.

---

236 Craig, *supra*, p. 446.

237 Gervais, le Droit d'auteur au Canada, *supra*, pp. 39–41.

238 Gervais, the purpose of copyright law in Canada, *supra*, p. 332.

239 Craig, *supra*, pp. 438–439; see also Gervais, towards a new core international copyright norm, *supra*.

240 Craig, *ibid*, p. 439.

241 Canada, Standing Committee on Communication and Culture, *A Charter of Rights for Creators*, Minister of Supply and Services, (Ottawa, 1985). The relevant text on fair dealing in contained in paras 63–66.

242 Consumer and Corporate Affairs Canada, *From Gutenberg to Telidon: A White Paper on Copyright*, Ottawa, 1984.

243 See for example Okediji, Toward an international fair use doctrine, *supra*, p. 169, (advocating for an international fair use standard that reflects a balance–not between users and owners as the domestic law is designed to do–but instead a balance between the domestic and the international regime); Gervais, Towards a new core international copyright norm, *supra*, p.4 (arguing that a new international copyright norm could be created based on the Berne Convention's three-step test in harmony with the U.S. fair use doctrine).

6.5. A "Fairness" Model for Copyright and Access to Education in Developing Countries

The difference between U.S. judicial practice on fair use and that of Canada on fair dealing is that in the latter case no single factor takes precedence over another. Of particular importance for developing countries, there is no emphasis on the economic impact of the dealing on the author. Rather, emphasis is placed on balancing the interests of the author and public interests. This prevents application of a three-step test kind of standard, which would be unworkable for developing countries. On the other hand, a major shortcoming of the Canadian legislation is that it allows fair dealing only for research and study.[244] The U.S. Copyright Act provides only an illustrative list of purposes for which fair use is allowed. While courts can interpret research and study in an expansive way according to the purpose to be achieved by the use, an open ended provision in legislation is to be preferred as it allows for the inclusion of more uses without necessarily going to court. In the case of Canada, Craig has rightly proposed legislative change in Canadian law to follow the U.S. example by adopting a broad fair use provision that would include the current fair dealing exceptions but also permit other fair uses to be assessed on the basis of criteria identified by the Federal Court of Appeal and cited by the Supreme Court of Canada in *CCH Canadian*.[245]

With regard to access to educational and teaching materials in developing countries, it is essential to articulate models or guidelines for 'fairness'. These guidelines or models should take into account the particular circumstances of developing countries and should acknowledge disparities between member countries in a regional economic unit, differentiating relatively industrialized countries from the less industrialized ones. In relation to our discussion, it is best to differentiate between developing, least developed and countries with economies in transition. The best strategy would be for each country to include a 'fairness' provision in its legislation. We therefore propose an open-ended 'fairness' provision, along the lines of the Israeli copyright Act,[246] with an illustrative list of factors to consider when determining fairness but without provision for or reference to the profit or non-profit use of the work. Each country should then define the purpose of copyright in its legislation, but without foreclosing the possibility of the courts doing the same.[247] Court should be guided by the models or guidelines which should reflect the policy underpinnings of each country. The courts should as much as possible adopt a

---

244 Although as demonstrated by the Supreme Court in *CCH Canadian*, a court interpreting the Copyright Act with a view to balancing the interests of right holders and users, will interpret 'research' or 'study' broadly.

245 Craig, *supra*, p. 460.

246 Article 19 of the Israeli Copyright Act 2007, provides an open-ended list of uses that can be fair but excludes the test of commercial or non-commercial nature of the use. See discussion under 6.2. (Factual acceptance of fair use and fair dealing by developing countries.)

247 The risk of leaving it to the courts to define the purpose of copyright, like in Canada is the possibility of having different definitions depending on the judge at the time. Since developing countries are more vulnerable to external economic and political pressure courts are more likely to be influenced by copyright interest groups than when the provisions are laid down in legislation.

"purposeful" interpretation of limitations and exceptions when they have to decide on a fairness issue. Public policy goals such as promoting research, education through access to education materials are a few examples of what can guide a "purposeful" interpretation. Indeed some developing countries are taking this trend. This is the case with India.

6.5.1. *Developing Countries Can Devise Educational Exceptions through Purposeful Interpretation of Legislation: The Case of India*

The Copyright Act of India excludes from copyright infringement the performance in the course of the activities of an educational institution by the staff and students of the institution; or performance of a literary, dramatic or musical work by an amateur club or society if the performance is given to a non-paying audience or for the benefit of a religious institution.[248] The copyright Act does not define private use or "amateur club or society". However, in the case of *Academy of General Education, Manipal and anor v. B. Manini Mallya,*[249] the Court qualified the educational institution as "amateur club" which exempted it from copyright violation.

Unfortunately, quite often developing countries act as agencies for intellectual property protection and public interest through access to copyrighted works. Two landmark cases in Mauritius further illustrate the failure of courts to devise case-by-case educational exceptions/public interest exceptions.[250]

In *Polo/Laurent Co Ltd Partnership v. Dinoo and others*[251] and *Polo/Laurent Co Ltd Partnership v. Regent Ltd and two others.*[252] An injunction issued against the respondents to prevent them from trading in products bearing the various 'Polo' marks. The respondents argued, *inter alia,* that if an injunction was granted, it would result in the loss of thousands of jobs. The court found that the use of the 'Polo' marks was in breach of the Copyright Act 1997. Concerning the issue of jobs, the court stated:

> If thousands of people will be affected by the stopping of an illegality in the granting of an interlocutory order protecting the rights of the copyright owner ... the fault does not lie with the copyright owner ... but with those purveyors of other people's ideas and works who have related the situation and who have been enjoying a very lucrative market. Furthermore, especially in matters relating to the infringement of copyright or trademark, no person must be allowed to steal and reap the fruits of those who through their skill, judgment, expense and know-how had created the work ... [I]t is fraudulent to appropriate what belonged to another and its use is contrary to commercial morality. No person should be allowed to obtain a free ride on the good will associated with the products of another.

All the 108 outlets that had been trading in Polo/Ralph Laurent garments in Mauritius were closed by the end of December 2004. It is estimated that each outlet employed on average five people. While there were no statistics to show how many people lost their

---

248 India, Copyright Act, 1957 (as amended), section 52 (i) and (l).

249 *Academy of General Education, Manipal and anor v. B. Manini Mallya,* [2009] 39 PTC 393 (SC).

250 See also the Uganda case of John Murray and the Thai cases of Ganokchai Petchdawong and Somsak Thanasarasenee discussed in section 2.3.

251 *Polo/Laurent Co Ltd Partnership v. Dinoo and others,* 2004 SCJ 44.

252 *Polo/Laurent Co Ltd Partnership v. Regent Ltd and two others,* 2004 SCJ 45.

jobs as a result of the court judgment, there appears to have been loss in the thousands as had been feared.[253]

The preceding example strongly points to the need to equip national institutions, especially courts to devise educational or public interest exceptions. It is well known that L&Es in developing country legislation are either absent or are narrowly and vaguely crafted.[254] National courts in developing countries are becoming more and more involved in enforcing IPRs. Where there are no adequate L&Es, courts will always play a key role in devising educational exceptions. This necessitates equipping them with the necessary tools to do this. Training of judges on IP and public interests like education is a first step.

6.6. Compulsory Licensing for Copyright in Printed Works beyond the Berne Appendix

We have to remember that neither the Berne Convention nor the TRIPS Agreement provides for compulsory licensing for reproduction of hard copies except under the Berne Appendix which is addressed to developing countries. However, developed countries are not prohibited from using compulsory licensing.[255] Therefore, some developed countries like Australia issue compulsory licences for reproduction of works in printed form, even if the Berne Convention does not provide for such an exception. Below we survey Australian legislation on CL for copyright with a view to identifying possible positive practice for developing countries for access to printed materials.

6.6.1. *Compulsory Licensing (CL) for Reproduction of Printed Material: Lessons from Australia*

In Australia, a compulsory licence can be issued for multiple reproductions of hard copies for or on behalf of educational institutions, in certain cases. A compulsory licence can also be issued for multiple production of printed periodical articles by or on behalf of a body administering an educational institution. Reproduction is limited to only one article contained in the same periodical publication, unless the articles relate to the same subject matter.[256] CLs can also be issued to an educational institution for a work contained in printed anthologies.[257] A CL can likewise be granted for multiple reproductions of the whole or part of a literary, dramatic, musical or artistic work (other than an article contained in a periodical publication) by or on behalf of a body administering an educational institution. The provision does not apply in relation to reproductions of the whole or more than a *reasonable portion* of a work that has been separately published unless the person who makes the reproductions, or causes the reproductions to be made for, or on behalf of, the educational institution, is satisfied *after reasonable investigation* that reproductions (other than second-hand reproductions) of the work cannot be obtained within

253 Kaushik Goburdhun, *supra,* 140.

254 Armstrong *et al, supra.*

255 For example, Japan has used compulsory licensing in a way similar to that allowed under the Berne Appendix. See Watal, *supra,* pp. 288–9.

256 Australia, Copyright Act 1968 Act No. 63 of 1968 as amended, Part VB, Division 2, Section 135ZJ.

257 Australia, Copyright Act 1968, *ibid,* Section 135ZK.

a reasonable time at an ordinary commercial price.[258] The terms reasonable portion or reasonable investigation are not defined, leaving it to the courts to decide. This procedure is suitable for a developed country where there exists a competent body to perform the investigation, but not for developing countries which lack such bodies. All cases of compulsory licensing for hard copies are administered through collecting societies, which determine the amount of remuneration. Before a reproduction takes place, the collecting society, or its representative, must first issue a remuneration notice.[259]

In Australia, the CL scheme for hard copies is governed by the Copyright Agency Limited (CAL).[260] The scope of the licence in terms of the extent of copying is as follows: for literary and dramatic works, 10% of number of words; all of the work, if not separately available for purchase; all of the work, if not available within a *reasonable period of time*. For periodical publications: one article, or more if of the same subject matter. For musical works: 10% of all the work, if not available for purchase; all of the work, if not available within a reasonable period of time. For artistic works: all of an artistic work.[261]

This scheme presents a number of challenges for access to education. In the case of literary, dramatic, periodical publications and musical works, it is clear that when a work is available for sale the amount allowed for copying is only 10% of the number of words of the work or one article. As we have demonstrated in chapter two, developing countries need bulk access to copyrighted works since they are basically consumers and not producers of such works. Allowing limited copying does not solve their problem regarding access to educational and learning materials.

Despite the procedural requirements mentioned above, one particular element of the Australian system, if copied, would serve the needs of developing countries. The Statute allows for the possibility of a compulsory licence for *multiple* reproduction of the *whole or part* of a literary work (if there is no commercial copy available).[262] This provision is similar to the Berne Appendix, which allows CL if the copyrighted work has not been available on the market.[263] The advantage of issuing CL along the lines of the Australian Copyright Act is that the procedural and administrative requirements are less costly than under the Berne Appendix. The Australian CL is managed by collecting societies which are located in Australia. This not only makes it relatively easy to find the relevant authority to grant clearance for CL, but it also eliminates such administrative costs as those involved in sending requests.

---

258 Australia, Copyright Act 1968, *supra,* Section 135ZL.

259 Australia, Copyright Act 1968 Act No. 63 of 1968 as amended, Part VB, Division 2, Sections 135ZJ(a), 135ZK(a), and 135ZL(a).

260 For detailed information on the work of the CAL in relation to various types of copyright and access procedures, see Garnett, Nic "Automated Rights Management Systems and Copyright Limitations and Exceptions," WIPO Standing Committee on Copyright and Related Rights, Fourteenth Session, Geneva, May 1 to 5, 2006, WIPO document SCCR/14/5, pp. 57–60.

261 Australia, Copyright Act 1968, *supra,* Section 135ZG, 135ZH and 135ZL, read together.

262 Australia, Copyright Act 1968, *ibid,* Section 135ZK (emphasis added).

263 The Berne Convention, *supra,* Appendix, article III(2).

6.6.1.1. A Case for Quasi Compulsory Licensing System for Developing Countries

The challenge with respect to CL in developing countries is that most of the books for which such licences would be issued are imported. Therefore, the problems associated with obtaining access to the owners to gain permission would remain. A potential solution would be to implement what we would call *a quasi compulsory licensing system*. This would involve a combination of compulsory licensing and negotiated compensation. There are two main reasons why a quasi compulsory licensing system would favour access to printed materials. First, while there are no collective management societies that government would entrust with managing compulsory licenses, there are collective societies for negotiated licences. The majority of these are representatives of international copyright management organizations. For example, in southern Africa, reproduction rights, which are of direct relevance to access to printed material in developing countries, are monitored by local organizations operating on behalf of the International Federation of Reproduction Rights Organizations (IFRRO) based in Brussels.[264] The second reason is that the mere possibility of a compulsory licence for reproduction would force a decline in the price of textbooks or more favourable voluntary licensing terms.[265]

6.6.2. *Developing Countries Can Issue Compulsory Licences for Printed Copyrighted Material outside the System Provided by the Berne Appendix*

One pertinent legal question is whether developing countries can issue compulsory licences for reproduction of printed material outside the system prescribed by the Berne Appendix. Does the fact that there is a special regime governing compulsory licences preclude developing countries from granting CL outside the Berne Appendix, since in this case the Berne provisions are *lex specialis?*[266] We are of the opinion that the Berne Convention does not preclude developing countries from using CL outside the system provided for in the Appendix. If read according to the ordinary meaning to be attached to the terms of a treaty,[267] one can conclude that there is no obligation to use the Appendix. Article I of the Appendix stipulates:

---

264 IFRRO has representatives in at least 28 developing countries. The information is available at http://www.ifrro.org.

265 While there are no local publishers for the kind of education books needed in tertiary institutions, there are a number of reprographic or photocopying businesses like those in Makerere University. See discussion in 6.3.5.

266 *Lex specialis* in this case is understood to mean specific treaty provisions governing use of CL by developing countries. A detailed discussion of *lex specialis* is beyond the scope of this research. But on possible uses of the term, see Pauwelyn, Conflict of Norms, *supra*, p. 387; and Ruth Okediji, "History Lessons for the WIPO development Agenda," in Neil Weinstock Netanel, ed. *The development Agenda: Global Intellectual Property and Developing Countries,* (Oxford: Oxford University Press, 2009). 137–161, at 137, footnote 4 (hereinafter referred to as Okediji, History lessons for WIPO DA).

267 The Vienna Convention on the Law of Treaties, 1969, 1155 *U.N.T.S, no.* 331. Article 31(1) requires a treaty to be interpreted in good faith in accordance with the ordinary meaning to be given to the terms of the treaty in their context.

> (1) Any country regarded as a developing country [...] *may*, by notification deposited with the Director General [...] *declare that it will avail itself of the faculty provided* for in Article II, or of the faculty provided for in Article III, or of both of those faculties.[268]

The word 'may' connotes an option. The obligation under the Appendix arises only for developing countries which make a declaration that they will use the special provisions on CL. In such a case, they are under an obligation to follow the rules and procedure for issuing CL as laid down in the Appendix.

Indeed, some developing countries have provisions for compulsory licences for translation and reproduction of copyrighted works outside the Berne Appendix. Examples include: China (providing for translation of Chinese Works into minority nationality languages),[269] Indonesia (providing for translation and/or reproduction of a work for education, science, research and developmental activities),[270] Malaysia (providing for a compulsory licence to produce and translate a publication)[271] and Pakistan (providing for grant of a compulsory licence, in the public interest, to an individual or government institution to reprint, translate, adapt or publish a textbook or other dramatic work, on non-profit basis).[272]

6.6.3. *"Compulsory Licences" in Place of Injunctions to Avoid Public Injury: Examples from the United States and India*

Some countries have used compulsory licensing to promote public interest. In this subsection, we illustrate with the case of the United States and India.

6.6.3.1. The Case of Abend v. MCA, Inc

In the case of *Abend v. MCA, Inc*,[273] the plaintiff/appellant was the owner of a renewal copyright on the original story, "It has to be Murder". The defendants/appellees, MCA and others, were the publishers of a film, "Rear Window", which was based on the original story, "It has to be Murder". The film version was broadcast with a lot of success. In 1971, Abend informed the defendants that he owned the copyright renewal, but the defendants nonetheless proceeded to enter into a second licence with broadcasters to broadcast the movie. Abend brought a suit, claiming infringement of the story's copyright and seeking compensatory damages, an accounting of the defendants' profits and a permanent injunction which, among other things, would enjoin the defendants from exhibiting, distributing, selling or marketing "Rear Window" in the United States.

This case raised many other issues beyond our interest in this discussion. At present, we limit our focus to the court's refusal to grant an injunction in the public interest.

268 Emphasis added.
269 China, Copyright Law, Article 22(11).
270 Indonesian Copyright Act, Article 16 (1)(c).
271 Malaysia, Copyright Act, section 31.
272 Pakistan, Copyright Ordinance, sections 36, 37 and 57(2).
273 *Abend v. MCA, Inc.*, United States Court of Appeals for the Ninth Circuit, 863 F.2d 1465; 1988 U.S. App. LEXIS 17515.

The U.S. Copyright Act provides that the court "*may* ... grant temporary or final injunctions on such terms as it may deem reasonable to prevent or restrain infringement of a copyright".[274] An injunction is only one of the possible remedies available to a plaintiff in case of an infringement, but the court is not obliged to give it. The Court of Appeals for the ninth circuit, while acknowledging that a finding of infringement presumptively entitles the plaintiff to an injunction, stated that "where great public injury would be worked by an injunction, the courts might ... award damages or a *continuing royalty instead of an injunction in such special circumstances.*"[275]

According to the Court, special circumstances existed that justified the denial of an injunction, one of which was the public injury that would arise from an injunction. The Court noted, "*an injunction could cause public injury by denying the public the opportunity to view a classic film for many years to come.*"[276] It therefore granted royalties instead of an injunction. In a sense, the court granted a compulsory licence, as royalties were a kind of licence decided by the court against the desire (or without permission) of the authors. The plaintiff would have preferred to stop the defendant from infringing upon his copyright rather than receiving payment while the unauthorized use continued. The court granted royalties instead of an injunction because of a public interest in viewing the film as opposed to the private interest of stopping infringement of the copyright.

6.6.3.2. The Case of eBay v. MercExchange, L.L.C.

In its Opinion of 15 May 2006 in the case of *eBay Inc. et al v. MercExchange, L.L.C.*,[277] the Supreme Court of the United States rejected the notion that an injunction automatically follows a determination that a copyright has been infringed.[278] To summarize the facts of the case, the petitioner, eBay operates a popular Internet Web site that allows private sellers to list goods they wish to sell, either through auction or at a fixed price. The other petitioner, Half.com, a wholly owned subsidiary of eBay, operates a similar Web site. The respondent, MercExchange L.L.C., holds a number of patents, including business method patents for an electronic market designed to facilitate the sale of goods between private individuals by establishing a central authority to promote trust among participants. MercExchange sought to licence its patent to eBay and Half.com but the parties failed to reach an agreement. MercExchange subsequently filed a patent infringement suit against eBay and Half.com, in the United States District Court for the Eastern District of Virginia, seeking, *inter alia*, a permanent injunction. The District Court denied MercExchange's motion for permanent injunctive relief.[279] The Court of Appeals for the Federal Circuit subsequently reversed, applying its "general rule that courts will issue

274 U.S. Copyright Act, section 502 (a) (emphasis added). The use of 'may' makes the availability of an injunction dependant on the discretion of the court.

275 *Abend v. MCA, Inc., supra*, para. 42, citing Nimmer, M., *Nimmer on Copyright*, 1988, paras 14–55 to 14–56.2 (emphasis added).

276 *Ibid*, para 43.

277 *eBay Inc. et al v. MercExchange, L.L.C*, 547 U.S. 388 (2006).

278 *Citing Campbell v. Acuff-Rose Music, Inc, supra.*

279 *eBay Inc. et al v. MercExchange*, 275 F. Supp. 2d 696 (2003).

permanent injunctions against patent infringement absent of exceptional circumstances."[280] The Court granted certiorari.

The Court stated that the decision whether to grant or deny injunctive relief rests within the equitable discretion of the district courts, and that such discretion must be exercised consistent with traditional principles of equity. The Court noted that under well-established principles of equity, a plaintiff seeking a permanent injunction must satisfy a four-factor test before a court may grant such relief:

> [a] plaintiff must demonstrate: (1) that is has suffered an irreparable injury; (2) that remedies available at law, such as monetary damages, are inadequate to compensate for that injury, (3) that, considering the balance of hardships between the plaintiff and defendant, a remedy in equity is warranted; and (4) that the public interest would not be disserved by a permanent injunction.[281]

Subsequent to *eBay,* courts have rejected a number of requests for injunctions in cases involving intellectual property rights, although there are more cases involving patents than copyrights.[282]

What is important to note from the above two examples is the option available to developing country courts to deny an injunction if this is in the public interest. While there is no hierarchy of importance for the factors for granting an injunction, the fact that an injunction is a discretionary relief grants an opportunity to the courts to make a decision based on public interest. Indeed, India has in the past used this option.

6.3.3.3 India: Civic Chandran v. Ammini Amma

In 1996 the High Court of Kerala found that substantial copying of copyrighted material was fair dealing because the work copied was necessary to pass a message in the public interest. In addition, the Court declined to issue an injunction against infringement because this would not be in the public interest.[283]

6.6.3.4. Compulsory Licensing Instead of Injunctions under International Copyright Law

Enforcement of intellectual property rights (IPRs) under the TRIPS Agreement is provided for under Part III of the Agreement. Article 44(1) enjoins judicial authorities of Members to order a party to desist from infringement of IPRs. In other words, judicial authorities can grant injunctions as a remedy for an infringement of IP. However, this is not the only available remedy under this article. Article 44(2) of TRIPS permits Members to limit remedies to payment of remuneration according to Article 31(h),[284] which relates

280 *eBay Inc. et al v. MercExchange,* 401 F.3d 1323, 1339 (2005).

281 eBay Inc. et al v. MercExchange, L.L.C, 547 U.S. 388 (2006), II.

282 For examples relating to patents, see James Love, "Compulsory licensing of copyright under Article 44.2 of the TRIPS, in light of eBay," KEI Research Note 2007:5, 28 May 2007, p. 4, available at http://www.keionline.org.

283 *Civic Chandran v. Ammini Amma,* [1996] 16 PTC 329 (Kerala).

284 Article 31(h) of the TRIPS Agreement stipulates that where a Member allows the use of a patented product without the authorization of the right holder, the latter shall be paid adequate remuneration taking into account the economic value of the authorization.

to patents. If the drafters of the TRIPS Agreement had stopped at this point, they would have limited non-injunctive remedies only to patents.[285] However, the provision continues;

> [i]n other cases, [such as in case of copyright] the remedies under this Part shall apply or, where these remedies are inconsistent with a Member's law, declaratory judgments and adequate compensation shall be available.[286]

This means that a court can make a declaratory judgement and grant "adequate compensation" instead of an injunction. This provision is similar to U.S. legislation and practice as far as it relates to remedies for copyright infringement. Indeed, this provision was inspired by U.S. law and practice.[287] For example, whenever a copyright in any work protected under the copyright laws of the United States is infringed by the United States or its authorized agents, the sole remedy is "an action by the copyright owner against the United States in the Court of Federal Claims for the recovery of his reasonable and entire compensation as damages for such infringement".[288] The provision allows for government use of a copyrighted work. For developing countries, this is a possibility worth exploring. Since TRIPS does not define reasonable or adequate compensation, it is left to the discretion of the judicial authorities to determine what this amounts to.

6.7. Conclusions on Models of Practice

In this chapter, we have explored models of practice for access to copyrighted material by developing countries. There are numerous proposals for broad exemptions in national law.[289] This chapter has emphasized of role of courts, as opposed to national legislation. In particular, we have examined the use of 'fairness' principles by developed countries like the United States and Canada. Developing countries could adopt open-ended provisions like fair use in their national legislation. While the actual application of fair use in U.S. courts resembles the three-step test, it would still be advantageous for developing countries to adopt it. Developing country courts would be able to decide each situation of use on a case-by-case basis, in light of their domestic circumstances. Where provisions on exceptions in national legislation are narrow, courts should adopt expansive and purposeful interpretation of such legislation like the Supreme Court of Canada does in CCH

285 Article 31 of the TRIPS Agreement provides for compulsory licences in case of patents. It does not apply to copyrights.

286 TRIPS Agreement, article 44(2) (emphasis added).

287 The text was included in the U.S. proposal for the enforcement of IPRs under TRIPS. See UNCTAD-ICTSD, *Resource Book on TRIPS and Development*, (Cambridge: Cambridge University Press, 2005), p.591, footnote 68.

288 Title 28 USC, (Judiciary and Judicial Procedure), section 1498(b).

289 On a sweeping exemption for scientific research, see for example Reto M. Hilty *et al*, "European Commission – Green Paper: Copyright in the Knowledge Economy – Comments by Max Plunck Institute for Intellectual Property, Competition and Tax Law, available at: http://www.ip.mpg.de/shared/data/pdf/comments_on_the_green_paper2.pdf; Jerome H. Reichman and Ruth L. Okediji, "When Copyright Law and Science Collide: Empowering Digitally Integrated Research Methods on a Global Scale," *University of Minnesota Law Review*, (2012, forthcoming).

Canadian. Combining elements from fair use (an open-ended list of uses) with those of fair dealing (expansive interpretation of narrow exceptions) could facilitate access to copyrighted materials for the purpose of education.

Additionally, use of compulsory or quasi-compulsory licensing outside the provisions of the Berne Appendix is something developing countries could explore. One particular advantage is that CL outside the Berne Appendix is not subject to cumbersome procedural requirements. Developing countries can deny injunctions, like USA and India do, in order to meet public interest. The courts can then decide on amount of compensation. This approach avoids the cumbersome procedural requirements of the Berne Appendix.

CHAPTER SEVEN

INSTITUTIONAL AND NORMATIVE SOLUTIONS FOR ACCESS TO COPYRIGHTED MATERIAL FOR EDUCATIONAL PURPOSES

7.1. Introduction

In the previous chapter, we investigated possible models of state practice for access to printed copyrighted material for education. We, nevertheless, believe that there should be an international solution for access to copyrighted material. The problem of copyright and access to education in developing countries lies in the nature of international legal instruments and the international IP system as a whole. As demonstrated, the international IP system stresses the protection of IP and not access to the same. For this reason we believe that solutions to access to IP lie largely within the international IP system and institutions. This further explains why we do not attempt to find solutions in the human rights regime and institutions.

In this chapter, we explore possible institutional and normative solutions within the WTO and WIPO for access to copyrighted materials for education. In the case of WTO, we examine the Doha Declaration on the TRIPS Agreement and Public Health, and the extension of the transition period for the implementation of the TRIPS Agreement. In the case of WIPO, we examine recent developments, in particular the WIPO Development Agenda (DA) and proposals for work on limitations and exceptions in the Standing Committee on Copyrights and Related Rights (SCCR).

7.2. Solutions in the World Trade Organization for Access to Health: Lessons for Copyright and Access to Education

In the following paragraphs, we examine the attempts by the WTO to facilitate access to protected works for the public interest. We realize that the work done in this respect, for example through the Doha Declaration on TRIPS and Public Health, relates to public health and patents, except for the extension of the transition period for LDCs. However, it is conceivable that lessons may be drawn from Doha for access to education. Toward this end, we highlight features of the Declaration on Public Health, the Decision on paragraph 6 of the Declaration, and the amendment to the TRIPS Agreement that are relevant to copyright and access to education. We also discuss the extension of the transition period for application of TRIPS by LDCs to see to what extent it facilitates access to education.

7.2.1. *Doha Declaration on TRIPS and Public Health*

On 20 November 2001, the WTO trade ministers sitting at Doha pronounced the Doha Declaration on the TRIPS Agreement and Public Health.[1] Before getting into a discussion of Declaration as it relates to this study, we first say a word about parallel importation and compulsory licensing in case of patents.

Article 6 of the TRIPS Agreement provides that, for the purpose of dispute settlement, nothing in the Agreement shall be used to address the issue of the exhaustion of intellectual property rights. There are three main options for the exhaustion of intellectual property rights: a) National exhaustion of rights, which limits the circulation of products covered by, for example a patent in one country to only those placed on the market by the patent owner or its authorized agents in that same country. In this case, it is not possible to parallel import; b) Regional exhaustion, which allows the possibility of importing into the national territory a patented product originating from any member state of a regional agreement; and c) International exhaustion, which allows any party to import into the national territory a patented product from any other country in which the product was placed on the market by the patent holder. Under the international exhaustion regime, the first sale by the patent holder in any country will exhaust any parallel intellectual property rights in the importing country. This means that IP rights may not be used to block importation. A right holder may have the exclusive right to manufacture his product and to put it on the market. But once the product is placed on the market, the principle of exhaustion means that the right holder has no further right over the product.

Parallel importation is a mechanism used to prevent market division and price discrimination. The price of the same product can vary widely from country to country depending on various factors such as differences in income or the degree of competition in the particular market.[2] For example, in 2002, the price of Pfizer's Azythromycin 250 mg capsule for a patient in Kenya was about Kshs 648 (USD7.85) while in India, where there is more competition, it retailed at Kshs 204 (USD2.47).[3]

In the case of patents, article 31 of TRIPS permits a Member to allow use of the subject matter of the patent without the authorization of the patent holder (compulsory licensing), including use by the government or third parties authorized by the government under a number of conditions, including that: (a) any such use is authorized predominantly for the supply of the domestic market of the Member authorizing such use; and (b) the right holder is paid adequate remuneration in the circumstances of each case, taking into account the economic value of the authorization.[4]

---

1 Declaration on the TRIPS Agreement and Public Health, *supra*.

2 Sisule Fredrick Musungu, "The Industrial Property Act 2001 and Access to Essential Medicines in Kenya: An Analysis of the Public Health Safeguards," South Centre, 2002, p. 11.

3 Médecins sans Frontières Access Campaign, 2001, available at www.msf.org.

4 TRIPS Agreement, article 31(f) and (h).

7.2.1.1. Challenges to the Use of Parallel Imports and Compulsory Licensing in South Africa and Brazil

The use of parallel imports and compulsory licensing are, therefore, consistent with the TRIPS Agreement.[5] However, a number of governments and pharmaceutical industries have strongly objected to their use in some developing countries, such as South Africa and Brazil. In the case of South Africa, the clash between the interests of patent holders and the use of flexibilities to promote developmental goals like access to medicines relates to an amendment to South Africa's Medicines Act in 1997 allowing parallel imports and compulsory licensing of pharmaceuticals. The purpose of the amendment was to facilitate the "supply of *more affordable medicines* in certain circumstances so as to protect the health of the public."[6] The United States Government denounced the measure as an infringement of patent rights and the Office of the US Trade Representative (USTR) designated South Africa as a Special 301 'watch list' country – a status that could lead to trade sanctions. The dispute was temporarily settled by a political understanding between the two governments.[7] However, on 18 February 1998, 39 pharmaceutical companies filed a suit against the South African president and the Department of Health.[8] As a result of civil society mobilization, the legal Action was withdrawn.[9]

---

5 TRIPS Agreement, articles 6 and 31 respectively.

6 Medicines and Related Substances Control Amendment Act, 1997, Act No 90, 1997, Government Gazette vol. 390, No. 18505, 12 December 1997. Article 15C of the Act provides:

> The Minister may prescribe conditions for the supply of more affordable medicines in certain circumstances so as to protect the health of the public, and in particular may
>
> a) notwithstanding anything to the contrary in the Patents Act, 1978 (Act No. 57 of 1978), determine that the rights with regard to any medicine under a patent granted in the Republic shall not extend to acts in respect of such medicine which has been put onto the market by the owner of the medicine, or with his or her consent;
> b) prescribe the conditions on which any medicine which is identical in composition, meets the same quality standard and is intended to have the same proprietary name as that of another medicine already registered in the Republic, but which is imported by a person other than the person who is the holder of the registration certificate of the medicine already registered and which originated from any site of manufacture of the original manufacturers as approved by the council in the prescribed manner, may be imported;
> c) prescribe the registration procedure for, as well as the use of, the medicine referred to in paragraph (b) (emphasis added).

7 Pedro Roffe, Christophe Spennemann and Johanna von Braun, "From Paris to Doha; The WTO Doha Declaration on the TRIPS Agreement and Public Health," in Roffe, Pedro *et al* eds. *Negotiating Health: Intellectual Property and Access to Medicines*. (London: Earthscan, 2005). 9–26, at 16 (hereinafter referred to as Pedro *et al*, From Paris to Doha).

8 *Pharmaceutical Manufacturer's Association of South Africa and others v. President of the Republic of South Africa*, (Transvaal Provincial Division), Case no. 4183/98, Notice of Motion.

9 For a detailed analysis of the political circumstance surrounding the dispute and legal issues arising therefrom, see for example Botoy Ituku, Propriété Intellectuelle et Droits de L'homme, *supra*, Part three, chapter II; and Hestermeyer, Human Rights and the WTO, *supra*, pp. 11–14.

In the case of Brazil, the U.S. challenged the Brazilian Industrial Property Law,[10] which authorized granting of compulsory licences and parallel imports in instances where the patent holders had not worked or produced the patented invention in Brazil. In other words, lack of "local working" is a ground for grant of a compulsory licence under the Brazilian Patent Law.[11] On 30 May 2000, the U.S. brought a complaint against Brazil before the WTO, alleging that article 68(1) (I) of the Brazilian legislation was inconsistent with Brazil's obligations under articles 27 (which defines patentable subject matter) and 28 (which defines the rights conferred by a patent) of the TRIPS Agreement and Article III of the GATT 1994.[12] The U.S. requested the establishment of a panel,[13] but the complaint was later withdrawn after the parties found a mutually agreed solution.[14]

The main issue in both of the preceding cases was the use of flexibilities in the TRIPS Agreement. In particular, governments of developing countries tried to use exceptions in the TRIPS Agreement to enable their populations to access drugs at affordable prices.[15] In both cases, the two developing country Members of WTO were making use of some of the flexibilities in the TRIPS Agreement to promote the public interest of access to medicine. They were not violating the TRIPS Agreement as such. Yet, they were subjected to intimidation and litigation. The possibility of litigation and/or trade sanctions serves to discourage other weak WTO Members from making full use of TRIPS flexibilities at the national level. It is this conflict, arising from the use of flexibilities, which led to negotiation of the Doha Declaration on the TRIPS Agreement and Public Health. The Declaration and the subsequent decisions are a test on the WTO as a development institution.

7.2.1.2. Major Provisions of the Declaration Relevant to Public Health

Under the Doha Declaration on the TRIPS Agreement and Public Health, the WTO Members affirmed that the TRIPS Agreement can and should be interpreted and

---

10 Brazil, Industrial Property Law (number 9,279 of 14 May 1996, effective as of 15 May 1997), as amended by law No. 196 of February 14 2001. Article 68 provides that a patentee will be subject to having its patent compulsorily licensed if he exercises rights resulting there from in an abusive manner or by means of abuse of economic power proven under the terms of the law by an administrative or court decision. The following may also result in a compulsory licence; I. Non-exploitation of the subject matter or the patent in the territory of Brazil, by lack of manufacture or incomplete manufacture of the product or, furthermore, by the lack of complete use of a patented process, except in the case f non-exploitation due to economic unfeasibility, when importation will be permitted; […]

11 This is consisted with article 5A (2) of the Paris Convention. Under the provision, failure to work a patent is an abuse of patent rights for which a compulsory licence can issue.

12 *Brazil – Measures Affecting Patent Protection,* Request for Consultations by the United States, G/L/385, IP/D/23, WT/DS199/1, 8 June 2000.

13 *Brazil – Measures Affecting Patent Protection,* Request for the Establishment of a Panel by the United States, WT/DS199/3, 9 January 2001.

14 *Brazil – Measures Affecting Patent Protection,* Notification of Mutually Agreed Solution, G/L/454, IP/D/23/Add.1, WT/DS/199/4, 19 July 2001.

15 See also in this sense, Frederick M. Abbott, "Trade Diplomacy, the Rule of Law and the Problem of Asymmetric Risks in TRIPS," Quaker United Nations Office (QUNO), Occasional Paper 13, (2003) p. 3. available at http://www.quno.org/economicissues/intellectual-property/intellectualLinks.htm (hereinafter referred to as Abbott, Trade diplomacy).

implemented in a manner supportive of WTO Members' right to protect public health and, in particular, to promote access to medicine for all.[16] As some authors have stated, the Declaration recognized the gravity of the public health problems afflicting many developing countries and the need to address these problems.[17] In this connection, the Declaration affirmed the 'right' of Members to use, to the fullest extent, the provisions of the TRIPS Agreement which provide flexibility for this purpose.

Under the Declaration, WTO Members are free to establish their own regimes on exhaustion of intellectual property rights or use parallel imports.[18]

7.2.1.4. Legal Status and Effect of the Declaration

The Declaration clarified the relationship between the TRIPS Agreement and Public health and stressed the need to strike a balance between intellectual property and wider policy objectives such as public health. In other words, the Declaration interpreted the relevant provisions.[19] Professor Pauwelyn[20] questions the possibility of the Declaration interpreting the TRIPS Agreement, since the Council for TRIPS does not, in his view, appear to have made a recommendation to the Ministerial Conference for such an interpretation as is required by article IX:2 of the Marrakesh Agreement Establishing the World Trade Organization.[21] However, we submit that since the Declaration was negotiated within the Council for TRIPS and the Ministerial Conference simply adopted what had been agreed upon in the Council, there was an implied recommendation. A recommendation does not need to be in writing.

The Declaration reaffirmed some of the provisions of the TRIPS Agreement.[22] In confirming that the Agreement has left room for flexibility at the national level, such as the

---

16 Declaration on the TRIPS Agreement and Public Health, *supra*, paragraph 4.

17 Roffe *et al*, From Paris to Doha; *supra*, p. 10.

18 *ibid*, paragraph 5(d). Article 6 of the TRIPS Agreement allows for parallel imports. The owner of an IP right loses that right when he puts his product to sell. It is said that he has exhausted his rights. It is then no violation of an IP right to for a person other than the right holder imports a product put on the market by the consent of the IP owner.

19 The ICJ defined 'interpretation' as a way to obtain clarification of the meaning and scope of [something, in this case] what the court had decided. *Request for Interpretation of the Judgment of November 20th, 1950 in the Asylum Case*, (Colombia v. Peru), Judgment of 27 November 1950, I.C.J Reports 1950, p.395 at 402.

20 Pauwelyn, Conflict of Norms, *supra*, p. 47.

21 Marrakesh Agreement Establishing the World Trade Organization, 15 April 1994, in *The Results of the Uruguay Round of Multilateral Negotiations, The Legal Texts*, (World Trade Organization, 1999). Article IX:2 stipulates that the Ministerial Conference and the General Council have the exclusive power to adopt interpretations of multilateral trade agreements like TRIPS. In the case of the TRIPS Agreement, the authority to interpret is given by a recommendation by the TRIPS Council.

22 Articles 7 and 8 of the TRIPS Agreement refer, *inter alia*, to a need to balance rights and obligations and the need to adopt measures necessary to protect public health and nutrition. See also Paul Vandoren and Jean Charles Van Eeckhaute, "The WTO Decision on paragraph 6 of the Doha Declaration on the TRIPS Agreement and Public Health: Making it work," *Journal of World Intellectual Property*, vol.6, no 4 (2003), 779–793, saying that the Declaration broke new grounds in clarifying this relationship (p. 1); Roffe, *et al*, From Paris to Doha; *supra*, pp. 18, (stating that

determination of the grounds for compulsory licensing and the admission of parallel imports, the Declaration has important political and legal implications. It indicates that the pressures exerted by some developed countries like the USA and the EU on developing countries to refrain from using available flexibilities run counter to the spirit and purpose of the TRIPS Agreement, especially in light of the recognized "gravity of the problems" which developing countries and LDCs face in the area of public health.[23]

In legal terms, this means that panels and the Appellate Body must interpret the TRIPS Agreement and the laws and regulations adopted to implement it in the light of the public health needs of individual Members.[24] However, the Declaration *does not* establish an automatic superiority of public health over the TRIPS Agreement,[25] or interests of right holders.[26] This is reminiscent of flexibilities in copyright law – they are favours which do not place the user in a superior position than the owner of rights. For this reason, the use of the flexibility for public interests like access to medication or education remains a permissible act and not a right.[27] In other words, this does not change the nature of flexibilities in international intellectual property law; they are only permissible and not mandatory.

7.2.2. *Legal Recognition of the Ineffectiveness of Flexibilities in Developing Countries: The Decision on Paragraph 6*[28]

The major issue dealt with in the Doha Declaration on TRIPS and Public Health was how countries with insufficient manufacturing capacity in the pharmaceutical sector would be

---

the Declaration reiterates what is already stipulated in the TRIPS Agreement and recognizes considerable room for the pursuit by Member Countries of public policy objectives, especially those related to public health). We, however, wish to emphasize that articles 7 and 8 of TRIPS do not apply to copyright or education.

23 Carlos Correa, "Recent International Developments in the Area of Intellectual Property Rights," Contribution to the second UNCTAD-ICTSD Bellagio Series on Development and Intellectual Property, 18–21 September 2003, p. 1, available at www.iprsonline.org/unctadictsd/bellagio/docs/Correa_Bellagio2.pdf. (hereinafter referred to as Correa, recent developments). These pressures are mainly exerted through what is referred to as 'TRIPS-plus', a term used to mean those provisions in bilateral or free trade agreements or measures, which provide for or require countries, especially LDCs and developing countries, to provide stronger IP protection than already exists in the TRIPS Agreement.

24 Doha Declaration on the TRIPS Agreement and Public Health, *supra*, paragraph 4. See also Correa, Recent International Developments, *supra*.

25 Roger Kampf, "Patents versus Patients," quoted in Hestermeyer, Human Rights and the WTO, *supra* p. 261 (emphasis added).

26 For example in the case of article 8, any measure taken to protect public health has to be consistent with the provisions of TRIPS. See TRIPS Agreement, article 8(1).

27 As we demonstrated in chapter 3, flexibilities or limitations and exceptions to copyright are only permissible, meaning a country is not penalized for not granting them. On the other hand, granting copyright protection is mandatory. Similarly in the case of patents, Members may (but are not obliged) provide limited exceptions (TRIPS article 30); Members may adopt measures necessary to protect public health and nutrition (TRIPS article 8).

28 "Implementation of paragraph 6 of the Doha Declaration on the TRIPS Agreement and Public Health," General Council Decision IP/C/W/405 of 30 August 2003. (The 30 August 2003 decision.)

able to make full use of compulsory licensing.[29] The aforesaid countries essentially include developing and least developed countries. As an attempt at resolving this problem, the Ministerial Conference at Doha instructed the Council for TRIPS to find an expeditious solution to the problem before the end of 2002.[30]

What is important to note at this point is that there was an international recognition that some of the flexibilities provided for in international intellectual property law fail to be effective for developing countries, not because they lack legal weight but because of the special economic circumstances (in this case, lack of manufacturing capacity) of those countries. The WTO, as an institution, acknowledged the fact that the economic circumstances of developing countries make legal solutions for access to protected IP inapplicable.

The result of paragraph 6 of the Declaration on TRIPS and Public Health was the 30 August 2003 Decision by the Council for TRIPS. The Declaration had requested that the Council for TRIPS find an 'expeditious solution', but the Decision was made two years after the Declaration. The Declaration was made three years after the challenge was made to the use by South Africa of the flexibilities provided for in international IP law. In total, therefore, South Africa had to wait for five years for the WTO to solve the problem, if at all.[31]

The Decision provides an interim solution in the form of waivers relating to article 31 of the TRIPS Agreement. The first waiver relates to article 31(f)[32] and the second relates to article 31(h).[33]

There are detailed procedural requirements attached to the use of the waiver Decision. These include self-identification, like under the Berne Appendix, as a country that qualifies to use the system under the waiver, making of notification of intention to use the system, and details as to the amounts of products, labelling of products and remuneration under the compulsory licensing system.

7.2.2.3. Evaluation of the Decision

Indeed, the predominant criticism of the Decision concerns the cumbersome legal and procedural requirements which could hinder the effective use of the system. As one author has rightly stated, "[the various] notifications along with the additional conditions for the issuance of a compulsory licence and safeguards against re-exportation, make the

29 According to article 31(f) of the TRIPS Agreement, compulsory licensing should be granted predominantly for the supply of the domestic market of the Member authorizing or granting the compulsory licence, which presupposes the existence of manufacturing capacity. It follows that it is not possible for a country that is able to manufacture, for example, a pharmaceutical product, to issue a compulsory licence in order to supply a third country which needs the product but has no capacity to produce it.

30 Declaration on the TRIPS Agreement and Public Health, *supra,* para. 6 (emphasis added).

31 Later on we demonstrate that the procedural requirements of the Decision render it ineffective. (*Infra,* section 7.2.2.2.). In effect, the solution provided by the Decision is of limited value.

32 The 30 August 2003 decision, *supra,* preamble and para. 2.

33 *Ibid,* preamble and para. 3. Article 31(h) provides for payment of adequate remuneration to the patent holder when a compulsory licence in granted.

Decision a highly cumbersome and inoperable mechanism with which to ensure supply of cheap drugs to developing countries."[34]

The practical implication of this cumbersome procedure is the reduction of the effectiveness of the system. To provide details regarding importing Member(s), quotas, special labelling and packaging, notifications and so on, is not only administratively time consuming but also imposes extra costs on the exporting country and the suppliers/licensee(s). In turn this either discourages exporting Member(s) from using the system or makes the generic drugs expensive for the importing Member. Indeed, during the negotiation of the Decision, developing countries Members were concerned about possible restrictions of the conditions on the solution to paragraph 6 of the Declaration.[35] This concern was not unfounded. In July 2007, four years after the Decision, Rwanda made a notification requesting supply of a certain medicine.[36] Canada promptly responded to Rwanda's request by notifying in October 2007 that it would supply the requested medicine.[37] However, it was not until September 2008, more than a year after the request, that the first batch of medicine was shipped to Rwanda. The reasons given for this delay by the top management of Apotex, the only generic drug company that has sought to supply medicine under the Decision, were the complex and costly administrative process.[38]

The waiver of the obligation under article 31(f) means only that a WTO Member will not complain against another Member using the system; but it does not prevent a private party from blocking the exportation or importation of drugs if national laws do not specifically permit such exports or imports under compulsory licences.[39] The lessons for copyright and access to education is that national laws should permit the use of flexibilities provided for at the international level. Like in the case of compulsory licensing for copyright under the Berne Appendix, the patent owner is given the opportunity to block the use of compulsory licensing under the waiver Decision.

---

34 Gopakumar, *supra,* p. 108.

35 Communication from Brazil on behalf of Developing Countries – Paragraph 6 of the Ministerial Declaration on the TRIPS Agreement and Public Health, document IP/C/W/355 of 24 June 2002.

36 Notification under paragraph 2(A) of the Decision of 30 August 2003 on the Implementation of Paragraph 6 of the Doha Declaration on the TRIPS Agreement and Public Health, WTO document no. IP/N/10/RWA/1, dated 19 July 2007 (information available at http://www.wto.org/english/tratop_e/trips_e/public_health_e.htm).

37 Notification under paragraph 2(C) of the Decision of 30 August 2003 on the Implementation Of Paragraph 6 of the Doha Declaration on the TRIPS Agreement and Public Health, WTO document no. IP/N/10/CAN/1, dated 8 October 2007 (information available at http://www.wto.org/english/tratop_e/trips_e/public_health_e.htm).

38 Jack Kay, the Chief of Apotex stated that the reason other companies have not tried to provide medicines under the regime [of the Decision] is because "it is too complex and has to be repeated for every request that comes in from a country. For Canada to truly be able to provide help, the regime must be changed." On his part, Elie Bettio, the director of public affairs of Apotex, says "It's a huge process, with huge costs involved," so Apotex will not supply the medicine again. See International Centre for Trade and Sustainable Development, "First Generic Drugs en Route to Africa under 5-year-old WTO deal," Bridges Weekly Trade News Digest, volume 12, no. 31, 25 September 2008, available at www.ictsd.net.

39 Correa, Recent International Developments, *supra,* p. 3, and Correa, Correa, Implementation of WTO General Council Decision, *supra,* p. 5.

The Decision was adopted as a temporary solution, to be replaced by a permanent solution in the form of an amendment to the TRIPS Agreement.[40] It is within this context that the General Council, acting on behalf of the Ministerial Conference,[41] adopted an amendment to the TRIPS Agreement.

7.2.3. *Amendment of the TRIPS Agreement*

On 8 December 2005, the WTO General Council adopted a Protocol amending the TRIPS Agreement by adding article 31*bis* to the Agreement.[42] The adoption of the amendment does not terminate the Decision. The Decision will cease to apply to a WTO Member on the date on which the amendment to the TRIPS Agreement takes effect for that Member.[43] The Protocol shall take effect when it is accepted by two thirds of the Members, in accordance with the provisions of paragraph 3 of Article X of the WTO Agreement.[44] As of 28 February 2012, more than 6 years after the amendment decision, only 41 out of 153 WTO Members had accepted the Protocol.[45] This is reminiscent of the Stockholm Protocol which could not enter into force for lack of signature.[46]

One should not ignore the legal value of the Declaration and the Decision, from which the amendment to the TRIPS Agreement was born. The Declaration and subsequent Decision gave permission to countries with manufacturing capacity in the pharmaceutical field to issue compulsory licences to generic manufacturers *to manufacture and export to countries without manufacturing capacity*. However, neither Declaration nor the Decision created any obligations for any Member to use the system. Obligations only arise if a Member *chooses* to use the Decision, either as a potential exporter or importer. Such obligations relate to the procedure for how to use the system under the Decision. Just as in

---

40 30 August 2003, *supra*, paragraph 11.

41 Under article IV(2) of the WTO Agreement, the General Council of WTO acts on behalf of the Ministerial Conference between sessions of the latter.

42 Amendment to the TRIPS Agreement, Decision of 6 December 2005, document no. WT/L/641 of 8 December 2005. The amending protocol is an attachment to this document. Article 31*bis* is Annex the Amending Protocol. The Hong Kong Ministerial Conference welcomed the decision of the TRIPS Council to amend the TRIPS Agreement. See Hong Kong Ministerial Declaration, Doha Work Programme, adopted on 18 December 2005, WTO document WT/MIN/05/DEC of 22 December 2005, paragraph 40.

43 30 August 2003, *supra*, paragraph 11.

44 Amendment to the TRIPS Agreement, Decision of 6 December 2005, document no. WT/L/641 of 8 December 2005, paragraph 3. Article X(3) of the WTO Agreement provides:
Amendments to provisions of this Agreement, or of the Multilateral Trade Agreements in Annexes 1A and 1C,[44] [...] of a nature that would alter the rights and obligations of the Members, shall take effect for the Members that have accepted them upon acceptance by two thirds of the Members and thereafter for each other Member upon acceptance by it. The Ministerial Conference may decide by a three-fourths majority of the Members that any amendment made effective under this paragraph is of such a nature that any Member which has not accepted it within a period specified by the Ministerial Conference in each case shall be free to withdraw with the consent of the Ministerial Conference.

45 See information available at http://www.wto.org/english/tratop_e/trips_e/amendment_e.htm.

46 See discussion in chapter 5 on the Stockholm Protocol.

case of the copyright or the Berne Appendix in particular, there is no obligation to use the flexibilities or the compulsory licensing system.

Rather than asking whether and how the Declaration and Decision have been used to promote health, it should be queried "why"? It is essential to consider the economic cost. We have already demonstrated that the procedure under the system is so cumbersome that it acts to discourage potential generic manufacturers. For the potential exporting countries to use the system, economic incentives are required. Otherwise, they will act merely for 'humanitarian' reasons and not out of legal obligation. Indeed, Canada has amended its legislation to allow compulsory licensing for export under the Decision. The title of the amending legislation[47] is revealing of the 'humanitarian' element. The first clause, which adds a new part to the Patent Act, is entitled "Use of Patents for International Humanitarian Purposes to Address Public Health Problems." However, the Canadian law provides for the right of first refusal,[48] which gives the patent holder the option to be the supplier of the requested pharmaceutical product,[49] and the listing of medicines for which a compulsory licence may be obtained.[50] These provisions go beyond the requirements of the Decision[51] and reduce incentives for generic manufacturers.

In short, where the system is not economically rewarding, it is not legally effective. So this solution does not solve the problem of dependence on political will of the exporting country. The success of the system depends on its acceptance by countries with manufacturing capacity. It is not surprising that, more than eight years after the Decision, there have been only two notifications – one from Rwanda and the other from Canada in response to Rwanda's request.

This points to the need to devise solutions that will not hold developing countries at the mercy of developed countries or owners of IP works when using flexibilities.

7.2.4. *Extension of the Transition Period for LDCs*

The TRIPS Agreement provides transition periods within which Members should implement the Agreement according to their level of development.[52] In relation to LDCs, the transition period was supposed to expire in 2005. However, TRIPS provides that "[t]he Council for TRIPS shall, upon duly motivated request by a least developed country

47 Bill C-9: An Act to amend the Patent Act and the Food and Drugs Act.

48 Patent Act Patent Act 1985, C. P-4, as amended by the Patents Act (Consolidation) of 30 April 1996), section 21.04(6)(a).

49 This is ironical, as there is no guarantee that the patent holder would be willing to manufacture the required product at a price affordable to the intending importer and within a reasonable time.

50 Patent Act Patent Act 1985, C. P-4, as amended by the Patents Act (Consolidation) Act, section 21.04(6)(a), section 21.03. Schedule 1 contains a list of patented products that could be used to address public health problems under the legislation. The list currently includes all products on the World Health Organization's (WHO) list of essential medicines that are currently under patent in Canada.

51 Although we have to remember that the Decision, like the international IP instruments, provides only minimum standards.

52 TRIPS Agreement, articles 65 and 66.

Member, accord extensions of this period."[53] On 30 November 2005, WTO Members, through the Council for TRIPS, accorded LDCs an extension of seven and a half years, until 2013, to apply intellectual property rules under the TRIPS Agreement.[54] In submitting the request on behalf of the WTO's 32 LDC Members, Zambia cited "[...] serious economic, financial and administrative constraints as well as a need for flexibility to create a viable technological base."[55]

For the following reasons, the granting of this extension does not render unnecessary a discussion of intellectual property rights and access to education. First, when this new transition period expires, the LDCs will have to implement the provisions of the TRIPS Agreement. Indeed under the Decision, LDCs were required to provide the Council for TRIPS, preferably by 1 January 2008, as much information as possible on their individual priority needs for technical and financial cooperation in order to assist them in taking *steps necessary to implement the TRIPS Agreement.*[56] Second, this extension only relates to the TRIPS Agreement and not the WIPO treaties. Thus, LDCs which are parties to the Berne Convention still have to comply with their obligations under the Convention. As demonstrated above, no flexibilities exist under the Berne Convention that developing countries and LDCs in particular can use to promote access to copyrighted works in the analogue environment. Third, by the time the extension was granted, a number of LDCs had already changed their laws to implement the TRIPS Agreement. Yet, under the extending decision, LDCs are "[...] to ensure that any changes in their laws, regulations and practice made during the additional transition period do not result in a lesser degree of consistency with the provisions of the TRIPS Agreement".[57] In other words, this so-called 'stand-still clause'[58] will freeze intellectual property-related laws that LDCs have already implemented, preventing them from reducing their scope or level of protection. The extension came too late for most LDCs.

---

53 TRIPS Agreement, article 66(1).

54 Extension of the Transition Period Under Article 66.1 for Least-developed Country Members: Decision of the Council for TRIPS of 29 November 2005, document no. IP/C/40 dated 30 November 2005, paragraph 1. Article 66(1) of the TRIPS Agreement allows LDC Members to request for an extension of the transitional period after which they have to apply the TRIPS Agreement.

55 Council for TRIPS. Request for an extension of the transitional period under Article 66.1 of the TRIPS Agreement. Communication from the Delegation of Zambia on behalf of the Least-Developed Country Members document IP/C/W/457 of 21 October 2005. Zambia requested for an extension of 15 years.

56 Decision on Extension of Transition Period for LDCs, *supra,* paragraph 2, (emphasis added). The extension anticipates that LDCs will still implement the Agreement. The emphasis is not on derogation or use of flexibility. The extension is a 'flexibility' in itself, but it does not solve the challenges – economic, administrative etc, LDCs meet in implementing the Agreement and at the same time providing public interest needs like access to education.

57 Decision on Extension of Transition Period for LDCs, *supra,* paragraph 5.

58 Bridges Weekly Trade News Digest, International Centre for Trade and Sustainable Development (ICTSD), Volume 9, no. 21, 23 November 2005, page 1, available at http://www.ictsd.net/weekly/05-11-30/story3.htm

7.2.5. *Lessons from the WTO for Copyright and Education*

The Doha Declaration on the TRIPS Agreement and Public Health,[59] the subsequent Decision on paragraph 6 of the Declaration,[60] and the resulting Protocol amending the TRIPS Agreement[61] represent attempts by the WTO to provide access to protected works, in this case patented goods, for public interest goals like improving public health. Though only addressing patents and health, the substantive elements of the Declaration, Decision, and Protocol may serve as lessons for bettering access to education through copyright.[62]

First, the Decision on paragraph 6 of the Declaration represents international recognition that some of the flexibilities in international intellectual property law fail to be effective for developing countries because of their special economic circumstances. The WTO acknowledged the fact that these circumstances make legal solutions for access to protected goods inapplicable or unworkable.[63] There may, therefore, be a need to develop special regimes for these countries. In WIPO in the area of copyright, a similar recognition was acknowledged historically through the Stockholm Protocol[64] and the Berne Appendix.[65]

Second, the Decision on paragraph 6 and the Berne Appendix represent failures at both the institutional and normative level to address the challenge of access to protected works. As has been well-noted by others, neither regime solved this challenge of enabling developing countries to promote their domestic public interests. The procedural requirements associated with both regimes rendered the substantive provisions sufficiently complex to administer with high transaction costs involved in complying with the various stipulations. In addition, many of the corresponding requirements imposed within the

---

59 Declaration on the TRIPS Agreement and Public Health, adopted on 14 November at the 4th WTO Ministerial Conference, Doha, 9–14 November 2001, document no. WT/MIN(01)/DEC/2, dated 20 November 2001. (available at http://www.wto.org/english/thewto_e/minist_e/min01_e/mindecl_trips_e.pdf)

60 Implementation of paragraph 6 of the Doha Declaration on the TRIPS Agreement and Public Health. General Council Decision IP/C/W/405 of 30 August 2003.

61 Amendment to the TRIPS Agreement, Decision of 6 December 2005, document no. WT/L/641 of 8 December 2005, Attachment.

62 Articles 7, 8 and 31 of TRIPS are addressed to patents. Articles 7 and 8 refer to promotion of technological innovation and to the transfer and dissemination of technology; and public health and nutrition. As such, they are not addressed to copyright. Also in the same line, see Carlos Correa, *Trade related aspects of intellectual property rights: a commentary on the TRIPS Agreement,* (Oxford: Oxford University Press, 2007), p. 92.

63 The major issue dealt with in the Doha Declaration on TRIPS and Public Health was how countries with insufficient manufacturing capacity in the pharmaceutical sector would be able to make full use of compulsory licensing. The subsequent Decision on paragraph 6 of the Declaration was meant to provide a solution.

64 Protocol Regarding Developing Countries, article 1(b)(ii)-(ix), reproduced in Records of the Intellectual Property Conference of Stockholm, 1967, *supra,* vol. II, Report of the Work of Main Committee II, p. 1197.

65 The Berne Convention, *supra,* Appendix.

regimes were designed to ensure that producers of those works would lack sufficient economies of scale, thus discouraging local entrepreneurs from taking advantage of the licensing models. Finally, under a strict interpretation approach, those flexibilities that do exist outside specialized regimes are best characterized as favours, which can be effectively used by developing countries solely to the extent that they do not conflict with the interests of developed countries, who own the knowledge-based products, as stipulated in articles 9(2) of the Berne Convention (BC) and 13 of TRIPS.

Third, like the Stockholm Protocol and the Berne Appendix, the Doha Declaration reflects a long-standing reluctance on the part of developed countries to explore meaningful institutional reform to solve challenges to realizing public interest goals traditionally associated with the international IP regime. In the case of Doha, the lack of convergence on public interest priorities was evidenced by the fact that even after the Declaration, and during negotiations on paragraph 6, developed countries continued to conclude Free Trade Agreements (FTAs) that prevented the use of flexibilities, including the application of the Doha Decision.[66] In the case of the Stockholm Protocol, developed countries campaigned against the signing of the Protocol.[67] The difference between the Stockholm Protocol and the Doha Declaration (and Protocol amending TRIPS) is that the former would automatically culminate in a legal instrument that would be directly enforceable by the developing countries, while the effective implementation of the Declaration depended on the cooperation of the developed countries.[68]

The failure of the solution to address public health needs provided under the WTO regime is a clear sign that there is a need to look for international solutions within other institutional frameworks. Notably, these failures show that the WTO, an organization whose major purpose is to protect and promote trade, is not in the best position to provide a global solution on IP issues without the need to address corresponding side-bargains in other areas of its competence.[69] At a minimum, this suggests that multilateral bargains for specialized regimes for developing countries may, in the end, be too politically costly for an organization with a broad mandate. It thus is not surprising that

66 A discussion on FTAs is beyond the scope of this article. For a discussion on the same in light of the Doha Declaration, see Frederick M. Abbott, "The Doha Declaration on the TRIPS Agreement and Public Health and the Contradictory Trend in Bilateral and Regional Trade Agreements," QUNO, Occasional Paper no. 14, (2004), p.4, available at http://www.quno.org.

67 For detailed narrative of the developments following the adoption of the Stockholm Protocol, see Sam Ricketson, *The Berne Convention, supra,* 621–623.

68 This situation will not change even if the amendment to the TRIPS Agreement becomes effective. The procedural requirements of the Decision are the same as under the Amendment.

69 But for an analysis comparing institutional design features of the WTO and WIPO for purposes of generating welfare-oriented norms, see Ruth L. Okediji, "WIPO-WTO Relations and the Future of Global Intellectual property Norms," *Netherlands Yearbook of International Law,* (The Hague: Nijhoff, cop, 2008). 69 - 125, (hereafter referred to as Okediji, WIPO-WTO Relations).

solutions such as the Doha Declaration (and the extension of transition periods)[70] have been a failure.[71]

The principal IP deliverable of the WTO, the TRIPS Agreement, is based on a system established by WIPO. Given this fact, it is implausible to think that WIPO can be excluded when trying to find a solution for new or newly-contested issues in international IP regulation. If there is going to be an international solution to copyright regulation and issues of access, WIPO has to take the lead.[72] As Professor Boyle rightly stated, "[T]here are systematic errors in the contemporary intellectual property policy and ... WIPO has an important role in helping to correct them".[73] Even in recognizing the strategic importance of the WTO, another leading scholar has noted that "it is still WIPO that defines what [international] IP *is*."[74] WIPO has to lead in reforming the Berne Convention and other IP systems to provide clear access principles to protected works. This reform mandate should include an express authority for WIPO to interpret the Conventions administered by it, instead of leaving this task to the WTO Dispute Settlement Body.[75]

But normative solutions alone are not enough. If WIPO is to improve access to IP for educational purposes, this will have to occur through a "cocktail" of mechanisms: conventional, quasi-conventional and non-conventional. In the following sections, we analyse in detail recent developments in WIPO, in particular the adoption of the WIPO Development Agenda (DA) and proposals for work on L&Es in the Standing Committee on Copyright

70 Extension of the Transition Period Under Article 66.1 for Least-developed Country Members: Decision of the Council for TRIPS of 29 November 2005, document no. IP/C/40 dated 30 November 2005.

71 In the same sense although in the context of patents and technology transfer, see Keith E. Maskus, "The WIPO Development Agenda: A cautionary Note," in Neil Weinstock Netanel, ed, *The Development Agenda: Global Intellectual Property and Developing Countries, supra,* 163–174, at 164, (saying that the relative inability of the WTO process to move forward in the Doha Round means that it has not served as a sensible forum for advocating global reform).

72 This is the case notwithstanding the shortcomings of the Stockholm Protocol and the Berne Appendix. There is a shift in WIPO towards promoting access to protected works.

73 See James Boyle, "A Manifesto on WIPO and the future of intellectual property," *Duke Law and Technology Review*, no. 9, (2004). 1–12, p. 1.

74 Okediji, WIPO-WTO Relations, *supra,*. 118.

75 For example, the WTO panel recently interpreted article 17 of the Berne Convention restrictively. See *China – Measures affecting the protection and enforcement of Intellectual Property Rights*, Report of the Panel, WT/DS362/R, 26 January, 2009. The provision allows Members to censor the circulation, presentation or exhibition of copyrighted works for reasons of public order. In an earlier case the WTO panel interpreted article 9(2) of the Berne Convention. See *United States – Section 110(5) of the US Copyright Act,* Report of the Panel, WT/DS160/R, 15 June 2000. The panel interpreted article 9(2) of the Berne Convention through an economic lens. One cannot ignore the sociological effect on a WTO panellist. A panellist deciding a dispute in a trade environment is very likely to take the decision with a trade bias without regard being given to social concerns like health or education. If WIPO is to lead in reform of the Berne Convention to facilitate access to protected works, it cannot leave the interpretation of the Convention to WTO which has a trade orientation. The WIPO Convention should be amended to vest the authority to interpret the Berne Convention in WIPO instead of the ICJ as is currently the case under article 33 of the Berne Convention.

and Related Rights (SCCR), in an attempt to understand the implications for WIPO's role in facilitating access to protected IP works.

7.3. The WIPO DA: Recent Adoption by WIPO of Development Approaches to Copyrighted Works

In September 2007, the General Assembly of WIPO adopted the Development Agenda (DA).[76] The DA is a set of 45 recommendations addressed to WIPO, asking it to perform or facilitate the performance of development-oriented activities. If the recommendations are properly implemented, there will be more access to protected works, although not necessarily in the analogue environment. In the following pages, we discuss the origins and legal basis of the DA as well as the extent to which it can facilitate more access to protected works, especially public goods.

7.3.2. *Legal Basis of the Development Agenda: A Constitutional Reform of WIPO*

A proposal for a development agenda for WIPO was first launched at the WIPO 2004 General Assembly by "Friends of Development" which included Argentina, Brazil and other developing countries.[77] In justifying the development dimension of IP, it was argued, "Development concerns should be fully incorporated into all WIPO activities. WIPO's role, therefore, is not to be limited to the promotion of intellectual property protection."[78] In particular, it was suggested that WIPO consider the possibility of amending the WIPO Convention (1967) to ensure that the "development dimension" is unequivocally determined to constitute an essential element of the Organization's work program. The proposal called upon the WIPO General Assembly to take immediate action in providing for the incorporation of a "Development Agenda" in the Organization's work program.[79] As such, WIPO was asked to modify its mandate and the way it operates to include a development-oriented approach to IP which would equally allow access to protected works. In legal terms, WIPO was being asked to modify the WIPO Convention.

The WIPO Member states, through the General Assembly, agreed to hold a series of inter-sessional intergovernmental meetings (IIMs) to examine proposals submitted by developing countries.[80] The decision represented a watershed in the intellectual property

---

76 WIPO General Assembly, Thirty-Fourth (18th Ordinary) Session, Geneva, September 24 to October 3, 2005, Report, World Intellectual Property Organization, Document no. WO/GA/32/13, dated November 12, 2005.

77 WIPO General Assembly. Thirty-First (15th Ordinary) Session, Geneva, September 27 to October 5, 2004. Proposal by Argentina and Brazil for the Establishment of a Development Agenda for WIPO, World Intellectual Property Organization, Document no. WO/GA/31/11, dated September 27, 2004. The Proposal for the establishment of a development agenda was presented by Brazil and Argentina, and co-sponsored by Bolivia, Cuba, the Dominican Republic, Ecuador, Egypt, Iran (Islamic Republic of), Kenya, Peru, Sierra Leone, South Africa, Tanzania and Venezuela. This group of countries are referred to as the Group of Friends of Development.

78 WIPO General Assembly. Thirty-First (15th Ordinary) Session, *supra,* Proposal by Argentina and Brazil for the Establishment of a Development Agenda for WIPO, Annex, para. III.

79 *Ibid.*

80 WIPO General Assembly. Thirty-First (15th Ordinary) Session, *supra,* paras 148–218.

and development debate.[81] For the first time, Members of WIPO, including developed countries with particular interests in strong IP protection, formally expressed a change in perception of the purpose of IP. The approval by the General Assembly of a discussion on the development dimension of IP meant legal acceptance that WIPO could discuss the social implications of IP and not merely focus on its protection and enforcement. In other words, the General Assembly officially accepted to modify the mandate of WIPO[82] to include a development dimension of IP. In this respect, the DA can be viewed as a constitutional reform in WIPO, or at least a move towards such reform.

The result of this reform was a new focus on the integration of the development dimension of intellectual property into the international IP scheme. For example, at the 2005 session of the WIPO GA, Argentina, speaking on behalf of the "Friends of Development," stressed the integration of the development dimension. Further, Argentina stated that this would ensure that the concerns of developing countries, consumers, and civil society would be fully taken into account when formulating new global intellectual property rules.[83]

In order to accelerate and complete discussions on submitted proposals, the 2005 session of the WIPO General Assembly agreed to establish a Provisional Committee on Proposals for a WIPO Development Agenda (PCDA).[84] Again, the General Assembly showed open support for the work of the DA. In other words, the highest organ of WIPO recognized the need to discuss development issues related to IP. After several meetings,[85] the PCDA came up with an agreement on a set of 45 recommendations, which were adopted by the WIPO General Assembly in September 2007.[86]

7.3.3. *A Survey of Some 'Agenda' Items Relevant to Education*

If the 45 proposals of the DA are implemented appropriately, this could result in profound changes at WIPO and in the international intellectual property regime. In particular, the DA comprises one way of contributing to development of developing and least developed

[81] In the past, WIPO has superficially shown interest in development issues of developing countries related to their economic challenges, but its work focused on the perception that IP protection was indispensable for economic growth. See Okediji, History lessons, *supra,* pp. 141–145.

[82] The original purpose of WIPO is "to promote the protection of intellectual property throughout the world through cooperation among States and, where appropriate, in collaboration with any other international organization". See WIPO Convention, *supra,* article 3(i).

[83] WIPO General Assembly. Thirty-Second (17th Ordinary) Session, *supra,* Report, Document no. WO/GA/32/13 (E), dated October 5, 2005, para. 112.

[84] *Ibid.*

[85] The PCDA held four meetings; two in 2006 and two in 2007. The different sessions were held on February 20 to 24, 2006, June 26 to 30, 2006, February 19 to 23, 2007 and June 11 to 15, 2007.

[86] Assemblies of the Member States of WIPO, Forty-Third Series of meetings, Geneva, September 24 to October 3, 2007, Report, World Intellectual Property Organization, Document no. A/43/6 (E) dated November 12, 2007, Annex A.

countries by facilitating access to public interest goods like education and health systems.[87]

The DA requires WIPO to analyse the potential benefits of a rich and accessible public domain, to protect a robust public domain when it creates new IP norms, and to provide balanced technical assistance to its member states, including information about the flexibilities and options open to them to protect the public interests of their citizens. The DA also requires WIPO to increase transparency in its work, the consultants it uses, and the information it provides to its Members as part of technical assistance programs. The items of the DA are therefore a means to hold WIPO accountable[88] (to its Members). Stated differently, the DA proposals require WIPO to take a balanced approach in promoting access to IP works, creativity and innovation, instead of focusing only on the maximization of IPRs.

The 45 recommendations are grouped in six clusters: (a) Technical Assistance and capacity building; (b) Norm setting, flexibilities, public policy and public domain; (c) Technology transfer, information and communications technologies (ICT) and access to knowledge; (d) Assessment, evaluation and impact studies; (e) Institutional matters including mandate and governance; and (f) Other issues. The 45 recommendations are also organized into two sets of 19 and 26. The 19 recommendations are considered to be "immediately actionable," as they do not require extra financial and human resources from WIPO, while the 26 items are not "immediately actionable" as WIPO has to assess the financial and human resource requirements.[89] Linking implementation of the proposals to availability of funds and/or human resources poses a risk of their not being implemented, as it would be possible to plead lack of funds.[90] In the following paragraphs, we discuss some of the recommendations that could be directly relevant to education in the analogue environment.

---

87 While it is acknowledged that intellectual property alone cannot bring about the solution to differential levels of development, the DA is a means through which WIPO can contribute, through IP, to meeting certain development concerns of poor countries. On this point, see for example Francis Gurry's acceptance speech to the WIPO General Assembly on his appointment as Director General of WIPO, available at http://www.wipo.int/about wipo/en/dgo/dg_gurry _profile.html

88 Comments made by Dalindyebo Shabalala, Director of the IP programme at the Centre for International Environmental Law, at a meeting organized on 13 March 2008 by the International Environmental Law Research Centre (IELRC) and 3D -> Trade - Human Rights - Equitable Economy in cooperation with the United Nations Office of the High Commissioner for Human Rights, under the title "Intellectual Property v. Human Rights".

89 Assemblies of the Member States of WIPO, Forty-Third Series of meetings, *supra*, Report, Document no. A/43/6 (E) dated November 12, 2007, para. 334.

90 This is the more likely considering the fact that the developed countries have a strong influence on the activities of the Programme and Budget Committee, which is responsible for approving activities that should be funded by WIPO. A recent demonstration of their influence is when budget for the 2008/2009 could not be approved until there was assurance that the then Director General of WIPO would retire before his term was over. This also shows that the Programme and Budget Committee can be used as a tool to reject programs that are against producers of copyrighted works. In other words, the implementation of the recommendations or success of the DA will require more than just legal means.

7.3.3.1. Technical Assistance

As mentioned earlier, WIPO is the main provider of technical assistance in the field of intellectual property at the multilateral level. By virtue of an agreement with the WTO,[91] it plays an important role in providing developing countries with technical assistance to implement the TRIPS Agreement. WIPO, through its Secretariat or International Bureau, provides technical assistance to developing countries in the areas of legislative advice, human resource development and training, institutional development and automation, and enforcement, primarily to national and regional intellectual property authorities.[92] WIPO's provision of technical assistance in the form of legislative assistance and support has come under significant criticism These criticisms include WIPO's predominant emphasis on the benefits of higher intellectual property standards with little consideration of costs, limitations, and public interest goals; the lack of attention paid to different levels of development and cultural differences; and the limited group of beneficiaries (with minimal assistance to, or participation from, civil society organizations).[93]

In other words, technical assistance should, at a minimum, ensure that national laws dealing with IP are tailored to meeting each country's level of development and are responsive to specific needs and problems of individual societies such as financial constraints and public interest goals like access to education. Technical assistance should also be directed towards assisting developing countries in making full use of the flexibilities in existing intellectual property agreements, such as those facilitating access to medicines or education.[94]

Accordingly, a number of proposals on technical assistance seek to address these problems. Proposal 10 asks WIPO to assist Member States to develop and improve national IP institutional capacity through further development of infrastructure and other facilities with a view to making national IP institutions more efficient and *promote fair balance between IP protection and the public interest.*[95] Proposals 1 and 13 are worded in a similar manner, except that one refers to technical assistance (in general) and the other to legislative assistance. Read together, the two proposals require that WIPO technical and/or legislative assistance shall be, *inter alia,* development-oriented, demand-driven and transparent, taking into account the priorities and the special needs of developing countries, especially LDCs, as well as the different levels of development of Member States, and activities should include time frames for completion. In relation to technical assistance,

---

91 Agreement Between the World Intellectual Property Organization and the World Trade Organization, concluded 22 December 1995, entered into force on 1 January 1996, World Intellectual Property Organization, Geneva 1997. Publication of the World Intellectual Property Organization no. 223 (E).

92 Information available at www.wipo.int/ip-devepment/en.

93 See for example statement of the delegation of Argentina on behalf of the Group of Friends of Development, WIPO General Assembly, Thirty-Second (17th Ordinary) Session, *supra,* Report, Document no. WO/GA/32/13, dated October 5, 2005, para. 112.

94 Much as there are no flexibilities facilitating access to copyrighted works for educational purposes in developing countries (see discussions in chapters 3 and 4), there are flexibilities for access to education in developed countries, especially for works on the internet.

95 Emphasis added. We discuss the implementation of this recommendation at a latter stage.

the design, delivery mechanisms and evaluation processes of technical assistance programs should be country specific.

These proposals aim at avoiding standard model laws in the guise of technical assistance.[96] They therefore challenge WIPO to avoid widespread uniform protection of IP given significant differences in cultural, technological and economic conditions prevailing in member countries. If these proposals were implemented, it would be a step forward in ensuring that the specific needs of developing countries are not overshadowed by strong IP protection on a global scale.[97] The proposals also challenged developing countries to make their priorities and demands clear to WIPO when asking for technical or legislative assistance. To do this effectively, developing countries need expert advice. They need to verify the suitability of draft laws for their public interest needs. However, since they usually lack the necessary expertise or manpower to do this, the involvement of intellectual property experts focused on the public interest objectives of IP protection becomes important[98] if WIPO will successfully meet these new expectations.

Concerning technical assistance in general, there exist a number of programs and activities that are planned or have been implemented since the adoption of the Development Agenda in October 2007.[99] However, these activities are generalized

---

96 See discussion in section 2.6.5.

97 This will not be useful where strong IP laws already exist.

98 Civil society organisations have been instrumental in scrutinizing draft IP legislation and their efforts led to the enactment of public interest oriented IP laws. Examples include the Kenya Coalition for Access to Essential Medicines (KCAEM), which successfully lobbied for incorporation of public health safeguards in the Kenya Industrial Property Act. (See Industrial Property Act 2001, Act no. 3 of 2001 (entered into force on 1 May 2002)). Another example is the Treatment Action Campaign which made comments on the draft Indian Patent Act (The Patents Act, 1970, (No. 39 of 1970) as amended by the Patents (Amendment) Act, 2005, (Act No. 15 of 2005)). See "Statement: A critical view of new Indian Patent (Amendment) Act 2005," access to Medicines and Treatment Action Campaign (AMTC), Alternative Law Forum, Lawyers Collective HIV/AIDS Unit, 24 March 2005. In recent years, civil society representing different public interests (like access to information, access to education), has linked up under the umbrella of "Access to Knowledge" (A2K) to advocate for public interest IP rules at national and international level. The Doha Declaration on TRIPS and Public Health and the WIPO DA are examples of their success. For a detailed account of the origins of the A2K and the effect of mobilization, see generally, Amy Kapczynski, "The access to knowledge mobilization and the new politics of intellectual property," *Yale Law Journal*, vol. 117, no. 5, (2008). 804–885. For a description of how coalitions of NGOs have reshaped the debate about the impact of international intellectual property rights on developing countries, see Duncan Matthews, *Intellectual Property, human rights and Development: the Role of NGOs and Social Movements*, (Cheltenham: Edward Elgar, 2011), especially chapters 2 and 3.

99 Activities relating to copyright include IP Strategy and Development plans which are being implemented in Côte d'Ivoire, Democratic Republic of Congo, Ethiopia, Ghana, Kenya, Mozambique, Nigeria, Rwanda, Sierra Leone, Uganda, and United Republic of Tanzania. Others include the modernization of IP system in Bangladesh, the creation and strengthening of collective management of copyright in Central American and Caribbean countries; publication in the publishing industry which is intended to stimulate and encourage greater awareness of the importance of IP in the business of publishing. See Information on activities for implementation of the first proposal, contained in Committee on Development and Intellectual Property (CDIP), First Session, Geneva, March 3 to 7, 2008, Initial Working Documents for the Committee

without particular attention to copyright in the analogue environment. Second, the activities, like those related to publishing, are meant to protect publishers and not facilitate access to published works. Let us now discuss another set of recommendations relating to norm setting.

7.3.3.2. Norm Setting, Flexibilities, Public Policy and Public Domain

The PCDA instructed WIPO to, *inter alia,* ensure that norm setting activities take into account the different levels of development and make norm setting activities a participatory process which *takes into consideration the interests and priorities of all WIPO Member States* and the *view points of non-Member States* like inter-governmental organizations (IGOs) and non-governmental organizations (NGOs).[100] Taking the views of non-Members into account is a significant development in a Member-driven organization. Even if the IGOs and NGOs participate in meetings as observers, the fact that their views are to be taken into account means that they can influence the outcome of norm setting processes. In proposing the Development Agenda, the "Friends of Development"[101] asked WIPO to foster the active participation of public interest non-governmental organizations in its subsidiary bodies to ensure that in IP norm setting a proper balance is struck between the producers and users of technological knowledge, in a manner that fully services the public interest.[102]

While the DA may not bring immediate results,[103] ensuring this balanced representative is an important development. Public interest NGOs are able to provide evidence-based countervailing research on the impact of IP on the public interest and propose relevant policies in ways that elude developing countries. At the minimum, then, increased NGO participation may serve as an important proxy for concerns articulated by developing countries and therefore aid in establishing the balance between producers and users of knowledge products.[104]

---

on Intellectual Property and Development, (Prepared by the Chair of the Provisional Committee on Proposals Related to a WIPO Development Agenda (CPDA)), World Intellectual Property Organization, document no. CDIP/1/3 dated March 3, 2008, Annex III, pp. 1–21.

100 Provisional Committee on Proposals Related to a WIPO Development Agenda (PCDA), Fourth session, Geneva, June 11 to 15, 2007, Report, World Intellectual Property Organization, Document PCDA/4/3 dated September 4, 2007, Annex 1, recommendation 15 (emphasis added).

101 As the reader may recall, 'Friends of Development' refers to a group of 14 developing countries which tabled the proposals for the WIPO Development Agenda.

102 WIPO General Assembly, Thirty-First (15th Ordinary) Session, *supra,* Proposal by Argentina and Brazil for the Establishment of a Development Agenda for WIPO, Document no. WO/GA/31/11, dated September 27, 2004, para. VIII.

103 The DA is a long process, like any other norm setting process. The DA is not intended to culminate in a treaty, but it is a quasi revision process of the WIPO constitution and mandate.

104 See for example Consumers International, Project on Access to Knowledge, *supra.*

7.3.5. *Establishment of the Committee on Development and Intellectual Property: A Formal Amendment of the WIPO Convention and Modification of Objectives of WIPO*

At its fourth session, the PCDA recommended that a Committee on Development and Intellectual Property (CDIP) be established to: (i) develop a work programme for implementation of the adopted recommendations; (ii) monitor, assess, discuss and report on the implementation of all the recommendations adopted, in coordination with relevant WIPO bodies; and (iii) discuss intellectual property and development related issues as agreed in the Committee, as well as those decided by the GA.[105]

Accordingly, the WIPO GA, at its forty-third session, approved the establishment of the CDIP, with a mandate as recommended by the PCDA.[106] In doing so, the GA legally recognized the 45 recommendations and the discussions on IP from a development perspective, and in addition established a permanent body, the CDIP, to implement those proposals. On an institutional level, WIPO, in reforming the way it operates, acknowledged the need for a development approach to intellectual property. So while the WIPO Convention has not been formally amended, its goals have been modified. Likewise, WIPO's mandate has also been modified. The adoption of the Agenda and the establishment of the CDIP is evidence that the Member States of WIPO, at a minimum, acquiesced to a reorientation of the objectives of WIPO from intellectual property protection per se, to include promoting the development of countries by facilitating access to intellectual property. The legal value of the DA and the CDIP derives from the fact that the two were adopted without a vote.[107] It could thus be argued that there was consent by all the WIPO Member States to a 'customary law form' of modification of the WIPO Convention.[108]

The CDIP is composed of Member States of WIPO and is open to participation by all accredited IGOs and NGOs.[109] The CDIP must report, but *may* make recommendations,

---

105 Provisional Committee on Proposals related to a WIPO DA (PCDA), Fourth Session, *supra*, Report, Document PCDA/4/3, (E), dated September 4, 2007, para. 76.

106 Assemblies of the Member States of WIPO, Forty-Third Series of meetings, *supra*, Report, Document no. A/43/16 (E) dated November 12, 2007. para 334.

107 The only concern raised by Member States with high IP protection standards, was related to financial implications of implementing the DA, but not on its substance. See Assemblies of the Member States of WIPO, Forty-Third Series of meetings, *supra*, Report, Document no. A/43/16 (E) dated November 12, 2007, para. 319 (statement by the USA). In any case the Budget for the biennium 2008/2009 was revised and approved so as to include financing of certain activities of the DA. This means that there was no objection.

108 A unanimous vote which is not accompanied by contradictory statements of the Members is evidence of agreement, which give legal value to document being voted. In the same sense, see Jorge Castañeda, "Valeur juridique des résolutions des Nations Unies," *RCADI*, vol. 129, (1971-I). 206–527, at 303. On the legal value of a decision of an organ of an international organization see *Texaco-Calasiatic c. Gouvernment libye*, sentence arbitral au fond du 19 Janvier 1977, arbitral award by René-Jean Dupuy, paras. 86–88 (reported in *Journal du droit international* (*Clunet*), vol. 104, no. 2 (1977), 350–389). The Arbitrator, after analysing the conditions of vote of four resolutions, comes to the same conclusion as Casteñeda.

109 Assemblies of the Member States of WIPO, Forty-Third Series of meetings, *supra*, General Report, Document no. A/43/16 (E) dated November 12, 2007. para 334.

annually to the GA.[110] Imposing an obligation to report to the GA ensures that substantial progress can be made during discussions within the CDIP, and places a check or measure of accountability regarding its work. The discretion to make recommendations to the GA offers an opportunity for the CDIP to contribute directly to development-oriented activities for consideration by the GA.

Of central concern was how the TA issues outlined in recommendation 1[111] could be integrated into WIPO's activities and general principles. It was, therefore, agreed that the Secretariat would make suggestions on the most appropriate documents in which the principles stated under Recommendation 1 could be incorporated as a reference for staff and consultants.[112] A major development concerning this recommendation was the effort being made by WIPO to make TA a transparent process. According to the secretariat, "[i]n order to ensure greater transparency in the field of TA, the organization [will] work on making more information on TA activities readily available to Member States ... through the database [...]"[113] In addition, WIPO created a system to regulate the conduct of those it contracts with to implement its policies in the area of TA. Thus, the Secretariat set up an "Office Instruction", which is a document detailing standards of conduct for consultants and national experts.[114] In addition, the names and profiles of consultants engaged by WIPO are posted on the WIPO website.

The Member States of WIPO, including those most interested in strong IP protection, consented, and even supported, the adoption of the DA and setting up a permanent body to ensure the correct implementation of its policies. For example, the CDIP already discussed the implementation of five recommendations, requiring extra human and financial resources, by December 2008.[115] Accordingly, the Program and Budget for the

---

110 Assemblies of the Members States of WIPO, Forty-Third Series of meetings, *supra,* Report, Document no. A/43/16 (E) dated November 12, 2007, para 334, (emphasis added).

111 Recommendation 1 stipulates that WIPO technical assistance shall be, *inter alia,* development-oriented, demand-driven and transparent, taking into account the priorities and the special needs of developing countries, especially LDCs, as well as the different levels of development of Member States and activities should include time frames for completion. In this regard, design, delivery mechanisms and evaluation processes of technical assistance programs should be country specific.

112 Committee on Development and Intellectual Property (CDIP), First Session, *supra,* Report, World Document no. CDIP/1/4 (E) dated July 7, 2008, para. 107.

113 Committee on Development and Intellectual Property (CDIP), Second Session, *supra,* Initial Working Document for the Committee on Development and Intellectual Property (CDIP): Revised text in respect of recommendations considered in the First Session of the CDIP, World Intellectual Property Organization, Document no. CDIP/2/2 (E) dated June 20, 2008, Annex I.

114 Committee on Development and Intellectual Property (CDIP), Second Session, *ibid,* Report Document no. CDIP/2/2 Prov. (E) dated August 22, 2008, para. 160.

115 These include recommendations 2, 5, 8, 9 and 10. Recommendation 10 requires WIPO "To assist Members States to develop and improve national IP institutional capacity through further development of infrastructure and other facilities with a *view to making national IP institutions more efficient and promote fair balance between IP protection and the public interest."*

biennium 2008–2009 was revised[116] to include implementation of the five recommendations.[117] The revised Program and Budget was endorsed by all WIPO Members, including major producers of intellectual works such as the United States and France.[118] The acceptance of the budget even by members with strong interests in IP protection, and therefore presumably with the least interest in facilitating easy access to IP works, evidences the normative importance of implementing the DA[119] and supports the argument that there is tacit acceptance by WIPO Member States of the idea that the protection of IP cannot be isolated from questions of access.

Under its new work program, the Development Agenda Coordination Program, WIPO has made it a priority to support development interests in all of its activities. The new Program, which is under the direct supervision of the Director General, is dedicated to ensuring effective coordination of work to implement the WIPO DA.[120] A clear indication of the high priority given to the implementation of the DA is that there have been various reforms in the internal structure of WIPO and new rules have been issued for all employees of WIPO to ensure transparency in providing TA.[121]

WIPO's stated goal is no longer simply the protection of intellectual property throughout the world[122] but includes "developing a balanced and accessible international

---

116 WIPO's program and budget are on a biennial basis. The current cycle covers the 2008/09 period. The session of the Assemblies that falls in the first year of a budgetary cycle typically considers a revised program and budget for the following year. In light of the change in WIPO's leadership on October 1, 2008, the Member States agreed to postpone the Program and Budget Committee (PBC) to December 10 to 11, 2008, to allow the new Director General to present a revised program and budget proposals. See background available at http://www.wipo.int/pressroom/en/articles/2008/article_0067.html.

117 For a copy of the revised Program and Budget see Program and Budget Committee, Thirteenth Session, Geneva, December 10 to 11, 2008, Revised Program and Budget for the 2008/2009 Biennium, World Intellectual Property Organization, Document no. WO/PBC/13/4 (E) dated November 13, 2008. Table 7 outlines a program for implementing recommendations 2, 5, 8, 9 and 10, all of which require WIPO to provide more funds and human resources., *ibid,* p. 28.

118 The PBC's recommendations to approve the proposed program and budget were endorsed by Member States in an extraordinary session of the Assemblies. See Assemblies of Member States of WIPO, Forty-Sixth Series of Meetings, Geneva, December 12, 2008; Draft General Report, World Intellectual Property Organization, Document no. A/46/12 Prov. (E) dated December 23, 2008, para. 38.

119 The developed countries' interests are specifically affected by the implementation of the DA. In another context, the ICJ stated that a very wide spread and representative participation in a [Convention] including that of states whose interests are specifically affected, is evidence of acceptance of a rule. See *North Sea Continental Shelf (Federal Republic of Germany v. Denmark and Federal Republic of Germany v. the Netherlands)*, Judgement of 20 February 1969, I.C.J Reports 1969, p.3, para 73. Much as the DA as such does not represent a rule of international law, one can draw an analogy from this statement of the ICJ in determining the existence of a consensus or acceptance to do something.

120 WIPO, "WIPO Launches Strategic Change Program," Geneva, December 15, 2008, PR/2008/580, available at http://www.wipo.int/pressroom/en/articles/2008/article_0067.html.

121 Committee on Development and Intellectual Property (CDIP), Third Session, Geneva, April 27 to May 1, 2009, Progress Report on recommendations for immediate implementation, World Intellectual Property Organization, Document no. CDIP/5/5 (E) dated March 23, 2009.

122 WIPO Convention, article 3.

intellectual property system, which rewards creativity, stimulates innovation and *contributes to economic development while safeguarding the public interest.*"[123] While 'public interest' is not defined, it should be understood as including access to protected works.

7.3.7. *Evaluation: The DA Is a Model for Future Development of Access Standards in International Copyright Law*

The actual implementation of the DA is a long term experiment and is still a politically sensitive process. However, this does not mean that the DA is of no value in improving access to education. The recommendations of the DA are a set of standards for WIPO's current and future activities. The recommendations, if adhered to, should produce meaningful solutions to the profound legal and policy challenges facing the international copyright system in general, and access to copyright for education in particular. The DA can act as a model for structuring future regulation of the international copyright system and development of access standards.

The recommendations that constitute the DA are not addressed to a specific organ of WIPO. This means that organs like the Standing Committee on Copyright and Related Rights (SCCR) can provide a forum for discussions on the relevant norm setting activities associated with the DA,[124] including norm setting activities related to L&Es for access to knowledge.[125] This view is supported by the fact that a prospective treaty or international instrument on limitations along such lines was proposed by a number of delegations and civil society organizations during discussions on the PCDA.[126]

In elaborating the activities planned or being carried out by WIPO in relation to the proposals of the PCDA, the work of the SCCR is of particular interest. The SCCR is the Committee with primary responsibility for norm setting activities in the field of copyright and related rights. The SCCR has stated that its work aims to support the interests of different actors in WIPO, such as creators, business and consumers, "but its duty is to ensure

123 Information available at: http://www.wipo.int/about-wipo/en/what/ (emphasis added).

124 Indeed at the second session of the Committee on Development and Intellectual Property (CDIP) several delegations expressed the belief that development was a cross-cutting issue and that the development dimension permeated all areas of IP. As such, the development dimension should not be confined to the discussions of the CDIP. See Committee on Development and Intellectual Property (CDIP), Second Session, *supra,* Report, World Intellectual Property Organization, Document CDIP/2/4/Prov. (E) dated August 22, 2008, particularly paras 257, 259 and 263.

125 In the case of patents, the Standing Committee on the law of Patents (SCP) has included a study on L&Es in its work programme. See for example, Exclusions from patentable subject matter and L&Es to rights, Standing Committee on the Law of Patents, Thirteenth Session, Geneva, March 23 to 27, 2009, World Intellectual Property Organization, WIPO Document SCP/13/3 E, dated February 4, 2009.

126 See for example Provisional Committee on Proposals Related to a WIPO DA (PCDA), Third session, *supra,* Report, Document PCDA/3/3 dated June 11, 2007, comments of the delegation of Brazil, (para. 32), Consumers International (para. 53) and the delegation of Chile (para. 86); Provisional Committee on Proposals Related to a WIPO DA (PCDA), Fourth session, *supra, Report,* Document PCDA/4/3 dated September 4, 2007, comments by Third World Network (para. 33), International Federation of Library Associations and Institutions (para. 35), Electronic Frontier Foundation (para. 36) and Knowledge Ecology International (para. 37).

that Member States' national interests fit within the global agenda".[127] This "global agenda", in our view, now includes access to protected works. WIPO has included the issue of L&Es to copyright and related rights for the purposes of education, libraries and disabled persons in its work.[128]

WIPO recognized the need to use both legal and quasi-legal means to respond to challenges facing the IP system. For example, in the case of the digital environment, while admitting that legal and normative activities are crucial to WIPO's work in the area of copyright, it is exploring the use of soft law approaches, the development of new business models and flexible licensing practices.[129] So while the work undertaken by WIPO at the moment may not directly relate to copyright in the print environment, there is place for discussion and consideration of access issues that could impact printed works. WIPO has developed a new interpretation of its mandate, which should allow it to move beyond the traditional practice of focusing only on traditional views of protection and promotion of IP.[130] Indeed, an important trajectory of WIPOs activities arising from the adoption of the DA is the growing acceptance that certain models of protection and access can converge

---

127 Information on activities for implementation of the first proposal contained in Committee on Development and Intellectual Property (CDIP), First Session, Geneva, March 3 to 7, 2008, Initial Working Documents for the Committee on Development and Intellectual Property, (Prepared by the Chair of the Provisional Committee on Proposals Related to a WIPO DA (CPDA)), World Intellectual Property Organization, document no. CDIP/1/3 dated March 3, 2008, Annex III, p. 24. In other words, consumers have become actors, and not only observers in the way WIPO operates.

128 Information on activities for implementation of the first proposal contained in Committee on Development and Intellectual Property (CDIP), First Session, Geneva, March 3 to 7, 2008, Initial Working Documents for the Committee on Intellectual Property and Development, (Prepared by the Chair of the Provisional Committee on Proposals Related to a WIPO DA (CPDA)), World Intellectual Property Organization, document no. CDIP/1/3 dated March 3, 2008, Annex III, p. 24.

129 Information on activities for implementation of the first proposal, contained in Committee on Development and Intellectual Property (CDIP), First Session, *supra,* Initial Working Documents for the Committee on Intellectual Property and Development, (Prepared by the Chair of the Provisional Committee on Proposals Related to a WIPO DA (CPDA)), document no. CDIP/1/3 dated March 3, 2008, Annex III, p. 24. Although this is to do with copyright under the WCT, it is interesting to note the effort to protect the interests of consumers or users of copyrighted works, as apposed to only promoting those of copyright owners.

130 Discussions on the DA have taken place alongside proposals for reform in organs of WIPO, such as the SCCR, to include work on L&Es. As part of the implementation of the DA, studies on L&Es have been proposed or commissioned in the Standing Committee on the law of Patents (SCP) and the Standing Committee on the law of Trade Marks (SCT), in addition to the SCCR. (See summary in Committee on Development and Intellectual Property (CDIP), Third Session, *supra,* April 27 to May 1, 2009, Progress Report on recommendations for immediate implementation, Document no. CDIP/3/5 (E) dated March 23, 2009.) It is, therefore, arguable that WIPO has not only adopted a new interpretation of the WIPO Convention so as to facilitate access to protected IP works, but there has developed a new custom, a *coutume sauvage,* dictated by the need to urgently respond to the needs of developing countries. On the concept of *coutume sauvage* (custom that developed without established practice or *opinion juris*), see René-Jean Dupuy, "Coutume sage et coutume sauvage," in *Mélanges offerts à Charles Rousseau: La communauté internationale*, (Paris: editions A. Pedone, 1974). 75–87.

simultaneously in an IP regime. The Open Source movement is, at the moment, the leading example of such a model of IP regulation.

7.4.7. *Standing Committee on Copyright and Related Rights (SCCR): Developing Access Principles and Rules for Copyright and Education*

If a new approach to norm setting is to emerge in the field of copyright in WIPO, it will have to be through the Standing Committee on Copyright and Related Rights (SCCR), the WIPO body charged with norm setting in the area of copyright and related rights. The SCCR was created through the Program and Budget for the 1998-1999 biennium.[131] The Assemblies of the Member States of WIPO and the Unions administered by WIPO at their Thirty-Second Series of Meetings approved[132] a proposal by the Program and Budget Committee to take "new approaches to the progressive development of international intellectual property law."[133] The "new approaches" were considered necessary as "the pace of change in the international intellectual domain necessitates consideration of new options for accelerating the development of international harmonized principles and rules of intellectual property law, so that the system is more responsive to the ever-changing demands placed upon it."[134]

The work of the SCCR aims to examine questions of substantive law or harmonization in WIPO's main fields of activity.[135] In particular, the SCCR was established to consider *emerging issues* in the field of copyright and related rights, and absorb and carry out the function of progressive development of international law in copyright and related rights.[136] The activities envisaged for the SCCR at that time were: (a) Protection of audio-visual performances; (b) Protection of databases; (c) Protection of the Rights of Broadcasting Organizations; and (d) Copyright, Related Rights and Digital Technology.[137] In relation to digital technology, the Committee was to consider in particular the impact

---

131 For the report of the Program and Budget see Assemblies of the Members States of WIPO, Thirty-Second Series of meetings, Geneva, March 25 to 27, 1998, Draft Program and Budget, World Intellectual Property Organization, Document no. A/32/2-WO/BC/18/2, p. vii.

132 The approval of the proposal is contained in Assemblies of the Members States of WIPO, Thirty-Second Series of meetings, Geneva, March 25 to 27, 1998, Report, World Intellectual Property Organization, Document no. A/32/2 dated March 27, 1998, para. 93.

133 Assemblies of the Members States of WIPO, Thirty-Second Series of meetings, Geneva, March 25 to 27, 1998, Draft Program and Budget, World Intellectual Property Organization, Document no. A/32/2-WO/BC/18/2, p. vii.

134 Assemblies of the Member States of WIPO, Thirty-Second Series of meetings, *supra,* Geneva, Draft Programme and Budget, Document no. A/32/2-WO/BC/18/2, p. vii.

135 Assemblies of the Members States of WIPO, Thirty-Second Series of meetings, *supra,* Draft Programme and Budget, Document no. A/32/2-WO/BC/18/2, p. viii.

136 For the report of the Program and Budget see Assemblies of the Members States of WIPO, Thirty-Second Series of meetings, *ibid,* Document no. A/32/2- WO/BC/18/2, main program 10 (emphasis added).

137 Assemblies of the Member States of WIPO, Thirty-Second Series of meetings, *supra,* Geneva, March 25 to 27, 1998, Draft Program and Budget, Document no. A/32/2-WO/BC/18/2, main Program, paras 10.2 to 10.5.

of digital technology and global information networks on copyright and related rights.[138] We can deduce two important features of the original mandate of the SCCR. Its work is concerned with (a) the rights of authors and not access to such works or limitations and exceptions, and (b) issues related to the digital environment as opposed to the analogue environment.

The question thus arises whether there is room in the SCCR for discussion on or development of access principles and rules on copyright and education. More specifically, is there a space for the development of an international legal mechanism for access to copyright in the analogue environment for purposes of education? If so, such a possibility would open the door for overcoming the short comings of the Berne Convention and the TRIPS Agreement. To address this question, we now explore the different developments in the SCCR related to limitations and exceptions.

In 2003, five years after the establishment of the SCCR, WIPO published its first study on limitations and exceptions. This study focused on limitations and exceptions in the digital environment,[139] which was expected considering the mandate of the SCCR. Its purpose consisted of showing how the existing limitations and exceptions could be applied to the digital environment.[140] In other words, the study sought to highlight possible solutions to the challenges raised for copyright protection in the digital environment, but not necessarily how to facilitate access to educational materials let alone material in the analogue environment. Of course, the irony of the matter is that, for developing countries, there are no exceptions that permit access to protected works for educational purposes.[141] If the existing limitations are to be applied to the digital environment, this means that developing countries will only be further excluded from the benefits of any limitations.

7.3.7.2. Proposals for Work on Limitations and Exceptions for Education, Libraries and Disabled Persons: Transforming Flexibilities to User Rights

The next step in the SCCR towards developing access principles was the proposal by Chile, at the SCCR's Twelfth Session in 2004, to include the subject of limitations and exceptions to copyright and related rights for the purposes of *education, libraries and disabled persons* on the agenda of the SCCR.[142] This was the first time education was expressly mentioned when considering limitations and exceptions to copyright. There was only a brief discussion of the proposal, but it was agreed that an item on limitations and exceptions for the purposes of education, libraries and disabled persons would be placed on the agenda of

138 Assemblies of the Member States of WIPO, Thirty-Second Series of meetings, *ibid,* main Program, para. 10.5.

139 Ricketson, WIPO Study, *supra*.

140 For example, how would an exception allowing copying of a few pages of printed material for private use be applied to the digital environment?

141 See discussion in chapters three and four.

142 Standing Committee on Copyright and Related Rights, Twelfth Session, Geneva, November 17 to 19, 2004, Proposal by Chile on the subject "limitations and exceptions to copyright and related rights," World Intellectual Property Organization, Document no. SCCR/12/3 (E) dated November 2, 2004 (emphasis added).

the Thirteenth Session of the Standing Committee.[143] This was an important development, as inclusion of the subject of limitations and exceptions would allow Members States and interested civil society organizations to give their views on the subject at a WIPO forum. Second, this marked the first time that a WIPO body agreed to discuss limitations and exceptions specifically for purposes of education, although as we see later, Chile was focused on works in digital form. At the aforesaid Thirteenth Session of the SCCR, Chile presented a proposal for an analysis of limitations and exceptions. Chile suggested three areas of work be undertaken by the SCCR: (1) Identification, from national intellectual property systems of Member States, of national models and practices concerning limitations and exceptions;

(2) Analysis of the limitations and exceptions needed to promote creation and innovation and the dissemination of developments stemming there from; and

(3) Establishment of agreement on limitations and exceptions for purposes of public interest that must be envisaged as a minimum in all national legislation for the benefit of the community, especially to give access to the most vulnerable or socially prioritized sectors.[144]

Let us take up the last area of work. By asking for establishment of an agreement on limitations and exceptions, WIPO was being asked to put the rights of copyright owners at the same level as exemptions and limitations to their enjoyment, by creating a mandatory legal instrument to facilitate access to protected works.[145]

In justifying its proposal, Chile focused upon access to works in the digital environment.[146] Thus discussions in the SCCR on Chile's proposal naturally focused on access to works in digital form, and the related, yet highly important, concerns of access by people with disabilities – especially the blind. Proposals were made for a study on a range of limitations and exceptions for libraries, archives, disabled people and educational users.[147] However, an outstanding aspect of discussions on activity (3) was the idea of international harmonization of limitations and exceptions, either by way of an international treaty providing mandatory minimum limitations and exceptions or some kind of instrument

143 Standing Committee on Copyright and Related Rights, Twelfth Session, *ibid,* Report, Document no. SCCR/12/4 (E) dated March 1, 2005, para. 275.

144 Standing Committee on Copyright and Related Rights, Thirteenth Session, *supra,* Proposal by Chile on the analysis of limitations and exceptions, Document no. SCCR/13/5 (E) dated November 22, 2005, Annex.

145 Recall that traditionally, only granting protection is mandatory while allowing access to copyrighted works is only permissible. Even where countries would prefer to grant access to protected works, the rules are so stringent that in many cases it is not possible, (see discussions in chapters 3, 4, 5 and 6).

146 Standing Committee on Copyright and Related Rights, Thirteenth Session, *supra,* Proposal by Chile on the analysis of limitations and exceptions, World Intellectual Property Organization, Document no. SCCR/13/5 (E) dated November 22, 2005, Annex, pp. 2 and 3.

147 Proposal was tabled by the Electronic Frontier Foundation, but with strong support especially from Brazil and the European Community. See Standing Committee on Copyright and Related Rights, Thirteenth Session, Geneva, *ibid,* November 21 to 23, 2005, Report, Document no. SCCR/13/6 (E) dated June 9, 2005, paras 24, 42 and 44.

providing uniform standards of access to copyrighted material.[148] Conspicuously absent was any discussion on access to works in the analogue environment, although there were general references to the rights of the disabled to information, knowledge and education;[149] exceptions for libraries, archives, disabled people and educational users.[150] However, we wish to underline that the idea of a mandatory international instrument on limitations and exceptions amounts to elevating limitations and exceptions from the level of favours which can be enjoyed only when they do not inconvenience the right holders to some type of 'user right' which must be protected internationally at the same level as rights of copyright owners. This is a noteworthy development, especially in an organization such as WIPO, whose primary mission has been to promote the protection of IPRs.[151]

Between 2005 and its Sixteenth Session in March 2008, the SCCR commissioned three other studies, in addition to one carried out in 2003, on L&Es focusing on automated rights management;[152] the visually impaired;[153] and library use.[154] However, after 2005 there were no further discussions in the SCCR on the subject of L&Es.[155] A proposal for

---

148 Standing Committee on Copyright and Related Rights, Thirteenth Session, *supra,* Report, Document no. SCCR/13/6 (E) dated June 9, 2005. Eight out of fifteen civil society organizations supported the idea of international harmonization of limitations and exceptions; these included the International Library Associations and institutions, Electronic Information for Libraries (para. 20), World Blind Union (para. 21), Electronic Frontier Foundation (para. 24), Consumers International (para. 25), IP Justice (para. 28), Civil Society Coalition (para. 30), European Digital Rights (para 34), The only civil society organisations that were against the idea of international harmonisation of limitations and exceptions were the International Confederation of Societies of Authors and Composers (para 26), the International Federation of Reprographic Rights Organisations (para. 27), International Federation of the Phonographic Industry (para. 31), and International Publisher Association (para. 32). The International Federation of Film Producers (para. 29), and the Union for the Public Domain (para. 33) neither expressly supported nor opposed international harmonization, but reminded that any limitations or exceptions had to conform to the three-step test (discussed in chapter 3). Brazil was at the forefront of supporting studies on limitations and exceptions and their international harmonization (para. 42).

149 See the comments of Mexico (para. 22) on the proposal for a study on limitations and exceptions for the visually impaired by the World Blind Union (WBU) (para. 21).

150 See for example Electronic Frontier Foundation (EFF) (para. 24), the USA (para. 36).

151 See WIPO Convention, preamble. But as demonstrated, the Development Agenda represents a constitutional reform in WIPO towards promotion of access to protected works as well.

152 Automated Rights Management Systems and Copyright L&Es, Standing Committee on Copyright and Related Rights, Fourteenth Session, Geneva, May 1 to 5, 2006, prepared by Garnett, Nic, WIPO Document SCCR/14/5 (E) dated April 27, 2006.

153 Study on Copyright L&Es of Copyrights for Visually Impaired, Standing Committee on Copyright and Related Rights, Fifteenth Session, Geneva, September 11 to 13, 2006, prepared by Sullivan, Judith, WIPO Document SCCR/15/7 (E) dated February 20, 2007.

154 Study on Copyright L&Es for Libraries and Archives, Standing Committee on Copyright and Related Rights, Seventeenth Session, Geneva, November 3 to 7, 2008, prepared by Kenneth Crews, WIPO Document SCCR/17/2 (E) dated August 26, 2008.

155 Indeed, at the Third Session of the PCDA, the Third World Network raised concern at the fact that since 2004, when Chile presented a proposal for an instrument on L&Es, there were no serious discussions on the subject in the SCCR, whose focus has been on the Broadcasting treaty. See Report of the Provisional Committee on Proposals Related to a WIPO DA (PCDA), Fourth session, *supra,* Document no. PCDA/4/3 dated September 4, 2007, para. 33.

consideration of L&Es appeared again on the agenda of the SCCR at its 16th Session in March 2008. The SCCR considered, among other things, a proposal from Brazil, Chile, Nicaragua, and Uruguay on L&Es.[156] The proposal elaborated further the 2005 proposal by Chile. In particular, the SCCR was asked to implement a plan taking into consideration the three levels of activities outlined in Chile's 2005 submission.[157] The plan was to be implemented with the objective of achieving consensus on *minimum mandatory L&Es particularly with regard to educational activities, people with disabilities, libraries and archives,* and exceptions that foster technological innovation.[158] Though not expressly defining "educational activities," the proposal expressly mentioned them as a category. Examples of the 'mandatory exceptions', also referred to as 'user rights' in the proposal, include the "right of the disabled community to export and import works produced under a copyright exception, or an exception in favour of libraries to the public lending right when it has been recognized." The idea of L&Es being "user rights" is emphasized.

An important advancement concerning access to education in developing countries was the Committee's approval of a study specifically dedicated to L&Es. The study was created for the benefit of educational activities, including distance education and its trans-border aspect *in particular for developing and least developed countries*.[159] This study offered an opportunity for Member States to evaluate the usefulness of L&Es at the international level. In particular, developing and least developed countries could explain why they had not used the Berne Appendix. The Berne Appendix in theory grants permission to issue compulsory licenses for reproduction and translation of printed copyrighted works, but it is in practice difficult to use because of stringent procedural requirements.[160] This was also an opportunity for developing countries to propose L&Es that can facilitate access to educational materials, especially in print form. In this way L&Es will contribute

156 Standing Committee on Copyright and Related Rights, Sixteenth Session, Geneva March 10 to 12, 2008, Proposal by Brazil, Chile, Nicaragua and Uruguay for work related to L&Es, World Intellectual Property Organization, Document no. SCCR/16/2 (E) dated July 17, 2008.

157 Chile proposed that the Committee undertakes work on three areas:
1. Identification, from national intellectual property systems of Member States, of national models and practices concerning L&Es; 2. Analysis of the L&Es needed to promote creation and innovation and the dissemination of developments stemming there from and; 3. Establishment of agreement on L&Es for purposes of public interest that must be envisaged as minimum in all national legislations for the benefit of the community; especially to give access to the most vulnerable or socially prioritized sectors. See Standing Committee on Copyright and Related Rights, Thirteenth Session, Geneva, November 21 to 23, 2005, Proposal by Chile on the analysis of L&Es, World Intellectual Property Organization, Document no. SCCR/13/5 (E) dated November 22, 2005.

158 Standing Committee on Copyright and Related Rights, Sixteenth Session, *supra,* Proposal by Brazil, Chile, Nicaragua and Uruguay for work related to L&Es, WIPO Document no. SCCR/16/2 (E), dated July 17, 2008 (emphasis added).

159 Standing Committee on Copyright and Related Rights, Seventeenth Session, Geneva, November 3 to 7, 2008, Summary of the Chair.

160 The Appendix to the Berne Convention allows developing countries, under very strict conditions, to grant compulsory licenses for reproduction and translation of printed material. But the stringent procedural requirements render it improbable that developing countries will ever find this sort of instrument useful.

more meaningfully to the progressive development of access principles to copyrighted works.[161]

7.4. Evaluation of Recent Developments in WIPO and Some Recommendations

The various developments in WIPO presented above indicate an agreement that there should be minimum international standards on limitations and exceptions. At the least, there is agreement that access to copyrighted works can no longer be regarded as less important than protection of such works. For this reason, there should be minimum access standards to copyrighted works just as there are minimum protection standards.

It is clear that solving access problems related to the digital environment was the priority for WIPO. But as Judge Guillaume rightly observed, "[i]nternational law must be geared to meet the needs of our modern world. It must also take into account the problems arising in specific regions or in specific fields."[162] Hence, while it is important to address the challenges that technology poses for access to protected works, WIPO needs to take into account problems of access for developing countries in the analogue environment as well. Indeed, Member States seem to acknowledge this need and there is effort at working out a solution for access to protected works in both digital and print environment. At the Twenty-First Session of the SCCR, GRULAC, who are the proponents of a treaty for the visually impaired and the African Group, which has been advocating for a "holistic approach" came up with a joint proposal for work on L&Es covering various access needs. The emphasis on printed education material is not yet evident in the negotiations, but there is hope that this will become clear during discussions on an instrument for educational activities.

Since the original mandate of the SCCR was to consider emerging issues (at the time) and, specifically "to consider in particular the impact of digital technology and global information networks on copyright and related rights",[163] it would seem that there is no place for limitations and exceptions in the analogue environment. However, as argued earlier, WIPO's adoption of the DA has de facto expanded its mandate beyond the traditional role of ensuring protection of IP to include facilitating access to protected works. It is, therefore, arguable that, the SCCR's mandate can be and has been expanded similarly. Since the DA's recommendations are not addressed to a particular organ of WIPO, the SCCR is best situated to discuss issues of limitations and exceptions to copyrights. Discussions on access to copyright for printed material should not, therefore, be strange

---

161 Four of the studies were presented at the information session of the nineteenth Session of the Standing Committee on Copyright and Related Rights, Geneva, December 14 to 18, 2009 (Information Meeting on Limitations and Exceptions for Educational Activities). Member states were given only until 8 January 2010 to provide further information (see Summary of the Chair). Member States can still propose L&Es for education, including for works in printed formats, which are suited to their economic circumstances.

162 Gilbert Guillaume, "The future of international judicial institutions," *International and Comparative Law Quarterly*, vol. 44 no. 4, (1995). 848–862 at 862.

163 Standing Committee on Copyright and Related Rights, First Session, *supra,* WIPO Document SCCR/1/2 (E), dated September 4, 1998, paras. 2 and 3.

to the SCCR's work. It is possible, within the SCCR, to work out an international mechanism for access to copyrighted works for educational purposes. The approval by the SCCR of a study on limitations and exceptions for the benefit of educational activities, in particular in developing and least developed countries, is supportive of this conclusion.[164] The result was five studies representing different regions of the world.[165] Unfortunately, they were narrowly focused and done in a hurry.[166] As such, there was limited input of developing countries.[167] WIPO Members have agreed to work towards international instruments on L&Es for Visually Impaired,[168] Libraries and Archives[169] and Education.[170]

Negotiating an international treaty is a trade-off between harmonization of norms and renunciation of a state's freedom to decide on public policy and thus public interest at the national level. This is more so for developing countries, whose national interests will often not match the standards set at the international level. Thus developing countries should be cautious not to negotiate treaties that will further limit this freedom.

---

164 Four of the studies were presented at the information session of the nineteenth Session of the Standing Committee on Copyright and Related Rights, Geneva, December 14 to 18, 2009 (Information Meeting on Limitations and Exceptions for Educational Activities). Member states were given only until 8 January 2010 to provide further information (see Summary of the Chair). Member States can still propose L&Es for education, including for works in printed formats, which are suited to their economic circumstances.

165 Standing Committed on Copyright and Related Rights, Nineteenths Session, Geneva, December 16 to 20, 2009. Although the original mandate was to conduct studies on L&Es for educational activities, the focus of the resulting studies ranged from just teaching (WIPO Document SCCR/19/5) to education and research (WIPO Document SCCR/19/4) and educational activities/purposes in general (WIPO Documents SCCR/19/6, SCCR/19/7 and SCCR/19/8).

166 Susan Isiko Štrba, "Commentary on the WIPO study on limitations and exceptions to copyright and related rights for the benefit of teaching in Africa." IQsensato. (2009) <http://www.iqsensato.org/blog/2009/12/13/commentary-on-sccr-study-on-le-for-africa/>; and "Commentary on the WIPO -SCCR Information Meeting on Limitations and Exceptions for Educational Activities." IQsensato (2009). <http://www.iqsensato.org/blog/2009/12/16/commentary-on-the-wipo-sccr-information -meeting-on-le-for -education/>

167 Member States had the opportunity to provide supplementary information on the studies but there is limited input from developing countries. See Supplementary Information on the Studies on Limitations and Exceptions for Educational Activities, WIPO Document SCCR/20/3.

168 Standing Committee on Copyright and Related Rights, Twenty- First Session, Geneva, November 8 to 12, 2010, Conclusions; and Standing Committee on Copyright and Related Rights, Twenty-Third Session, Geneva November 21 to 25, 28, 29 and December 2, 2011. Working document on an international instrument on limitations and exceptions for visually impaired persons/persons with print disabilities. WIPO Document SCCR/23/7. This document will constitute the basis for the future text-based work on the matter to be undertaken by the SCCR in its 24th Session, with an aim to agree and finalise a proposal on an international instrument on L&Es for visually impaired persons/persons with print disabilities.

169 Standing Committee on Copyright and Related Rights, Twenty- First Session, Geneva, November 8 to 12, 2010, Conclusions; and Standing Committee on Copyright and Related Rights, Twenty-Third Session, Geneva November 21 to 25, 28, 29 and December 2, 2011. Provisional working document containing comments on and textual suggestions towards an appropriate international legal instrument (in whatever form) on exceptions and limitations for libraries and archives, WIPO Document SCCR/23/8 Prov.

170 Standing Committee on Copyright and Related Rights, Twenty- First Session, Geneva, November 8 to 12, 2010, Conclusions.

Developing countries should be more vigilant in the future treaty negotiation and norm setting. For example, developing countries should make a list of issues that are not covered in international treaties but can allow them to develop public policy that is open to national implementation and in the public interest. Developing countries should not merely react to negotiations but should instead present original proposals on what they wish to achieve and defend their proposal together as developing countries.[171] Accordingly, the current trend in WIPO, whereby developing countries are investing greater efforts in negotiation and taking the lead in presenting their needs, may be seen as a promising aspect in the development of international IP law.

What guarantee do we have that implementation of the DA or the work of the SCCR will lead to increased access to protected works? One would hope that the increased participation of developing countries in negotiations offers such a guarantee. In the past, developing countries were not very active in negotiating IP norms for various reasons. For example, the representation from Asia, Africa and Central and South America at the 1948 intellectual property conference at Brussels was meagre.[172] Reasons for this poor participation varied, but include lack of the necessary expertise to follow the negotiations.[173] In similar fashion, very few developing countries took part in the negotiations on the TRIPS Agreement. Many did not understand the technical part of the negotiations, and at essential moments of decision making, many were not even present.[174] Only 9 out of

---

171 The tendency of developing countries has been is to oppose what developed countries propose. The fact is that when developed countries propose something, they have already agreed on it, even if they may have differences on other issues. But they defend what they have agreed upon. It is hard for developing countries to negotiate compromises if they do not clearly state what they want, let alone agree on it as developing countries. This lack of preparedness and disagreement is displayed in the statements made by developing countries during discussions of the DA. Take for example statements of regional coordinators. Algeria, speaking on the behalf of the Africa group at the fourth session of the PCDA was very general statements. The same can be said for the representatives of GRULAC and Asia. See Provisional Committee on Proposals related to a WIPO Development Agenda (PCDA), Fourth Session, *supra,* Document no. PCDA/4/3, (E), dated September 4, 2007, paras. 19, 20 and 21 respectively.

172 Daniel Gervais, *The TRIPS Agreement: Drafting History and Analysis*. 2nd ed. (London: Sweet and Maxwell, 2003). 12–26.

173 On the part of Africa, this was attributed to the fact that there were very few independent African countries were in a position to send to the Conference specialists capable of following its work. See closing speech by Mr. Ledoux (Senegal) on behalf of the African delegation in Records of the Intellectual Property Conference of Stockholm, 1967, *supra,* Volume II, Summary Minutes (Plenaries), World Intellectual Property Organization, Geneva, 1971, p.799.

174 On the negotiation of the TRIPS Agreement in general, see Abbott, Protecting First World Assets, *supra,* On reasons for inclusion of IP in GATT, see Cattaneo, Olivier, Le règlement des différends entre Etats en matière de propriété intellectuelle, Thèse, Université de Genève et Institut universitaire de hautes études internationales, Geneva, 2002, pp. 19–34. On the role of the IP industry in shaping the TRIPS Agreement and inclusion of IP in WTO, see Susan K. Sell, *Private Power, Public Law: the Globalization of Intellectual Property Rights.* (Cambridge: Cambridge University Press, 2003). pp. 1 and 2. On the participation of countries of Sub-Saharan Africa in TRIPS negotiations, see Murigande, Aimé, Developing countries and their participation in the world trading system: an African perspective, Mémoire, Institut universitaire de hautes etudes internationals, Geneva, 2000, pp.29–33.

38 countries of sub-Saharan Africa participated in the Uruguay Round negotiations.[175] According to the African delegates to the GATT/WTO, developed countries benefitted from the support of various national and lobby groups who often provided their negotiators with critical and significant technical guidance.[176] Other reasons include the fact that most negotiations were conducted during informal groups between developed countries. The participation of African countries in the informal groups was restricted by limited human and financial resources.[177] Therefore, negotiations on the WIPO Development Agenda and in the SCCR show that such participation could produce more balanced results than historically had been the case. The participation of civil society organizations, which are willing to provide free technical advice to developing countries and to supplement their limited manpower, will surely aid this outcome.[178]

In summary, the international solution to international copyright regulation and access to copyrighted works can be either one or combination of (a) institutional reform; (b) a soft law instrument, or (c) a treaty on access. A lot of effort is going into negotiating international instruments on L&Es. This work does not propose an international instrument for access to copyright for education at this point. It is not self-evident that concluding international instruments on L&Es should be the main short term target in an attempt to facilitate access to copyrighted works, especially for education. Concluding such instruments will take long[179] and the outcome is uncertain.[180] The content of an international

175 Despite significant technical assistance from UNCTAD and the GATT, the national negotiating capabilities of African countries were relatively weak in comparison to developed countries whose resources were considerably greater. Developed countries, had undertaken significant preparatory work so they were able to identify their trade interests with respect to various issues under negotiation, which was not the case with developing countries. See Oyejide, A "The participation of developing countries in the Uruguay Round: An African perspective," *The World Economy,* vol. 13 no. 3, September 1990, quoted in Murigande, *ibid,* p. 30.

176 Murigande, *ibid.*

177 T. Stewart, *the GATT Uruguay Round: A negotiating history (1986–1992).* (Boston: Kluwer Law and Taxations Publishers, 1993). 2073.

178 Even today, developing countries are under-represented at meetings for lack of manpower. For example the list of participants at the PCDA shows that most developing countries delegations were composed of on average one person, as opposed to those of developed countries that were composed of at least five people, plus expert advisors from interested IP holders. See Provisional Committee on Proposals Related to a WIPO Development Agenda (PCDA), Fourth session, *supra,* Report, World Intellectual Property Organization, Document PCDA/4/3 dated September 4, 2007, Annex II.

179 In the case of WIPO in particular, Edward Kwakwa has rightly recommended that the Organization adapts its traditional rulemaking process by adopting more rapid, transparent, effective and politically acceptable means of norm creation, see Edward Kwakwa, "Some comments on rulemaking at the World Intellectual Property Organization," *Duke Journal of Comparative and International Law,* volume 12, issue 1, (2002). 179–95, at 179.

180 An example is the Stockholm Protocol which was aimed at facilitating access to printed copyrighted material for educational purposes. The Protocol was opposed by producers of copyright works and never came into force. A recent example is the Doha Declaration on the TRIPS Agreement and Public Health and the subsequent amendment of TRIPS. There is a risk of developing countries being coerced, through the threat of trade sanctions, to accept a treaty text whose provisions do not enable them to address national interests like access to copyrighted material for education. For examples of such coercion in intellectual property

instrument should be the result of careful studies on the needs of users of IP. It is important to substantiate the current studies with more evidence of, not only legislation, but policies and practices.[181] As demonstrated in chapter 6, courts have an important role in devising case-by-case educational exceptions. These should then feed into the international solution as evidence of what works.

On the other hand, the risk remains that enforcement of an international instrument on limitations and exceptions, or any access principles, would rest with Member States. For developing countries there is an undeniable risk of being subjected to trade or political sanctions by developed countries on behalf of owners of IP works if they try to enforce an international instrument on access principles. This becomes more likely if we consider the fact that, in the past, developing countries have been threatened with trade sanctions when they attempted to allow access to protected IP works. For example, Pakistan was threatened with section 301 procedures[182] when it amended its Copyright Ordinance in 2000[183] to provide for government use of copyrighted material for purposes of education.[184]

For a start, the focus should be on sustaining efforts at institutional reform already taking place in WIPO and on concluding a soft law instrument under the auspices of WIPO. Institutional reform should include, among priorities for technical assistance, sensitizing

---

negotiations, the excellent account of Peter Drahos, "Negotiating Intellectual Property Rights: Between Coercion and Dialogue" in H. Hansen, ed. *International Intellectual Property law & policy*. vol.7, (Juris Publishing 2002), Chapter 82, pp. 82–8 and 9.

181 States should devise case-by-case educational exceptions, policies (by government, educational institutions and libraries) and practices. A WIPO questionnaire on L&Es focuses on national statutes. Only 61 Members answered the questionnaire, with a number of them providing only partial responses. (see Standing Committee on Copyright and Related Rights, Twenty-First Session, Geneva, November 8 to 12, 2010, Updated Questionnaire on Limitations and Exceptions, WIPO Document SCCR/21/7, dated October 2, 2010.). As I have suggested elsewhere, country delegates or negotiators should come more prepared to table informed and researched proposals. (see IP-Watch, "Copyright Exceptions Needed to Ensure Balance in Africa – Panellists Say," (IP-Watch 2009) <http://www.ip-watch.org/weblog/2009/05/25/copyright-exceptions-needed-to-ensure-balance-in-africa-panel-says/>. Accessed 20 December 2011. They can seek technical assistance from WIPO or help of NGOs to get ready for the meetings.

182 See discussion in section 2.3.

183 Pakistan, the Copyright Ordinance, 1962, Ordinance No. XXXIV of 1962, (as amended by Copyright (Amendment) Ordinance, 2000 dated 29th September, 2000).

184 The Government of Pakistan amended its Copyright Ordinance in 2000 to include a provision (Section 36(3)), which allows a royalty-free compulsory licence of books for government use. Specifically, it provides, "[t]he Federal Government or the Board may, upon an application by any government or statutory institution, in the public interest, grant a licence to reprint, translate, adapt or publish any textbook on non-profit basis." Included in "government or statutory institution" is the National Book Foundation (NBF), which is part of the Ministry of Education. The IIPA recommended that Pakistan modifies its law, as it had not availed itself of the Berne Appendix. See International Intellectual Property Alliance, "IIPA's 2006 Special 301 Report, on copyright protection and enforcement, submitted to the U.S. Trade Representative, on February 13, 2006 by the International Intellectual Property Alliance," available at http://www.iipa.com/special301.html. As we have demonstrated in section 6.6.2, developing countries have no obligation to use the Berne Appendix in order to provide for access to copyrighted works.

and training of judges in using copyright limitations and exceptions for public interest. If correctly done, this should help national courts in not only interpreting limitations and exceptions in statutes in the public interest, but also to devise case-by-case educational exceptions. Effort is going into revising the WIPO model law. While this is a laudable effort, the priority should be placed on testing what works at the national level for each country. This is where technical and legislative assistance should follow public interest goals, which includes access to educational materials.

The DA has an advantage over an international instrument in that the DA is under the direct implementation of WIPO, the organization monitoring the protection of IP. The DA charges WIPO with the task of ensuring access to IP works in a manner consistent with the interest of the majority of its member states which are developing countries. WIPO has a strong interest in balancing both protection of and access to IP, and, through the DA has committed itself to doing so. A proposal for a soft law instrument is not new, but it is new to WIPO. What is also new is the need particular attention to providing access mechanisms solutions to printed copyright material.[185] The development Agenda together with the studies in the SCCR offers preliminary glimpses into the elements that could be included in the design of a prospective soft law instrument.

185 See Bernt P Hugenholtz, and Ruth L. Okediji, *Conceiving an international instrument on limitations and exceptions to copyright.* Final Report, study commissioned by the Open Society Institute, March 6, 2008 (available at www.ivir.nl). An abridged version is published under the title "Contours of an international instrument on limitations and exceptions," in Neil Weinstock Netanel, ed., *The Development Agenda: Global Intellectual Property and Developing Countries, supra,* 473–497. The proposal does not clearly state that WIPO should lead in drafting a soft law instrument. In addition, the report does not focus only on access to printed copyrighted materials. In fact, it is not clear if this particular issue is taken into account.

GENERAL CONCLUSIONS

The primary objectives of this study were to contribute to the understanding of the legal relationship between copyright regulation and access to education in developing countries and to explore possible ways to make access possible within the international copyright system. Towards these ends, the study had two main tasks. The first was to address the question whether flexibilities in international intellectual property law can be used to balance the private interest of intellectual property (IP) holders and the public interest of IP users. In particular, can limitations or exceptions (flexibilities) in international copyright law serve to facilitate access to printed educational material by developing countries? Second, the study explored possible solutions, within the international copyright system, for access to education in developing countries.

The present study began by demonstrating that early copyright protection was in fact geared towards promoting a public interest goal. Examples include the encouragement of learning and promotion of the progress of science and useful arts. Copyrights were granted for a limited time to encourage those who produced the public goods such as books. There always existed regulation on how the copyright was used. In other words, there were limitations imposed on the enjoyment of the copyright. However, copyright protection at the international level did not have the same objective as at the national level. International protection was meant to protect the works of one country (producer) in another (user) country. The first multilateral copyright statute, the Berne Convention, was a harmonization of different national and bilateral agreements. It contained minimum standards likely to be acceptable to the major negotiating states. The original standards of the Berne Convention, therefore, consisted of national norms and practices of negotiating states, common elements of existing bilateral agreements and principles of bilateral commercial treaties. Naturally, the national realities of developing countries as we know them today were not taken into account since they were not party to the negotiation.

In reality, because of their special economic circumstances, developing countries require extensive freedom to access copyrighted works in order to meet their educational needs. If developing countries had the opportunity to design limitations and exceptions to copyrights, they would be most interested in obtaining exceptions to the translation right and to the reproduction right. This is because developing countries need bulk access to photocopied and translated works. There are various reasons for this. First, book publishing in developing countries is negligible.[1] The number of books in circulation and for sale is low, and books are unaffordable for the average person.[2] Being basically users and not producers of copyrighted materials, developing countries and least developed countries are dependent upon books published in industrialized countries.[3] Accordingly, they require permission to use the protected materials. The administrative costs involved in obtaining this permission from the rights owners, who are mainly multinationals in developed countries[4] are high. Second, developing countries depend primarily on printed copies of copyrighted works, as opposed to electronic works, for educational purposes. Therefore, the textbook represents the most important source of information. Since many persons in developing countries cannot afford to purchase textbooks, they depend entirely on photocopied course-packs and access to information in their institutions' libraries. Consequently, what is needed is bulk access to printed material for purposes of

---

1 Olian Jr., *supra,* p. 90 (stating that of the new books distributed in developing countries, sometimes as many as ninety-five percent are translations from foreign works, the majority of which are imported rather than published within the developing countries); UNCTAD/ICTSD, "Intellectual Property Rights: Implications for Development," Policy discussion paper, August 2003, p.129. Two recent studies on access to knowledge in Indonesia and Thailand revealed the same situation: most of the books, for tertiary education, especially technical education are imported. Even then, the imported books are mainly supplied to a small fraction of the population in the major cities. See Consumers International, Project on copyright and access to knowledge in Indonesia, *supra,* pp. 12–13; and Consumers International, Project on access to knowledge, Thailand, *supra,* pp. 12–13 and 18. This emphasizes the need for reproduction of imported books.

2 United Nations Development Programme, News Bulletin, 18 October 2004, (http://www.undp.org/dpa/pressrelease/releases/2004/october/pr18oct04.html), reporting that every other person in the sub-Saharan region of Africa lives on less than one US dollar a day. This situation applies even to South Africa, the most developed country in Africa. On this point, see Francois Hendrikz, "The Book Chain in South Africa," in Stringer Roger, ed. *The Book Chain in Anglophone Africa.* (Oxford, International Network for the Availability of Scientific Publications, 2002). 72–82. Hendrikz reports that the South African book market is relatively small. It is estimated that only 5% of the population could be regarded as a book-buying market. This may be due to illiteracy, leading to the lack of a reading culture, as well as the high cost of books, p. 77. See also Denise Rosemary Nicholson, "Free Trade Agreements and TRIPS-plus: implications for developing countries in Africa," a paper presented at the World Library and Information Congress: 71th IFLA General Conference and Council under the theme "Libraries – A voyage of discovery," Oslo, Norway, August 14–18 2005, pp. 2 and 5, (available at www.ifla.org/IV/ifla71/Programme.htm. The author uses the example of South Arica, the most developed country in Africa, to demonstrate the illiteracy crisis and how 'restrictive' copyright laws affect access to information. See also Rens *et al,* IP, education and access, *supra,* pp. 14–15. It is reported that textbooks, particularly for tertiary education are routinely unavailable. They cite the example of Zambia.

3 UNESCO, "Basic Learning Materials Initiative," Chapter 6, Available at http://www.unesco.org/education/blm/chap6_en.php; Olian Jr., *supra,* pp. 81–112, p. 90. (of new books distributed in developing countries, sometimes as many as ninety-five percent are translations of foreign works, the majority of which are imported rather than published within the developing country).

4 UNESCO, *World Information Report 1997/98,* UNESCO, Paris, 1998, available at http://www.unesco.org/webworld/com_info_reports/wirenglish/chap23.pdf; Commission on Intellectual Property Rights, *supra.*

education – not merely a few copies. Developing countries must be able to access copyrighted material at affordable prices, but without discouraging creativity.[5]

Third, in relation to translation, developing countries require considerable freedom to translate protected works. This is more so owing to the fact that, in developing countries, the language of instruction in school is not necessarily the language in which the teaching or reading material has been written. Since most of the educational material is imported, it needs to be translated from the language of publication into the local language of instruction. In this case, translation is a very important element of access to copyrighted educational material.

Finally, imported books are more expensive than reproduced or translated books. This stems from a number of factors, including the administrative costs involved. In the end reproduction and translation become the only access mechanisms to printed works in developing countries.

While copyright protection is not the main barrier to accessing and use of printed materials, it reinforces other problems such as cost of materials, overall economic conditions within poor countries and the scarcity of photocopiers to reproduce and assist in the wider distribution of existing materials.

This study has demonstrated that limitations and exceptions provided as solutions for access to copyrighted material for public interest goals like education are ineffective. Uncompensated exceptions that can be useful for access to educational material in printed form are the exceptions for quotations or illustrations in teaching. However, these do not serve the purpose of providing bulk access to copyrighted material because they only apply to limited quantities; otherwise uses are subject to the three-step test. The principle impact of the three-step test is to limit the quantity of what can be used for free. For this reason, the use of a copyrighted work as quotations or by way of illustration amounts to fair practice only as long as the amount of text used is short. But this is not the kind of access developing countries need. As was demonstrated in chapter 2r and reiterated above, developing countries need bulk access to copyrighted works.

Similarly, the three-step test under article 9(2) BC and 13 of TRIPS cannot be effectively used to facilitate access to copyrighted educational material in developing countries. The three-step test must be read and understood within the context of the Berne Convention and the TRIPS Agreement. The open ended and vague provision in article 9(2) of the Berne Convention is a result of the fact that its formulators, who are the producers of intellectual material, had no intention of providing wide spread access to protected works beyond their national borders. Hence, at the Stockholm Conference for the revision of the Berne Convention, where for the first time in the Berne Convention's history limitations on the right of reproduction were discussed, the Members came up with a vague and open-ended provision as a general exception to the reproduction right. This was one way to fulfil the objective of the Berne Convention: "to protect, in as effective and uniform a manner possible, the rights of authors in their literary and artistic works."[6]

---

5 In another context, Professor Okediji refers to use of copyrighted material on terms that "do not erode downstream creativity". See Okediji, Sustainable Access, *supra*, p. 149.

6 Berne Convention, Preamble.

Second, the three-step test under article 13 of TRIPS is not only based on article 9(2) BC, but restricts the already narrow exceptions provided under the latter provision. Article 13 of TRIPS has to be understood within the context of the whole Agreement, which is an annex to the WTO Agreement. The purpose of TRIPS is to promote international trade. So limitations and exceptions under article 13 are only acceptable if they do not affect the economic interests of right holders, who are commercial entities. In addition, because of its trade orientation, TRIPS is not equipped to take care of social interests like access to education.[7]

If one considers the three-step test as merely providing guidelines which facilitate the task of striking a proper balance,[8] one can then argue that states in general and developing countries in particular could use it to strike a balance between the protection of authors' rights and access to educational material. This would make sense if we were to assume that the three-step test under the Berne Convention and the TRIPS Agreement provide simple guidelines. Unfortunately, this is not the case. The three-step test, at least in relation to copyright, provides strict guidelines from which it is not easy to derogate. This is more so if considered in relation to the rights of reproduction and translation, exceptions to which are particularly important for developing countries. In sum, the three-step test cannot be used by developing countries to facilitate access to educational material in the analogue environment.

This led us to conclude that the three-step test cannot be used by developing countries to provide access to educational material, either because it focuses on the market effect of the use or only a small amount of copies is permitted. Even then, the use should not result in competition with the market of the protected work.

We then examined previous attempts, within the Berne legal system, to provide solutions for access to copyrighted material by developing countries for educational purposes. We analysed the special legal regimes provided for under the international copyright system. The Stockholm Protocol was the first attempt at providing such solution at the international level. It provided certain exceptions allowing use of copyrighted material for education under certain conditions, but it was more liberal than the three-step test. If the Protocol had come into force, it would have been a solution to the special access needs of developing countries. However, while developed countries recognized the fact that developing countries have special access needs, they remained unwilling to facilitate such access at the expense of their authors and publishing industries. For this reason, the Stockholm Protocol was not accepted by developed countries. As a result, it never became a legal instrument. The alternative solution was the Appendix to the Berne Convention, which provides "special provisions regarding developing countries" to permit compulsory licensing for translation and reproduction of copyrighted works in hard copy. The Appendix cannot be used by developing countries. Its complicated administrative and procedural requirements render its use prohibitively expensive for developing countries.

7 Although there is a possibility of taking care of social interests like health, as long as this is done according to the provisions of TRIPS. See TRIPS Agreement, article 8 and 30.

8 Senftleben, *supra,* p.212.

In other words, none of the special regimes for developing countries serves the purpose of facilitating access to educational material in printed form.

The next step of the study was to explore possible solutions for access at the domestic level while taking into account the special economic needs of developing countries. The focus was on solutions that would entail a minimum of financial burden for developing countries but at the same time would be acceptable, especially among producers of copyrighted material. We identified two main solutions – the use of fairness principles and compulsory licensing beyond the Berne Appendix. Therefore, we explored models of practice for access to copyrighted material by developing countries. In particular, we examined the use of 'fairness' principles by developed countries like the United States and Canada. At the national level, developing countries can use the "fairness" standards along the lines of fair use and fair dealing but adjusted to suit their national realities. We concluded that developing countries could adopt open-ended provisions like fair use in their national legislation. While the actual application of fair use in U.S. courts raises it to the standard of the three-step test, there remains an advantage to developing countries adopting it. Developing countries would be able to decide on each situation of use on a case-by-case basis, in light of their domestic circumstances. On the other hand, while the Canadian fair dealing provision is very limited, its application by the courts in some cases is quite liberal, allowing wide use of protected works for public interest. Combining elements from fair use with those of fair dealing can facilitate access to copyrighted materials for the purpose of education.

Developing countries can also apply compulsory licensing outside the Berne Appendix. This includes quasi compulsory licensing regimes, which entail compulsory licensing plus negotiated prices; the use of declaratory judgements and issuing of compulsory licences instead of injunctions.

Fair use, fair dealing and compulsory licensing require relatively minimal financial input for implementation. As such, they respond better to the economic needs of developing countries. At the same time, the use of fairness principles and compulsory licensing to facilitate access to copyrighted material are widely acceptable practices, especially among developed countries that are the major producers of copyrighted material. These solutions do not completely solve the problem of bulk access, but if used in combination, they are useful steps towards achieving bulky access.

Nevertheless, we believe there should be an international solution to access to copyrighted material. The problem of copyright and access to education in developing countries lies in the nature of international legal instruments and the international IP system as a whole. As demonstrated earlier, international IP system stresses the protection of IP and not access. In relation to copyrights, there is strong emphasis on protection of rights without providing for access to those rights or concerns of public interest. So the study proceeded to explore international institutional and normative solutions. In particular, the study explored the possibility of providing solutions through the WTO and WIPO, the two main organizations that regulate international copyright law.

The failure of access solutions for health provided under the WTO is a clear sign of the need to look for international solutions elsewhere. Whereas it is not denied that there is a need for an international solution to access to IP works, this solution cannot only be from the WTO, an organization whose major purpose is to protect and promote trade.

It is unsurprising that solutions such as the Declaration on the TRIPS Agreement and Public Health, amendment to the TRIPS Agreement and extension of transition periods for implementation of TRIPS by LDCs have failed. Notably, these failures show that the WTO, an organization whose major purpose is to protect and promote trade, is not in the best position to provide a global solution on IP issues without the need to address corresponding side-bargains in other areas of its competence. There is need to reform the international IP system as a whole and the copyright system in particular. The TRIPS Agreement is based on a system established by WIPO: the Paris Convention and the Berne Convention being only two examples of treaties concluded under WIPO. WIPO is the most feasible institution to take the lead in international copyright reform through finding an international solution to copyright regulation and issues of access. This is why the present study analysed in detail recent developments and reforms in WIPO in an attempt to understand the legal implications for access to protected IP works.

We have argued that the establishment of the WIPO Development Agenda and a mechanism for its implementation is a formal amendment to the WIPO Convention and consequently a modification of the objectives of WIPO. In September 2007, the WIPO General Assembly, without vote, adopted 45 recommendations of the WIPO Development Agenda (DA) and established a permanent body, the Committee on Development and Intellectual Property (CDIP), to implement the DA's recommendations. The DA asks WIPO to modify the way it operates in order to focus on access to intellectual property in its work and not only on promotion of IP.

On an institutional level, WIPO acknowledged the need for a development approach to intellectual property in reforming the way it operates. So while the WIPO Convention has not been amended in its terms, its goals have been modified. Likewise, WIPO's mandate has also been modified. The adoption of the Agenda and establishment of a permanent body, the CDIP, is evidence that the Member States of WIPO agreed to modify the objectives of WIPO, from simply protecting intellectual property to allowing access to it as a way to promote development in developing countries. The legal value of the DA and the CDIP is deduced from the fact that the DA and the CDIP were adopted without vote.[9] We are of the opinion that there is consent of all the parties to modify the WIPO Convention.[10]

The Member States of WIPO, including those most interested in strong protection of intellectual property, not only consented to the adoption of the DA and setting up a permanent body to ensure its implementation, but actually supported efforts being carried out by WIPO to implement the DA. The DA is, therefore, a model for the future development of access standards in international copyright law.

9 The only concern raised by Member States having most interest in high standards of IP protection, was related to financial implications of implementing the DA, but not on its substance. See Assemblies of the Member States of WIPO, Forty-Third Series of meetings, *supra,* General Report, Document no. A/43/16 (E) dated November 12, 2007, para. 319 (statement by the USA).

10 A unanimous vote which is not accompanied by contradictory statements of the Members is evidence of agreement. In the same sense, see Castañeda, *supra,* p. 303. On the legal value of a decision of an organ of an international organization see *Texaco-Calasiatic c. Gouvernment libye*, sentence arbitral au fond du 19 Janvier 1977, *supra.*

The recommendations of the DA are not addressed to a specific organ of WIPO. This means that organs like the Standing Committee on Copyright and Related Rights (SCCR), the primary organ responsible for norm setting activities in the field of copyright and related rights in WIPO can provide a forum for discussion on the relevant norm setting activities.[11] This brings to mind norm setting activities related to limitations and exceptions or access to knowledge.[12]

The present study argued that WIPO recognized the need to use legal and quasi-legal means to respond to challenges to the IP system. Thus, while the work undertaken by WIPO at present may not directly relate to copyright in the analogue environment, there exists space for discussion and consideration of access issues in the analogue environment. WIPO has developed a new interpretation of its mandate, which allows it to move beyond the traditional practice of focusing only on protection and promotion of IP.[13] Accordingly, it is not impossible to discuss issues of access to copyright in the analogue environment. WIPO has accepted to and is indeed taking the lead in reforming the international IP system by viewing IP through a development lens.

Indeed, the SCCR has stated that its work aims to support the interests of different actors in WIPO – creators, business and consumers – "so its duty is to ensure that Member States' national interests fit within the global agenda". This "global agenda", in our view, now includes access to protected works.

The recent developments in the SCCR represent, in our view, a process towards the development of an international legal mechanism for access to copyright in general and in the analogue environment in particular, for purposes of education. These developments include proposals for studies on limitations and exceptions with the objective of

---

11 Indeed at the second session of the Committee on Development and Intellectual Property (CDIP) several delegations expressed the belief that development was a cross-cutting issue and that the development dimension permeated all areas of IP. As such, the development dimension should not be confined to the discussions of the CDIP. See Committee on Development and Intellectual Property (CDIP), Second Session, *supra,* Report, particularly paras 257, 259 and 263.

12 In the case of patents, Standing Committee on Patents (SCP) has included a study on limitations and exceptions in its work programme. See for example, Exclusions from patentable subject matter and limitations and exceptions to rights, Standing Committee on the Law of Patents, Thirteenth Session, Geneva, March 23 to 27, 2009, World Intellectual Property Organization, WIPO Document SCP/13/3 E, dated February 4, 2009.

13 Discussions on the DA have been done alongside proposals for reform in organs of WIPO like the SCCR to include work on limitations and exceptions. As part of the implementation of the DA, studies for the study on limitations and exceptions have been proposed or commissioned in the Standing Committee on the law of Patents (SCP) and the Standing Committee on the law of Trade Marks (SCT), in addition to the SCCR. (See summary in, Committee on Development and Intellectual Property (CDIP), Third Session, *supra,* Progress Report on recommendations for immediate implementation, World Intellectual Property Organization, Document no. CDIP/5/5 (E) dated March 23, 2009.) It is, therefore, arguable that WIPO has not only adopted a new interpretation of the WIPO Convention so as to facilitate access to protected IP works, but there has developed a new custom, a *coutume sauvage,* dictated by the need to respond to the needs of developing countries as Members of WIPO. On the concept of *coutume sauvage* (custom that developed without established practice or *opinion juris*), see René-Jean Dupuy, "Coutume sage et coutume sauvage," in *Mélanges offerts a Charles Rousseau: La communauté Internationale, supra,* 75–87.

achieving agreement on minimum mandatory limitations and exceptions with regard to educational activities, libraries and archives. The approval by the SCCR of a study on limitations and exceptions for the benefit of educational activities, in particular in developing and least developed countries, is proof of the importance currently attached to access to copyrighted material for education purposes. Furthermore, the SCCR approved work on international instruments on L&Es for libraries and archives as well as for education. These developments emphasize the efforts being made by WIPO as an institution to find access solutions.

The various developments in WIPO indicate agreement that there should be minimum international standards on limitations and exceptions. In other words, there is at least agreement that access to copyrighted works can no longer be regarded as less important than protection of those works. For this reason, there should be minimum access standards for copyrighted works just as there are minimum protection standards.

As we have stated and now emphasize, the international solution to access to copyrighted material should include one or a combination of institutional reform, a soft law instrument or treaty on access. For a start, the focus should be on sustaining efforts at institutional reform as is already taking place in WIPO, and on concluding a soft law instrument under the auspices of WIPO. While a proposal for a soft law instrument is not new, it is new to WIPO.

This study contributes to the general debate on the role of copyright in the development aspirations of developing countries, in this case, access to education. In particular, it (a) draws the attention of the international community to the important, yet ignored question, of whether and how copyright law can be used to address the problem of access to *printed copyrighted material for educational purposes*; (b) highlights the need to incorporate/include the issue of access to printed copyrighted material for educational use in debates on access solutions at the international level; and (c) proposes possible solutions for access.

APPENDIX

Table 1. Summary of How the Berne Appendix Works

General requirement for use of the Appendix	Declaration to WIPO Director General, renewable every 10 years	
	Translation licence	Reproduction licence
Purpose for grant of CL	Teaching, scholarship and research	Use in systematic instructional activities[1]
Waiting period (before application)	– Generally 3 years – 1 year if language in general use is not English, French or Spanish	– 3 years for works of natural or physical science – 5 years for work of art – 7 years for works of fiction, poetry, drama and music – 7 years for all other works
Waiting period (after application has been deposited)	– 6 months where application is made after 3 years – 9 months where application is made after 1 year	6 months in all cases
Grace Period (for rights holder)	– CL not granted if rights holder exercises his right within the waiting period of 6 or 9 months – Rights holder can withdraw works from market after Cl has been granted during waiting period.	
Administrative structure to administer use of CL	Competent Authority	

(*Continued*)

[1] The Appendix does not define "Systematic Instructional Activities".

Table 1. (*Cont.*)

General requirement for use of the Appendix	Declaration to WIPO Director General, renewable every 10 years
General conditions for application for CL	– Request a voluntary licence or prove that right holder could not be found after due diligence on part of applicant – Alert national or international information Centre of application – Send by registered mail copies of application to the publisher or his representatives
General Conditions for use of CL	– Copies made under CL must be labelled – In case of translation licence, the title must be indicated in the original language as well – Copies made under CL cannot be exported, (except in case of translation where government can export to a national abroad under certain conditions) – Payment of just compensation consistent with standards of royalties for freely negotiated licences (sent in internationally convertible currency or equivalent)

Table 2. Past Notifications under the Berne Appendix

Notification No.	Country	Notification Date	Provision in National legislation (including provisions that use language similar to Appendix)
194	Algeria	30 March, 1998	Yes
212	Argentina	19 Nov, 1999	
177	Bahrain	2 Dec 1996	
140	China	15 June, 1992	Yes
128	Egypt	14 March, 1990	Yes
100	Guinea	20 Aug, 1980	
108, 110	India	6 Feb, 1984 (renewed 20 June 184)	Yes
152	Jamaica	1 Oct, 1993	
124	Lesotho	28 June, 1989	Yes
122	Liberia	8 Dec, 1988	
130	Malaysia	29 June, 1990	
123	Mauritius	10 Feb, 19989	
79, 109A	Mexico	3 June, 1976 (renewed 18 June, 1984)	
91	Niger	17 March, 1978	
198	Singapore	21 Sept, 1998	
83	Surinam	23 Nov, 1996	

Table 2. (*Cont.*)

Notification No.	Country	Notification Date	Provision in National legislation (including provisions that use language similar to Appendix)
156	Tanzania	25 April, 1994	
74	Tunisia	16 May, 19975	Yes

Source: Author's compilation from the WIPO website: http://www.wipo.int/treaties/en/noticiations/berne.

Table 3. Current Notifications under the Berne Appendix

Notification No.	Country	Notification Date	Provision in National legislation (including provisions that use language similar to Appendix)
200, 234	Bangladesh	4 Feb, 1999 (renewed on 1 June, 2004)	Yes
176, 238	Cuba	20 Nov, 1996 (renewed on 28 on, 2004)	Yes
204, 232	Jordan	28 April, 1999 (renewed on 27 April 2004)	Yes
224	Korea	28 Jan, 2003	
190, 237	Mongolia	12 June, 1997 (renewed on 25 June, 2004)	
233	Oman	6 May, 2004	
23	Philippines	16 June, 2004	
250	Samoa	21 April, 2006	
248	Sri Lanka	27 Sept, 2005	Yes
240	Sudan	26 July, 2004	Yes
245	Syria	3 Nov, 2004	Yes
167, 239	Thailand	2 June, 1995 (renewed on 8 July, 2004)	Yes
236	United Arab Emirates	16 June, 2004	Yes
244	Uzbekistan	19 Jan, 2005	
241	Vietnam	26 July, 2004y	Yes
254	Yemen	14 April, 2008	

Source: Author's compilation from the WIPO website: http://www.wipo.int/treaties/en/noticiations/berne.

BIBLIOGRAPHY

A. Primary Sources

1. *Official Documents*

Laws and Other Multilateral Instruments

United Nations Education, Scientific and Cultural Organization (UNESCO)

Universal Copyright Convention, concluded at Geneva on 6 September 1952, entered into force on 16 September 1955, and as revised at Paris on 24 July 1971, entered into force on 24 July 1974, *U.N.T.S 13444*.

World Declaration on Education for All and Framework for Action to Meet Basic Learning Needs. Adopted by the World Conference on Education for All: Meeting Basic Learning Needs, published as Appendix to the Final Report of the World Conference on Education for All: Meeting Basic Learning Needs, Jomtiem, Thailand, 5–9 March 1990, Inter-Agency Commission (UNDP, UNESCO, UNICEF, World bank) for the World Conference on Education for All, New York 1990, 166p.

United Nations Organization

Universal Declaration of Human Rights, adopted by General Assembly Resolution 217A (III), 10 December 1948.

General Comment no. 3, The nature of States parties obligations (art. 2. para. 1 of the Covenant) in UN Doc. E/1991/23, Report of the Committee on Economic, Social and Cultural Rights, Fifth session, 1990, pp 83–87.

UN Doc. A/CONF.157/23, World Conference on Human Rights, Vienna, 14–25 June 1993, Declaration and Program of Action.

UN Doc. A/51/506/Add.1, appendix, United Nations Decade for Human Rights: Human Rights Questions: Human Rights Questions including alternative approaches for improving the effective enjoyment of human rights and fundamental freedoms, dated 12 December, 1996.

General Comment no. 13, The right to education (art. 13 of the Covenant) in UN Doc. E/2000/22, Report of the Committee on Economic, Social and Cultural Rights, Twenty-first session, 1999, pp 111–127.

UN. Doc. E/C.12/2000/12, "Approaching Intellectual Property as a Human Right: Obligations related to article 15(1)(c)," Discussion paper presented by Audrey R. Chapman to the 24th Session of the Committee on Economic, Social and Cultural Rights.

UN. Doc. E/CN.4/Sub.2/2000/13, Globalization and its impact on the full enjoyment of human rights, Preliminary report submitted to by Joseph Oloka-Onyango and Deepika Udagama to the 52nd Session of the Sub-Commission on the Promotion and Protection of Human Rights.

UN Doc. E/CN.4/SUB.2/2001/12, Intellectual property rights and human rights, Report of the Secretary-General submitted to the Sub-Commission on the Promotion and protection of Human Rights at its 52nd session, 2001.

UN Doc. E/CN.4/Sub.2001/12, "Intellectual property rights and human rights," Report of the Secretary-General submitted to the Sub-Commission on the Promotion and protection of Human Rights at its 53rd session, 14 June 2001.

UN Doc. E/CN.4/Sub.2/2001/13. "The Impact of the Agreement on Trade-Related Aspects of Intellectual Property Rights on Human Rights," Commission on Human Rights, Report of the High Commissioner for Human Rights presented to the Sub-Commission on the Promotion and Protection of Human Rights at its 52nd Session, 27 June 2001.

UN.Doc.E/C.12/2001/15, Human rights and intellectual property, Statement by the Committee on Economic, Social and Cultural Rights, submitted as a follow-up to the day of general discussion on article 15.1(c) of the CESCR.

General Comment no. 17, The right of everyone o benefit from the protection of the moral and material interests resulting from any scientific, literary or artistic production of which he or she is the author (art. 15, paragraph 1 (c), of the Covenant) in UN Doc. E/C.12/GC/17, Committee on Economic, Social and Cultural Rights, Twenty-fifth session, 7-25 November 2005.

World Intellectual Property Organization

Berne Convention for the Protection of Literary and Artistic Works (9 September 1886), as revised by the Act of Stockholm (1967), and by the Paris Act (1971) and amended in 1979, Publication of the World Intellectual Property Organization no. 287(E).

Convention Establishing the World Intellectual Property Organization, signed at Stockholm on 14 July 1967 and as amended on 28 September 1979, Publication of the World Intellectual Property Organization, no. 250(E).

Guide to the Berne Convention for the Protection of Literary and Artistic Works (Paris Act, 1971), World Intellectual Property Organization, 1978, Publication of the World Intellectual Organization no. 615(E).

The International Convention for the Protection of Performers, Producers of Phonograms and Broadcasting Organizations (Rome Convention, 1961), done at Rome, 26 October 1961. Publication of the World Intellectual Property Organization no. 328(E).

Records of the Intellectual Property Conference of Stockholm, June 11 to July 14, 1967, (vol. I and II), World Intellectual Property Organizations, Geneva, 1971.

Protocol Regarding Developing Countries, reproduced in Records of the Intellectual Property Conference of Stockholm, June 11 to July 14, 1967, vol. II, Report of the Work of Main Committee II, World Intellectual Property Organizations, Geneva, 1971, p. 1197.

Paris Convention for the Protection of Industrial Property, (20 March 1883), Stockholm Act (1967), modified in 1979, Publication of the World Intellectual Property Organization no. 201(E).

Records of the Diplomatic Conference for the Revision of the Berne Convention, Paris, July 5 to 24, 1971, World Intellectual Property Organization, Geneva, 1974, WIPO Publications No. 385 (E).

Agreement Between the World Intellectual Property Organization and the World Trade Organization, concluded 22 December 1995, entered into force on 1 January 1996, World Intellectual Property Organization, Geneva 1997. Publication of the World Intellectual Property Organization no. 223 (E).

WIPO Copyright Treaty, adopted in Geneva on 20 December 1996, entered into force on 6 March 2002. WIPO Publication no. 226(E).

Standing Committee on Copyright and Related Rights, First Session, Geneva, November 2 to 10, 1998, Organizational and procedural matters and overview of substantive issues, WIPO Document SCCR/1/2 (E), dated September 4, 1998.

Standing Committee on Copyright and Related Rights, 9th Session, Geneva, June 23 to 27, 2003, Study on limitations and exceptions of copyright and related rights in the digital environment, prepared by Sam Ricketson, WIPO Document SCCR/9/7 (E) dated April 5, 2003.

General Assembly, Thirty-First (15th Ordinary) Session, Geneva, September 27 to October 5, 2004, Proposal by Argentina and Brazil for the Establishment of a Development Agenda for WIPO, World Intellectual Property Organization, Document no. WO/GA/31/11, dated September 27, 2004.

Standing Committee on Copyright and Related Rights, Twelfth Session, Geneva November 17 to 19, 2004, Proposal by Chile on the subject "Limitations and exceptions to copyright and related rights," World Intellectual Property Organization, WIPO Document no. SCCR/12/3 (E) dated November 2, 2004, Annex.

Information on WIPO's Development Cooperation Activities, January 2000–June 2005, World Intellectual Property Organization, Geneva, WIPO Document WIPO/EDS/INF/1 Rev (E) dated September 23, 2005 (available at www.wipo.int/ip-development).

General Assembly, Thirty-Second (17th Ordinary) Session, Geneva, September 26 to October 5, 2005, Report, World Intellectual Property Organization, Document no. WO/GA/32/13, dated October 5, 2005.

Standing Committee on Copyright and Related Rights, Fourteenth Session, Geneva, May 1 to 5, 2006, Study on Automated Rights Management Systems and Copyright Limitations and Exceptions, prepared by Garnett, Nic. World Intellectual Property Organization Document SCCR/14/5, (E) dated April 27, 2006.

Standing Committee on Copyright and Related Rights, Fifteenth Session, Geneva, September 11 to 13, 2006, Study on Limitations and Exceptions of Copyrights for Visually Impaired, prepared by Sullivan, Judith, World Intellectual Property Organization, Document SCCR/15/7, (E) dated February 20, 2007.

Provisional Committee on Proposals related to a WIPO Development Agenda (PCDA), Third Session, Geneva, February 9 to 13, 2007, World Intellectual Property Organization, Document no. PCDA/3/3, (E), dated June 11, 2007.

Provisional Committee on Proposals related to a WIPO Development Agenda (PCDA), Fourth Session, Geneva, June 11 to 15, 2007, World Intellectual Property Organization, Document no. PCDA/4/3, (E), dated September 4, 2007.

Assemblies of the Members States of WIPO, Forty-Third Series of meetings, Geneva, September 24 to October 3, 2007, General Report, World Intellectual Property Organization, Document no. A/43/16 (E) dated November 12, 2007.

Committee on Development and Intellectual Property (CDIP), First Session, Geneva, March 3 to 7, 2008, Initial Working Document for the Committee on Development and Intellectual Property (CDIP), World Intellectual Property Organization, Document no. CDIP/1/3 (E) dated March 3, 2008.

Committee on Development and Intellectual Property (CDIP), First Session, Geneva, March 3 to 7, 2008, Draft Report, World Intellectual Property Organization, Document no. CDIP/1/4 Prov (E) dated April 11, 2008.

Standing Committee on Copyright and Related Rights, Sixteenth Session, Geneva March 10 to 12, 2008, Proposal by Brazil, Chile, Nicaragua and Uruguay for work related to limitations and exceptions, World Intellectual Property Organization, WIPO Document no. SCCR/16/2 (E) dated July 17, 2008.

Committee on Development and Intellectual Property (CDIP), Second Session, Geneva, July 7 to 11, 2008, Initial Working Document for the Committee on Development and Intellectual Property (CDIP): Information Document Related to adopted Recommendation 10, World Intellectual Property Organization, Document no. CDIP/2/INF/1 (E) dated May 16, 2008.

Committee on Development and Intellectual Property (CDIP), Second Session, Geneva, July 7 to 11, 2008, Initial Working Document for the Committee on Development and Intellectual Property (CDIP): Revised text in respect of recommendations considered in the First Session of the CDIP, World Intellectual Property Organization, Document no. CDIP/2/2 (E) dated June 20, 2008.

Committee on Development and Intellectual Property (CDIP), First Session, Geneva, March 3 to 7, 2008, Report, World Intellectual Property Organization, Document no. CDIP/1/4 (E) dated July 7, 2008.

Committee on Development and Intellectual Property (CDIP), Second Session, Geneva, July 7 to 11, 2008, Draft Report, World Intellectual Property Organization, Document no. CDIP/2/4/Prov. (E) dated August 22, 2008.

Study on Copyright Limitations and Exceptions for Libraries and Archives, Standing Committee on Copyright and Related Rights, Seventeenth Session, Geneva, November 3 to 7, 2008, prepared by Crews, Kenneth, WIPO Document SCCR/17/2 (E) dated August 26, 2008.

Program and Budget Committee, Thirteenth Session, Geneva, December 10 to 11, 2008, Revised Program and Budget for the 2008/2009 Biennium, World Intellectual Property Organization, Document no. WO/PBC/13/4 (E) dated November 13, 2008.

Standing Committee on the Law of Patents, Thirteenth Session, Geneva, March 23 to 27, 2009, Exclusions from patentable subject matter and limitations and exceptions to rights, World Intellectual Property Organization, WIPO Document SCP/13/3 E, dated February 4, 2009.

Committee on Development and Intellectual Property (CDIP), Third Session, Geneva, April 27 to May 1, 2009, Progress Report on recommendations for immediate implementation, World Intellectual Property Organization, Document no. CDIP/5/5 (E) dated March 23, 2009.

Standing Committee on Copyright and Related Rights, Eighteenth Session, Geneva May 25 to 29, 2009, Proposal by Brazil, Ecuador and Paraguay, relating to limitations and Exceptions: Treaty proposed by the World Blind Union, World Intellectual Property Organization, Document no. SCCR/28/5 (E), dated May 25, 2009.

World Trade Organization

The Results of the Uruguay Round of Multilateral Negotiations, The Legal Texts, The World Trade Organization, 1995.

Council for TRIPS, Review of Legislation on Copyright and Related Rights – Replies to Questions Posed to the United States by Brazil, the European Communities and their Members States, Australia and Korea, WTO Doc. IP/Q/USA/1, dated October 30, 1996.

Agreement on Trade-Related Aspects of Intellectual Property Rights, Annex 1C to the Marrakesh Agreement Establishing the World Trade Organization, 15 April 1994, in *The Results of the Uruguay Round of Multilateral Negotiations, The Legal Texts.* World Trade Organization, 1995.

Ministerial Declaration adopted on 14 November at the 4th WTO Ministerial Conference, Doha, 9–14 November 2001, document no. WT/MIN(01)/DEC/1, dated 20 November 2001.

Declaration on the TRIPS Agreement and Public Health, adopted on 14 November at the 4th WTO Ministerial Conference, Doha, 9–14 November 2001, document no. WT/MIN(01)/DEC/2, dated 20 November 2001. ((available at http://www.wto.org/english/thewto_e/minist_e/min01_e/mindecl_trips_e.pdf)

Paragraph 6 of the Ministerial Declaration on the TRIPS Agreement and Public Health, (Communication from Brazil on behalf of Developing Countries), document IP/C/W/355 dated 24 June 2002.

Extension of the transition period under article 66.1 of the TRIPS Agreement for Least Developed Country Members for certain obligations with respect to pharmaceutical products, Decision of Council for TRIPS of 27 June 2002. document no. IP/C/W/25 dated 1 July 2002.

Least developed Country Members – the Obligations Under Article 70.9 of the TRIPS Agreement with Respect to Pharmaceutical products, General Council Decision of 8 July 2002, document no. WT/L/478 dated 12 July 2002.

Argentina – Patent Protection for Pharmaceuticals and Test Data Protection for Agricultural Chemicals (WT/DS171), and Argentina – Certain Measures on the Protection of Patents and Test Data (WT/DS196): Notification of Mutually Agreed Solution according to the Conditions Set Forth in the Agreement. Document no. IP/D/18/Add.1, IP/D/22/Add.1, dated 20 June 2002.

Implementation of paragraph 6 of the Doha Declaration on the TRIPS Agreement and Public Health, General Council Decision of 30 August 2003, Document no. WT/L/540 dated 2 September 2003.

The General Council's Chairperson's Statement (which accompanied the 30 August 2003 Decision), Minutes of the General Council, document WT/GC/M/82 dated 13 November 2003, pp. 6 and 7.

Council for Trade Related Aspects of Intellectual Property Rights. Annual review of the decision on the implementation of paragraph 6 of the Doha Declaration on the TRIPS Agreement and public health, document. IP/C/37, dated 3 November 2005.

Council for TRIPS, Request for an extension of the transitional period under Article 66.1 of the TRIPS Agreement, Communication from the Delegation of Zambia on behalf of the Least-Developed Country Members, document no. IP/C/W/457 of 21 October 2005.

Council for TRIPS, Extension of the Transition Period Under Article 66.1 for Least-developed Country Members: Decision of 29 November 2005, document no. IP/C/40 dated 30 November 2005.

Amendment to the TRIPS Agreement. Decision of the General Council of 6 December 2005, document no. WT/L/641 dated 8 December 2005.

Hong Kong Ministerial Declaration, Doha Work Programme, adopted on 18 December 2005, document WT/MIN/05/DEC dated 22 December 2005.

Notification under paragraph 2(a) of the Decision of 30 August 2003 on the implementation of paragraph 6 of the Doha Declaration on the TRIPS Agreement and Public Health: Rwanda, document IP/N/9/RWA/1, dated 19 July 2007.

National Laws and Other Regional and National Instruments

Algeria

Copyright and Neighbouring Rights Act of July 19, 2003

Australia

Copyright Act 1968 Act no.63 of 1968 (as amended)

Copyright Amendment (Digital Agenda) Act 2000, no. 110 of 2000.

Belgium

Loi du 22 mai 2005 transposant en droit belge la Directive 2001/29/CE du 22 mai sur l'harmonisation de certains aspects du droit d'auteur et des droits voisins dans la société de l'information, (Published in the *Moniteur Belge* (*Official Journal*), 27/05/2005, p. 24997.)

Bolivia

Copyright Act No. 1322 of 1992

Brazil

Industrial Property Law no. 9.279/96 of May 14, 1996, (effective as of 15 May 1997) as amended by the Industrial Property, Law (Amendment), no. 10.196 of 14 February 2001.

Canada

Patent Act, 1985. C. P-4, as amended by the Patents Act (Consolidation) of 30 April 1996).

Copyright Act, 1985 (R.S., c. C–30, s. 1).

China(the People's Republic of)

Copyright Law of the People's Republic of China, 7 September 1990, as amended in 2010.

Decree of the State Council of the People's Republic of China, no. 468: Regulations on Protection of the Right of Communication through Information Network, adopted at the 135 Executive Meeting of the State Council on 10 May, 2006.

Colombia

Copyright Law No. 23 of 1982 on Copyright

Cuba

Law No.14 of 1977 on Copyright

Djibouti

Law No. 154/AN/06 of 23 July, 2006 on Protection of Copyright and Neighbouring Rights

Dominican Republic

Copyright Law No. 65 of 2000

Egypt

Law on the Protection of Intellectual Property Rights, Law no. 82 of 2002.

El Salvador

Law on the Promotion and Protection of Intellectual Property, (Legislative Decree No 604 of 15 July 1993).

Ethiopia (the Federal Democratic Republic of)

Proclamation concerning inventions, minor inventions and industrial designs, Proclamation no. 123/1995.

European Community

Directive 91/250/EEC of 14 May 1991 on the legal protection of Computer Programs, *Official Journal. L 122, 17/05/1991 P. 0042–0046.*

Directive 93/98/EEC of 29 May 1993 on harmonizing the term of protection of copyright and certain related rights, *Official Journal L 290,* 24/11/1993 P. 0009–0013.

Directive 96/9/EC of the European Parliament and of the Council of 11 March, 1996 on the Legal Protection of Databases, 1996 *Official Journal* L77/20, 27/03/1996 P.0020–0028.

Directive 2001/29/EC of the European Parliament and of the Council of 22 May 2001 on the harmonization of certain aspects of copyright and related rights in the information society, *Official Journal* L 167, 22/06/2001 P. 0010–0019.

Commission of the European Communities, Green Paper in Copyright in the Knowledge Economy, Brussels, COM(2008) 466/3.

France

Law on the Intellectual Property Code (Legislative Part), (No. 92–597 of July 1, 1992, as last amended by Laws Nos. 94–361 of May 10, 1994, 95–4 of January 3, 1995, and 97–1106 of December 18, 1996).

Copyright Act 2005, Act 690.

Germany

Law on Copyright and Neighbouring Rights (Copyright Law) of September 9, 1965, as last amended by the Law of May 8, 1998.

Honduras

Decree No 4-99E, Copyright and Neighbouring Rights Law

India

India, Copyright Act, 1957 (as amended)

The Patents (Amendment) Act, 2005, (Act No. 15 of 2005), Published in the Gazette of India, April 5 2005.

Japan

Copyright Law. (Law no. 48 of May 6, 1970, as amended by Laws no. 49 of May 18, 1978, no. 45 of May 19, 1981, no. 78 of December 2, 1983, no. 23 of May 1, 1984, no. 46 of May 25, 1984, no. 62 of June 14, 1985, no. 64 of May 23, 1986, no. 65 of May 23, 1986, no. 87 of November 1, 1988, no. 43 of June 28, 1989, no. 63 of May 2, 1991, no. 106 of December 16, 1992, no. 89 of November 12, 1993, no. 112 of December 14, 1994, and no. 91 of May 12, 1995).

Jordan

Copyright Law, Law No. 22 of 1992 (as amended by laws No.14 of 1998, No. 29 of 1999 and 52 of 2001),

Kenya

Industrial Property Act 2001, Act no. 3 of 2001.

The Copyright Act, 2001, Act no. 12 of 2001.

Kuwait
Law No 64 of 1999 Concerning Intellectual Property Rights including Explanatory Memorandum

Lesotho
Copyright Order of 1989, No. 13 of May 1989

Mongolia
Law of Mongolia on Copyright, 1999.
Nepal
The Copyright Act 2002, Act no. 8 of 2002, entered into force on 15 August 2002
Copyright Rules, 2004.

Netherlands
The Copyright Act, 1912 (as last amended by the Law of October 27, 1972).

Norway
Norway Patent Act of 19 December 2003, entered into force on 1 February 2004.

Panama
Law No. 15 of 1994 on Copyright and Neighbouring Rights.

Pakistan
The Copyright Ordinance, 1962, Ordinance No. XXXIV of 1962, (as amended by Copyright (Amendment) Ordinance, 2000 dated 29th September, 2000).

Philippines
Intellectual Property Code of the Philippines 1997, Republic Act no. 8293 of June 6, 1997 (entered into force on January 1, 1998.
Copyright Safeguard and Regulations of August 13, 1999.

Republic of South Africa
Medicines and Related Substances Control Amendment Act, 1997, Act No 90, 1997, Government Gazette vol. 390, no. 18505, 12 December 1997.
Copyright, Act (Consolidation), 20/06/1978 (1992), no. 98 (No. 125).

Sri Lanka
Code of Intellectual Property

Sudan
Copyright and Neighbouring Rights Act 1996

Syria (the Arab Republic of)
Copyright Law No 12 of 2001

Thailand
Copyright Act, B.E. 2537 (1994).

Tunisia
Tunisia Law No. 2009-33 dated 23 June 2009 amending and completing Law No. 94-36 dated 24 February 1994 relating to Literary and Artistic Property.

Uganda
Uganda, Copyright and Neighbouring Rights Act 2006

United Arab Emirates
Federal Law no. 7 of 2002 concerning copyrights and neighbouring rights.

United Kingdom

Statute of Anne, found in The Founders' Constitution, Vol.3, Document available at http://press-pubs.uchicago.edu/founders/documents/a1_8_8s2.html

Copyright, Designs and Patents Act 1988 (c. 48) as amended.

United States of America

The Constitution of the United States of America.

House of Representatives Report on the 1976 Copyright Bill, House Committee on the Judiciary, House Report No. 94-1476 to accompany s. 22, 94th Congress, 2nd Session, September 3 1976.

Copyright Act of 1976, Act of 19 October 1976, as amended through to13 December 2003, Title 17 United States Code (USC), ch. 1 to 13.

Fairness in Music Licensing Act of 27 October 1998, Pub.L. 105-298, 112 Stat. 2830, 105th Cong., 2nd Session (1998).

The Digital Millennium Copyright Act, Public law 105-304, October 28, 1998.

The Technology, Education and Copyright Harmonization Act, 2002.

Vietnam

Law No. 50/2005/QH11 of 29 November 2005 on Intellectual Property, as amended by Law No. 36/2009/QH12.

Agreement between the United States of America and the Socialist Republic of Vietnam on Trade Relations.

2. *Treaties*

International Covenant on Economic, Social and Cultural Rights, 1966, 993 *U.N.T.S no.* 3.

The Vienna Convention on the Law of Treaties, 1969, 1155 *U.N.T.S, no.* 331.

Convention on the Rights of the Child, adopted by General Assembly resolution A/RES/44/25 of 20 November 1989, entered into force on 2 September 1990, 1577 *U.N.T.S, no.* 3.

3. *Cases*

International

Arbitral Awards

Texaco-Calasiatic c. Gouvernment libye, sentence arbitral au fond du 19 janvier 1977, arbitral award by René-Jean Dupuy, reported in *Journal du droit international* (*Clunet*), vol. 104, no. 2 (1977), pp. 350–389.

International Court of Justice

Request for Interpretation of the Judgment of November 20th, 1950 in the Asylum Case, (Colombia v. Peru), Judgment of 27 November 1950, I.C.J Reports 1950, p. 395.

Ambatielos (*Greece v. United Kingdom*), (Preliminary objection), Judgement of 1 July 1952, I.C.J Reports 1952, p. 28.

North Sea Continental Shelf (*Federal Republic of Germany v. Denmark and Federal Republic of Germany v. the Netherlands*), Judgment of 20 February 1969, I.C.J Reports 1969, p. 3.

Applicability of the obligation to arbitrate under section 21 of the United Nations Headquarters Agreement of 26 June 1947, Advisory Opinion of 26 April 1988, I.C.J. Reports, 1988.

Gabcíkovo-Nagymaros Project (Hungary/Slovakia), Judgment of 25 September 1997, I.C.J Reports 1997, p. 7.

World Trade Organization

India – Patent Protection for Pharmaceutical and Agricultural Chemical Products, (complaint by the European Communities), WT/DS79/R, 24 August 1998.

Argentina – Patent Protection for Pharmaceuticals and Test Data Protection for Agricultural Chemicals, Request for Consultations by the United States, WT/DS171/1, 6 May 1999.

Canada – Patent Protection of Pharmaceutical Products, Complaint by the European Communities and their Member States, Report of the Panel, WT/DS114/R, Geneva, 17 March 2000.
Argentina – Certain Measures on the Protection of Patents and Test Data, Request for Consultations by the United States, WT/DS196/1, 30 May 2000.
Brazil – Measures Affecting Patent Protection, Request for Consultations by the United States, WT/DS1991, G/L/385, IP/D/23, 8 June 2000.
United States – Section 110(5) of the US Copyright Act, Report of the Panel, WT/DS160/R, Geneva, 15 June 2000.
Brazil – Measures Affecting Patent Protection, Request for the Establishment of a Panel by the United States, WT/DS199/39, 9 January 2001.
Brazil – Measures Affecting Patent Protection, Notification of Mutually Agreed Solution, G/L/454, IP/D/23/Add.1, WT/DS/199/4, 19 July 2001.
China – Measures affecting the protection and enforcement of Intellectual Property Rights, Report of the Panel, WT/DS362/R, 26 January, 2009.

National Decisions

Belgium

Test Achats v. EMI Music Belgium et al, Tribunal de Première Instance de Bruxelles, 25 May 2004, case 2004/46/A.
Test Achats v. EMI Recorded Music Belgium et al, Cour d'Appel de Bruxelles, (9th Chamber), 9 September 2005, case 2004/AR/1649.

Canada

Compagnie Générale des Etablissement Michelin-Michelin & Cie v. National Automobile, Aerospace, Transportation and General Workers Union of Canada (CAW-Canada), 1997, 71 C.P.R (3d) 348.
Tele-Direct (Publications) Inc. v. American Business Information, Inc. (C.A.) 79 C.P.R. 3d 296 (1997), Court of Appeal, October 27, 1997.
Théberge v. Galerie d'Art du Petit Champlain inc., 2002 SCC 34.
CCH Canadian Ltd v. Law Society of Upper Canada, 2004 SCC 13.
Society of Composers, Authors and Music Publishers of Canada v. Canadian Association of Internet Providers, 2004 SCC 45, [2004] 2 S.C.R. 427.
Euro-Excellence Inc. v. Kraft Canada Inc., 2007 SCC 37.

France

Studio Canal et al v. S. Parquin and Union fédérale des consommateurs (UFC) Que choisir, Paris Court of Appeal, 4 April 2007, Gaz. Pal. 18 July 2007, no. 199.

India

Academy of General Education, Manipal and anor v. B. Manini Mallya, [2009] 39 PTC 393 (SC).

Mauritius

Polo/Laurent Co Ltd Partnership v. Dinoo and others, 2004 SCJ 44.
Polo/Laurent Co Ltd Partnership v. Regent Ltd and two others, 2004 SCJ 45.

Republic of South Africa

Pharmaceutical Manufacturer's Association of South Africa and others v. President of the Republic of South Africa, (Transvaal Provincial Division), Case no. 4183/98, Notice of Motion.

Thailand

Public Prosecutor v. Somsak Thanasarasenee, Supreme Court of Thailand, case No. 1732/2000, Judgement of April 4, 2000.
Public Prosecutor v. Ganokchai Petchdawong, The Supreme Court of Thailand, case No. 5843/2543 (2000) J.S.C., decided on September 18, 2000.

Uganda

John Murray (Publishers) Ltd and others v George William Senkindu and another, Misc. Application HCCS 1018 of 1997 (unreported)

United States of America

Sony Corp. v. Universal City Studios, 464 U.S. 417 (1984).
Harper & Row, Publishers, Inc. v. Nation Enterprises, 471 U.S 539 (1985).
Abend v. MCA, Inc., United States Court of Appeals for the Ninth Circuit, 863 F.2d 1465; 1988 U.S. App. LEXIS 17515.
Feist Publications v. Rural Telephone Service Co., 499 U.S. 340 (1991), U.S. Supreme Court.
Basic Books, Inc. v. Kinko's Graphics Corporation, 758 F. Supp. 1522, S.D.N.Y, 1991.
American Geophysical Union v. Texaco Inc., 60 F.3d 913, 918 (2d Cir. 1994).
Campbell v. Acuff-Rose Music, Inc, 510 U.S. 569 (1994).
Princeton University Press v. Michigan Document Service, 1996 FED App. 0046P (6th Cir.).
United States of America v. The Thomson Corporation and West Publishing Company, Federal Register, July 5, 1996.
Universal City Studios, Inc., et al. v. Shawn C. Reimerdes, et al., United States District Court, Southern District of New York, Civ. 0277 (LAK), Opinion, 17 August 2000.
Worldwide Church of God v. Philadelphia Church of God, Inc, 227 F 3d 1110 (9th Cir. 2000).
Kelly v. Arriba Soft Corporation, 336 F.3d 881 (9th Cir. 2003).
Eldred et al. v. Ashcroft, Attorney General, Supreme Court of the United States, Case no. 01-618, 15 January 2003, 537 *U.S.* 1ff. (2003).
CoStar Group v. LoopNet, 373 F.3d 544, 4th Cir (2004).
eBay, Inc., et al v. MercExchange, L.L.C. 275 F. Supp. 2d 696 (2003).
eBay, Inc., et al v. MercExchange, L.L.C. 401 F.3d 1323, 1339 (2005).
eBay, Inc. v. MercExchange, L.L.C, 547 U.S. 388 (2006).
Lenz v. Universal Music Corp., et al, 572 F.Supp.2d 1150 (2008).
London-Sire Records, Inc., et al v. Doe 1 et al, 542 F.Supp.2d 153 (2008).
Capitol Records, Inc., v. Jammie Thomas, 579 F.Supp.2d 1210 (2008).

B. Secondary Sources

1. *Books and Collective Works*

Armstrong, Chris, Jeremy de Beer, Dick Kawooya, Achal Prabhala and Tobias Schonwetter, eds. *Access to knowledge in African: the Role of Copyright.* Claremont: UCT Press, 2010.
Bellmann, Christophe, Graham Dutifield and Ricardo Meléndez-Ortiz, eds. *Trading in Knowledge: Development Perspectives on TRIPS, Trade and Sustainable Development.* London: Earthscan Publications Ltd, 2003.
Bently, Lionel and Brad Sherman. *Intellectual Property Law.* 2nd ed. Oxford: Oxford University Press, 2004.
Botoy Ituku, Elangi *Propriété Intellectuelle et Droits de L'homme: L'impact des brevets pharmaceutiques sur le droit à la santé dans le contexte du VIH/SIDA en Afrique.* Bruxelles: Bruylant, Bruxelles, 2007.
Cavalli Jean, *La genèse de la Convention de Berne pour la protection des oeuvres littéraires et artistiques du 9 septembre 1886.* PhD thesis, University of Lausanne, Imprimeries Réunies, 1986.
Chandler, Martin Trent, *Toward a context-specific language policy for developing countries with an emphasis on language-in-education.* A thesis presented to the Faculty of the School of International Studies, Department of TESOL and applied linguistics, Biola University, May 1992. (available on www.eric.ed.gov).
Clapham, Andrew, *Human Rights Obligations of Non-Sate Actors.* Oxford: Oxford University Press, 2006.

Cornish, W.R., *Intellectual Property: Patents, Copyrights, Trademarks and Allied Right.*, 4th ed. London: Sweet and Maxwell,1999.
Correa, Carlos, *Implementing the TRIPS Agreement: General Context and Implications for Developing Countries.* Penang: Third World Network, 1998.
——, *Intellectual Property Rights, the WTO and Developing Countries: The TRIPS Agreement and Policy Options.* Penang: ZED Books Ltd, 2000.
——, *Integrating Public Health Concerns into Patent Legislation in developing Countries.* 2nd ed. Geneva: South Centre, 2001.
——, *Implications of the Doha Declaration on the TRIPS Agreement and Public Health.* Geneva: World Health Organization, *Health, Economics, and Drugs* (EDM), EDM Series no.12, June 2002.
——, *Implementation of WTO General Council Decision on Paragraph 6 of the Doha Declaration on the TRIPS Agreement and Public Health*, Geneva: World Health Organization, *Health, Economics, and Drugs* (EDM), EDM Series no.16, 2004.
——, *Trade related aspects of intellectual property rights: a commentary on the TRIPS Agreement.* Oxford: Oxford University Press, 2007.
Cottier, Thomas, ed. *The Challenge of WTO Law: collected essays.* London: Cameron May, 2007.
Cottier, Thomas, Joost Pauwelyn, and Elizabeth Bürgi Bonanomi, eds. *Human Rights and International Trade.* Oxford: Oxford University Press, 2005.
Desbois, Henri, *Le droit d'auteur en France.* 2nd ed. Paris : Dalloz, 1966.
Dessemontet, Francois, *Intellectual Property Law in Switzerland.* The Hague: Kluwer Law International and Stämpli, 2000.
Dinwoodie, Graeme B. and Rochelle C. Dreyfuss, *A Neofederalist Vision of TRIPs: Building a Resilient International Intellectual Property System,* Oxford University Press, Oxford, 2012 Forthcoming.
Drahos, Peter and Ruth Mayne, eds. *Global Intellectual Property Rights: Knowledge, Access and Development.* New York: Palgrave Macmillan and Oxfam, 2002.
Ficsor, Mihály, *The Law of Copyright and the Internet – The WIPO Copyright Treaties, their interpretation and implementation.* Oxford: Oxford University Press, 2002.
Garcia-Rubio, Mariano, *On the Application of Customary Rules of State Responsibility by the WTO Dispute Settlement Organs: A General International Law Perspective.* Geneva: Graduate Institute of International Studies, 2001.
Geist, Michael, ed. *In the Public Interest: The Future of Canadian Copyright Law.* Toronto: Irwin Law, 2005.
Gervais, Daniel, ed., *Intellectual property, trade and development: strategies to optimize economic development in a TRIPS-Plus era.* Oxford: Oxford University Press, 2007.
Gervais, Daniel. *The TRIPS Agreement: Drafting History and Analysis.* 2nd ed. London: Sweet and Maxwell, 2003.
Gervais, Daniel. *The TRIPS Agreement: Drafting History and Analysis.* 3rd ed. London: Sweet and Maxwell, 2008.
Goburdhun, Kaushik. *Access to knowledge in Africa: how to free a continent from the shackles of copyright.* LLM thesis, Kent Law School, University of Kent, 2006.
Goldstein, Paul. *International intellectual property law: cases and materials.* New York: Foundation press, 2001.
Goldstein, Paul. *International Copyright: Principles, Law and Practice.* Oxford: Oxford University Press, 2001.
Gordon, Wendy J. and Richard Watt. *The Economics of Copyright: Developments in Research and Analysis.* Cheltenham,: Edward Edgar, 2003.
Groves, Peter J. *Sourcebook on Intellectual Property Law.* London: Cavendish Publishing Limited, 2003.
Guibault, Lucie M.C. *Copyright Limitations and Contracts: An analysis of the contractual overridability of limitations on copyright.* The Hague: Kluwer Law International, 2002.
Hansen, Hugh C. ed. *International Intellectual Property law & policy.* vol.6, Huntington: Juris Publishing, 2001.

Hestermeyer, Holger. *Human Rights and the WTO. The case of Patents and Access to Medicines.* Oxford: Oxford University Press, 2007.

Hugenholtz, Bernt P and Ruth L. Okediji. *Conceiving an international instrument on limitations and exceptions to copyright,* Final Report, study commissioned by the Open Society Institute, March 6, 2008 (available at www.ivir.nl).

Isiko Štrba, Susan. Dispute Settlement Under the TRIPS Agreement in Relation to Human Rights. Mémoire of Master Degree at the Graduate Institute of International Studies, Geneva, 2001.

Jones, Peter. *Rights.* London: Macmillan, 1994.

Kennedy, Daniel L. M. and James D. Southwick, eds. *The political economy of international trade law: Essays in honour of Robert E. Hudec.* Cambridge: Cambridge University Press, 2002.

Lettermann, Gregory G. *Basics of International Intellectual Property Law.* Ardsley: Transnational Publishers, 2001.

Lopez Hurtado, Carlos Justino. *The WTO Legal System and International Human Rights.* PhD Thesis, Graduate Institute of International Studies, Geneva, 2006.

MacMillan, Fiona, ed. *New Directions in Copyright Law.* vol. 1. London: Edward Elgar, 2005.

Maskus, Keith E. *Intellectual Property Rights in the Global Economy.* Washington, DC: Institute for International Economics, 2000.

Matthews Duncan. *Intellectual Property, human rights and Development: the Role of NGOs and Social Movements,* Cheltenham: Edward Elgar, 2011.

McCalmam, Phillip. *The Doha Declaration and Development: Prospects for intellectual property rights reform.* Manila: Asian Development Bank, 2002.

Mélanges offerts a Charles Rousseau: la communauté internationale. Paris: editions A. Pedone, 1974.

Murigande, Aimé. *Developing countries and their participation in the world trading system: an African perspective.* Geneva: Graduate Institute of International Studies 2000.

Netanel, Neil Weinstock ed. *The development Agenda: Global Intellectual Property and Developing Countries.* Oxford: Oxford University Press, 2009.

Pauwelyn, Joost. *Conflict of Norms in Public International Law: How WTO Law Relates to other Rules of International Law.* Cambridge: Cambridge University Press 2003.

Perez Pugatch, Meir ed. *The Intellectual Property Debate: Perspectives from Law, Economics and Political Economy.* Cheltenham: Edward Elgar, 2006.

Piotraut, Jean-Luc. *Droit de la propriété intellectuelle.* Paris: Ellipses, 2004.

Reichman, J. H. and Keith Maskus, eds. *International Public Goods and Transfer of Technology Under a Globalized Intellectual Property Regime.* Cambridge: Cambridge University Press, 2005.

Ricketson, Sam. *The Berne Convention for the Protection of Literary and Artistic Works: 1886–1986.* Centre for Commercial Law Studies, Queen Mary College, Kluwer, 1987.

Ricketson, Sam and Jane C. Ginsburg. *International Copyright and Neighbouring Rights: the Berne Convention and Beyond.* 2nd ed, (volume I). Oxford: Oxford University Press, 2006.

Ricketson, Sam and Jane C. Ginsburg, *International Copyright and Neighbouring Rights: the Berne Convention and Beyond.* 2nd ed (volume II). Oxford: Oxford University Press, 2006.

Rizk, Nagla and Lea Shaver, eds, *Access to Knowledge in Egypt: New Research on Intellectual Property, innovation and Development,* London: Bloomsbury Academic, 2010.

Roffe, Pedro, Geoff Tansey and David Vivas-Eugui eds. *Negotiating Health: Intellectual Property and Access to Medicines.* London: Earthscan, 2006.

Roger, Stringer, ed. *The Book Chain in Anglophone Africa.* International Network for the Availability of Scientific Publications, Oxford: Oxford University Press, 2002.

Sell, Susan K. *Private Power, Public Law: the Globalization of Intellectual Property Rights.* Cambridge: Cambridge University Press, 2003.

Senftleben, Martin. *Copyright, limitations and the Three-Step Test.* The Hague: Kluwer Law International, 2004.

Shaw, Malcolm N., *International Law.* 4th ed. Cambridge: Cambridge University Press, 1999.

Sterling, J.A.L. *World Copyright Law: Protection of authors' works, performances, phonograms, films, video, broadcasts and published editions in national, international and regional law.* 2nd ed. London: Sweet & Maxwell, 2003.

Stewart, T. *The GATT Uruguay Round: A negotiating history (1986–1992)*. Boston: Kluwer Law and Taxations Publishers, 1993.
Stoll, Peter-Tobias, Jan Busche and Katrin Arend, eds. *WTO-trade-related aspects of intellectual property rights*. Max Planck Institute for Comparative Public Law and International Law, Leiden: Martinus Nijhoff Publishers, 2009.
Story, Alan, Colin Darch and Debora Halbert, eds. *The Copy/South Dossier: Issues in economics, politics and ideology of copyright in the global south*. The Copy/South Research Group, 2006.
Symonides, Janusz, and Vladimir Volodin, eds. *UNESCO and human rights: Standard setting instruments, major meetings, publications*. 2nd ed. Paris: UNESCO, 1999.
The Oxford English Dictionary. vol. 3. Oxford: Clarendon Press, 1978.
The Oxford English Dictionary. vol. 7. Oxford: Clarendon Press, 1978.
The New Shorter Oxford English Dictionary on historical principles. vol. Oxford: Clarendon Press, 1993.
Tomaševski, Katarina. *Education Denied: Costs and Remedies*. London: Zed Books, 2003.
Torremans, Paul, ed. *Intellectual Property and Human Rights: Enhanced edition of Copyright and Human Right*. The Hague, Kluwer Law International, 2004.
Torremans, Paul, ed. *Intellectual Property and Human Rights: Enhanced edition of Copyright and Human Right,* The Hague, Kluwer Law International, 2008.
UNCTAD-ICTSD. *Resource Book on TRIPS and Development*. Cambridge: Cambridge University Press, 2005.
UNCTAD. Statistical Profiles of Least Developed Countries, 2005, United Nations, New York and Geneva, 2006.
UNESCO. *World Information Report 1997/98*. Paris: UNESCO, 1998.
UNDP. *Human Development Report 2007/2008: Fighting climate change: Human solidarity in a divided world*. New York: Palgrave Macmillan, 2007.
Vorburger-Rajagopalan, Divvya. *A Human Rights perspective on Farmers' Rights and the World Trade Organization*. PhD Thesis, Graduate Institute of International and Development Studies, Geneva, 2009.
Watal Jayashree, *Intellectual Property Rights in the WTO and Developing Countries*, The Hague: Kluwer Law International, 2001.
Webster's Desk Dictionary of the English language. New York: Portland House, 1990
Westkamp, Guido. *Implementation of Directive 2001/29/EC in the Members States,* Queen Mary Intellectual Property Institute, Centre for Commercial Law Studies, Queen Mary, University of London, February 2007.
World Intellectual Property Organization. *Implications of the TRIPS Agreement on Treaties Administered by WIPO*. Geneva: WIPO, Publication no. 464(E), 1997.
World Intellectual Property Organization. *WIPO Intellectual Property handbook: Policy, Law and Use*. 2nd ed. Geneva: WIPO Publication no. 489 (E), 2004.
Yusuf, Abdulqawi A., ed. *African Yearbook of International Law*. vol. 12 (2004), Leiden: Martinus Nijhoff Publishers, 2006.

2. *Collected Courses of the Hague Academy of International Law*

Castañeda, Jorge, "Valeur juridique des résolutions des Nations Unies," *RCADI*, vol. 129, (1971-I). 206–527.

3. *Articles and Contributions to Collective Works*

Abbott, Frederick M. "Protecting First World Assets in the Third World: Intellectual Property Negotiations in the GATT Multilateral Framework," 22 *Vanderbilt Journal of Transnational Law,* (1989): 689–746.
——, "WTO Dispute Settlement and the Agreement on Trade-Related Aspects of Intellectual Property Rights," in Petersmann, Ernst-Ulrich, *International Trade Law and the GATT/WTO Dispute Settlement System*. London: Kluwer Law International, 1997.

——, "The TRIPS-legality of measures taken to address public health crises: Responding to USTR-State-industry positions that undermine the WTO," in Kennedy, L. M. Daniel and James D. Southwick, eds., *The political economy of international trade law: Essays in honour of Robert E. Hudec*. Cambridge: Cambridge University Press, 2002. 311–348.

—— "WTO TRIPS Agreement and its Implications for Access to Medicines in Developing Countries," "Study Paper on Intellectual Property Rights, the Internet, and Copyright," Study Paper 2a, Prepared as a background paper for the Commission on Intellectual Property Rights, available at http://www.iprcommission.org/graphic/documents/study_papers.htm

—— "The Doha Declaration on the TRIPS Agreement and Public Health: Lighting a Dark Corner at the WTO," *Journal of International Economic Law*, vol.5, no.2, (2002): 469–505.

—— "Legal options for implementing paragraph 6 of the Doha Declaration on the TRIPS Agreement and Public Health," QUNO, (2002): available at http://www.geneva.quno.inf/pdf/Legal%options%20Abbott.pdf

—— "Trade Diplomacy, the Rule of Law and the Problem of Asymmetric Risks in TRIPS," Quaker United Nations Office (QUNO), Occasional Paper no. 13, (2003) available at http://www.quno.org/economicissues/intellectual-property/intellectualLinks.htm

—— "The Doha Declaration on the TRIPS Agreement and Public Health and the Contradictory Trend in Bilateral and Regional Trade Agreements," QUNO, Occasional Paper no. 14, (2004): available at http://www.quno.org.

—— "The WTO Medicines Decision: World Pharmaceutical and the Protection of Public Health," *American Journal of International Law*, vol. 99, no. 2 (April 2005): 317–358.

Abi-Saab, Georges. "Technological development and the right to development," in Sicilianos, Linos-Alexander and Maria Gavouneli, eds. *Scientific and Technological Development and Human Rights*. Athens: Ant. N. Sakkoulas Publishers, 2001. 259–273.

Abdel Latif, Ahmed. "Egypt's Role in the A2K Movement: an Analysis of Positions and Policies," in Nagla Rizk and Lea Shaver, eds. *Access to Knowledge in Egypt: New Research on Intellectual Property, innovation and Development*, London: Bloomsbury Academic, 2010. 16–55

African Copyright and Access to Knowledge Project (2009), (available at www.aca2k.org).

Akada, Yasukazu. " 'Fair use' stipulation planned for intellectual property," *The Asahi Shimbun*, 28 May 2008, available at http://www.asahi.com/english/Herald-asahi/TKY200805280068.html

Anderson, Michael G., Paul F Brown and Andre P. Cores. "Market substitution and copyright: predicting fair use case law," *University of Miami Entertainment & Sports Law* Review, vol. 10 no. 33, (1993). 33–50.

Australian Copyright Council, "Digital Agenda amendments: and overview," Information Sheet, G65, March 2006, p.3. Available at www.copyright.org.au

Awad, Bassam, Moatasem El-Gheriani and Perihan abou Zeid, "Egypt," in Armstrong, Chris, Jeremy de Beer, Dick Kawooya, Achal Prabhala and Tobias Schonwetter, eds. *Access to knowledge in African: the Role of Copyright*. Claremont: UCT Press, 2010. 22–56.

Balasubramaniam, K. "Access to Medicines and Public Policy Safeguards under TRIPS" in Bellmann, Christophe, Graham Dutifield and Ricardo Meléndez-Ortiz, eds. *Trading in Knowledge: Development Perspectives on TRIPS, Trade and Sustainable Development*. London: Earthscan Publications Ltd, 2003. 135–142.

Band, Jonathan. "educational fair use today," Association of research libraries, available at http://www.policybandwidth.com/doc/20080203-educationalfairusetoday.pdf

Band Jonathan. "The right copyright law," *Jerusalem Post*, 28 March 2008. Available at http://www.policybandwidth.com/doc/20080410-Israel-Fair-Use.pdf

Beeckman Katrien. "Mother tongue instruction in Africa: human rights treaty bodies and the language problem in education," *African Yearbook of International Law*, (2005).163-192.

Benabou Valérie-Laure. "Chronique de France," in *Revue Internationale du droit d'auteur*, vol. 215, (January 2008). 154–259.

Boyle James. "A Manifesto on WIPO and the future of intellectual property," *Duke Law and Technology Review*, no. 9, (2004). 1–12.

Boyle, Alan, "Some Reflections on Relationship between Treaties and Soft Law," in Gowlland-Debbas, Vera ed. *Multilateral Treaty-making: The Current Status of Challenges to and Reforms needed in the International Legislative Process*. The Hague: Nijhoff Cop, 2000. 122p.

Brennan David J. "The Three-Step Test Frenzy - Why the TRIPS Panel Decision Might be Considered Per Incuriam," Faculty of Law, The University of Melbourne Public Law and Legal Theory Working Paper no. 22, 2002, available at http://papers.ssrn.com/sol3/delivery.cfm/SSRN_ID299543_code020206140.pdf?abstractid=299543

Brown, Lesley, ed. *The New Shorter Oxford English Dictionary on Historical Principles*. vol.2, This Edition. Oxford: Clarendon Press, 1993.

Center for International Environmental Law (CIEL), "Intellectual Property in European Economic Partnership Agreements with Africa, Caribbean and Pacific countries: What way forward after the CARIFORUM EPA and the interim EPAs?" April 2008.

Cerda Silva Alberto, "Beyond the Unrealistic Solution for Development provided by the Appendix to the Berne Convention on Copyright," *American University International Law Review*, (forthcoming 2012)

Chapman, Audrey. "A Human Rights Perspective on Intellectual Property, Scientific Progress and Access to the Benefits of Science," in *Intellectual Property and Human Rights*. The proceedings of a panel discussion, organized by the World Intellectual Property Organization in collaboration with the Office of the United Nations High Commissioner for Human Rights, on 9 November 1998, to commemorate the 50th anniversary of the proclamation of the Universal Declaration of Human Rights, WIPO Publication no.762(E), 1999. 127–174.

Charnovitz Steve. "The legal status of the Doha Declaration," *Journal of International Economic Law*, vol.5, no.1, (2002). 207–211.

Chon. Margaret. "Copyright and Capability for Education: and Approach from Below." In *Intellectual Property and Human Development: Current Trends and Future Scenarios*. Cambridge: Cambridge University Press, 2010. 1–29.

Combe, Emmanuel and Étienne Pfister. "Le renforcement international des droits de propriété intellectuelle," *Economie Internationale*, no. 85, (2001). 63-81.

Commission on Intellectual Property Rights. *Integrating Intellectual Property Rights and Development Policy*. Report of the Commission on intellectual Property Rights, London, September 2002, available at http://www.iprcommission.org.

Consumers International, Project on access to knowledge in Indonesia, 2006, available at www.consumersinternational.org

Consumers International, Project on access to knowledge, Thailand, 2006, available at www.consumersinternational.org

Cornell University, "After failed negotiations, CU library cancels Elsvier Journal Package," *Cornell Chronicle*, vol. 35, No. 17, December 11, 2003. available at www.news.cornell.edu/Chronicle/03/12/.11.03/CULElsevier.html.

Council of Ministers of Education, Canada, "Educational use of the internet: "fair dealing" just may not be enough," *Copyright Bulletin 3*, March 14, 2008. available at http://www.cmec.ca/copyright/bulletins2008/bulletin-03.en.pdf

Coomans, Fons, "In Search of the Core Content of the Right to Education," in Chapman, Audrey and Russell, Sage (eds.) *Core Obligations: Building a Framework for Economic, Social and Cultural Rights*, Intersentia, Oxford, 2002, pp217–246.

Correa, Carlos. "Recent International Developments in the Area of Intellectual Property Rights," Contribution to the second UNCTAD-ICTSD Bellagio Series on Development and Intellectual Property, 18–21 September 2003, available at www.iprsonline.org/unctadictsd/bellagio/docs/Correa_Bellagio2.pdf.

Cottier Thomas. "Trade and Human Rights: A Relationship to Discover," *Journal of International Economic Law*, vol. 5, no.1, (2002). 111–132.

Craig, Carys. "The changing face of fair dealing in Canadian copyright law: a proposal for legislative reform," in Geist, Michael ed. *In the public interests: the future of Canadian copyright law*. Toronto: Irwin Law, 2005. 437–461.

—— and Krista Nadakavukaren Schefer. "The relationship between World Trade Organization law, national and regional law," *Journal of International Economic Law,* vol. 1, no. 1, (1998). 83–122.

Cullet, Philippe. "The Doha Declaration of the WTO and access to medicines," International Environmental Law Research Centre, Briefing Paper 2002-1.

de Vuyst Bruno, Alea M. Fairchild, and Gunther Meyer. "Exceptions to intellectual property rights: lessons from WTO-TRIPS panels," *Murdoch University Electronic Journal of Law,* volume 10, no. 4 (December 2003).

Dhar, Biswajit and K.M. Gopakumar. "Post-2005 TRIPS scenario in patent protection in the pharmaceutical sector: the case of the generic pharmaceutical industry in India." ICTSD, UNCTAD and International Development Research Centre (IDRC), UNCTAD/ICTSD project on intellectual property rights and sustainable development, Geneva, 2006.

Dietz A. "The moral rights of the author: moral rights and the civil law countries," *Columbia-VLA Journal of Law and Arts,* vol. 19(1995). 199–228.

Dinwoodie, Graeme, B. "The international intellectual property system: treaties, norms, national courts and private ordering," in Gervais, Daniel, ed. *Intellectual property, trade and development: strategies to optimize economic development in a TRIPS-Plus era.* Oxford: Oxford University Press, 2007. 61–114.

Dinwoodie Graeme B. and Rochelle C. Dreyfuss. "Designing a Global Intellectual Property System Responsive to Change: the WTO, WIPO and Beyond," *Houston Law Review,* vol. 46 no. 4 (2009). 1187–1234.

Donnelly Jack and Rhoda E Howard. "Assessing National Human Rights Performance: A Theoretical Framework," *10 Human Rights Quarterly,* (1988). 214–248.

Drahos, Peter. "Negotiating Intellectual Property Rights: Between Coercion and Dialogue," in H. Hansen, ed. *International Intellectual Property law & policy,* vol.7, Huntington: Juris Publishing, (2002). Chapter 82.

Drassinower, Abraham. "Taking User Rights Seriously," in Geist, Michael, ed. *In the Public Interest: The Future of Canadian Copyright Law.* Toronto: Irwin Law, Toronto, 2005. 462–479.

Dupuy, René-Jean. "Coutume sage et coutume sauvage," in *Mélanges offerts a Charles Rousseau: La communauté internationale.* Paris: editions A. Pedone, 1974. 75–87.

Dussolier Séverine. "Copie privée *versus* mesure techniques de protection: l'exception est-elle un droit?," *Auteurs & Media,* vol. 4, (2004). 341–345.

Dworkin, Gerald. "Exceptions to copyright exclusivity: Is fair use consistent with article 9(2) Berne and the new international order?" in Hansen, H., ed. *International Intellectual Property law & policy.* vol.6, Huntington: Juris Publishing, (2001), Chapter 66.

Fink, Carsten and Patrick Reichenmiller. "Tightening TRIPS: Intellectual Property Provisions of U.S. Free Trade Agreements, World Bank, Trade Note, 7 February 2005. 289–303.

Fisher III William. W., "Reconstructing the Fair Use Doctrine," *Harvard Law Review,* vol. 101, (1988). 1659–1795.

Fisher William. "Theories of intellectual property," available at http://cyber.law.harvard.edu/people/tfisher/iptheory.pdf

Garnett, Nic, "Automated Rights Management Systems and Copyright Limitations and Exceptions," WIPO Standing Committee on Copyright and Related Rights, Fourteenth Session, Geneva, May 1 to 5, 2006, WIPO document SCCR/14/5, (E) dated April 27, 2006.

Gasaway Laura N. "Anti-Circumvention: a view from librarians and educators" ALAI 2001 Congress: Adjuncts and Alternatives to Copyright, June 13-17, 2001. (available at www.law.columbia.edu/conferences/2001/1_program_eng.htm

Geiger Christophe. "Right to copy v. Three-step Test: the future of the private copy exception in the Digital environment," *Computer Law Review International (CRi),* vol. 1 no.7, (2005): 1- 13.

—— "Droit d'auteur et droit du public à l'information: pour un rattachement du droit d'auteur aux droits fondamentaux." *Recueil Dalloz,* vol. no. 38, (2005): 2686–2689.

—— "The private copy exception, an area of freedom (Temporarily) preserved in the digital environment." *International Review of Intellectual Property and Competition Law,* vol. 37, no.4 (2006): 371–406.

—— "The three step test, a threat to a balanced copyright law?" International Review of Intellectual Property and Competition Law, vol. 37, no. 5, (2006): 683–699.
——, "Copyright and free access to information: for a balance of interest in the globalized world," European Intellectual Property Review, vol. 28, no. 7 (2006): 366–373.
——, " "Constitutionalising" intellectual property? The influence of fundamental rights on intellectual property in the European Union," *International Review of Intellectual Property and Competition Law,* vol. 37, no. 4, (2006): 371–406.
——, "The role of the three-step test in the adaptation of copyright law to the information society," UNESCO *e-Copyright Bulletin,* January – March 2007: 1–21.
Gervais Daniel J. "The Internationalization of intellectual property: New challenges from the very old and the very new," *Fordham Intellectual Property and Entertainment Law Journal,* vol. 12, (Spring 2002): 929–990.
Gervais Daniel. "Le Droit d'auteur au Canada: le point après CCH," *Revue Internationale du droit d'auteur,* vol. 203, (2005): 3–61.
——, "The purpose of copyright law in Canada," *University of Ottawa Law & Technology Journal,* vol. 2 no.2, (2005). 315–356.
——, "Towards a new core international copyright norm: the reverse three-step test," Marquette Intellectual Property Law Review, vol. 9, no. 1, (2005). 1–36.
Ginsburg Jane C. "Toward supranational copyright law? The WTO Panel decision and the "three-step test" for copyright exceptions," *Revue Internationale du droit d'auteur,* vol. 187, (2001): 3–65.
Gopakumar, K.M. "The WTO deal on cheap drugs: A critique," *Journal of World Intellectual Property,* vol7, no.1 (2004): 99–149.
Grosheide Willem., "Copyright law from a user's perspective: access rights for users," *European Intellectual Property Review,* vol. 23, issue 7, (2001): 321–325.
Guibault, Lucie, The limitations and exceptions to copyright: 'Limitations found outside of copyright law', General Report, ALAI Study Days, Cambridge, September 14–17, 1998.
Guillaume Gilbert. "The future of international judicial institutions," *International and Comparative Law Quarterly,* vol. 44 no. 4, (1995): 848–862.
Harris Lesley Ellen. "Comparing fair dealing and fair use," *The Copyright & new media law newsletter,* volume 10, issue 4, (2006).
Harvard University, "Libraries take a stand: Journals present rising costs to libraries - and to scholarship," Harvard Gazette Archives, February 5, 2004, available at www.news.harvard.edu/gazette/2004/02.05/10-libraries.html
Helfer, Laurence R. "World Music on a U.S. Stage: An Analysis of the Section 110(5) WTO Dispute," in Hansen, H., ed. *International Intellectual Property law & policy.* vol.6, Huntington: Juris Publishing, (2001), Chapter 48.
——, "World music on a US stage: a Berne/TRIPS and economic analysis of the Fairness in Music licensing Act," *Boston university law review,* vol. 80, issue 1, (2000): 93–204.
Hendrikz, Francois, "The Book Chain in South Africa," in Roger, Stringer, ed. *The Book Chain in Anglophone Africa.* Oxford: International Network for the Availability of Scientific Publications, 2002.-72–82.
Hilty Reto M., Sebastian Krujatz, Benjamin Bajon, Alfred Früh, Annette Kur, Josef Drexl, Christophe Geiger and Nadine Klass, "European Commission – Green Paper: Copyright in the Knowledge Economy – Comments by Max Plunck Institute for Intellectual Property, Competition and Tax Law, available at: http://www.ip.mpg.de/shared/data/pdf/comments_on_the_green_paper2.pdf
Hugenholtz Bernt P., "Copyright, Contract and Code: What will remain of the public domain," *Brooklyn Journal of International Law,* vol. 26, (2000): 77–90.
International Intellectual Property Alliance, "IIPA's 2009 Special 301 Report, on copyright protection and enforcement, submitted to the U.S. Trade Representative on February 17, 2009 by the International Intellectual Property Alliance," available at http://www.iipa.com/special301.html.
Intellectual Property Watch, "Panellists outline strategies on limitations and exceptions to copyright," 20 March 2008, (available at www.ip-watch.org).
Iwasawa Yuji. "WTO Dispute Settlement as Judicial Supervision," *Journal of International Economic Law,* vol.5, no.2, (2002): 281–299.

Kapczynski Amy. "The access to knowledge mobilization and the new politics of intellectual property," *Yale Law Journal*, vol. 117, no. 5, (2008): 804–885.

Kebler, Florian, "Article 7: Objectives," in Stoll, Peter-Tobias, Jan Busche and Katrin Arend, eds. *WTO-trade-related aspects of intellectual property rights*. Max Planck Institute for Comparative Public Law and International Law. Leiden: Martinus Nijhoff Publishers, (2009): 179–187.

Klingsporn G.K. "The Conference on fair use (CONFU) and the future of fair use guidelines," *Columbia VLA - Journal of Law and the Arts*, (1999): 101–126.

Knapp John C. Jr. "Laugh, and the whole world ... scowls at you?: a defense of the United States' fair use exception for parody under TRIPS," *Denver Journal of International Law & Policy*, vol. 33, no. 2, (2005): 347–366.

Kongolo Tshimanga. "Public interest versus the Pharmaceutical Industry's Monopoly in South Africa," *Journal of World Intellectual Property*, vol.4, issue 5, (2001): 605–627.

Kongolo Tshimanga, "TRIPS, the Doha Declaration and public health," *Journal of World Intellectual Property*, vol.2, issue 2, (2003): 373–378.

Kumar, N. "Intellectual Property Rights, Technology and Economic Development: Experiences of Asian Countries," Commission on Intellectual Property Rights (CIPR) background paper 1b, CIPR, London, 2002. Available at: http://www.iprcommission.org/graphics/documents/study_papers.htm

Kwakwa Edward, "Some comments on rulemaking at the World Intellectual Property Organization," *Duke Journal of Comparative and International Law*, vol. 12, issue 1, (2002): 179–195.

—— "Institutional Perspectives of International Economic Law," in Qureshi, Asif H., ed. *Perspectives in International Economic Law*. London: Kluwer Law International, 2002. 45–62.

Lawal-Solarin, Yinka Otunba, 'Copyright and Education - A publisher's perspective from a developing world', (November 2005), available at http://www.wipo.int/edocs/mdocs/copyright/en/educ_cr_im_05/educ_cr_im_05_www_53637.doc.

Lepage, Anne. "Overview of exceptions and limitation to copyright in the digital environment," UNESCO, e-bulletin, January – March 2003.

Leval Pierre N. "Towards a Fair Use Standard," *Harvard Law Review*, vol. 103, (1990): 1105–1124.

Litman, Jessica, "The Breadth of the Anti-Trafficking Provisions and the Moral High Ground" ALAI 2001 Congress: Adjuncts and Alternatives to Copyright, June 13-17, 2001. (available at www.law.columbia.edu/conferences/2001/1_program_eng.htm)

Liu Joseph P. "Copyright and time: a proposal," *Michigan Law Review*, vol. 101, no. 2, (2002): 404–481.

Love James. "Risks and Opportunities for access to knowledge," available at www.wsispapers.choike.org.

——, "Access to medicine and compliance with the WTO TRIPS accord: models for state practice in developing countries," in Drahos, Peter and Ruth Mayne, eds. *Global Intellectual Property Rights: Knowledge, Access and Development*. Palgrave Macmillan, New York, (2002): 74–89.

——, "Compulsory licensing of copyright under Article 44.2 of the TRIPS, in light of eBay," KEI Research Note 2007:5, 28 May 2007, available at http://www.keionline.org.

——, "Norm setting on copyright limitations and exceptions at WIPO: what is ready?" in *Knowledge Ecology Notes*, January 2009, available at http://www.keionline.org/blogs/2009/01/28/sccr_norm-setting-lne

Marc Patrick. "Compulsory licensing and the South African Medicine Act of 1997: violation or compliance of the Trade Related Aspects of Intellectual Property Rights Agreement?" *New York Law School Journal of International and Comparative Law*, vol. 21 no. 1, (2001): 109–125.

Maskus, Keith E. "The WIPO Development Agenda: A cautionary Note," in Netanel, Neil Weinstock, ed. *The development Agenda: Global Intellectual Property and Developing Countries*. Oxford: Oxford University Press, (2009) 163–174.

Max Planck Institute for Intellectual Property, Competition and Tax law "Declaration on a balanced interpretation of the "three-step test" in copyright law." July 2008. Available at http://www.ip.mpg.de/ww/de/pub/aktuelles/declaration_on_the_three_step_.cfm

Musungu, Sisule F., "The Industrial Property Act 2001 and Access to Essential Medicines in Kenya: An Analysis of the Public Health Safeguards," South Center, 2000.

Nabhan Victor. "La photocopie et la droit d'auteur au Canada," *Revue Internationale du droit d'auteur*, vol. 99 (1979) : 3–27.
Netanel, Neil Weinstock, "TRIPs Interpretation and Dispute Settlement Panel Report on U.S. Copyright Act § 110(5)," in Hansen, H., ed. *International Intellectual Property law & policy*. vol.7, Huntington: Juris Publishing, 2002, Chapter 74.
Newby Tyler G., "What's fair here is not fair everywhere: Does the American fair use doctrine violate international copyright law," *Stanford Law Review*, vol. 51, (1999). 1633–1663.
Nicholson, Denise, "Does copyright have any significance in the lives of illiterate or visually-impaired persons?" http://www.wipout.net/essays/1128nicholson.htm
Nicholson, Denise Rosemary, "Free Trade Agreements and TRIPS-plus: implications for developing countries in Africa," a paper presented at the World Library and Information Congress: 71st IFLA General Conference and Council under the theme "Libraries – A voyage of discovery," Oslo, Norway, August 14–18, 2005, p.2 (available at www.ifla.org/IV/ifla71/Programme.htm.
Nimmer David. " 'Fairest of them all' And other fairy tales of fair use," *Law & Contemporary Problems*, vol. 66 No. 263, (Winter/Spring 2003): 263–287.
Office of the High Representative for the Least Developed Countries, Landlocked Developing Countries and Small Island Developing Countries, available at www.unohrlls.org.
Oh, Cecilia, "Will TRIPS Amendment on Compulsory Licensing Work?" in International Centre for Trade and Sustainable Development (ICTSD) *Bridges Monthly Review, no.*1, January – February 2006. 22–23.
Okediji Ruth L., "Toward an international fair use doctrine," *Columbia Journal of Transnational Law*, vol. 39, (2000). 75–175.
——, "New treaty development and harmonization of intellectual property law," in Bellmann, Christophe, Graham Dutifield and Ricardo Meléndez-Ortiz, eds. *Trading in Knowledge: Development Perspectives on TRIPS, Trade and Sustainable Development*. London: Earthscan Publications Ltd, 2003. 89–98.
——, "Development in the Information Age: Issues in the Regulation of Intellectual Property Rights, Software and Electronic Commerce," ICTSD/UNCTAD Project on Intellectual Property and Sustainable Development. Issue Paper no.9, May 2004. (available at: www.ictsd .net)
——, "Fostering Access to Education, Research and Dissemination of Knowledge through Copyright," UNCTAD-ICTSD Dialogue on Moving the pro-development IP agenda forward: Preserving Public Goods in health, education and learning, Bellagio, 29 November – 3 December 2004. (available at: www.ictsd.net)
——, "Back to bilateralism? Pendulum swings in international intellectual property protection," *University of Ottawa Law and Technology Journal*, vol.1, (2004): 125–147.
——, "Sustainable Access to Copyrighted Digital Information Works in Developing Countries," in Reichman, J. H. and Maskus, Keith, *International Public Goods and Transfer of Technology Under a Globalized Intellectual Property Regime*, Cambridge University Press, Cambridge, (2005): 142–187.
——, "The International Copyright System: Limitations, Exceptions and Public Interest Considerations for Developing Countries in the Digital Environment," ICTSD/UNCTAD Project on Intellectual Property and Sustainable Development. Issue Paper no.9, September 2005. (available at: http://www.ictsd.net)
——, "Africa and the Global Intellectual Property System: Beyond the Agency Model," in Yusuf, Abdulqawi A., (ed.) *African Yearbook of International Law*, vol. 12 (2004), Martinus Nijhoff Publishers, Leiden, (2006): 207–251.
——, "WIPO-WTO Relations and the Future of Global Intellectual property Norms," *Netherlands Yearbook of International Law*, (2008): 69–125.
——, "History Lessons for the WIPO development Agenda," in Netanel, Neil Weinstock, ed. *The development Agenda: Global Intellectual Property and Developing Countries*. Oxford: Oxford University Press, (2009): 137–161.
——, "The regulation of creativity under the WIPO Internet Treaties," *Fordham Law Review*, vol. 77, (2009): 2379–2410.

Olian Jr. Irwin A. "International Copyright and the needs of developing countries: the awakening at Stockholm and Paris," *Cornell International Law Journal*, vol. 7, no. 2, (1973/1974): 81–112.

Perez Pugatch, Meir, "Conclusion: placing IPRS at the heart of the public discourse," in Perez Pugatch, Meir, ed. *The Intellectual Property Debate: Perspectives from Law, Economics and Political Economy*. Cheltenham: Edward Elgar, UK and Northampton, US, (2006): 361–363.

Petersmann, Ernst-Ulrich, "The WTO Constitution and Human Rights," *Journal of International Economic Law*, vol.3, no.1, (2000): 19–25.

——, "From 'Negative' to 'Positive integration in the WTO: Time for 'mainstreaming' human rights into WTO law?," *Common Market Law Review*, vol.37, No.6. (December 2000): 1363–1382.

——, "Human rights and international economic law in the 21st century – need for clarifying their interrelationships," *Journal of International Economic Law*, vol. 1 no. 1, (2001): 3–39.

——, "Time for a United Nations 'Global Compact' for integrating human rights into the law of worldwide organizations: lessons from European integration," *European Journal of International Law*, vol. 13, no. 3, (2002): 621–650.

——, "Human rights and international trade: defining and connecting the two fields," in Cottier, Thomas, Joost Pauwelyn, and Elizabeth Bürgi Bonanomi, eds. *Human Rights and International Trade*. Oxford: Oxford University Press, 2005.

Prabhala, Achal and Tobias Schonwetter. Common Wealth of Learning Copyright Audit on Copyright Law and Education. December 2006, p.1, (available at http://www.col.org/colweb/site/pid/4198).

Pradhan, Pustun. "Nepal's New Law on Copyright: Some reflections," UNESCO e.Copyright Bulletin, January – March 2004.

Primo Braga Carlos A. "Reforming Intellectual Property Rights Regimes: Challenges for Developing Countries," *Journal of International Economic Law*, vol.1, no.4, (1998): 537–554.

Ranjan, Prabhash. "International Trade and Human Rights: Conflicting Obligations" in Cottier, Thomas, Joost Pauwelyn, and Elizabeth Bürgi Bonanomi, eds. *Human Rights and International Trade*. Oxford: Oxford University Press, 2005. 311–321.

Reichman, Jerome H. and Ruth L. Okediji, "When Copyright Law and Science Collide: Empowering Digitally Integrated Research Methods on a Global Scale," *University of Minnesota Law Review*, (forthcoming, 2012).

Rens Andrew. "Implementing the WIPO Development Agenda: treaty provisions on minimum limitations and exceptions for education," Shuttle Foundation Working Paper on Intellectual Property, (2008).

——, Achal Prabhala and Dick Kawooya. "Intellectual property, Education and Access to Knowledge in Southern Africa," ICTSD, UNCTAD and Trade Law Centre for Southern Africa (TRALAC), 2006 (available at www.ictsd.net.)

Rich Lloyd L., "How much of someone else's work may I use without asking permission?: the fair use doctrine," Part I, The publishing Law Centre, (1996). available at http://www.publilaw.com/work.html

Ricketson Sam. "The boundaries of copyright: Its proper limitations and exceptions: International Conventions and Treaties," *Intellectual Property Quarterly*, (1999): 56–94.

——, "Letter from Australia/Chronique d'Australie, *Revue Internationale de Droit d'Auter*, vol. 188, (2001):117–245.

——, "The Three-Step Test, Deemed Quantities, Libraries and Closed Exceptions," Advice prepared for the Centre for Copyright Studies Ltd, 2002, (available at www.copyright.com.au/reports%20&%20papers/CCS0202Berne.pdf.)

——, "WIPO Study on limitations and exceptions of copyright and related rights in the digital environment," Standing Committee on Copyright and Related Rights, 9th Session, Geneva, June 23 to 27, 2003, WIPO document SCCR/9/7 (E) dated April 5, 2003.

Ringer Barbara A. "The role of the United States in international copyright–past, present and future," *Geo. Law Journal*, vol. 56, (1968): 1050–1079.

Roffe, Pedro, Christophe Spennemann and Johanna von Braun, "From Paris to Doha; The WTO Doha Declaration on the TRIPS Agreement and Public Health," in Roffe, Pedro, Geoff Tansey and David Vivas-Eugui eds. *Negotiating Health: Intellectual Property and Access to Medicines*. London: Earthscan, 2006. 9–26.

Roffe, Pedro, "Bilateral agreements and the TRIPS-plus world: the Chile-USA Free Trade Agreement," TRIPS Issues Papers, No. 4, Quaker International Affairs Programme, Ottawa, 2004, (available at www.quno.org).

Schonwetter, Tobias, Caroline Ncube and Pria Chetty, "South Africa," in Armstrong Chris, Jeremy de Beer, Dick Kawooya, Achal Prabhala and Tobias Schonwetter, eds. *Access to knowledge in African: the Role of Copyright*. Claremont: UCT Press, 2010. 231–280.

Simma, Bruno, and Andreas L. Paulus, "The 'International Community': facing the challenges of globalization," *European Journal of International Law*, vol. 9, (1998): 266–277.

South centre, "The threat of technological protection measures to a development-oriented information society," Policy Brief No. 9, August 2007.

Spitz Brad, "Droit d'auteur, copyright et parodie, ou le mythe de l'usage loyal," *Revue international du droit d'auteur*, vol. 204, (2005). 55–153.

Story, Alan. "Don't ignore copyright, the 'Sleeping Giant' on the TRIPS and International education agenda," in Drahos, Peter and Ruth Mayne, eds., *Global Intellectual Property Rights: Knowledge, Access and Development*. New York: Palgrave Macmillan, 2002. 125–143.

——, "Study Paper on Intellectual Property Rights, the Internet, and Copyright," Study Paper 5, Prepared as a background paper for the Commission on Intellectual Property Rights, available at http://www.iprcommission.org/graphic/documents/study_papers.htm

——, "Burn Berne: why the leading international copyright Agreement must be repealed," *Houston Law Review*, vol. 40, no. 3, (2003): 763–801.

Tawfik, Myra J. "International Copyright law and 'fair dealing' as a 'user right', UNESCO, e-Copyright Bulletin, April – June 2005.

Tocups Nora Maija, "The development of special provisions in international copyright law for the benefit of developing countries," *Journal of the Copyright Society of the U.S.A.*, vol. 29, (1981/1982): 402–421.

Trosow, Samuel E. "The changing landscape of academic libraries and copyright policy: interlibrary loans, electronic reserves, and distance education," in Geist, Michael, ed. *In the Public Interest: The Future of Canadian Copyright Law*, Toronto: Irwin Law, 2005. 373–407.

Turner, Scott, "Library sees red over rising journal price," available at www.brown.edu/Administration/George_Journal/vol24/24GSJ19c.html

United Nations Development Programme, News Bulletin, 18 October 2004, (http://www.undp.org/dpa/pressrelease/releases/2004/october/pr18oct04.html)

Vandoren, Paul and Jean Charles Van Eeckhaute. "The WTO Decision on paragraph 6 of the Doha Declaration on the TRIPS Agreement and Public Health: Making it work," *Journal of World Intellectual Property*, vol.6, no 4(2003): 779–793.

INDEX